MIGRANT KINGDOM:
MZILIKAZI'S NDEBELE IN SOUTH AFRICA

MIGRANT KINGDOM:

Mzilikazi's Ndebele in South Africa

R. KENT RASMUSSEN

REX COLLINGS LONDON *with* DAVID PHILIP CAPE TOWN 1978

First published in Great Britain by Rex Collings Ltd
69 Marylebone High Street, London W1

ISBN 086036061 X

Typesetting by Malvern Typesetting Services
Printed in Great Britain by
Billing and Sons Ltd
Guildford, London and Worcester

For Nancy, and for both her parents and mine

CONTENTS

FOREWORD

To most white men in nineteenth century Southern Africa the Ndebele people were creatures of legend. Then white men visited the Ndebele, traded with them, preached to them, extracted Concessions from them, conquered them, expropriated them—and wrote about them. The Ndebele, it seemed, had moved out of legend and into history. But for a complex of reasons—ignorance, carelessness, private interest, romanticism once it was safe to admire a defeated foe—what the white man wrote about the Ndebele constituted a myth in itself. Then in the odd dialectic of colonialism the Ndebele themselves embraced this new white myth and began to live up to it. By the time the new academic African historiography began it seemed as if we knew a good deal about the Ndebele and their 'tradition'. Even a revolutionary new historiography has to take and make use of a very great deal of the old assumptions—and old assumptions and assertions about the Ndebele were on the whole taken and made use of. Some of the new Africanist historians devoted themselves to the task of doing justice to the history of the Shona speaking peoples of Rhodesia, who had hitherto stood so much in the shadow of the Ndebele. Others devoted themselves to re-examining the history of white relations with the Ndebele and revealing elaborate fraud and duplicity. The Shona were no longer thought of as craven fugitives; the whites were no longer thought of as heroic pioneers. But the Ndebele went on being thought of as simple but glamorous soldiers.

One of the most complete and significant historiographical revolutions of the recent period of research into Southern Africa has been the erosion and explosion of this old myth of the Ndebele. After the work of Kent Rasmussen on the Ndebele south of the Limpopo and the work of Julian Cobbing on the Ndebele state in Rhodesia it is no exaggeration to say that all previous historical work on the Ndebele has to be discounted. Nothing is what it seemed to be; the Ndebele did not originate in the way we imagined; they did not move from here to there and settle there and here as we had been told; they farmed and traded much more and fought and raided much less than we had believed; their monarchy and their armies and their religious beliefs were none of them what for decades we had fondly supposed them to be.

A few months ago I was asked to record some comments on the Ndebele and the Shona for a programme on the British Broadcasting Programme. The interviewer had read my book, *Revolt in Southern Rhodesia*, coming up in the train and arrived full of excitement at the audience appeal of the Ndebele military state as it appeared in its pages. He was increasingly despondent as I told him of the new historiography of the Ndebele and repented of my own earlier endorsement of the 'simple soldier' image. At last he complained. 'I've no doubt its all true,' he said, 'but I liked the Ndebele much better the way they were before. Now they sound like everybody else.'

Some readers may feel at first that Dr Rasmussen's rigorous examination of evidence and detail and his demolition of previous accounts of Ndebele history are no substitute for the old blood and thunder epics of the interior. But most will come to feel, I think, a different sort of excitement as they read on. Dr Rasmussen is a scout not on the trail of an Ndebele impi but of all the journalists and travellers and historians who have beaten out their misleading track. What he is doing is essential for African history to come of age; to take nothing on trust; to scrutinise everything. And when he and Dr Cobbing have done with their revisions the Ndebele certainly do not look much like our old image of them, but they still look reassuringly different from everybody else.

Terence Ranger
University of Manchester

LIST OF MAPS

LIST OF ABBREVIATIONS*

ABC	American Board of Commissioners for Foreign Missions
Acc.	Accession item
Bloemhof	Report of the Bloemhof Commission, 1871
CA	Cape Archives
CNC	Chief Native Commissioner (Southern Rhodesia)
CO	Colonial Office
dd.	dated
Evid.	Evidence
facs. rep.	Facsimile reprint
GTJ	*Grahamstown Journal*
Herin.	Herinneringe (memories)
jnl.	journal
LMS	London Missionary Society
MS., MSS.	manuscript(s)
NAR	National Archives of Rhodesia
NC	Native Commissioner (Southern Rhodesia)
n.d.	no date given
n.l.	no location of publication given
PA	Pretoria Archives
SA	South Africa
TNAD	Transvaal Native Affairs Department
ts.	typescript
WMMS	Wesleyan Methodist Missionary Society

*Specific archival abbreviations are explained in bibliography; other abbreviations used in this study should be self-explanatory.

NOTE ON ORTHOGRAPHY

No single set of rules for the rendering of African words into English is yet accepted. In this study I attempt merely to follow the usages of the best available modern scholarship. For Nguni terms I tend to follow Pelling's *Practical Ndebele Dictionary* and Doke & Vilakazi's *Zulu-English Dictionary*. Similar guides are not available for Nguni proper names, so I strive mainly for consistency in my own usage. For Sotho/Tswana names I tend to follow the examples contained in William F. Lye's and Isaac Schapera's various writings.

One emerging rule for rendering Bantu words in English is to drop the prefixes. This I do for proper names, leaving 'Ndebele' for *Amandebele*, 'Sotho' for *Basotho, etc*. However, where the dropping of prefixes from familiar nouns would render them unrecognizable, I retain their singular prefixes (adding 's' to make them into English plurals); hence: *impi*(s), *induna*(s), *etc*.

Personal names found in historical documents often present special difficulties because their spellings are barely recognizable. Quotations and footnotes in this study thus give names exactly as they are found in documents. Modern spellings are added (in brackets) only when identifications can confidently be made. For an illustration of the depth of this problem, see my article, 'From Cillicaats to Zelkaats', which documents 325 spelling variations of 'Mzilikazi'.

ACKNOWLEDGEMENTS

I owe thanks to many people and many institutions. I feel especially indebted to David Beach and William F. Lye. Both have been remarkably generous with their time, advice, and encouragement during the nearly five years I have worked on this project. Some of the conclusions on early Ndebele history to be found in the present book differ markedly from those presented in Dr Lye's writings; however, perceptive readers will recognize that it was he who showed me the way.

I visited many libraries and archives during my research. Each seemed determined to outdo the others in extending to me courtesy and practical assistance. To all their staffs go my sincere thanks.

This book is a slightly altered version of a doctoral thesis I presented to the history department of the University of California at Los Angeles in 1975. For encouragement and assistance with the manuscript, I am indebted to my faculty advisers, E. A. Alpers, Christopher Ehret, Hilda Kuper, and T. O. Ranger. I am especially grateful to Professor Ranger for continuing to assist me even after he left UCLA for Manchester University.

A grant from the Fulbright-Hays Dissertation Research Abroad programme made possible my research in England and South Africa. Additional financial support from my parents and my wife's parents enabled me to buy a car and to spend a brief but rewarding period in Rhodesia. Finally, it has been the patient support and encouragement of my wife Nancy which has allowed me to complete this project with the care I believe it deserves.

INTRODUCTION

Mzilikazi and the Ndebele* people need little introduction. With a history aptly described as 'spectacular', they have been the subject of numerous popular books, including several novels. Under Mzilikazi's leadership the Ndebele kingdom arose during the Zulu wars of the late 1810s and early 1820s, and helped to spread these disorders among the predominantly Sotho-speaking inhabitants of the South African interior. For two decades the kingdom grew rapidly as it absorbed conquered peoples and other Nguni refugees. In stages it moved across the Transvaal from east to west, until finally it settled permanently in present Matabeleland, north of the Limpopo River. Along the way the Ndebele engaged in life-or-death struggles with armies of the Zulu empire, with Sotho and Griqua/Korana marauding bands, and even with the first wave of white settlers to reach the deep interior—the Afrikaner Voortrekkers. Indeed, one would be hard pressed to find a book on almost any aspect of the early nineteenth century South African interior in which the Ndebele do not figure prominently. Moreover, outside of South Africa the Ndebele are even more famous for their role in the creation of present-day Rhodesia during the later nineteenth century.

With so much already written on the Ndebele, it is fair to ask what yet another book can contribute. The answer is simple. Most of what has already been written on early Ndebele history is so erroneous that it is almost worthless. It is time to wipe the slate clean for a fresh start.

This is not at all the kind of book I set out to write when I started my research on Ndebele history five years ago. I entered the field impressed by the comparative wealth of information already available on the Ndebele, and I planned an interpretative study of Ndebele warfare, with an emphasis on the trans-Limpopo period.

---

* The use of this name in this study is discussed in Appendix A

Soon, however, I discovered that I was labouring under two great misconceptions. The first of these was my notion that the main outlines of Ndebele history were already so well-established that it remained merely for me to help fill in minor gaps in the record, while concentrating on broad thematic issues. My second misconception was that the early decades of Ndebele migrations were of only peripheral importance to the longer and—so I thought—more important period of settlement north of the Limpopo.

The first misconception was revealed to me as I found mounting evidence for such matters as Ndebele settlements in places they should not have been, different outcomes for wars they fought, and, generally, a wholly different chronology for the events of the first several decades than that generally accepted. I decided that there must be something terribly wrong with the existing literature on the Ndebele—particularly that pertaining to the sub-Limpopo period. Historians seemed to know very little indeed about what actually happened in Ndebele history. And it seemed that almost everything written about the Ndebele over the past fifty or so years derived from the same few authorities. I dropped my plans to do an interpretative study. My first priority became to get the facts straight.

The second misconception emerged as I realized that many patterns and phenomena thought peculiar to the Ndebele experience north of the Limpopo had important antecedents south of that river. I concluded that any proper study of the Ndebele kingdom had to begin with a thorough investigation of its history in South Africa. That such a task alone requires a full-scale study is demonstrated by this present book.

This book is thus essentially a narrative history of the first two decades of Mzilikazi's kingdom—a period which coincides with its phase of active migrations. These migrations started in Zululand in about 1821, and concluded when Mzilikazi himself arrived in Matabeleland about mid-1839. A background chapter on Mzilikazi's earlier career is also offered to help place the whole subject in a broader perspective.

Two themes—migration and warfare—dominate this study. Clearly, the Ndebele devoted only a small part of their time and energy in these pursuits. The overwhelming concerns of their lives were the business of producing food, building homes, and organizing their ever-expanding society. Nevertheless, Ndebele migrations and wars were the activities most thoroughly discussed by contemporary literate chroniclers; they were the phenomena having the greatest impact upon the many peoples whom the Ndebele encountered during their travels; and they are the activities best remembered by the Ndebele themselves. I do not mean to contend that these are the only aspects of Ndebele history worth studying, or even that they are necessarily the most important ones. I do, however, argue that a sound understanding of these subjects is essential to any wider appreciation of Ndebele history, and that their accurate and detailed reconstruction is the most appropriate starting point for any serious research into the Ndebele past. Furthermore, since Ndebele operations during this brief migratory period directly affected at least fifty other African societies—not to mention the course of white expansion into the interior—Ndebele history also offers an important key to a wide range of other topics.

Early Ndebele history is important for yet another reason. Mzilikazi's kingdom is a rare example of an African state whose moment of formation can be dated almost exactly, and whose far-flung migrations can be traced with some precision. The era of Zulu wars, or *Mfecane* (*Difaqane* to the Sotho), threw up a number of similar states around the same time the Ndebele kingdom formed. Among the best-known of these were Soshangane's Gaza kingdom, which soon settled in southern Mozambique; Zwangendaba's Ngoni kingdom, which split into five independent states after reaching southern Tanzania; and Sebitwane's Kololo kingdom, which occupied western Zambia until its collapse. These states all resembled the Ndebele kingdom in their origins, military orientations, and proclivities for rapid migration; however, none has so well-documented an early history. Alone among the major *Mfecane*-spawned migratory states, the Ndebele kingdom operated near major pockets of literate Europeans during its formative decades. This crucial fact helped to produce an invaluable record of Ndebele operations during the 1820s and 1830s. Early Ndebele history therefore offers a unique opportunity to study the processes of state-formation and large-scale migration. This study is probably the most detailed yet written on a southern African migrant state during its formative period; as such, it should help to illuminate similar processes elsewhere.

I must now add a cautionary note. Although evidence for early Ndebele history is quite good compared to that available for other migrant states, it is very meagre indeed by European or American historical standards. It is not merely by choice that this study emphasizes *events* rather than social issues. There are simply not sufficient data to support intelligent discussion of most issues. I have, for example, found it impossible to develop more than a superficial picture of the processes by which strangers were incorporated into Ndebele society. In general, where this book discusses a pertinent issue very briefly, it is because evidence is limited. It should be kept in mind that evidence for the period treated in this book does not compare to that available for the late nineteenth century Ndebele. It would be tempting to flesh out the bare-bones narrative presented here by extrapolating back in time with evidence drawn from later years, but to do so would defeat the book's purpose. Throughout this study I attempt to restrict all assertions to evidence directly relevant to the period under study—a practice to which African historians do not always adhere. I do not want to introduce new misconceptions while working to dispel old ones. Ndebele history is, if anything, a study in rapid and often dramatic change. The possibility of erring through invalid chronological extrapolations is great. Much as I would have preferred to comment more fully on state-building, social organization, and other issues, I have repeatedly had to bow to the severe paucity of data.

The amount of misinformation previously published on early Ndebele history is enormous. The reconstruction of the subject presented in this book will be found to differ radically from all previous accounts. (Readers wishing to see a quick summary of the revisions proposed may find it helpful first to read the introductory sections of all the chapters.) In order to make my arguments as strong as possible, I have gone well beyond citing merely those sources which support my own conclusions. I have also attempted to show where other historians have erred badly, why they have done so, and why my own conclusions are the more correct. The result is a much more massively documented piece of work than I would like to have written, but one which I feel is justified, if challenges to my revisions are to be met. I hope general readers will not be deterred by the heavy documentation found in the footnotes. The text should make perfectly good sense without frequent reference to the footnotes. I have, in fact, tried to make the text itself as simple as possible by not bringing in unnecessary and unfamiliar names, and by relegating minor issues to the footnotes.

To a certain extent this study is an exercise in the writing of history from diverse and ostensibly unpromising sources. Hopefully, historians of southern Africa will find it useful as a discussion of both the possibilities and limitations inherent in the resources available for the nineteenth century interior. I have attempted, wherever possible, to test each piece of information by asking Who was its original source? What was its chain of transmission over time and space? How might errors or distortions have altered it before or during its eventual reduction to written form? And, finally, how does it compare to such other pieces of evidence as are available for a given issue? Such standards are hardly original; however, the existing state of early Ndebele historiography suggests that they have rarely been applied.

A comprehensive discussion of the most important sources used in this study is offered in Appendix B. Some readers may wish to peruse that section before beginning the book itself.

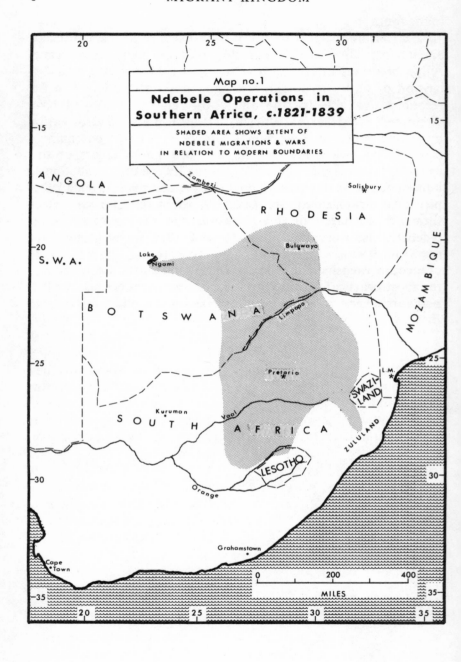

Map no.1

**Ndebele Operations in
Southern Africa, c.1821-1839**

SHADED AREA SHOWS EXTENT OF
NDEBELE MIGRATIONS & WARS
IN RELATION TO MODERN BOUNDARIES

CHAPTER I

PRELUDE TO THE NDEBELE KINGDOM: MZILIKAZI'S EARLY LIFE

There are many uncertainties in our picture of the early Ndebele kingdom, but on one point there can be no doubt: King Mzilikazi was the central figure in the state. His personal leadership—more than any other recognizable force—defined the state and held it together. He was, of course, far from solely responsible for everything that happened in early Ndebele history, and it is easy to exaggerate his personal role. Nevertheless, his life story serves as the most practical starting point around which to reconstruct his kingdom's history, and it is to his early life that we must turn to find the kingdom's origins.

Mzilikazi grew up in Northern Nguni country of eastern South Africa during a period of far-reaching political changes. It was a period of military innovation, characterized by apparently new developments in weaponry, organization and mobilization, and tactics and strategy. A new generation of rulers fought wars of total conquest and undertook unprecedentedly large-scale territorial aggrandizement. The most outstanding of these new rulers was Shaka, the founder of the Zulu empire.

The Northern Nguni wars of the late 1810s and early 1820s created an era of widespread disturbances remembered as the *Mfecane*. As the *Mfecane* rocked Nguni country, a number of Northern Nguni bands fled the region and carried the wars to the predominantly Sotho-speaking South African interior and to regions north of the Limpopo River.

Mzilikazi led one such band into the present Transvaal, where his followers became known as the Ndebele. The kingdom he built in the Transvaal bore many similarities—particularly in military techniques—to Shaka's growing Zulu empire, so historians have naturally raised the question of what connections existed between the two state systems. This question can only be answered after a thorough examination of what Mzilikazi experienced up to the time he founded the Ndebele state.

Most historians who have dealt with the origins of the Ndebele state perceive a special relationship between Mzilikazi and Shaka. Mzilikazi and his original followers clearly served under Shaka immediately before they became independent, so it has often been suggested that they had a unique opportunity to learn innovative military and political ideas from their Zulu master. According to this theory Mzilikazi was a close confidant of Shaka, he held a high post in the Zulu political/military hierarchy, and he spent about five years under Shaka's tutelage.[1]

The major conclusion of this chapter is that Mzilikazi had no special relationship with Shaka. He appears to have held only a minor position, he was posted far from Shaka's headquarters, and he may have served under the Zulu king for as little as two years. The implications of these points should be readily apparent. Whatever similarities between the Zulu, Ndebele, and other breakaway Northern Nguni state systems are observable, they were probably not derived from innovations promulgated by Shaka. Instead, such ideas must have derived from an older and broader pool of common Northern Nguni practices to which Shaka himself was an heir.[2]

The evidence used to advance these points is spotty and far from conclusive. There is no contemporary written evidence whatsoever for the period discussed in this chapter. Mzilikazi and his followers left Zululand several years before the first literate observers visited Shaka's domain in 1824; Mzilikazi himself was not visited by literate travellers until 1829. Mzilikazi's early career is therefore documented solely by near-contemporary and traditional evidence recorded after those dates.

The chronology for this chapter presents special problems which would have to be more fully resolved if the chapter's main arguments are to be carried. The dates given here are inferred from two kinds of data: (1) that pertaining to the stages of Mzilikazi's personal life and to the sequences of events occurring around him; and (2) backward extrapolations from the firmer chronology of subsequent events. Evidence adduced in the next chapter suggests that Mzilikazi must have left Zululand by about 1821—at date two years earlier than that most frequently assigned to the event. The dates given for earlier events are progressively less precise as their remoteness in time increases.

The most important source of traditional evidence employed in this chapter is A. T. Bryant's *Olden Times in Zululand and Natal*, a work based largely upon Northern Nguni clan histories. Bryant's work excels recorded Ndebele traditions in that his sources place Mzilikazi's early life in the broadest possible context. Unfortunately, Bryant rarely identifies his specific sources, and it is clear that he also introduces material from early European authorities—notably Henry Fynn—as well.[3] Although little serious criticism of Bryant's writings has been undertaken, his views on the *Mfecane* period have dominated all modern historical interpretations. The present study reviews Bryant's material on Ndebele history carefully, but a broader analysis of his work would be beyond its scope. I have therefore had to accept without demur much of Bryant's material on Mzilikazi's early life and times.[4]

Ndebele-derived sources of evidence on Mzilikazi's early career are pervaded with striking contradictions; one generally finds in such evidence at least two versions of each major turning point in his life. Two historical factors seem to be behind these discrepancies. The first is the patriotic tendency of the Ndebele to magnify Mzilikazi's early achievements and to portray him as Shaka's equal.[5] The second factor is the inherent confusion in Ndebele memories. Within a decade of his departure from Zululand Mzilikazi's original followers constituted only a fraction of his whole following. He continuously incorporated other peoples into his state, and many of these newcomers were also Nguni refugees from the *Mfecane* wars. These other Nguni had their own memories of Zululand and of their flights from there, and their memories became mixed up with what we might call the mainstream of Ndebele tradition. Near-contemporary evidence collected from Ndebele by Europeans during the 1830s reflects the differing experiences of Mzilikazi's various followers. Perhaps unknowingly the European chroniclers presented such evidence as representing a single historical experience. Similar confusion of divergent memories is reflected in traditions collected from the late nineteenth century. A complete history of the Ndebele people would attempt to sort out the separate histories of the society's component members; for now, however, it is enough to reconstruct Mzilikazi's life. The primary aim of this chapter, therefore, is simply to determine how much we can confidently accept as being true about Mzilikazi's early life.

Mzilikazi's youth and his relationship with Zwide

Mzilikazi was born near the centre of present Zululand sometime during the 1790s.[6] According to the patrilineal descent system of the northern Nguni-speaking peoples, he was a member of the Khumalo clan. The Khumalo were, as was the case with most Nguni clans, divided into several autonomous branches, each of which was organized under a chief. Mzilikazi's father, Mashobane, was a member of a branch headed by a man named Magugu. Mashobane and other men of his generation were dissatisfied with Magagu's leadership and they wished to establish new chiefdoms elsewhere. Soon after Mzilikazi's birth Mashobane and several other leading Khumalo each led a group of Khumalo away from Magugu and founded new chiefdoms between the sources of the Mkuze River and the Ngome Forest of northern Natal.[7]

The formation of new chiefdoms by Mashobane and his peers typified the traditional Northern Nguni practice of political fission with its resultant dispersion of peoples. At this time, however, a new political process was emerging in the region as militarily powerful chiefs consolidated chiefdoms of unrelated clans into larger units. The new Khumalo chiefs now found themselves close to the growing Ndwandwe league of Zwide in the east, and the Mthethwa confederation of Dingiswayo to the southeast.[8]

The nature of the relationship between the Khumalo of Mashobane and the Ndwandwe of Zwide poses the first riddle in Mzilikazi's career, for their relationship seems to have laid the basis for Mzilikazi's own connection with Zwide at a later date. Since Zwide was one of the greatest of the Northern Nguni empire-builders, we should naturally want to know to what extent, if any, his career influenced that of the future Ndebele king. A recent Ndebele historian suggests that Mzilikazi learned a great deal about government directly from Zwide; however, lack of evidence for this supposition makes it almost pure speculation.[9]

Mzilikazi's father, Mashobane, is mentioned in so many independent sources that there can be no reasonable doubt of his identity. But, as one might expect of a patrilineal society, Mzilikazi's mother is rarely identified. The few sources who mention her give different names; the consensus favours Nompethu, a 'daughter' of Zwide.[10] What ultimately became of her is unknown; she seems either to have remained in Natal when Mzilikazi left in c.1821, or to have died at some earlier date.[11]

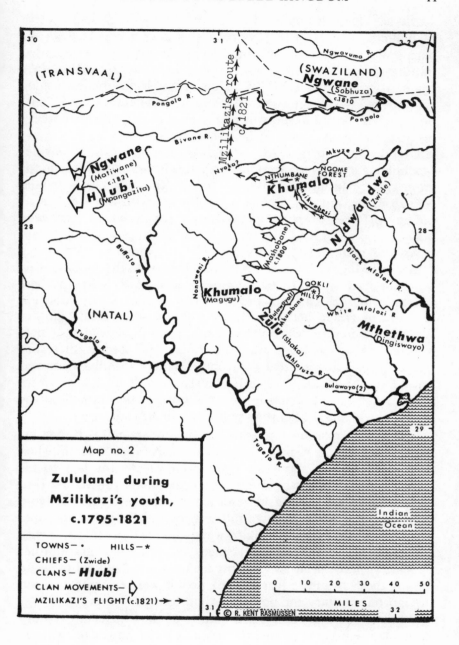

Map no. 2

Zululand during Mzilikazi's youth, c.1795-1821

TOWNS— •   HILLS— *
CHIEFS— (Zwide)
CLANS— *Hlubi*
CLAN MOVEMENTS— ⬠
MZILIKAZI'S FLIGHT (c.1821)— →

© R. KENT RASMUSSEN

Mzilikazi himself married one or two of Zwide's other 'daughters', one of whom bore a son later recognized as his heir.[12] Whatever the names of these various individuals were, two important points are clear. First, the fact that Mzilikazi's mother came from the house of Zwide made her Mashobane's senior wife; thus Mzilikazi was Mashobane's acknowledged heir. Second, Mzilikazi himself was tied to the house of Zwide both by his maternal ancestry and by his own marriage links.[13]

Despite his marriage to a daughter of the house of Zwide, Mashobane's own connections with the Ndwandwe remain far from clear. Mashobane, like his fellow Khumalo chiefs by the Mkuze River, must have concerned himself with the problem of playing off the two rival, expansionist powers which were near him.

As was mentioned, Mzilikazi was born sometime before his father left Magugu's chiefdom to found his own. Bryant dates this separation to about 1800, a date which accords with the best estimates of Mzilikazi's birthdate.[14] Thus we can safely conclude that the marriage between Mashobane and Mzilikazi's mother took place before Mashobane became an independent chief. Mashobane's marriage into the house of Zwide therefore probably had no political overtones. When Mashobane moved away from Magugu, he resettled closer to the Ndwandwe centre than he had been previously, but his move in that direction was likely coincidental rather than politically significant.

Mzilikazi's relationship with Zwide underwent two phases, coinciding with the years before and after his father's death, when he himself was in about his early twenties. As the heir to his father's chiefship, it would have been customary for Mzilikazi to have been raised among his mother's people in order to avoid potential intrigues at his own father's court.[15] Indeed, traditional evidence confirms that Mzilikazi went with his mother to live with his maternal grandfather.[16] Since his maternal grandfather appears to have been Zwide, this means that Mzilikazi grew up among the Ndwandwe just as these people were entering a period of vigorous military and political expansion.

By the middle of the second decade of the nineteenth century Zwide was emerging as one of the three most powerful rulers in northern Natal. The others were Sobhuza of the Ngwane, and Dingiswayo of the Mthethwa. Zwide drove Sobhuza north of the Pongolo River , where the latter founded the modern Swazi kingdom. He then advanced against Dingiswayo. Dingiswayo was captured and killed by the Ndwandwe. However, before his Mthethwa confederation could disintegrate, it was taken over and rebuilt by a subordinate chief. This was Shaka of the Zulu clan. By A. T. Bryant's reckoning, these events occurred in roughly 1816.

Again according to Bryant, Zwide set a trap for Shaka similar to that with which he had captured Dingiswayo. However, Shaka was saved when a Khumalo chief revealed the plot to him. This chief was Donda, a nephew of Mashobane and also the latter's neighbour by the Mkuze River. The relationship between these two Khumalo chiefs is significant. Zwide is said to have regarded Donda's action as treason. He retaliated by killing *both* Donda and Mashobane.[17] Bryant is generally vague on the nature of the relationship between Zwide and Mashobane, but from this story it can be inferred that Zwide regarded both Donda and the latter as his vassals. This story, such as it is, is really the only evidence which suggests that Mashobane recognized Zwide as his overlord.

Another version of Mashobane's death is supported by sources written well before Bryant. According to this version Zwide killed Mashobane during a campaign of conquest.[18] Mashobane thus would have died not as an Ndwandwe subject suspected of disloyalty, but as an independent chief fighting off an aggressor. Both versions of Mashobane's death share the theme that after Zwide had him killed, he had his body mutilated.[19]

Either version of Mashobane's death seems compatible with the conclusion that Mzilikazi was raised in or around Zwide's court. There he seems to have won favour with Zwide, who confirmed his accession to the Khumalo chiefship left vacant by Mashobane's death.[20] Perhaps Zwide saw in Mzilikazi a malleable instrument of his own policy whose potential value as a puppet chief justified killing off Mashobane. If so, events were to prove that he had underrated Mzilikazi's capacity for independent action.

Zwide's support of Mzilikazi's claim to the Khumalo chiefship carried a condition—he made his grandson his vassal.[21] Whatever had been their former status, Mashobane's people were now firmly a part of the growing Ndwandwe domain, Mzilikazi returned to the Mkuze region personally to take up the leadership of his small chiefdom. There is little record of what he did while under Zwide's rule. One traditional authority tells us, however, that he led a successful cattle raid against Sobhuza.[22] Anything else said about his activities then is speculation.

Mzilikazi defects from Zwide to Shaka

The first truly large-scale wars in Southern African history were fought between Shaka and Zwide in about 1818 and 1819.[23] Mzilikazi was serving under Zwide when the wars began; he was under Shaka by the time they were over. Although he was clearly near the centres of action during these wars, we know almost nothing about the extent of his or his followers's participation in them. In view of his later reputation as a military leader, it is ironic that his rôle in the Zulu-Ndwandwe wars is so mysterious.

Zwide and Shaka spent the year or two after Dingiswayo's death preparing for the major confrontation which had failed to come off during the first meeting of the rival power blocs. Finally, Zwide sent a large force across the White Mfolozi River into Shaka's territory. Shaka met the Ndwandwe army at a place called Qokli Hill. There he staged a brilliant defensive effort, whittling down successive Ndwandwe onslaughts until the enemy withdrew. Losses were great on both sides, but this first war ended indecisively.[24]

A year later Zwide mounted a larger invasion force, this time under the command of Soshangane. Shaka withdrew his own forces deep into his own territory, stripping bare the country behind him. As Soshangane was drawn in, his men were harassed and worn down by Zulu bands. Finally, after the Ndwandwe army had become demoralized and weakened by hunger, Shaka attacked and overwhelmed it. He followed this victory with a rapid counter-invasion into Ndwandwe country, where he dispersed most of his enemies. Zwide himself was forced to flee north of Swaziland, where he eventually died in comparative obscurity.[25] The remnants of Soshangane's army returned to find their homes in ruins. Soshangane and one of his subordinate officers, Zwangendaba, each gathered what followers they could muster and headed towards Delagoa Bay, where they started to build the Gaza and Ngoni kingdoms, respectively.[26]

Shaka's victory in this second Zulu-Ndwandwe war left him in virtually uncontested control of northern Natal. From this point he went on to consolidate and to expand his holdings, and to restructure his composite state into a more nearly unitary kingdom.

At some point during the Zulu-Ndwandwe wars Mzilikazi and his Khumalo switched their allegiance from Zwide to Shaka.[27] The exact timing and the reasons for this shift of allegiance are muddled by contradictory streams of evidence; however, certain points can be immediately sorted out. For example, while some authorities hold that Mzilikazi joined Shaka after the second war, none suggests that he did so before the first war.[28] Such evidence allows us to infer, therefore, that Mzilikazi joined Shaka during or shortly after the two wars, and that the wars themselves may have had something to do with his action. The question of exactly *when* Mzilikazi made his shift is partly answered by an analysis of *why* he joined Shaka.

One stream of evidence contends that Mzilikazi fought *against* Shaka during the Zulu-Ndwandwe wars. Variations of this stream further hold that he was *conquered* by Shaka, and that this was how the Khumalo fell under Zulu rule.[29] By contrast, another stream of evidence does not refer to Mzilikazi's having fought Shaka during these wars, but insists that he joined Shaka *voluntarily*. Mzilikazi's distrust of Zwide—the murderer of his father—is the motive usually assigned to him for his deserting the Ndwandwe ruler.[30] In addition, there is some evidence that Mzilikazi fought on Shaka's side against the Ndwandwe in at least the second of the two major wars.[31]

A simple interpretation of these events reconciles all this apparently contradictory evidence. Mzilikazi probably changed sides *between* the two wars.[32] This interpretation would explain how Mzilikazi would have fought on both sides during the Zulu-Ndwandwe wars. The question of whether he joined Shaka voluntarily or was conquered might be explained as a difference in perspectives. Given that he went over to the Zulu quite voluntarily after the first war, he was probably still associated in many peoples' minds with Zwide. Then, when Zwide was finally crushed, Mzilikazi and he followers carried some of the Ndwandwe stigma of defeat. I suspect that the general confusion of this period left many people uncertain about Mzilikazi's rôle in these wars—he was, after all, only a minor chief at the time—and that some of this uncertainty was shared by Nguni refugees who joined Mzilikazi at a later date.

Mzilikazi could have had two motives for switching his

allegiance to Shaka when he did. The first has already been mentioned: his fear of Zwide's duplicity. The second would have been his desire to be on the winning side at the conclusion of the wars. Had he sensed the coming of the ultimate Zulu victory, he would have realized that a speedy and voluntary submission to Shaka would greatly enhance his chances for preserving as much as possible of his own chiefdom's autonomy. The physical location of his chiefdom near the Zulu-Ndwandwe frontier made such a shift easy in any case. Mzilikazi's desire to maintain his own freedom is certainly one of the most striking features of his whole life's story. Indeed, one modern Ndebele authority suggests that Mzilikazi only 'pretended to submit' to Shaka when he joined him.[33]

Zwide's second invasion of Zulu territory took place about a year after the Battle of Qokli Hill; this would have been roughly mid-1818 or mid-1819.[34] Curiously, the only two authorities who place Mzilikazi in the thick of the action of this war are the authors of popular biographies of Shaka and Mzilikazi. Normally one should like to avoid drawing conclusions from such sources, but in this case it is significant that both authors cite African informants to make their case. According to one of these authors, Peter Becker, 'Mzilikazi proved so dauntless a warrior that he won Shaka's admiration and became his favourite.'[35] The other author, E. A. Ritter, identifies his informant as an elderly Zulu who, as a child, observed Mzilikazi directly at Shaka's side on the eve of the climactic battle.[36] Unfortunately, except for the implication that Mzilikazi's service to Shaka was sufficiently distinguished for him to be rewarded liberally with cattle, neither author details exactly what Mzilikazi did. Their evidence seems just strong enough to support the conclusion that Mzilikazi served under Shaka during this war, but any implication that he held a high rank or that he distinguished himself greatly is probably an exaggeration.

Mzilikazi and Shaka

The nature of Mzilikazi's relationship with Shaka is another of the great puzzles in his early life. Modern historians tend to impute a great deal of significance into the fact that Mzilikazi served under Shaka, but they are uniformly vague about the nature of his experience.[37] At least one Ndebele traditional authority denies that Mzilikazi ever served Shaka; however, this view need not be taken seriously, since the evidence for Mzilikazi's having served Shaka is overwhelming.[38] Unfortunately, most of this evidence pertains to Mzilikazi's violent separation from the Zulu, and we are left, again, to speculate about what hé was doing under Shaka between the first Zulu-Ndwandwe war and then.

Nineteenth century writers described Mzilikazi's position under Shaka as almost everything from 'servant' to 'commander-in-chief' of the entire Zulu army.[39] These extreme terms are certainly inaccurate, but it seems clear that while under Shaka Mzilikazi rose from a low position to one of comparative importance.[40] This latter view seems to fit what little we know of Mzilikazi at this stage of his career, and it has an inherently logical ring to it. Mzilikazi came to Shaka as a young and unimportant chief, but at a time when defections from the enemy would have been welcome to the Zulu. Furthermore, the chances are good that when the Khumalo defected from Zwide, they had to move quickly, leaving their goods, and perhaps their livestock, behind; in short, they were probably hard up. Within a short time, however, they were able to share in the fortunes of victory, as the Zulu forces displaced the Ndwandwe from northern Natal. After the defeat of the Ndwandwe, the Zulu empire continued to expand rapidly, so this would have been a time of rapid promotion of officials. And, as later events certainly demonstrated, Mzilikazi was a very capable leader.

When Mzilikazi went over the Shaka, he seems to have taken his entire chiefdom with him.[41] In fact, by one traditional account, it was the members of his chiefdom who took the initiative in proposing this move.[42] In any case, it is clear that Mzilikazi's chiefdom retained its corporate identity during its period of service under the Zulu, and that he remained its undisputed chief.[43]

There is some confusion in the evidence as to where Mzilikazi's people resided in Zululand. This confusion seems to derive from the fact that Mzilikazi's chiefdom was billeted first in central Zululand, and then later at the northern frontier. When Mzilikazi joined Shaka, he apparently moved directly to the latter's headquarters at Bulawayo, then situated on a tributary of the Mkumbane River, about thirty-five miles south of where the

Khumalo had been living previously.[44] Some modern authorities further assert that Mzilikazi actually became 'headman' at Bulawayo, but this seems unlikely.[45] Furthermore, his praise-poem describes him as one 'who refused to eat the leg at Bulawayo', suggesting that he refused the Bulawayo headmanship.[46]

Within a year or so of the Zulu victory over Zwide, Shaka moved his headquarters from the Mkumbane River to the Mhlatuze, near the coast; this new site became the second Bulawayo.[47] Mzilikazi appears to have taken the opportunity posed by Shaka's move to return to his former home between the Black Mfolozi and Mkuze Rivers.[48] Those sources which argue that Mzilikazi lived at some 'outpost', and not at Bulawayo, do not specify where this outpost was; however, it was almost certainly the original Khumalo territory to which they refer.[49] For, as will be shown, it is very clear that it was from this very region that Mzilikazi later defied Shaka on the eve of his leaving Zululand.

The idea that Mzilikazi was somehow a great 'favourite' of Shaka was being expressed at least as early as the 1860s and it is a popular theme in modern literature, particularly in Ritter's biography of Shaka.[50] Shaka is a major figure in Ndebele traditions; it is not surprising that the closeness of Mzilikazi's relationship to him has been exaggerated.[51] These men were among the most important movers of nineteenth century southern African history; the fact that their paths crossed as closely as they did invites invention. Unfortunately, the claim that Mzilikazi was Shaka's favourite and that he held an especially high position in the Zulu hierarchy exists without any details to support it. Furthermore, the fact that Mzilikazi and Shaka moved in opposite directions away from the first Bulawayo indicates that while Shaka may have trusted Mzilikazi, he had no special affection for him. Mzilikazi's new position as chief over what was then a frontier district of Zululand was a responsible one, but it was probably not at all exceptional.

Mzilikazi as a military commander

The years following the Ndwandwe downfall were a period of vigorous Zulu military activity. Shaka consolidated his new holdings and moved against previously independent chiefdoms around his borders, particularly in the south.[52] Once again, the evidence for what Mzilikazi was doing is skimpy and vague. He seems to have played no part in Shaka's campaigns of conquest, for he is known to have participated in but a single expedition: a cattle raid to the north. In view of the Mzilikazi's later military accomplishments, it is remarkable that modern scholars have failed to ask what he was doing under the illustrious Shaka.

Mzilikazi begins to come to life as an historical personality in accounts of the one campaign he is known to have commanded while under Shaka. Many diverse sources discuss this campaign. Their agreement on its main points is striking and deserves to be emphasized, since it contrasts with so much of the evidence pertaining to earlier events.[53] The consensus of these sources holds that Mzilikazi attacked a wealthy chiefdom—probably Sotho—somewhere north or northwest of Zululand; he captured many cattle, but when he returned home, he neglected to turn them over to Shaka as he should have. This act of defiance was the trigger, if not the root cause, of Mzilikazi's subsequent break from Shaka and his leaving Zululand.

Of the campaign itself we can say little. The community he raided was ruled by a chief named Somnisi (or Ramnisi), and was, according to Bryant, located 'near the Zulu border in the Transvaal'.[54] Other than the fact that Mzilikazi captured considerable livestock, no particulars of this campaign are remembered.[55]

The 'Somnisi' campaign was possibly the only one which Mzilikazi commanded during the few years he served under Shaka. In any case, none other is remembered.[56] The specialness of this campaign was apparently enhanced by its connection with an important rite of passage in Mzilikazi's life: his circumcision.

According to A. A. Campbell, the 'Somnisi' campaign followed Mzilikazi's circumcision rites because 'the shedding of blood' was their 'necessary consequence' in the case of a chief.[57] No other authority associates these two events in Mzilikazi's life, but Campbell's evidence is credible. Although circumcision seems to have been dying out as a custom among the Northern Nguni during this period, it was still required of Ndebele men old enough to marry, at least through the 1830s. In this the Ndebele state appears to have reflected the trend taking place among the Northern Nguni generally.[58] Mzilikazi would have been about twenty to twenty-five years of age at the time of the 'Somnisi' campaign, and thus at about the right age to undergo circumcision according to the changing practices.[59] As the nineteenth century wore on, the Ndebele practised the rite of circumcision less and less. Mzilikazi's son and successor as king, Lobengula, may have been one of the last Ndebele to have been ritually circumcized, for he was said to have been 'circumcized on behalf of the nation'.[60] By the early twentieth century circumcision was described as 'unknown' among the Ndebele.[61]

Mzilikazi's circumcision symbolized his coming of age both as an adult male and as the ruler of chiefdom. Perhaps it was not a coincidence that shortly thereafter he asserted his independence by defying Shaka and leaving Zululand with his people.

Mzilikazi defects from Shaka

What moved Mzilikazi to defy Shaka and to lead his people out of Zululand will be considered below. First I shall attempt to reconstruct the sequence of events between the time he returned from his campaign against Somnisi and the moment he achieved his political independence.

The flight of the Khumalo from Zululand is the first Ndebele national epic. It is the story of the birth of the nation; as such it has been subjected in Ndebele accounts to patriotic distortions. Contradictions pervade accounts of this episode, and not all of them can be satisfactorily explained. The reconstruction offered here is therefore quite tentative.[62]

After the raid against Somnisi Mzilikazi returned to his own town, which was located by the Insikwebesi River, a northern tributary of the Black Mfolozi.[63] As a vassal of Shaka he should then have turned over the captured livestock to his king, who would have exercised his prerogative to redistribute it as he saw fit. Customarily Mzilikazi could have expected to receive a generous part of the booty almost immediately. Indeed, a personal representative of Shaka accompanied the expedition, and this man reminded Mzilikazi of his obligation when the campaign was over. Mzilikazi, however, refused to acknowledge his full obligation and sent the agent back to Shaka with so few cattle that the offering amounted to an insult.[64] His failure to turn over the bulk of captured animals is a point affirmed by virtually all near-contemporary and traditional sources which discuss this episode.[65]

When Shaka learned of Mzilikazi's insubordination he is said to have sent several messengers to remind the Khumalo of their duty. A colourful tradition recalls Mzilikazi's dramatic and unmistakable defiance; turning to his own men, he said:

> Surround these dogs, and cut the tops from off their plumes. Slowly and without a word we hemmed them in, but not a hand was raised to touch those marks of royalty. Mzilikazi saw our hesitation, and red now grew his eyes with passion, and pressing his way through his people, with his own hands he plucked the crests from off their heads, and seizing a battle-axe, he laid them down . . . and hacked them through. When done he handed back the stumps and each in silence took it. . . .
> Then spoke Mzilikazi; 'Messengers, take these words to Tshaka. Show to him the stumps of plumes and say that Mzilikazi, son of Matshobana, thus addresses him. Mzilikazi has no king. In peace he will meet Tshaka as a brother, and in war he will find in him an enemy whom he cannot and will not despise. . . . Depart! and tell your king it rests with him whether it be peace or war.'[66]

Whether or not this particular story is apocryphal, it is clear that Mzilikazi defied Shaka and angered him.[67]

From this point in the narrative the evidence tends to separate into two distinct streams. Both streams agree that Shaka responded to Mzilikazi's actions violently, and that several battles were fought in mountainous terrain before Mzilikazi managed to escape into the Transvaal. What they disagree on is the location of the battles. One version holds that all the fighting was done around the Insikwebesi River; the other version places all the battles in the Drakensberg Mountains, a goodly distance to the northwest. It is clear that in leaving Zululand Mzilikazi and his followers passed through both of these regions, but it is significant that no single source holds that battles were fought in both regions. The similarities in themes and details between the two versions make it clear that both refer to the same events. Hence, the question is: in which of the two regions did these events take place? It is an issue which should have obvious implications in any assessment of the depth of Shaka's commitment to suppress Mzilikazi's revolt.

According to the first version of this episode, Shaka responded to Mzilikazi's defiance by sending an armed Zulu force against him. This force met the Khumalo at a hilltop fortress somewhere around the lower Insikwebesi from which Mzilikazi's people successfully defended themselves. As the Zulu retreated back to Shaka's headquarters, Mzilikazi moved his people upriver to Nthumbane Hill to await the next assault. Shaka seems to have dallied for a few weeks, perhaps even several months, before making his next move.[68] Finally, he sent a force, larger than his earlier one, which stormed Nthumbane Hill and routed the Khumalo. Some traditions add the detail that a Khumalo traitor named Nzeni revealed the hill's secret access way to the Zulu commander, making it possible for him to breach the defences. The survivors fled the hill in disorder, but Mzilikazi soon regrouped them and led them out of Zululand.[69]

The second version of the story says nothing about fighting in Zululand, but instead tells of the Zulu pursuing the Khumalo all the way into the Drakensbergs. When the two sides met and fought, the outcome was essentially the same as in the first version: an initial Khumalo victory was countered by an overwhelming Zulu success in which the Khumalo lost all their cattle. Unlike the first version, however, this one goes on to tell of how Mzilikazi directed a brilliant action against the Zulu rearguard from which most of the lost cattle were recaptured.[70] This last point is suspect, however, since near-contemporary evidence recorded in the 1830s emphasizes that Mzilikazi had lost *all* his cattle to Shaka by the time he was free.[71] By contrast, many sources—from both versions of the story—agree that many Khumalo people, especially women and old men, were killed by the Zulu.[72] These were losses which Mzilikazi could not have made up immediately.

These two versions of Mzilikazi's escape from Zululand are compatible in themes, but not in geography—an aspect on which only one of them can be correct. The correct version is almost certainly that which places the Zulu-Khumalo fighting by the Insikwebesi River. It is supported by an array of generally credible authorities, and it offers convincing geographical details which are lacking in the other version. There are a number of possible explanations as to how the Drakensberg Mountains incorrectly found their way into Ndebele traditions in the other version. Mzilikazi's people did eventually cross the Drakensbergs, and they were probably impressed by the range's immense size. In later recollections of fighting the Zulu in mountainous terrain perhaps the Drakensbergs seemed a more suitable setting for the epic of the Ndebele kingdom's founding.[73] It is a distortion which would serve well to glorify the nation's past.

The unlikely tradition of Mzilikazi's recapturing his cattle from his Zulu pursuers also probably derives from a patriotic distortion of what actually happened. Once Mzilikazi broke away from Nthumbane Hill, he was free of serious Zulu harassment. He appears to have led his remaining followers directly to attack the Ngweni town of chief Nyoka—about a day's march west from Nthumbane.[74] He stripped this Zulu vassal of all his cattle, so this fact would explain how the story of his recapturing his own cattle from the Zulu proper originated. His progress north from this community is discussed in the next chapter.

It is clear that Mzilikazi's defiance of Shaka indicates his desire to assert his independence. What is unclear is whether leaving Zululand was part of his original intent, or whether he was forced to leave because of Shaka's attacks. While the latter explanation appears to be the more plausible in view of the desperate circumstances of Mzilikazi's actual departure, there is some evidence that Mzilikazi was contemplating flight at the time of his raid on Somnisi, who, it should be remembered, lived on or near the escape route followed by Mzilíkazi when he finally left Zululand.

When Robert Moffat visited Mzilikazi in the Transvaal in 1829, he recorded a summary of the latter's history. Of Mzilikazi's defiance of Shaka he wrote:

> This [news] coming to Chaka's ears, he vowed vengeance and Moselekatse was half prepared to take refuge in the fine fertile country which he had already surveyed.[75]

Any preparations to migrate which Mzilikazi may have made were probably only contingency plans, else we should expect him to have left Zululand before having to deal with Shaka's soldiers.

The fact that Mzilikazi turned over even a small part of his booty from the Somnisi raid suggests either of two conclusions: (a) he thought a sop would appease Shaka and allow him to remain where he was unmolested; or (b) he was making preparations to migrate and he hoped the small gift would buy time. Indeed, the latter interpretation is given credence by another summary of Mzilikazi's career, this one written by American missionaries in 1836:

> Maselekatsi reserved for himself a part of the booty, of which Chakka got information, and intended to call him to an account.

Maselekatsi, being aware of the consequences, resolved to stand his ground till he could collect some other people in addition to his own followers, and then to escape from his superior enemy by flight . . .[76]

This piece of evidence offers a logical explanation of why Mzilikazi delayed his migration; however, neither it nor Moffat's evidence confirms that Mzilikazi necessarily determined to leave the country before he was forced to do so. It would have been natural for Ndebele informants to portray Mzilikazi's leaving Zululand as an action based upon his initiative rather than upon Zulu pressure.

The patriotic Ndebele view of their history offers a simple explanation of why Mzilikazi would have wanted to leave Zululand: so great and popular had he become under Shaka that the latter became jealous and plotted to kill him.[77] One version goes further, suggesting that Mzilikazi might even have challenged Shaka for the Zulu kingship![78] The likelihood of Shaka's having perceived Mzilikazi as a rival for power was remote in view of Mzilikazi's limited backing, his distance from the centre of Zululand, and the absence of any indication that he was attracting non-Khumalo support. The threat that Mzilikazi posed to Shaka was merely that of a subordinate whose independent behaviour might be emulated by others.

From the start of his career as a chief Mzilikazi probably wanted nothing more than to maximize his chiefdom's autonomy. Had he successfully defended his stronghold on Nthumbane Hill, he might never have left Zululand at all. His desire to stay where he was is indicated in the message he was purported to have sent Shaka when he cut the plumes from the headdresses of the latter's messengers. He disliked what he must have perceived as a mounting drift towards political centralization under Shaka. Shaka was said to have 'oppressed' Mzilikazi's people, 'and would have reduced them to slavery. But the young chief resisted, suffered heavy losses, and was compelled to retreat towards the north.'[79] Mzilikazi led migrations several times in his later career; each time, however, it took some kind of disaster or major threat to his security to encourage him to move. Despite his reputation as a wanderer, his normal inclination seems to have been to stay put wherever he was. Furthermore, the notion that Mzilikazi could reasonably have expected to maintain his political autonomy under the shadow of the Zulu is not as strange as it might appear. Two of Mzilikazi's fellow Khumalo chiefs, Beje and Mlotsha, did just that. According to Bryant, both lived in the Ngome Forest, just east of Nthumbane Hill, where they resisted full incorporation into the Zulu state until after Shaka's death in 1828.[80] If a similar political autonomy was all that Mzilikazi sought, then he was a failure. How much better Ndebele traditions read if we accept flight from Zululand as his original goal!

The roots of Ndebele society on the threshold of independence

When the first literate observers visited Mzilikazi in 1829 his followers numbered perhaps 20,000 people.[81] However, his following is known to have grown rapidly during the preceding years, so the number of people who accompanied him out of Zululand must have been a tiny fraction of this figure. There is but one near-contemporary estimate of the size of his refugee band; happily, it appears to be fairly accurate.

One of the first Europeans to reach Shaka's court was the English trader Henry Fynn, who arrived there in 1824, only about three years after Mzilikazi had left the region. Fynn, who learned much about Shaka's earlier career, later wrote that Mzilikazi left Zululand with about 300 people.[82] This estimate conforms pretty well with what we would expect to have been the case on the basis of what little is known about Mzilikazi's Khumalo chiefdom.

Extrapolating back from late nineteenth century population figures for Zululand, A. T. Bryant estimates that there were about 78,000 people there in 1816 (approximately the year Mzilikazi became a chief) of whom about 2050 were Khumalo.[83] Since we know that there were at least four Khumalo chiefdoms during Mashobane's time, and since there is no reason to suspect that the chiefdom inherited by Mzilikazi was larger than any of the others, that chiefdom would have contained about a fourth of the total Khumalo population. Hence, Mzilikazi would have inherited a chiefdom with about 500 people in it.

In the pre-Shakan days of independent clan-based chiefdoms membership in the chiefdoms was fluid; individuals and families moved easily from chief to chief, according to their preferences.[84] Some of this fluidity carried over into the early years of Shaka's rise. The composition of Mzilikazi's chiefdom no doubt changed constantly through this period, especially as he moved around during the Zulu-Ndwandwe wars. He appears generally to have been a popular leader, and to have gradually gained rather than lost adherents.[85] Despite the ease with which people could change their political allegiances, the principal of grouping along exogamous clan lines seems to have remained strong; Mzilikazi's new followers were probably mostly related Khumalo. According to a tradition recorded in the 1870s, Mzilikazi 'managed to rally round himself the best families of his own tribe . . .'[86] As we have already seen, he continued to gather adherents right up to the moment he left Zululand. No source mentions it, but it is reasonable to assume that he also lost some adherents as soon as he defied Shaka. The faint-hearted would not have had far to go to join other kinsmen living under Beje and Mlotsha in the nearby Ngome Forest.

Whatever population gains Mzilikazi's chiefdom made up to about 1821 were largely off-set by the severe losses suffered during the last battle with the Zulu. Fynn's figure of 300 for the number of people who actually left Zululand with Mzilikazi could therefore be very nearly correct. The occasional references to individual survivors of this period which dot later written accounts affirm that men, women, and children were all in this group, but, as we have seen, a high proportion of those killed by the Zulu were females and old people. Hence, most of the survivors were males. Shorn of many of the weaker members of their society, these remaining people were left tough, mobile, and determined—excellent qualities with which to meet the many challenges ahead.

FORMATION OF THE NDEBELE STATE IN THE EASTERN AND SOUTHERN TRANSVAAL, *c.*1821-1827

The years immediately following Mzilikazi's departure from Zululand are perhaps the least well understood in his career. Not only are these years undocumented by first-hand literate witnesses, but they are also poorly remembered by the Ndebele themselves. Near-contemporary testimony taken from Ndebele informants says little about Mzilikazi's activities during the early 1820s; traditional sources say even less. Traditional authoritites tend to compress events of those years into a story suggesting the Mzilikazi marched more or less directly from Zululand to the western Transvaal. In the words of one informant, it was a journey that 'took twelve months'.[1] Other authorities have Mzilikazi pausing from this rapid march only in order to attack the famous Sotho king Moshweshwe at Thaba Bosiu (an event datable to 1831).[2] In fact, it took Mzilikazi ten years to reach the western Transvaal. During the first five or so of those years he moved through the eastern and southern regions of the Transvaal, gathering new followers by conquest and by voluntary submission, and transforming his chiefdom into what soon came to be known as the Ndebele kingdom.[3]

The failure of the Ndebele to remember much about the formative years of the early 1820s must have been a consequence of the frantic confusion of the period. Mzilikazi migrated almost steadily for several years through completely unknown regions. He waged war with most of the strangers he encountered along the way , and his original following was quickly out-numbered by new adherents. Many of these new-comers were other Nguni refugees from the Shakan wars who brought with them their own perspectives on the disorders then spreading on the highveld. Mzilikazi's followers—both old and new—had little time to become familiar with their ever-changing surroundings and alien Sotho neighbours. In later years they remembered some of the most outstanding occurences of the period, but they forgot—or never perceived—the broader contexts in which they had taken place. Hence, from the earliest written records, Ndebele testimony on the 1820s is spotty and contradictory.

Fortunately we do not have to rely solely upon Ndebele evidence for this period. The Ndebele were not seen by literate observers until 1829, but reports of their activities filtered down into European areas as early as 1823, making possible at least a skeletal chronological framework. More important, however, is evidence taken from non-Ndebele Africans in later years. Whereas Mzilikazi's first years in the Transvaal were to his own followers confusing and only vaguely remembered, to the peoples among whom he travelled his passage was a traumatic and well-defined experience. The Ndebele may not have remembered the identities and locations of all their neighbours and adversaries, but these other peoples never forgot who Mzilikazi was or where they had encountered him. Through the near-contemporary and traditional evidence of the peoples of the eastern and southern Transvaal the course of early Ndebele migrations can be charted in some detail. Employment of such evidence makes possible a reconstruction of the period which is more accurate and far clearer than any previously written.

Current views on early Ndebele migrations have been shaped largely by A. T. Bryant's version in his book, *Olden Times in Zululand and Natal*. Historians recognize that Bryant's work contains major flaws, but in the apparent absence of alternative sources they have tended to accept his views on this subject as reflecting authentic Ndebele traditions and, therefore, as essentially correct.[4] In fact, Bryant's version of Ndebele migrations draws upon A. A. Campbell's early writings—not upon traditional material collected by himself—with modifications based upon a book written by two missionaries, Thomas Arbousset and F. Daumas, in 1842.[5] As will be seen, neither of these sources is fully reliable. Since Bryant's version of the period so clearly dominates modern literature on the subject, his account is worth summarizing here.

According to Bryant, Mzilikazi escaped from Zululand in about 1823, quickly crossing the Drakensberg Mountains onto the South African plateau, or highveld. There he and his followers fought their way north until they reached the 'upper Olifants River', where they built a temporary settlement known as *ekuPumuleni* ('the place of rest'). Shortly after founding this settlement,

Mzilikazi repelled a major attack by two local rulers, Makotoko and Sibindi. Around the time of this confrontation (Bryant's sequence of events is unclear here), Mzilikazi sent an army against the Pedi people living between the Olifants and lower Steelpoort Rivers, but this force was decisively defeated. During his two or so years at *ekuPumuleni* Mzilikazi's forces were more successful against many other Sotho communities, which they raided continuously. At some point during these years Mzilikazi clashed with another Nguni refugee leader, Nqaba, who afterwards veered off to the northeast. Finally, drought forced Mzilikazi to abandon *ekuPumuleni* in 1825, so he migrated west with his evergrowing following to the region immediately around present Pretoria in the central Transvaal. (There he built new settlements along a lengthy stretch of the Aapies River. In 1827 his troops returned against the Pedi, whom they conquered and impressed into service at the Aapies.)[6]

This version of early migrations, as stated by Bryant and as interpreted by later historians, contains a number of readily apparent problems. First, where exactly was *ekuPumuleni*? Bryant's allusions to its location are vague and somewhat contradictory. Later historians place it in numerous locations, some separated by as much as 150 miles.[7] Second, how was it possible for Mzilikazi continuously to send out raiding parties far and wide when his manpower must have been severely limited and his very survival threatened? Two recent authorities even hold that he sent forces 'long distances' from *ekuPumuleni*, including attacks on Molitsane and Sebitwane, who were then operating at least 200 miles west of the Olifants River.[8] Third, independent lines of evidence, as will be shown, contradict Bryant's basic geographical and chronological scheme of Ndebele movements.

By drawing upon evidence from the non-Ndebele peoples, this chapter offers a totally revised version of the first five years of Ndebele migrations. It argues that Mzilikazi must have left Zululand by 1821; that he never built a settlement like Bryant's *ekuPumuleni* in the eastern Transvaal; that his troops were never defeated by the Pedi; that he did not migrate directly from the eastern Transvaal to the Pretoria region; and that he left the eastern Transvaal in 1823.

Mzilikazi spent only about two years in the eastern Transvaal. Except during a one year occupation of Pediland he moved almost continuously. He did not send detached raiding parties over significant distances; instead his entire following seems to have fought as a single band of roving predators. When they quit the eastern Transvaal, they moved southwest to the middle bend of the Vaal River, on both sides of which they built their first semi-permanent settlements. Finally, it was from the Vaal—not from the eastern Transvaal—that the Ndebele moved to the Pretoria region in about mid-1827.

The most important contribution of this chapter is its revelation of the hitherto unrecognized period of Ndebele settlement by the Vaal River. Besides its obvious inherent significance to Ndebele history, this revelation helps to correct some of the problems implicit in Bryant's version of early Ndebele migrations. Evidence pertaining to the Vaal period of settlement provides a chronological framework against which Mzilikazi's prior movements can be dated more accurately. Also, it allows us to make some geographical sense out of Ndeble military operations during the early 1820s. Raids formerly ascribed to the so-called *ekuPumuleni* period of settlement can now be seen to have emanated from the Vaal settlements. Thus it is evident that the Ndeble experience in the eastern Transvaal was of a different nature from later periods, for the Ndebele began to coalesce as a quasi-sedentary society only after they reached the southern Transvaal.

Mzilikazi arrives in the Transvaal, c. 1821

The previous chapter carried the story of Mzilikazi's flight from Zululand up to the point where he attacked Nyoka near the head-waters of the Mkuze River. He seems to have occupied Nyoka's town only long enough to obtain supplies, for the danger of Zulu pursuit still existed. From Nyoka's Mzilikazi and his followers marched approximately north. They may have passed through Sobhuza's emerging Swazi kingdom along the Usutu River, but this is not certain. According to one traditional account, Mzilikazi had arranged with Sobhuza for passage through Swaziland prior to his departure from Zululand.[9] However, if this were so, one would expect the event to have been better remembered in traditions in view of their tendency to emphasize Mzilikazi's connections with other famous men. In any case, it is certain that Mzilikazi's followers at least skirted the western fringes of

Sobhuza's domain, as some Khumalo elected to remain in Swaziland.[10]

Mzilikazi probably crossed the Drakensbergs onto the interior plateau somewhere just west of the Usutu River, for he immediately fell upon a branch of the Phuthing people living on the Vaal/Olifants watershed.[11] The Phuthing scattered before the invaders. Some of them formed a predatory band under a sub-chief named Ratsebe, who led his followers across the Vaal River, where they became caught up in a general shift of Sotho peoples to the west.[12] Ratsebe later returned to the Vaal and encountered Mzilikazi a second time. As will be seen, firm chronological evidence for Ratsebe's activities during the interval between these two encounteres provides a major clue to dating Ndebele movements throughout this period. For the moment it need only be stressed that Mzilikazi occupied Phuthing territory briefly while his people rested, refreshed themselves with Phuthing foodstores, and rounded up livestock.[13]

From Phuthing territory the Ndebele proceeded north, following the course of the Steelpoort River to the site of present Roos-Senekal. There they attacked the Ndzundza chiefdom ruled by a man named Magodongo. The Ndzundza are a branch of the so-called Transvaal Ndebele—largely Sotho-ized Nguni whose ancestors migrated to the Transvaal from the eastern coast some centuries earlier.[14] These people were in many respects culturally identical to their Sotho neighbours, with whom they had inter-married extensively. Indeed, in various traditions Magodongo is commonly referred to as a 'Sotho' chief, and his name is usually given in one of its Sotho forms: Makotoko, Rankokoto, or Enkokoto.[15]

Mzilikazi's conquest of Magodongo is in Ndebele traditions the best-remembered event of his years in the eastern Transvaal. It is also well-remembered by the Ndzundza themselves, among whom 'the coming of Mzilikazi is spoken of as an event of yesterday, compared with the remote times to which [Transvaal] Ndebele tradition goes back.'[16] To Mzilikazi's Ndebele the encounter with Magodongo was a dramatic and peculiar event. One of the few Ndebele-penned histories of the kingdom devotes an entire chapter to the confrontation, stressing the idea that Magodongo was a magician whom Mzilikazi had to overcome by trickery.[17] The image of Magodongo as a magician probably derives from his attempt to repel Mzilikazi's invasion with a cattle stampede.

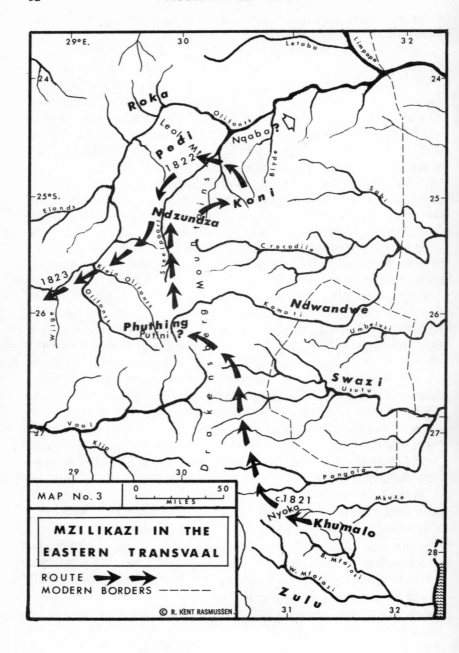

MAP No. 3

MZILIKAZI IN THE EASTERN TRANSVAAL

ROUTE
MODERN BORDERS - - - - -

© R. KENT RASMUSSEN

According to Ndebele tradition collected in 1898, Magodongo combined with a neighbouring Transvaal Ndebele chief, Sibindi, to fight Mzilikazi:

> These two chiefs sent out as a blind, in charge of an impi, a large troop of white oxen, as a peace offering. The oxen were driven right into Umziliga's [sic] people, and as they became separated and disorganized, the impi commenced stabbing them. The Mangoni [Mzilikazi's people] rallied, drove the Basutos beyond their kraals inflicting great loss, buring some of their kraals, and capturing all their cattle. They remained some months living in the sunburnt kraals of the Basutos.[18]

This account , recorded by A. A. Campbell, goes on to tell of how Mzilikazi eventually captured and executed Magodongo, apparently by impalement.[19]

Ndzundza traditions corroborate Ndebele traditions on the essential points of the above account. They tell of Mzilikazi's 'conquering the chief Magodongo with an overwhelming force, while on his way to the north. Magodongo himself was killed, and the tribe lost all their property.'[20] Sibindi's personal fate is not recorded, but it is clear that his chiefdom was soundly defeated.[21]

The first solid clue to the chronology of Mzilikazi's movements is the apparent connection between Mzilikazi's conquest of the Ndzundza and the period of time shortly after a solar eclipse. The French missionaries Arbousset and Daumas, who collected information from Transvaal refugees south of the Vaal in 1836, wrote that 'the natives allege that a short time before [Mzilikazi's invasion] an eclipse of the sun had presaged these misfortunes and those which followed.'[22] After the passage of several more decades the Ndzundza seem to have telescoped the eclipse and Mzilikazi's invasion into a single event. According to the amateur ethnologist George W. Stow (writing sometime before 1882):

> Enkokoto [Magodongo] was killed and his tribe ruined. A great eclipse of the sun having taken place the same day, the apparent extinction of the light of day and appalling darkness which accompanied it were veritable omens which predicted these disasters . . .[23]

Stow's informants almost certainly err in dating Mzilikazi's arrival to the day of the eclipse. The fact that the eclipse occurred *before* Mzilikazi arrived is implied by Stow's phrase, 'omens which *predicted* these disasters', and of course, is, made explicit in the earlier account written by Arbousset and Daumas. The telescoping of the two events is typical of the tendency in oral traditions to link together epical events.[24] Significantly, Ndebele tradition says nothing about any eclipse during Mzilikazi's early career.

The significance of Stow's account lies in its emphasis on the totality of the eclipse remembered by the Ndzundza, for the only eclipse of that general period which could have blacked out their territory was the solar eclipse of 14 March 1820.[25] It is safe to conclude that Mzilikazi reached Ndzundza country *after* that date on the basis of Ndzundza evidence. Furthermore, the failure of all Ndebele-derived evidence to comment on any eclipse suggests also that his break with Shaka and subsequent departure from Zululand took place some time after March 1820. As additional chronological evidence unfolds below, it will become clear that he probably arrived in the Transvaal sometime in 1821, and that he attacked Magodongo in either 1821 or 1822.

As it appears that Ndzundza country was the first region in which the Ndebele halted for any length of time— perhaps several months—we might wonder if this is the site which Bryant calls *ekuPumuleni*. Bryant caused a great deal of confusion by giving this settlement's location as on 'the upper Olifants River'. Since the 'upper' part of a river is generally construed to mean its headwaters, many historians have placed *ekuPumuleni* around the Olifants/Vaal watershed.[26] We know that Mzilikazi occupied Phuthing territory in that area, but he did so only very briefly. What Bryant apparently meant by 'upper Olifants' was the *northern* bend of that river. He describes the Pedi people as 'occupying the country about the *upper* Olifants and Steelpoort rivers' and as 'Mzilikazi's near neighbours' during his occupation of *ekuPumuleni*.[27] Ndzundza country was not, of course, on the Olifants River, but it was so placed as to make the Pedi Mzilikazi's 'near neighbours' during his occupation of the region. Furthermore, it fits Bryant's description of *ekuPumuleni* as the place from which Mzilikazi invaded the Pedi—which, as we shall see, he did.

Ndzundza country also fits Bryant's description of *ekuPumuleni* in other ways. It was indeed Mzilikazi's first 'place of rest', as the name itself connotes, although he clearly did not remain there the several years suggested by Bryant. Also, Bryant gives drought as Mzilikazi's reason for abandoning *ekuPumuleni*, and there are good reasons to believe that it was in fact a water shortage which encouraged him to leave the middle Steelpoort.[28] As we have seen, an Ndebele tradition quoted above describes the kraals of the Ndzundza as 'sunburnt'. This expression hints at a drought. A more convincing piece of evidence recorded by Andrew Smith in 1835 relates that when the Ndebele first entered the Transvaal, they 'took a course a good way to the eastward, but finding the country badly watered, they established themselves where Mr Moffat found them.'[29]

In sum, it appears that Bryant's *ekuPumuleni* has some basis in fact. However, Bryant clearly exaggerates the longevity of the settlement, thereby giving a misleading picture of the nature of Ndebele operations in the eastern Transvaal. The Ndebele appear never to have remained in one place long enough to establish a base from which they could raid beyond their immediate vicinity, or around which they could build a viable, self-sustaining economy.

The Ndebele occupy Pediland, c. 1822–23

While the Ndebele were advancing north from Zululand, a political transformation was occurring among the Pedi, who lived between the lower Steelpoort and middle Olifants Rivers. Under their great paramount chief Thulare the Pedi had built a small empire by reducing many of their neighbours to tributary status during the 1810s.[30] Shortly before the Ndebele arrived, Thulare died and his sons engaged in a debilitating fratricidal struggle for power. Within a few years of Thulare's death one of these sons, Phethedi, secured a tenuous hold on the Pedi paramountcy, while another, Makopole, crossed the Steelpoort River and established a new Pedi state over the Koni people near present Lydenburg.[31] Divided amongst themselves, the Pedi were ill-prepared to deal with a comparatively powerful aggressor.

According to Pedi tradition, Thulare died on the day of a solar eclipse.[32] This was almost certainly the same eclipse remembered by the Ndzundza: that of 14 March 1820.[33] Since the Pedi themselves date Mzilikazi's arrival in their country to two years after Thulare's death, it would follow that he got there in 1822.[34] Normally such traditional estimates of chronology cannot be relied upon implicitly; however, what we can piece together from subsequent Ndebele chronology suggests that 1822 was probably the correct date for this event.

As was mentioned at the beginning of this chapter, the 'Bryant version' of early Ndebele history holds that the Ndebele attacked the Pedi twice. The first time the Ndebele attacked from their base at *ekuPumuleni* but were decisively repelled. The second time, about four years later (in c.1827), the Ndebele attacked from their new base by the Aapies River and achieved total victory.[35]

The present account rejects this two-invasion theory. It argues that Mzilikazi attacked the Pedi but once, achieving a victory in about 1822. It further argues that the two-invasion theory probably derives from the Pedi confusing Mzilikazi's people with those of another migrant Nguni leader, Nqaba.

The Pedi remember Mzilikazi's invasion as a devastating blow from which their society barely recovered.[36] By contrast, the Ndebele hardly remember this episode.[37] This discrepancy is para-doxical, for it contradicts the normal tendency of tradition to stress victories while suppressing memory of defeats. In this case, however, the Pedi could scarcely forget an event which—however humiliating—constituted a major turning point in their history. To the Ndebele, victory over the Pedi was merely one unexceptional success in a string of major military confron-tations. The Ndebele evidently regarded the Pedi as less challeng-ing or less interesting adversaries than others they encountered during this period. Before reconstructing the history of the Ndebele invasion of Pediland, we must first return to the question of why they left Ndzundza territory.

As we have seen, drought may have been the reason the Ndebele were willing to abandon their occupation of the middle Steelpoort region. Another, related reason may have been that they exhausted the stores of food which they had found and were unprepared to commit themselves to producing their own food.[38] In any case, it is clear that their decision to move on was triggered by friction with their northeastern neighbours: the Pedi and Koni of Makopole. Mzilikazi grew irritated by Makopole's cattle raids, so he mobilized his entire following for a massed assault on his troublesome neighbours. The Ndebele stormed the Koni kraals around Lydenburg, killing Makopole and many other people and driving most of the surviviors northwest to central Pediland. This is the first Ndebele war for which we have explicit evidence that Mzilikazi captured non-Nguni people whom he incorporated into his own ranks.[39]

The Ndebele did not linger in Koni country. Instead, they pursued their escaping enemies across the Steelpoort River into Pediland.[40] They found the Pedi paramount chief Phethedi, his uncle Motodi, and other members of the Pedi royal family near the Steelpoort and quickly killed them all.[41] No meaningful details of the fighting survive, but the Ndebele appear to have capitalized on the failure of the Pedi to combine their defensive efforts. In successive engagements the Ndebele routed localized groups of Pedi until they found themselves the masters of all Pediland. Some Pedi survivors hid in the recesses of the Leoulu Mountains, which dominate central Pediland, throughout Mzilikazi's occupation of their country .[42] Other Pedi fled across the Olifants River to seek refuge among their neighbours. One small band was led by Thulare's sole surviving son, Sekwati, who later returned to rebuild the Pedi state. Sekwati may have paid tribute to Mzilikazi during this period of exile, but evidence on this point is not conclusive.[43]

That Mzilikazi's reasons for steadily migrating north and invading successive communities were largely economic is suggested by Ndebele behaviour during their occupation of Pediland. The Ndebele seem to have remained there long enough to consume local food supplies, to collect cattle, and to incorporate new members into their society. Their occupation lasted about one year.[44] The Pedi refugees hiding in the mountains eked out their own existence by gathering wild vegetables and occasionally pilfering stray cattle from the new Ndebele herds.[45] According to Ralolo, an elderly Pedi man interviewed around 1910:

> The Zulus [i.e., Ndebele] also had no grain and lived upon their enormous herds of cattle, sheep and goats. Mosilikatse stayed for one year. Some of the Bapedi and other [sic] went with him when he left . . .[46]

A more recent authority adds that during Mzilikazi's occupation of Pediland, the Ndebele 'completely denuded the country of all stock and grain.'[47] The impression that the Ndebele exhausted the resources of Pediland is further supported by Pedi descriptions of their country in the aftermath of Mzilikazi's occupation. The Pedi remember this as a time of social chaos and famine during which cannibal bands roamed the country, and grazing lands reverted to their natural state in the absence of livestock.[48] Once again it appears that the Ndebele did not attempt to sustain local food production in an occupied territory.

The reasons for Mzilikazi's abandonment of Pediland will be discussed below. First, however, it is necessary to comment upon the origin and significance of the two-invasion theory of Ndebele-Pedi relations which is found in the Bryant version of early Ndebele history.

Mzilikazi, the Pedi, and the Ngoni of Nqaba, c. 1822

The French missionaries Arbousset and Daumas originated the theory that the Ndebele had to invade the Pedi twice, in c.1822 and c.1827, before they achieved a victory.[49] Although no other original source corroborates their theory, their conclusions have been accepted by most historians who have written about this period of Ndebele history.[50] In view of the fact that Arbousset and Daumas collected their evidence only about fifteen years after the events they describe, it is strange that they could be so incorrect. Not only does no other known evidence support the two-invasion theory—as they express it—but such evidence as does exist on Ndebele-Pedi relations stresses that Mzilikazi conquered the Pedi during his *first* encounter with them, and that this encounter occurred while he was migrating north through the eastern Transvaal—not while he was living in the central Transvaal.

The key to this contradiction between the two-invasion theory and other existing evidence lies in the traditional account told by the Pedi informant Ralolo:

> . . . .the Zulus [sic] under Mosilikatse came and killed Makopole, the other side of Lydenburg. When a part of the Zulus came to Krugerust, Pethedi went and killed them. Some of these Zulus crossed the Olifants River and went into the low-brush field (now Portuguese). Gunganyane was their chief.
>
> Now the greater part of the Zulus under Mosilikatse came down the Watervall [River]. . . . Pethedi with his men went against them. He and all the sons of Tulare were then killed in a fierce fight except Sekwati.[51]

It will be observed that while Ralolo's statement agrees with many of the points made about Ndebele-Pedi relations above, it also contains several puzzles. His description of Mzilikazi's people as 'Zulus' presents no difficulties. But who were the 'Zulus' who crossed the Olifants, and how did the name of the late nineteenth century Gaza king Gungunyane find its way into his statement? A single explanation resolves both these questions and the problem of Arbousset and Daumas' two-invasion theory.

About the same time Mzilikazi was forming his Ndebele state in the eastern Transvaal, another Northern Nguni refugee leader, Nqaba (or Nxaba) of the Msene clan, was passing through this region.[52] According to A. T. Bryant, Nqaba and Mzilikazi 'came into violent collison, about Pediland' and Nqaba 'ricochetted again sharply off to the northeast, into Portuguese territory.'[53] No other independent source mentions this confrontation, but independent lines of evidence confirm Bryant's additional assertion that Nqaba at least briefly joined forces with the founder of the Gaza kingdom, Soshangane, in present Mozambique.[54]

Unfortunately, Bryant does not identify his sources for the above points.[55] Nevertheless, his account does appear credible, especially when interpreted in the light of Ralolo's statement. Viewed together, these two authorities suggest a coherent explanation of Arbousset and Daumas' two-invasion theory. It is possible—if not probable—that Mzilikazi and Nqaba met and formed some kind of alliance at the Steelpoort River, and that while Mzilikazi's own people were attacking Makopole at Lydenburg, Nqaba was leading his people (later known as Ngoni) against central Pediland. Nqaba's force would thus have been the first wave of 'Zulus' mentioned by Ralolo, and his defeat by Phethedi's Pedi would have been the Pedi victory which Arbousset and Daumas said was over Mzilikazi's people.[56] Nqaba's people would thus have been the 'Zulus' who crossed the Olifants River and entered Portuguese territory—where they are known actually to have gone about this time. Ralolo's reference to Nqaba as 'Gunganyane' (Soshangane's grandson) is not untypical of the kind of anachronistic identifications one finds in oral traditions. The Pedi evidently knew that Nqaba was associated with Soshangane, and a bare hint of this connection is also found in Ndebele traditions.[57] The two-invasion story is completed by Ralolo's clear description of Mzilikazi's leading the follow-up attack which resulted in the Pedi defeat.[58]

The above hypothesis explains the two-invasion theory, but it does not explain the nature of the presumed relationship between Mzilikazi and Nqaba. Bryant is the sole authority that such a relationship even existed, but he is vague both on the type of relationship the two leaders had and on the reasons for their separation.[59] Further speculation on this issue is justifiable, in view of the possibility that additional evidence may some day emerge.

The 1820s saw many shifts of political alignments among the Nguni refugee bands which were fleeing from Zululand. The personal qualities of individual band leaders were probably the most important determinants in holding together the unrelated members within aggregate groups. So long as these bands kept moving, the loyalties of their members went first to their immediate leaders, who were typically traditional clan chiefs. Mzilikazi's eventual success in building his chiefdom into a large kingdom lay largely in his early ability to attract other Nguni chiefs (many of whose names are now forgotten) to his own standard. However, even he was occasionally deserted by chiefs who had joined him voluntarily.[60] Nqaba may well have been one such deserter; indeed, his own later career was notable for his inability to sustain alliances with other leaders.[61] Assuming that Nqaba and Mzilikazi did form some kind of alliance prior to their attacks on the Pedi, Nqaba's defeat at the hands of the Pedi would certainly have placed him in an inferior bargaining position in relation to Mzilikazi; it might even have placed him in danger of retribution from the latter. In either case, he probably saw resuming his own migration to the northeast to be his safest course of action. This interpretation would explain why Bryant's references to hostilities between Nqaba and Mzilikazi are so vague.

In sum, then, Mzilikazi's own followers were never defeated by the Pedi. They conquered the latter during their initial migration north, in about 1822. Accounts of an Ndebele defeat actually pertain to other Nguni invaders, most likely the Ngoni of Nqaba. We can now turn our attention back to Mzilikazi's reasons for leaving Pediland.

The Ndebele leave the eastern Transvaal, c. 1823

As we have seen, the Ndebele occupation of Pediland lasted about one year. Various scraps of chronological evidence, while individually inconclusive, collectively point to 1822–1823 as the period of Ndebele occupation. Somewhat firmer evidence which shall be presented below supports this dating, suggesting that the Ndebele left Pediland in early or mid-1823.

Thus far in his career as an independent leader, Mzilikazi had operated as a roving predator. His followers appear to have moved and to have fought in a single compact—but growing—body. They moved north steadily, occupying existing towns, capturing other peoples and their livestock, and consuming conquered peoples' accumulated food stores. Nowhere did they exhibit any observable interest in establishing a self-supporting settlement. They apparently decided to abandon Pediland once they had used up all the supplies they had captured.

Hitherto it has been supposed by historians that from the eastern Transvaal the Ndebele moved directly to the region around present Pretoria where they were first visited by literate Europeans in 1829.[62] In the next section of this chapter conclusive evidence will demonstrate that from Pediland the Ndebele actually migrated southwest to the middle Vaal River before they settled in the central Transvaal. Less conclusive, however, is the evidence pertaining to the reasons for their abrupt turn away from what had been a consistently northerly migration over the previous several years.

The possibility that the Ndebele suffered through drought conditions in the eastern Transvaal has already been discussed with reference to their leaving Ndzundza territory. The evidence that they experienced a drought somewhere in the eastern Transvaal is good, but it is not clear whether this condition applied to their stay in Pediland. Furthermore, it does not follow that drought in that region should have influenced the Ndebele to turn southwest, rather than continuing to the north or northeast.

The somewhat mysterious relationship between Mzilikazi and Nqaba may have been an element in the Ndebele decision to migrate southwest. We know that Nqaba's Ngoni migrated northeast from Pediland. Possibly the Ndebele turned away from that direction to avoid a second confrontation with them. Furthermore, had the Ndebele followed Nqaba's route towards Mozambique, they probably would have risked losing their cattle in a tsetse-fly zone around the lower Olifants River.[63] By 1823 the Ndebele had large herds of livestock which they must have valued greatly. Nqaba, on the other hand, might well have been bereft of cattle after his repulse at the hands of the Pedi.

Finally, there is very tantalizing, but inadequate, evidence that the Ndebele encountered coastal-based slavers, against whom they suffered some military reverses. In 1833 the London Missionary Society South African superintendent John Philip wrote that Mzilikazi 'has been in a constant state of warfare with the Slave Traders'. Philip never visited the Ndebele. He relied upon missionary agents stationed in the far interior for his information. It appears that he drew this particular conclusion from information supplied to him by French missionaries who dealt with the Ndebele in 1832.[64] These same missionaries wrote that Mzilikazi 'has penetrated eastward as far as the coast'; that 'he has extended his conquests as far as the Portuguese settlement of Mozambique'; and that the Portuguese 'who have attempted to seize his cattle have been repelled'. They also alluded to Mzilikazi's having 'encountered a powerful nation which has checked his advance' to the north.[65] Unfortunately, while it is probable that all these statements allude to the period of Ndebele operations in the eastern Transvaal, their specific context is unclear, and no other known sources illuminate these points significantly.[66] At best we can surmise that conflicts with coastal peoples influenced the Ndebele not to migrate farther northeast.[67]

Taken as a whole, the issues discussed above suggest that the Ndebele regarded continued northerly or northeasterly migration as dangerous. Whether Mzilikazi sent out scouts in various directions to find a new home we can only guess.[68] Whatever the reasons, however, there is no doubt that the Ndebele next moved to the Vaal River.

The Ndebele settle along the Vaal River, c. 1823

When the Ndebele left Pediland they returned up the Steelpoort River and again passed through Ndzundza country. The Ndzundza were now under a chief named Somdegi. According to Ndzundza tradition, Somdegi 'was killed by Umzilikatze *on his return from the north*' (my italics)—a clear indication of the direction of Mzilikazi's migration.[69] From some spot on the Steelpoort the Ndebele turned away and advanced, apparently quickly, to the confluence of the Suikerbosrand and Vaal Rivers. There they confronted the Khudu people, who 'on the approach of Umzilikatzi . . . took refuge amongst the Barolong, where they remained until about 1896, when a great many of them returned to their old homes.'[70] Some Khudu, however, remained and 'offered allegiance to Mziligazi'.[71]

I have already discussed evidence which suggests that Mzilikazi occupied Pediland between 1822 and 1823. Since there is no reason to suppose that his migration from Pediland to the Vaal was other than rapid, it would follow that he arrived at the Vaal in about 1823. This conclusion is supported by another line of evidence taken from indirect but contemporary written sources.

The Phuthing whom the Ndebele had driven west from the Vaal/Olifants watershed in about 1821 combined with thousands of other Sotho refugees to form a vast throng which converged on the Tlhaping town Dithakong (near Kuruman) in mid-1823. In order to defend his mission station Robert Moffat assembled a force of Griqua horsemen who confronted the Sotho throng at Dithakong on 26 June 1823. Though they were greatly outnumbered by the Sotho, the Griqua used their combined advantages of mobility and firearms to scatter the throng.[72] Some prisoners taken during that battle were questioned about their origins; their testimony appears to allude to Mzilikazi's arrival in the Transvaal two years earlier:

> We learn from the prisoners that they with other marauding tribes have been driven from their country by a tribe they call Matabele, and, from the description they give of them, it is evident that they are none other than Caffrees or Mambookees.[73]

Most of the Sotho survivors from Dithakong fled to the north or to the east. Some of those who fled east met Mzilikazi at the Vaal. Within three months of the battle a report reached the Cape Colony that 'the defeated tribe met with another strange tribe *coming down in this direction*' (my italics)—*i.e.*, from the north or northeast.[74] The conclusion that this 'strange tribe' was Mzilikazi's Ndebele is supported by Mzilikazi himself. In 1829 he told Robert Moffat,

> that his was a very humane government, that he, while on the sources of the Yellow [Vaal] River, had avoided the Mantatees on the route northward, but after their defeat at Old Lattakoo [Dithakong] he surrounded a great number of them on their return, whom he took prisoners to prevent them doing more mischief![75]

Sotho traditions confirm that at least some of these refugees whom Mzilikazi captured were the Phuthing of Ratsebe.[76] Ratsebe himself was captured, and he served under Mzilikazi until 1831.[77]

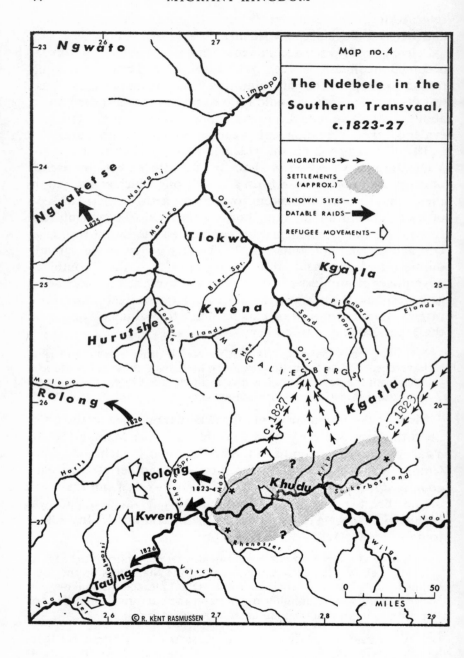

Map no. 4

The Ndebele in the
Southern Transvaal,
c.1823-27

MIGRATIONS—➤ →
SETTLEMENTS
(APPROX.)
KNOWN SITES— ✱
DATABLE RAIDS— ➤
REFUGEE MOVEMENTS— ◇

Ngwato

Limpopo

Ngwaketse

Nolwani

Marico

Oori

Tlokwa

Bier Spr.

Kgatla

Pienaars
Aapies
Elands

Kwena

Toelanie

Elands

Hurutshe

MAHEX

GALIESBERGS

Oori

Sand

Kgatla

c.1823

Molopo

Rolong

1826

c.1827

Harts

Rolong

Schoon Spr.

1823

Klip

Khudu

Suikerbosrand

Vaal

Kwena

Rhenoster

Wilge

1826

Taung

Vaal

Volsch

Vaal

0   50
MILES

© R. KENT RASMUSSEN

Viewed separately, each of the pieces of evidence presented above reveals little substantive information about Ndebele movements. Taken as a whole, however, they form a nearly complete picture of the Ndebele invasion of the middle Vaal region. And that picture suggests that Mzilikazi reached the Vaal around August 1823, about the same moment Ratsebe's Phuthing arrived from the west.[78]

The conclusion that the Ndebele reached the Vaal in 1823 is further supported by contemporary reports of their raiding activity at the end of that year. Agents of the Wesleyan Methodist Missionary Society had begun working among a Rolong community by the Makwassi River (a northern affluent of the Vaal) in 1822.[79] They were thus only about one hundred miles west of where the Ndebele were settling. From about the end of 1823 they began to report that Kwena and other Sotho peoples were fleeing west through Rolong territory before 'a powerful tribe called Matabele'.[80] Mzilikazi's name is not mentioned in their writings—nor in any other extant document written before 1829; however, circumstantial evidence pointing to his people as the aggressors here is good. His Ndebele were unquestionably occupying the region to the east of the Makwassi, and no other Nguni group or predatory Sotho band is known to have been operating in that vicinity at that time. Furthermore, the recorded tradition of one Kwena community names Mzilikazi's Ndebele as the enemy who drove the Kwena west through Rolong territory.[81]

Ndebele settlements by the Vaal

It is difficult fully to account for the failure of historians to observe that the Ndebele resided by the Vaal River. The evidence for their having lived there is diverse and comparatively abundant; it proves beyond any reasonable doubt that the Ndebele occupied the middle Vaal about five years— approximately the same length of time they remained at each of their later (and already well-known) settlements in the Transvaal.[82]

Although much was written about Ndebele history throughout the nineteenth century, nothing like a coherent account of the earliest years of the kingdom was recorded until A. A. Campbell and A. T. Bryant began writing in the early part of this century.

Campbell's writings contain allusions to the Vaal River settlement period, but these have been overlooked by other historians.[83] Bryant, as has been discussed many times already, is one of those historians who had access to Campbell's earliest summary of Ndebele history. He is also the first person to attempt to place Ndebele migrations in a straightforward and explicit framework—naming places and estimating dates. Unfortunately, he too failed to notice Campbell's allusions to the Vaal period, so he simply wrote that Mzilikazi moved directly from the eastern Transvaal to the Magaliesberg Mountains. Until now, his version has gone unchallenged.[84]

The failure of early chroniclers of Ndebele history to record a clearer picture of Mzilikazi's migrations can be attributed, in part, to the Ndebele themselves. Much earlier in this chapter I discussed the inherent confusion of this period to the Ndebele. Another problem was the reticence of the Ndebele to reveal to Europeans details of their past history. In 1829 Moffat wrote of Mzilikazi:

> Of the countries his warriors had visited in the course of their depredatory expeditions I could learn little from him as he seemed to wish me ignorant of his marauding disposition . . .[85]

With the notable exception of Andrew Smith, few European writers troubled to break through this veil of secrecy. Nevertheless, the Ndebele occasionally revealed important clues about their past history, particularly when they wanted to complain about harassment from Griqua and Sotho cattle raiders. In 1835, for example, Mzilikazi told Moffat about

> no less than six times being attacked from the Griqua side. The first time was by the Bergenaars [Griqua bandits] *when he was living on the Lekue and Kena rivers.* The Lekue is a branch of the Kena or Vaal River. [my ital.][86]

Later the same year Mncumbathe, a leading Ndebele official, told Andrew Smith a more detailed story:

> *Whilst on the Liqua* [Vaal] the Matabeli were attacked by parties from the Griqua country, particularly by Jan Bloom and Mulitsani. The first commando of these two attacked his uncle's post which was on the *south of the Liqua* . . . About 5 months afterwards returned to the same place [*sic*] and carried off another post of cattle . . . After that the commando returned and carried off some more cattle . . . These three commandoes went against his uncle who then fled to Mas. [Mzilikazi] who was living to the north of the Liqua. *Whilst still near the Liqua* another comando from Mulitsani carried

off a number of cattle . . . [other attacks are mentioned] . . . After this he [Mzilikazi] *fled inland* to the situation where Mr Moffat found him [in 1829] . . . [my ital.][87]

This account confirms that the Ndebele lived by the Vaal; it implies that they stayed there for some time; and it explicitly refers to their moving from the Vaal to the central Transvaal settlements.

Additional evidence for Ndebele settlement by the Vaal comes from non-Ndebele African sources. 'Ou Booi', a very old Sotho man interviewed sometime before 1925, claimed that as a child he was a witness when 'M'Zilikatze occupied and fortified the Heidelberg Hills' and that he saw 'the Matabele constructing and repairing the fortifications in the Zuikerboschrand'.[88] (The Suikerbosrand is a northern affluent of the Vaal.) Ou Booi's interviewer adds that local traditions attribute all stone fortifications in the region to Mzilikazi. The Ndebele are not known to have built in stone; it was probably their prestige as conquerors that gave rise to traditions linking them to the stone ruins.[89] However, while these traditions may err in connecting the Ndebele with stone ruins, they are not likely to err about the *location* of Ndebele settlements.

Another purportedly first-hand account was recorded by W. C. Scully before 1909. Scully's informant was one Madubangwe, a Hlubi man who had joined Mzilikazi at the Vaal River after his own chief, Mpangazitha, was killed by the Ngwane of Matiwane in the present Orange Free State Province.[90] According to Madubangwe, Mzilikazi had built his 'great place', *Ezinyosini* ('the place of the bees'), near the site of present Potchefstroom, *i.e.*, on the Mooi River, about fifty miles west of the Suikerbosrand.[91] In addition, he says that the Hlubi refugees who joined Mzilikazi were attached to 'an important cattle post commanded by an induna named Soxokozela' located 'on the Rhenoster River in the present district of Kroonstad', *i.e.*, south of the Vaal.[92] Madubangwe thus gives us an idea of the western extent of Ndebele settlements and he confirms Mncumbathe's statement (quoted above) about settlements south of the Vaal.

In order to present the final proof that the Ndebele settled by the Vaal prior to their arriving in the central Transvaal, it is necessary to anticipate a bit on the narrative. At the end of this chapter and at the beginning of the next it will be shown that the Ndebele moved north of the Magaliesberg Mountains in about mid-1827. Traditions collected from various Sotho peoples who had been living in that region naturally remember Mzilikazi's arrival and subsequent conquests there. In almost every instance in which these traditions indicate Mzilikazi's direction of approach, they specify that he came *from the south*. In several instances they further specify that he crossed the Magaliesbergs through Kommando Nek, a pass several miles west of the Oori River.[93] Bryant's version of Ndebele migrations holds that the Ndebele invaded the central Transvaal directly from where they had been living in the eastern Transvaal, *i.e.*, some place around Pediland, as we have seen. If his version were correct, then the central Transvaal peoples would have remembered Mzilikazi's invasion as coming from the northeast; however, no recorded tradition makes such a claim.

To summarize, several independent lines of evidence contain explicit and consistent statements concerning Ndebele settlements on both sides of the middle Vaal River. Of the existence of these settlements there can be no doubt. Unfortunately, little is known about the nature of the settlements themselves. Judging from the statements of Ou Booi and Madubangwe, the Ndebele settlements spanned an east-west breadth of about one hundred miles, between the present sites of Heidelberg and Potchefstroom.[94] This dimension conforms to what we know about the much better documented settlements later built in the central and western Transvaal, but it may not represent a single point in time. Conceivably the Ndebele resided first on the Suikerbosrand, where they displaced the Khudu, and later shifted west, where the Hlubi found them. The evidence further suggests that Ndebele settlements were clustered near the Vaal River, but this point also is not conclusive.

It would probably be safe to assume that the towns and cattle posts built by the Ndebele along the Vaal shared many of the characteristics of those later observed by Europeans in the central and western Transvaal. However, little value would attach to such speculation, so discussion of those later settlements themselves is reserved for the next two chapters. By contrast, it will be seen that we are on much firmer ground in reconstructing the *events* of the Vaal settlement period.

Ndebele raids and wars, c. 1823-1827

The *Difaqane* wars which rocked the interior of South Africa during the 1820s dislocated long-settled communities and transformed many traditional rulers into predatory band leaders. Mzilikazi was unique among the migrant leaders in the Transvaal in the degree to which he succeeded in building a stable and sedentary society. He achieved much of his success through his skillful deployment of military force and his persistence in taking the initiative against his adversaries. From time he reached the Vaal, his success can be measured by his ability to maintain that initiative. Each time he lost it to his enemies he was forced to move on.

Attainment of physical security was clearly Mzilikazi's primary objective throughout his early career. That goal was his justification for all his ostensibly aggressive wars. During the 1860s he told an Afrikaner hunter that

> all his warfare was purely defensive. To that end he conquered and exterminated . . . he excused his wholesale massacres in the Transvaal as an act of policy. 'I was like a blind man feeling my way with a stick. We had heard tales of great impis that suddenly popped up from underground or swept down on you from high mountains . . . and we had dread of the Korannas, mounted and armed with rifles. I had to keep open veld around me. Had I been attacked, every one of them [*sic*] would have been a spy and a recruit for my enemies.'[95]

Throughout their stay by the Vaal River, the Ndebele raided frequently in all directions—particularly to the west.[96] During 1823 and 1824 especially, they maintained heavy pressure on the Khudu, Kwena and other peoples in their vicinity, many of whom—as we have seen—fled west.[97] By late 1825 or early 1826 they were raiding as far northwest as the Molopo River, where they attacked Rolong chiefdoms, and into southeast Botswana, where they attacked the Ngwaketse.[98]

Ndebele occupation of the Vaal went unchallenged for two years; then Sotho and Griqua/Korana cattle raiders began to harass their outposts with increasing frequency. A tradition recorded by A. A. Campbell in 1898 gives a remarkably accurate overview of those years:

> Umziligas fled to the Transvaal to Umkwashla's, whose people surrendered to him on his arrival. They subdued and conquered all the surrounding Basuto tribes. After two years of a comparatively peaceful life, Umlizana [Molitsane] of the Heambese [Taung] sent an

Impi to fight Umziligas. This Impi arrived during the absence of a
large expedition to a Basuto chief named Manyoba. Umlizana looted
a large number of cattle and the Mandebele lost heavily in men. On
the return of the Impi who had been successful against Manyoba,
Umziligas collected all his people and followed up Umlizana, who on
seeing their approach fled. They succeeded in recapturing a portion of
their stolen cattle.[99]

'Umkwashla' was probably the name of the Khudu chief whom
the Ndebele drove out in 1823. As will be shown, 'Manyoba'
seems to have been the Ndebele name for the Ngwaketse ruler
Makaba, or for the Ngwaketse themselves. A variety of sources
confirm that the Ndebele attacked the Ngwaketse in 1825 while
their own territory was being raided by Molitsane and his allies.
Campbell's description of Ndebele retaliation against the latter is
also substantially correct. Ironically, Campbell altered his
account of this period in his later and more influential writings,
thus steering other historians away from the truth.[100]

The campaign against the Ngwaketse was the most distant one
undertaken by the Ndebele during their occupation of the Vaal.[101]
It appears also to have been the first major Ndebele military effort
unrelated to migrations. Under paramount chief Makaba II the
Ngwaketse had developed into one of the most powerful and
prosperous of the western Sotho (or Tswana) chiefdoms.[102] It was
probably the abundant cattle owned by the Ngwaketse which
attracted the Ndebele.

The Ndebele attacked the Ngwaketse in late 1825.[103] As in many
other instances, the Ndebele profited from the failure of their
adversaries to unite against them. One of Makaba's neighbours,
Motswasele I of the Kwena, declined to aid him until he knew how
the battle would develop. When Motswasele concluded that the
Ndebele would prevail, he joined in the attack on the Ngwaketse
and helped to round up livestock.[104] The Ndebele drew Makaba
into a trap and killed him.[105] Before he died, however, Makaba
had taken the precaution of sending Ngwaketse women and
children, as well as cattle, into the neighbouring desert. The
Ndebele were thus able to collect only a small booty and few
captives.[106] Nevertheless, they proved their ability to wage war
successfully against a comparatively strong chiefdom located far
from their own homes.

The proximity of the Ngwaketse to an immense desert gave
them a safe avenue of retreat against invaders. The Ndebele

attacked the Ngwaketse many times over the next twenty years, but they were never able to subdue them.

While Ndebele forces were fighting the Ngwaketse in late 1825 a new adversary appeared at the Vaal River. The Taung chief Molitsane allied with Griqua and Korana horsemen to raid Ndebele cattle posts.[107] Molitsane was the leader of one of the many predatory Sotho chiefdoms which had arisen on the highveld as a consequence of the widespread disorders of the early 1820s. He had obtained some success by emulating Nguni military formations and tactics and by adopting short stabbing spears.[108] His allies were outlaws from the many Griqua and Korana communities dotted along the northern fringes of the Cape Colony. The Korana were a branch of the Khoikhoi who had adopted many elements of European culture.[109] They were generally closely associated with people of mixed European and Khoikhoi descent known as Griqua.[110] The Griqua and Korana enjoyed the advantages of being skilled in the use of firearms and horses, but they suffered the disadvantage of being accepted fully by neither African nor European societies. Hence, they tended to cluster around the frontier zone which joined the Cape Colony with the independent northern regions. Many—but far from all—of these people subsisted by preying upon the livestock of neighbouring Sotho communities and were thus ready allies to men such as Molitsane.

According to Mncumbathe's account (quoted on p. 46), Molitsane and his Griqua/Korana allies raided the Ndebele —together or separately—at least seven times at the Vaal River.[111] Compared to much larger Griqua/Korana assaults on later Ndebele settlements, these early raids appear to have been merely harassing. Nevertheless, the first raids drove Mzilikazi's uncle across the Vaal to the northern bank, as we have seen. Perhaps this was the blow which persuaded the Ndebele to retaliate against Molitsane in early 1826.

Following the account of A. A. Campbell, it appears that soon after his soldiers returned from attacking the Ngwaketse, Mzilikazi sent a large force, or *impi*, in pursuit of Molitsane, then encamped just to his west. This *impi* temporarily drove Molitsane south of the Vaal; it appears also to have encountered the Fokeng chief Sebitwane at the same time.[112]

Sebitwane was originally the chief of a small branch of the Fokeng clan from south of the Vaal River. His chiefdom—like

that of the Phuthing discussed above—was one of the many
forced to move west by the disorders of the early 1820s. He joined
the Sotho throng which converged on Dithakong in June 1823,
and then entered the western Transvaal after the Sotho were
dispersed by the Griqua.[113] For a brief period Sebitwane joined
with Molitsane in plundering Transvaal peoples. Eventually,
however, they were defeated and separated by the Ndebele, so
Sebitwane led his people north.[114] This defeat apparently occurred
early in 1826, in conjunction with Mzilikazi's pursuit of
Molitsane. Sebitwane himself later told the missionary David
Livingstone that he had been defeated by Mzilikazi twice during
his early career, but he did not reveal the details of his encounters
with the Ndebele.[115] Unfortunately, Ndebele-derived evidence on
this subject is also weak.[116]

The apparent silence of Ndebele traditions on Mzilikazi's
earliest encounters with Sebitwane is a puzzle. For after Sebitwane
went on to found the Kololo kingdom, which conquered
Barotseland in present Zambia around 1840, the Ndebele fought a
number of major wars with him during the ensuing decade.[117] It is
sometimes suggested that Mzilikazi and Sebitwane regarded each
other as arch-rivals for three decades; however, this theory
probably exaggerates the significance of their contacts before the
1840s.[118]

While it is clear that the Ndebele were frequently engaged in
raids and defensive wars during their years along the Vaal, it is
also clear that they were busy in other activities. One such activity
was the incorporation of new people into their developing society.

The expansion of Ndebele society

Mzilikazi started adding new recruits to his Khumalo band almost
as soon as he arrived in the Transvaal. His hasty and violent exit
from Zululand had depleted his chiefdom of children, women,
and old people. Other people seem to have deserted him for
Sobhuza when he passed by Swaziland. He began to correct the
imbalances in his following and to enlarge it when he conquered
Magodongo's Ndzundza chiefdom. According to Campbell's
traditions:

> In course of time those belonging to the chiefs Magodonga and
> Sibindi came in and declared allegiance. The women worked as slaves,

and of the men a regiment was formed . . .
The women and children who by these different means had been acquired were given in marriage to our older men. The older ones were chosen for this office. Our ranks were thinned by war and other things, and we say that it was necessary to increase the tribe.[119]

Males incorporated from Sibindi and Magodongo's chiefdoms brought with them new patrilineal clan names. Though these people were themselves of Nguni origin, their descendants appear to have been later identified with Sotho rather than Nguni elements within Ndebele society.[120]

The Pedi provided Mzilikazi with additional recruits,[121] as did the Khudu.[122] It is difficult to find specific evidence on Mzilikazi's incorporation of other Sotho peoples, but it is probable that he took captives from most of the societies he fought.[123] A. T. Bryant asserts that during this period Mzilikazi's following became 'a profoundly Sutuized community, not in name alone, but in numbers, habits, language and blood; for many of its men were Sutu captives, and practically all its females.'[124] This statement may be a valid description of the Ndebele after 1827, but prior to then there was probably a higher proportion of Nguni-derived Ndebele than Bryant allows. Otherwise it would be difficult to explain the predominance of Nguni language, customs, and political power which characterized Ndebele society in later years.[125]

The modern Ndebele count more than sixty distinct names of clans whose members trace patrilineal descent back to the coastal Nguni.[126] Since Mzilikazi appears to have left Zululand in the company only of members of his own Khumalo clan, the other Nguni clan names were all introduced subsequently. The research of A. J. B. Hughes suggests that none of these new clan names was freshly created within Ndebele society, so their origins must lie in the bands of refugees who joined Mzilikazi.[127] Such evidence as exists on this subject further suggests that most of the Nguni refugees who joined Mzilikazi did so during the troubled 1820s.[128] The stories of several important Nguni recruits to Ndebele society during the Vaal period will be told a bit later on.

According to the ethnologist George Stow, Mzilikazi actively recruited new Nguni adherents directly from Zululand *after* he left Pediland:

After securing his retreat he managed to send secret envoys back again into the Zulu country to other of the Zulu regiments, informing them that he had discovered a country where the men could not fight, but one which was rich in cattle and wives! Many further desertions, according to native authority, followed, one of the principal of which was that of Gozane . . .[129]

Stow's statement is apparently uncorroborated by any other independent authority, but it is plausible. His description of the 'country where the men could not fight' might well have applied to what Mzilikazi knew of the Transvaal as a whole up to about 1823; and Mzilikazi's migration southwest from Pediland would have been the most logical time for him to send messengers back to Zululand. What effect such messengers had in securing new Ndebele adherents we can only surmise, but it is clear that by 1826 Mzilikazi was notably successful in attracting two major refugee groups to his banner.

The first group comprised Hlubi refugees. While Mzilikazi was settling the Vaal region, two other important Nguni migrant leaders were operating in the present Orange Free State. These were Mpangazitha and Matiwane of the Hlubi and Ngwane clans, respectively.[130] Their two bands vied for mastery of the Caledon River basin until 1825, when Matiwane's Ngwane routed the Hlubi in a single great battle, killing Mpangazitha in the process.[131]

The Hlubi informant named Madubangwe—discussed above—relates the fate of some of the Hlubi survivors. According to him, one section of the Hlubi regrouped under Mpangazitha's junior son Mehlomakhulu (or Sondaba). He led the Hlubi to the Vet River, where they were captured by an Ndebele *impi* returning from a campaign. The Ndebele soldiers took these Hlubi (and possibly some others) to Mzilikazi, before whom Mehlomakhulu submitted.[132] Madubangwe himself was among those captured:

> I was one of a party which wandered far after Matiwane scattered us . . . [and the Ndebele] captured us. One raised his spear and said: 'Let us kill the jackals.' But the leader said: 'No, we want boys to help in driving the cattle.' They gave us food, and we followed them to Ezinyosini where Umziligazi was.
>
> . . . Umziligazi loved to see dancing, so I was kept at the 'great place'. After a time I was given a spear and a shield. Then I got a wife—a woman captured from the Bangwaketse. This was because I could dance the 'Umsino' (the Hlubi tribal dance) so well.[133]

Mzilikazi allowed Mehlomakhulu's people to remain together—just as Mzilikazi had kept his own people together while under Shaka in Zululand. The Hlubi were, however, posted under an already established Ndebele official:

> Umziligazi . . . accepted his [Mehlomakhulu's] submission to the Matabele dominion. On the Rhenoster River, in the present district of Kroonstad, was an important cattle post commanded by an induna named Soxokozela, who stood high in the confidence of Umziligazi, and here Sondaba [Mehlomakhulu] and his following were located. The ablebodied men were trained under the Matabele military system, and Sondaba was given a minor command.[134]

Things went smoothly for the Hlubi for about a year. Then Mehlomakhulu purportedly feared that his own popularity was making Mzilikazi jealous. Mehlomakhulu learned that Mzilikazi was about to kill him—according to Madubangwe—so he took the initiative by fleeing. In order to make it dangerous for his own followers to stay behind he first killed Soxokozela. Most of the Hlubi then joined his flight back to the Caledon River.[135]

Two different stories are told to explain why Mehlomakhulu succeeded in eluding the *impi* Mzilikazi sent to pursue him. According to the first, Mzilikazi's own soldiers included other Hlubi men who went over to Mehlomakhulu just as the Ndebele *impi* caught up with him. Their defection turned the tables, allowing Mehlomakhulu to escape.[136] The second version is similar to the first, but it adds a third party: the Ngwane of Matiwane. By this version, Mehlomakhulu met another group of Hlubi soldiers while he was fleeing Mzilikazi. These other Hlubi were in the service of Matiwane, whom they had joined after Mpangazitha's death. They diverted the attention of the Ndebele away from Mehlomakhulu, allowing him and his people to escape completely.[137] This version is important for its contribution to our slender knowledge of Ndebele-Ngwane relations.

There is some question as to whether the Ndebele actually fought with Matiwane, or if Matiwane was attacked by the Zulu around this time.[138] Matiwane may or may not have brushed with the Zulu, but Ndebele-derived evidence makes it clear that he indeed fought—and was defeated by—subjects of Mzilikazi.[139] It is likely that this confrontation occurred in the present Free State in conjunction with the Ndebele pursuit of Mehlomakhulu. The present interpretation of Madubangwe's story dates Mehlomakhulu's flight to about early 1827; this date conforms to what is known about Matiwane's subsequent activities. For shortly after he was defeated—apparently by the Ndebele—he crossed the Orange River into the Cape Colony. This happened in mid-1827. The following year a British army force mistook Matiwane's people for Shaka's Zulu and overwhelmed them with artillery.[140] The Ngwane state was shattered. Many of the survivors fled inland. Some of them joined Mzilikazi, then living in the central Transvaal.[141]

Before relating the circumstances of Mzilikazi's migration away from the Vaal River, the story of one more group of Nguni refugees who joined him should be told. Recall that shortly after Mzilikazi defected from the Ndwandwe ruler Zwide to join Shaka in the late 1810s, the Zulu crushed the Ndwandwe and drove Zwide north. Zwide fled beyond Swaziland and regrouped his surviving followers by the Komati River.[142] He died in 1825 and was succeeded as chief by his son Sikhunyane.[143] A year later Sikhunyane mobilized a large force to invade Zululand, hoping to redress the humiliation suffered by the Ndwandwe years before. Warned of the impending invasion by an Ndwandwe defector, Shaka organized an immense army and marched north to meet the enemy. In October 1826 the Zulu army met the Ndwandwe near the Pongolo River and dealt them their final defeat.[144] Sikhunyane seems to have to returned to the Komati River, where he eventually died in obscurity. Other Ndwandwe fled farther inland. According to A. T. Bryant, 'Mzilikazi reaped a rich harvest in this final break-up of the Ndwandwe clan; for large numbers of its men and women, knowing nowhere else to go, betook themselves to him and added considerable strength to his ever-growing tribe.[145] Mzilikazi thus found himself heir to many of the subjects once ruled by the maternal grandfather whom he had deserted.[146]

The Ndebele leave the Vaal River, c. 1827

Continuous harassment from cattle rustlers was probably the main reason the Ndebele decided to abandon their Vaal settlements, as implied by Mncumbathe's statement (quoted above). Further incentive may have been provided by the news of Shaka's impressive victory over the Ndwandwe at a spot only 150 miles to the east.[147] As will be shown in the next chapter, the Ndebele apparently crossed the Magaliesbergs with the intention of continuing north indefinitely—a strong indication that they sought security as far from Zululand as possible. It appears to have been tsetse fly which halted their northward progress, forcing them to find their security on the northern slopes of the

Magaliesberg Mountains.

Chronologically, the migration away from the Vaal is circumscribed by two datable events which together point to around mid-1827 as its own date. The first event was the Ndebele pursuit of Mehlomakhulu's Hlubi. As we have seen, the Hlubi left the Ndebele while the latter were still settled by the Val, and this happened around early 1827.

Evidence for the second relevant event is much firmer. The statement on Ndebele troubles with the Griqua/Korana which Mncumbathe made to Andrew Smith in 1835 also specified that 'shortly after' the Ndebele resettled by the Magaliesbergs they were attacked by the Griqua of Jan Bloem.[148] Contemporary European documents clearly date this Griqua raid to July 1828.[149]

These two events leave a gap between early 1827 and mid-1828 during which the Ndebele could have migrated. Interpolative reasoning allows us to pin the date of the migration down to mid-1827 with some confidence. Bloem's raiding party had to travel several hundred miles from the southwest in order to reach the Ndebele at the latters' new settlements. It is unlikely that Bloem would have undertaken such a distant campaign without prior knowledge of where the Ndebele were; therefore, he probably knew the Ndebele were by the Magaliesbergs at least several months before July 1828. This means that the Ndebele removal to the Magaliesbergs probably occurred before the 1828 winter season. This is an important point, as the Ndebele are unlikely to have migrated during a season other than winter. The dry winters of South Africa were the most convenient periods for both military campaigns and migrations: river beds were easier to cross, the firmer soil was easier to travel over, summer crops were already harvested, and the veld still held fresh fodder for livestock. Furthermore, migrants needed to arrive at a new location during a winter season in order to have time to prepare farms for the following spring's plantings. Although the Ndebele left the Vaal under some duress, there is no indication that their move was panicky. In sum, they probably moved during a winter season, and the winter of mid 1827 is the most likely one during which they could have moved.[150]

CHAPTER III

INSECURITY IN THE CENTRAL TRANSVAAL, c. 1827–1832

Between about mid 1827 and mid 1832 the Ndebele lived around the sources of the Oori River and the northern slopes of the Magaliesberg Mountains in the central Transvaal. This period is the first in Ndebele history for which we have eye-witness written documentation. It is also a period for which there is an abundance of contemporary second-hand documentation and near-contemporary accounts from African informants. The problems of reconstructing the chronology and geography of this period are thus not nearly so formidable as is the case for earlier periods. Nevertheless, a number of important errors have crept into the historiography of this period, and this chapter seeks to dispel them.

The chronological errors found in existing literature on the central Transvaal phase of Ndebele history are mostly only a year or so off the correct dates of events. Such discrepancies may appear minor; however, in several cases they have produced bizarre and tangled reconstructions of related and unrelated events. Incorrect associations of unrelated events have in turn contributed to major misconceptions about Ndebele military power and the geographical scale of their warfare. A particularly striking instance is one historian's inflation of a single tenuous piece of evidence alluding to one Ndebele raid across the Limpopo River into the conclusion that the Ndebele raided from the central Transvaal into present Rhodesia on at least three different occasions. The same historian further concludes that during two of these purported trans-Limpopo raids the Ndebele homeland was invaded by foreign enemies, whom they repelled with severely depleted forces because most of their fighting men were gone. In this instance we can see how one error in chronological reconstruction leads to misleading assessments of the scale of distant Ndebele raiding activity, the strength of Ndebele manpower available at home at any given moment, and the extent of Ndebele experience north of the Limpopo prior to their actual settlement there after 1838.

This chapter pays particular attention to errors such as that discussed above. It attempts to demonstrate how they originated, to correct them, and to re-interpret the Ndebele experience in the central Transvaal in the light of these revisions. Furthermore, this chapter challenges the growing mystique concerning the importance of firearms in African history. It argues that the Ndebele were initially fascinated by guns, but that they lost interest in them as practical instruments of war as they discovered the tactical limitations of firearms in the hands of their Griqua/Korana enemies.

Finally, this chapter examines the geographical extent of Ndebele settlements. It attempts to show how hitherto historians have failed to confront obvious contradictions in the evidence about the locations of Ndebele towns, and how this failure has led to preposterous conclusions. It argues that Ndebele settlements were actually distributed over a more compact area than has been realized, and that prior estimates of the size of the Ndebele population are greatly exaggerated. It will be found that these revised assessments help to place the central Transvaal period more logically within the overall sequence of Ndebele settlements in the Transvaal.

The Ndebele invade the central Transvaal, c. mid-1827

Once the Ndebele decided to abandon their Vaal River settlements, they appear to have moved north rapidly. They advanced, probably as a single body, through a pass in the Magaliesberg Mountains later known as Kommando Nek, just west of the Oori River. The date of their migration was roughtly mid-1827.[1]

In contrast to their situation during their earlier migrations, they now had sufficient manpower to fan out in several directions at once as they entered the new country. Precise reconstruction of this sequence of events is impossible, but the Ndebele may well have conquered the entire Oori River basin in a single stroke. The numerous Sotho chiefdoms they found there had recently been weakened by a succession of foreign invaders, including the Pedi

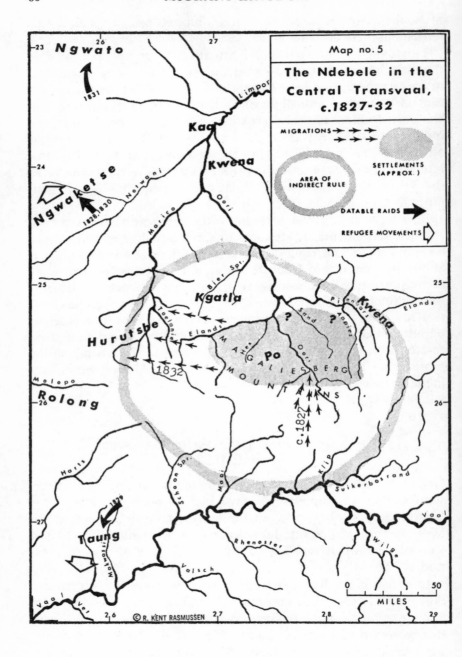

Map no. 5

The Ndebele in the Central Transvaal, c.1827-32

MIGRATIONS →→→ →→→

AREA OF INDIRECT RULE

SETTLEMENTS (APPROX.)

DATABLE RAIDS ➤

REFUGEE MOVEMENTS ⇨

© R. KENT RASMUSSEN

MILES

of Malekutu, the Fokeng of Sebitwane, and others.[2] The extension of the *Difaqane* into this region had turned neighbour against neighbour, resulting in the abandonment of agriculture by many societies and the ruination of many towns.[3] In the midst of such chaos it was almost impossible for the various chiefdoms to combine in defence against the Ndebele invation. The Ndebele thus met only token resistance from a few chiefdoms.[4] Most peoples either submitted meekly to Mzilikazi or fled the region.[5]

Members of individual Sotho chiefdoms often reacted quite differently to the Ndebele invasion. Chiefdoms were divided as individuals and small groups of people fled north and south, often leaving new chiefs behind to deal with the Ndebele. Most of those who fled were not to return to their homes until after Mzilikazi himself fled the Transvaal in 1838.[6] Not all the people who remained in the central Transvaal elected to co-operate with the Ndebele. Some attempted to hide in isolated mountain retreats where the Ndebele besieged and harassed them during their occupation of the region.[7]

After the Ndebele crossed the Magaliesbergs, they appear to have fought their way as far north as the Pienaars River before turning back to settle along the northern slopes of the mountains.[8] Circumstantial evidence suggests that they encountered tsetse fly just beyond the Pienaars River which endangered their livestock, forcing them to turn back.[9] If this were so, it was possibly the second time in their history that their northward migration was halted by that disease-carrying insect.

Within two years—probably sooner—Mzilikazi became the master of the entire region between the Aapies and Elands Rivers to the east and west, and between the Magaliesberg Mountains and the Pienaars River to the south and north. As will be shown, the Ndebele soon began to direct most of their aggressive campaigns against the Sotho/Tswana chiefdoms to their west and northwest, depleting them of both people and livestock. Throughout their residence in the central Transvaal the Ndebele worked consistently to extend their control into the western Transvaal.

Within, and just beyond, the region of direct control in the central Transvaal the Ndebele appropriated the livestock of every community they subdued and added new human recruits to their own population. Mzilikazi required some communities to pay him taxes in grain, skins, ivory, and iron tools.[10] Some communities he gave herds of livestock to tend, but ownership of such herds remained firmly with the Ndebele.[11] He had the chiefs of many groups killed, and had acceptable successors installed in their places.[12]

The Ndebele remained in the central Transvaal for five years. They found the land there fertile and well-watered. It was ideal for raising livestock and for farming and was clearly superior to the surrounding regions in these respects.[13] Furthermore, the central Transvaal suited the Ndebeles' immediate security needs. They had left the Vaal River because of Griqua/Korana harassment from the south; they probably felt that the Magaliesbergs offered them the added physical protection they required. To increase the difficulties for potential invaders, they cleared the territory between the Vaal and the Magaliesbergs of human settlements.[14] As it developed, these physical obstacles failed to provide the Ndebele with the security they required. However, until they were able to neutralize the threat of Griqua/Korana harassment, they were reluctant to migrate farther west.

Jan Bloem attacks the Ndebele, July 1828

The previous chapter discussed how Griqua/Korana and Sotho/Tswana marauders frequently raided Ndebele cattle posts around the Vaal River—temporarily culminating in Mzilikazi's driving Molitsane south of the Vaal. Shortly after the Ndebele left the Vaal in 1827, Molitsane and his Taung recrossed the river from the south and settled by the Makwassi River. Molitsane then resumed his raids on Ndebele outposts.[15] A pattern of Taung raids and Ndebele counter-raids persisted about a year. Finally, a particularly massive Ndebele strike against the Taung encouraged Molitsane again to ask the Korana chief Jan Bloem for assistance.[16]

Bloem readily agreed to help the Taung and he assembled a force comprising Griqua and Korana horsemen armed with guns and unmounted Sotho/Tswana armed with spears and battle-axes. His allied commando numbered several hundred men.[17] Under Bloem's direction, the commando advanced against the Ndebele up the Harts River from the southwest, rendezvousing with Molitsane's people at the Harts/Makwassi watershed in about July 1828.[18] From there the allies proceeded rapidly against Ndebele posts on the northern slopes of the Magaliesbergs between the Hex and Oori Rivers.[19]

The commando arrived in Ndebele country as Mzilikazi's main forces were again campaigning in the far west against the Ngwaketse. Bloem met little resistance. His followers collected about 3,000 head of cattle and then retreated in the direction from which they had come.[20]

Molitsane had experienced Ndebele pursuit before, so he wasted no time in returning with his share of the booty to the Makwassi River. By contrast, the easy success they had thus far experienced made the Griqua/Korana over-confident. They drove their cattle slowly towards the Schoonspruit River, only to be overtaken and scattered by an Ndebele force three nights later.[21]

The development of this conflict resembles later Ndebele-Griqua conflicts so closely that it bears detailed description. Griqua/Korana foolhardiness in these affairs coloured Ndebele attitudes towards firearms and inspired the strategy which Mzilikazi used against half-caste and European invaders over the next two decades.

A minor Korana chief named Haip, whose people were with the Taung early in 1828, described the year's hostilities later to Andrew Smith,[22]

. . . the Mollatzanis [i.e., the Taung] saw that some decisive effort was necessary for future protection. Not being confident of their own powers, the tried and experienced robber, John Bloom . . . was applied to; and, with his assistance and that of his people, a commando was gathered to attack the Solicatzi [i.e., the Ndebele]. To the country of the latter John Bloom and his commando immediately repaired; and, by cunning . . . they succeeded in surprising an outpost and carrying off a very considerable number of cattle, and a few women, which—and not actual warfare—was the chief object of their expedition. For about three days they enjoyed their booty unmolested; and in spite of the advice they received from the women thought that no attempt at rescue or retaliation would be made.

One of the captive females, however . . . zealously cautioned the commando against the probable consequences of the third night; well knowing that a Salatacatzi [Ndebele] invariably waited to accomplish his object at a time of apparent tranquility when he could compass it with great ease . . . To her admonitions, however, one and all were indifferent and the only observations they called forth were: 'Your words must be lies, for you would not inform against your own people.'

> Though thus discouraged, the woman still persevered in inculcating caution, and . . . answered, 'Why should I lie? having been taken by you I must now remain, for, were I to return to my own nation, I should be killed!'

This woman's explanation probably reflected her own fears rather than any actual Ndebele policy. There is no evidence which supports the conclusion that they ever harmed countrymen whom they recaptured.

During these three days, the Griqua and Korana travelled only about fifty miles southwest. Haip continues:

> The third night arrived without any direct evidence of danger. The party proceeded to slaughter and feast upon a part of the cattle they had secured and in that congenial occupation, they passed the greater part of the night . . . They betook themselves to rest just as the moon was descending below the horizon, but a short period before the break of day.
>
> With the appearance of morning the prophecy of the woman was to be fulfilled. When approaching day could just be faintly discerned and the revellers were buried in sleep, the Zooloos [Ndebele] rushed to the charge, and, as would be expected . . . flight rather than defence was immediately resorted to by the attacked.
>
> In the confusion a few shots were fired; but . . . perhaps more the result of inadvertancy than of any regular aim. Haip, accompanied by a bushman [sic], effected his escape from the camp; and, shortly afterwards, when daylight was fairly established, he discovered that, not only himself, but many of the Bituanas [Tswana], were within a circle of Zooloo warriors placed from six to ten yards apart, and ready to destroy whoever might be found flying.

Haip goes on to tell of how the men who attempted to breach the Ndebele ring drew the enemy in on them, thus opening a gap through which Haip and others escaped. The Ndebele then went on to kill about fifty of the invaders and to recapture all the cattle taken by this part of the commando.[23] The Griqua/Korana survivors of this fiasco escaped annihilation only because they had horses. In the next major Griqua/Korana attack on the Ndebele the invaders were not to be so fortunate.

The *impi* Mzilikazi sent after Bloem was apparently a 'scratch' force, whose composition is unknown. Normally he sent young men, or *majaha*, on aggressive campaigns, leaving older, married men, or *madoda*, at home. Since the *majaha* were apparently then off fighting the Ngwaketse, it was probably mostly *madoda* who defeated the commando. Korana participants in the commando also reported seeing very young Ndebele men observing the battle from a distance. These youths were evidently watching the fighting as part of their military training, while also staying close by in case they might be needed.[24]

The Ndebele force which recaptured the cattle from the Griqua/Korana did not continue its pursuit against the Taung, who had returned the additional hundred miles to the Makwassi River. Instead, Mzilikazi delayed his retaliation against Molitsane until the following year.

The Ndebele crush Molitsane, July 1829

Almost exactly a year after the Molitsane/Bloem invasion, a large Ndebele *impi* advanced against the Taung at the Makwassi River. Molitsane somehow learned of the Ndebele *impi* in time to collect his people and to recross the Vaal River to the south. This time the Ndebele pursued him deep into the present Orange Free State and routed his people by the Modder River. The association between this event and the Bloem/Molitsane commando of the previous year is fairly clear, but the time lag between the two events is vague in most sources. As a consequence, historians have tended to conclude that the Ndebele retaliated against Molitsane *immediately* after Bloem's force was scattered.[25] This is a serious error, for it implies that Mzilikazi's manpower was sufficient to wage distant campaigns in several directions simultaneously since it is known that the Ndebele were fighting the Ngwaketse in 1828. Furthermore, the notion that a hastily-assembled *impi* could defeat the Griqua/Korana and then immediately pursue a second enemy an additional 300 miles exaggerates the capabilities of Ndebele soldiers. A careful reconstruction of these campaigns helps to place Ndebele military power into a more accurate perspective.

Before discussing the Ndebele campaign against the Taung itself, it is necessary to fix its chronology. We have already seen that the date of Bloem and Molitsane's commando against the Ndebele is firmly fixed to mid-1828. Hitherto overlooked scraps of evidence date the retaliatory strike against Molitsane to July 1829.

The first piece of evidence is the testimony of an Afrikaner *trekboer* who visited the site of the Ndebele-Taung battle at the Modder River the day after it was fought. Ironically, though he could not later remember whether this happened in 1828 or 1829, he was confident that the correct month was July.[26] There is, however, no doubt that he alluded to 1829, for in August of that year two European traders met the Ndebele *impi* on its return from fighting Molitsane, and they even used their wagons to assist in carrying wounded men.[27]

Around June 1829, then, Mzilikazi decided to rid himself of the troublesome Molitsane once and for all. He mounted an immense *impi* of about four or five thousand men, including a thousand Ndebele of Nguni origin. Many of the incorporated Sotho/ Tswana troops were commanded by Ratsebe, the Phuthing chief whom Mzilikazi had captured by the Vaal River six years earlier.[28] Another non-Nguni chief who assisted the Ndebele was Matlabe, the head of one of the four main Rolong chiefdoms which the Ndebele had defeated in the western Transvaal. Matlabe himself was soon to flee from Mzilikazi's domain, but in 1829 he was content to recognize the latter's rule. Years later he recalled:

> I remained at Hartebeestfontein, and paid taxes to Moselekatse in karosses and beads, as I had no cattle , for Molitsane had taken them from me, and, he, Molitsani, afterwards stole Moselekatse's cattle.
>
> When Moselekatse attacked Molitsani, I was present, being a subject of Moselekatse, and we followed Molitsane across the Vaal River to the Modder River, a little below Bloemfontein, where we attacked him, capturing a number of cattle , killed a great many of his people, and followed him to beyond Bloemfontein . . .[29]

Another Tswana participant in the Ndebele *impi*, Magala of the Hurutshe, added additional details. He recounted how the 'large commando' of Ndebele fell upon Molitsane's town near the Vaal only to find it abandoned. They then pursued and overtook the fleeing Taung south of the Modder River, 'where we recaptured the cattle, and killed all the people.' They then returned home by the same westward-arcking route they had come, apparently in order to find easy fording spots for their cattle on the rivers.[30]

Before the Ndebele attacked the Taung, Molitsane and some of his people escaped from the scene of the battle. Unfortunately for them, however, they soon met Griqua from south of the Orange River who attacked them and took their remaining livestock.[31] After these simultaneous disasters Molitsane temporarily submitted to the Griqua chief Adam Kok at Philippolis; later he joined Moshweshwe in Lesotho and regained some of his former power.[32]

In several respects Mzilikazi's war with Bloem and Molitsane marked a turning point in Ndebele history. His successful repulse of Bloem's commando proved that men armed with guns were not invincible, and his defeat of Molitsane ended the raiding career of his last major enemy north of the Vaal River. Thereafter Ndebele dominance in the Transvaal was challenged only by opponents from south of the Vaal.

The campaign against Molitsane in 1829 is the first for which we have clear evidence of the participation of non-Nguni Ndebele troops. To a great extent Mzilikazi owed his dominance in the Transvaal to his success in mustering diverse and potentially rival forces under a single banner. No other Transvaal leader of the period matched his ability to recruit and to hold new followers. The unitary military command in the Ndebele state gave Mzilikazi an advantage which most of his rivals could not contest.

Finally, the 1829 campaign into the Free State appears to have been the most distant, and perhaps the largest-scale military effort undertaken by the Ndebele to that date. At least four thousand men marched more than 600 miles. This campaign assured that Mzilikazi's reputation would spread more rapidly than ever, especially to the south. Perhaps it was not a coincidence that Europeans first visited him later the same year.

First direct contacts with Europeans, 1829

Information about Europeans first reached the Ndebele from two directions. From the east they learned about European trading activities in Zululand which had commenced in 1824. By 1829 Mzilikazi even knew the names of several traders at Port Natal; he probably got his information from Zulu refugees who joined him in the Transvaal.[33] Through Tswana contacts to the southwest the Ndebele also knew about the European Cape Colony and about the Christian mission stations between themselves and the Colony.[34]

At some point during the 1820s Mzilikazi became very interested in the London Missionary Society (LMS) agent Robert Moffat, who had worked at Kuruman since 1817. The reasons for Mzilikazi's later devotion to Moffat have been a subject for considerable speculation by historians, but all interpretations of their relationship are distorted by our one-sided perspective: Moffat was literate and Mzilikazi was not. Hence, we know little about Mzilikazi's feelings towards Moffat beyond what Moffat himself chose to tell us. Moffat's description of his relationship with Mzilikazi is highly sanctimonious; his voluminous writings about Mzilikazi and the Ndebele are striking more for what they reveal about Moffat himself than what they tell us about the Ndebele.[35] In order to understand why Mzilikazi became interested in the man in the first place, we must look back to an event which occurred as the Ndebele were approaching the southern Transvaal in 1823.

In July 1823 a force of Griqua horsemen turned back an enormous body of Sotho refugees who were threatening Dithakong near Kuruman—a confrontation mentioned in the previous chapter. Moffat was not a combatant in that affair, but he played a prominent role in organizing the defence of Dithakong; his prestige as a mediator in the region enabled him to enlist the aid of the Griqua who saved the town. During the battle itself—in which the Sotho refugees took a severe beating—Moffat played a very visible role in futile attempts to negotiate a truce.[36] The ease with which the Griqua turned back the vastly more numerous Sotho made a deep impression on the latter.[37] The survivors of the battle scattered inland and—as we have seen some of them were absorbed into the Ndebele state. It is reasonable to assume that many of these people knew who Moffat was, and that they saw him as the architect of the Griqua victory at Dithakong. This view was probably passed on to Mzilikazi. The impression that Moffat was an important political figure in the South African interior grew over the ensuing years. Kuruman remained the northernmost European outpost in South Africa; it was the focus of all European activity in the interior and Moffat was known among Africans as the 'chief' of Kuruman. Occassionally he travelled farther north to discuss extending trade and missions with Tswana chiefs, thus spreading his reputation more widely. His success as a spiritual missionary developed slowly, but his secular prestige was great. The only other missionaries operating as far north as Moffat were the Wesleyan Methodists, but their efforts were so disrupted by the effects of the *Difaqane* that they were not able to establish their influence until the 1830s.[38] It is thus not surprising that when Mzilikazi decided to open communications with Europeans, he chose to deal with Moffat. Moffat appeared to exercise influence over both the Tswana and the Griqua unmatched by any other individual.

In July 1829 two European traders named Schoon and

McLuckie reached Hurutshe country in the western Transvaal. There they met Ndebele messengers who encouraged them to visit Mzilikazi at the Aapies River.[39] Widespread reports of the Ndebele king's wealth in cattle convinced them of the possibility of profitable trade, and, indeed, they were not to be disappointed. They arrived at Mzilikazi's headquarters early in August. Mzilikazi lavished gifts upon them; in return they demonstrated the use of guns, which he had never before seen fired.[40]

As the traders left Mzilikazi asked them to send missionaries back to him. At the Vaal River they chanced upon the Methodist agent James Archbell to whom they communicated Mzilikazi's request. Archbell was then seeking a new mission field, so he seized upon the invitation and rushed to the Aapies River, where he arrived in late October.[41] In the meantime, however, Mzilikazi had sent envoys to Kuruman to invite Robert Moffat to visit him.[42] The envoys, under the leadership of Mncumbathe, persuaded a reluctant Moffat to accompany them back to Mzilikazi, who received from them a favourable report of Kuruman.[43] Mzilikazi delayed admitting Archbell to his presence until Moffat arrived. Then he lavished his attention on the latter, against whose prestige Archbell had little to offer.[44]

During the missionaries' brief visit Mzilikazi vigorously defended himself as a peacemaker, stressing his desire to live on good terms with Europeans. He solicited the introduction of resident missionaries among the Ndebele, but the tone of his request implied that his interests were strictly secular. He probably surmised that missionaries were the only Europeans willing to reside permanently in the interior, so he would have seen them as the natural intermediaries in his relations with the European Cape Colony. Furthermore, at that date he was still favourably impressed by what he had seen of firearms and he expected that missionaries would assist him in obtaining them.[45]

It is indicative of Mzilikazi's respect for Moffat's position that he never asked the latter himself to serve as a missionary among the Ndebele. He regarded Moffat more as his political equal—a man with whom he might potentially exchange 'state' visits.[46] Mzilikazi summed up his attitude towards Moffat in his farewell statement to him:

> Tell the white king [*i.e.*, Colonial governor] I wish to live in friendship, and he must not allow the Bastards [Griqua] and Korannas to annoy me as they have done. Let the road to Kuruman remain open.[47]

Moffat did not again visit Mzilikazi until 1835, by which time the Ndebele had moved west to the Marico River. During the interim, however, Mzilikazi regarded him as his only completely trustworthy European contact and the two men maintained a regular correspondence.[48] Moffat acted as Mzilikazi's unofficial liason with all European traders, hunters, and missionaries who entered the interior. Hence , when agents of the Paris Evangelical Society came to South Africa in search of mission fields in 1830, Moffat worked to steer them towards the Ndebele. He might have succeeded in planting a French mission among the Ndebele, but Mzilikazi's developing troubles with his neighbours spoiled his efforts.

Ndebele campaigns in 1830 and 1831

It has already been mentioned that during his years by the Oori River Mzilikazi consistently maintained pressure on the Tswana communities to his west. Sometime before 1830, for example, he reduced the Hurutshe of Mokgatlha to tributary status and incorporated some of them into the Ndebele ranks.[49] Thereafter Mokgatlha had to make an annual delivery of a 'large part of his crops', and his activities were carefully overseen by Ndebele envoys.[50]

By 1830 Mzilikazi had so effectively crushed the resistance of the Hurutshe and Rolong of the western Transvaal that he was left with a free hand to extend his raiding efforts even farther west in search for ever more cattle. Sometime during 1830 he sent his third *impi* against the Ngwaketse. On this occasion the Ngwaketse chief Sebego once again escaped into the desert with most of his people. The Ndebele troops returned to Mzilikazi with some captured cattle, but he was irritated with their failure to capture Sebego himself—the last major holdout against Ndebele domination in the region.[51] Nevertheless, Ndebele pressure on the Ngwaketse took its toll; each raid forced the Ngwaketse to retreat farther into the Botswana desert and away from economically productive land.

Also during 1830 Mzilikazi gave the Hurutshe Ndebele cattle to tend, and he ordered that all Tswana to his west cease to trade with Europeans or Griqua without his express permission.[52] This attempt directly to control the region rekindled the anger of the

Griqua/Korana, who had hunted and traded in the western Transvaal, since it threatened their economic livelihood.[53]

At some point during either 1830 or 1831 an Ndebele *impi* assaulted the mountain stronghold of Moshweshwe in Lesotho. This is one of the most famous events of early Ndebele history; however, it is an episode which presents some important problems of reconstruction which have probably contributed to popular exaggerations of its intrinsic significance to both Ndebele and Southern Sotho history. For this reason it is worth discussing in some detail.

The year 1831 is the generally accepted date of this Ndebele campaign.[54] This date presents a difficulty, however, since—as will be shown—it was a year during which the Ndebele are known to have campaigned far to the north and to have experienced another major Griqua/Korana invasion. It is significant that although the campaign against Moshweshwe is well-remembered in Ndebele tradition, no authoritative source links it with the other wars of 1831.[55] Since major campaigns were typically waged during the winter months, it would follow that this campaign either was not major or was not fought in 1831. Such evidence as is available suggests that the campaign was a minor one and that it was waged during the autumn of either 1830 or 1831.

The best evidence for the campaign comes from Sotho-derived sources. According to these Mzilikazi sent what may have been a large *impi* deep into the Orange Free State to raid cattle.[56] The Ndebele marched south, attacking a number of Sotho chiefdoms before finally reaching the mountain fortress of Sekonyela's Tlokwa.[57] They attacked the Tlokwa at daybreak, but found their mountain too well fortified to take, so they broke off their assault and marched against Moshweshwe's stronghold at Thaba Bosiu, just to the east. Meanwhile, Sekonyela alerted Moshweshwe of the approaching Ndebele.[58]

Moshweshwe was able to prepare his own defences well enough to present the Ndebele with another impasse. This time the Ndebele encamped by the neighbouring river for several days to consider the situation.[59] Finally, their commander (whose name is not recorded) decided that success was imperative so he ordered an attack. According to Sotho accounts,

> The assault . . . was at first terrific. Nothing seemed able to arrest the rush of the enemy. Accustomed to victory, the Zulus [Ndebele] advanced in serried ranks, not appearing to observe the masses of

basalt, which came rolling down with a tremendous noise from the top of the mountain. But soon there was a general crush—an irresistible avalanche of stones, accompanied by a shower of javelins, sent back the assailants with more rapidity than they had advanced.

The chiefs might be seen rallying with fugitives, and snatching away the plumes with which their heads were decorated, and trampling them under foot in a rage, would lead their men again towards the formidable rampart. This desperate attempt succeeded no better than the former one. The blow was decisive.

The next day the Zulus resumed their march, and returned home . . .[60]

This same account goes on to tell how Moshweshwe extended to the defeated Ndebele a gesture which has become one of the most popular stories in southern African history:

At the moment of their departure, a Mosuto, driving some fat oxen, stopped before the first rank, and gave them this message—'Moshesh salutes you. Supposing that hunger has brought you into this country, he sends you these cattle, that you may eat them on your way home.[61]

This is an appealing anecdote, but it is probably apocryphal. It was written in 1861 by the French missionary Eugene Casalis. Casalis had arrived in Lesotho in 1833 in the company of Thomas Arbousset. Arbousset's own account of the Ndebele-Southern Sotho encounter—written in 1842—agrees with that of Casalis in most particulars, but it gives quite a different epilogue:

The chief of the Matebeles, filled with indignation, set fire to the millet growing at the foot of the mountain, and cried to the natives as he was going away, 'You slaves! you are still little and lean. They must fatten you, and I will come for you next year.'

It is said that the furious general, with his own hand, stript the soldiers of their plumes. As to what Mosolekatse did to them, no one knows . . .[62]

Arbousset's version does not mention Moshweshwe's offering cattle to the Ndebele; furthermore, it implies that the Ndebele did not need food. Why else would they have burned the millet field?

There are few modern accounts of Mzilikazi or Moshweshwe which fail to comment on the Ndebele assault at Thaba Bosiu. It is frequently suggested that Moshweshwe scored a brilliant tactical victory over the Ndebele and that his purported gift of cattle to the retreating enemy was a statesmanlike gesture which saved his people from future Ndebele harassment.[63] The latter interpretation raises the question of why the Ndebele attacked Moshweshwe in the first place. It appears more probable that the

Ndebele assault was largely accidental and that they would not have returned in any case.

The campaign against the Southern Sotho was an anomaly in Ndebele raiding patterns of the period. It not only took Ndebele troops farther south than at any other time, but it also was the only distant Ndebele campaign south of the Vaal not related to the pursuit of an enemy—such as Mehlomakulu or Molitsane—begun north of the Vaal.[64]

The descriptions of the campaign quoted above reinforce the impression that the Ndebele fell upon Thaba Bosiu accidentally—after having raided aimlessly around the Caledon River. There is no reason why Moshweshwe should have regarded the Ndebele as a serious threat to his security. If he actually gave the retreating *impi* cattle to eat, his gesture was gratuitous.[65]

There is no evidence which connects the campaign against Moshweshwe with the time of any of the major winter wars waged by the Ndebele during their residence in the central Transvaal.[66] This fact suggest that the campaign occurred during another season—a conclusion supported by Arbousset's reference to the Ndebele being at Thaba Bosiu while millet was growing. The timing of the campaign and its apparent aimlessness further suggest that it was a minor affair—perhaps a partly exploratory cattle raid into regions little known to the Ndebele. The campaign ended in failure, but the failure was not remembered by the Ndebele as having been of disastrous proportions. That the Ndebele and the Southern Sotho remembered their confrontation at all was probably due to the reputations of their kings, Moshweshwe and Mzilikazi.

The Griqua invade the Ndebele, July 1831: prelude

During the three years following Jan Bloem's abortive raid on the Ndebele, ill-feeling between the Griqua/Korana and Ndebele rose higher than ever before. Many Griqua/Korana who had not even been involved with Bloem's commando must have shared his embarrassment over the recent humiliation. Griqua continued to hunt in Rolong and Hurutshe country for elephant ivory, but Mzilikazi's increasing control over these regions restricted their efforts. On several occasions small Ndebele and Griqua/Korana parties clashed.[67] Men from both sides were killed, and the Griqua became particularly incensed when the Ndebele flogged one of their men.[68]

One of Bloem's main rivals for supremacy among the outlaw bands of the Griqua/Korana was Barend Barends, the Griqua chief of a town on the Harts River called Boetsap.[69] Barends had participated in the battle at Dithakong in 1823 in which the huge Sotho force had been turned back.[70] This experience had given him the confidence that his men could best any Bantu force—so long as his own people had guns and horses. This assumption was largely true when the Griqua restricted their fighting to open-field battles during daylight. Employing these advantages Barends' band subsisted through the 1820s by hunting and plundering. Occasionally he harassed other Griqua communities, but his favourite targets were Sotho/Tswana communities.

In late 1829 Barends visited Ndebele country in the company of the Methodist missionary James Archbell; there he was evidently impressed by the numbers of Ndebele cattle.[71] Afterwards he worked to mount a commando of unprecedented size against Mzilikazi.[72] Griqua/Korana men from every community except Griqua Town—whose chief Andries Waterboer was a strong supporter of Christianity—joined Barends' developing crusade.[73] Barends was particularly supported by Hendrik Hendriks, a Griqua official in the town of Philippolis, south of the Orange River. Hendriks personally led a large Griqua contingent from his own town, despite opposition from his chief Adam Kok.[74]

Initiative for the anti-Ndebele commando did not lie only with the Griqua. Barends was joined by several hundred Tswana men who wanted to avenge their own grievances against Mzilikazi. The Kgatla chief Pilane, for example, resented Mzilikazi's interference in his trading activities.[75] Other chiefs such as Sebego of the Ngwaketse and Tawane of the Rolong wished to avenge recent military setbacks.[76]

It is possible that some of these Tswana chiefs actually first proposed the idea of a commando to Barends, but evidence for this point is clouded by the biased testimony of the commando's participants after it was over. Hendriks, for example, later declared that the 'only motive' of the Griqua in attacking the Ndebele was 'to compel restitution of the cattle which had been stolen from other tribes by Mussellikats [Mzilikazi].'[77] His claim is, however, refuted by the statements of other Griqua who were more candid about their own avaricious aims.[78]

Barends himself may have been sincere about wanting to help the Tswana, but his judgement was probably affected by his advancing age and infirmity.[79] Robert Moffat later described Barends as

> labouring under an unaccountable delusion, that he was destined to sweep Moselekatse and his gang of blood-guilty warriors, from the fine pastures and glens of the Bakone [*i.e.*, Tswana] country, and thus emancipate the aborigines from their thralldom.[80]

Whether Barends seriously thought he could drive the Ndebele out of the central Transvaal is debatable. In any case, it is clear that few of his followers shared such a lofty ambition. According to Griqua testimony, after Barends had assembled his commando in one place he

> explained to the people his intention, which was to drive Masalacatzie out of the land which he had without right taken possession of, and if cattle were taken, they were to be given to the Buchuanas [Tawana], who had lived and lost them [*sic*]. No person spoke against that.
>
> When they had left the camp and Old Barend, the people of Dam [Adam Kok], Haip and Adam Kreger [Kruger] appeared dissatisfied with the arrangement that the cattle should be given to the Bechuanas. [They] had again a meeting of some of Barends' people stated the meaning of the chief: then the commando became of one mind a second time.[81]

This unanimity of purpose did not last long. However, since there was never to be a division of spoils, differences of opinion among the participants were never resolved. As will be shown, Griqua disunity adversely affected their discipline, thus contributing to their ultimate defeat by the Ndebele.

In mid-June 1831 Barends moved northeast from Boetsap, ostensibly leading a large hunting party into familiar territory.[82] It is difficult to determine exactly how large his allied force was; estimates of its size vary greatly. Since the same informants evidently passed information around, it is impossible even to identify the original authorities for the various estimates. According to the most conservative figures, however, Barends commanded 300 Griqua/Korana horsemen armed with guns and several hundred Tswana footmen armed only with spears.[83] Other estimates range much higher, but the estimates of the number of Griqua casualties (given below) which resulted from the ensuing engagement and the circumstances of the affair as a whole support the more conservative figures.

The members of the commando rendezvoused near the confluence of the Makwassi and Vaal Rivers, about 150 miles southwest of the Magaliesberg Mountains. The elderly Barends himself
remained there with the wagons while the main forces advanced to
the northeast on July 11—apparently under the command of one
Gert Hooyman.[84]

When the commando reached the Ndebele settlements it found
that most Ndebele fighting men were gone. Ndebele vulnerability
to attack at that moment suggests that the Griqua knew in
advance that the Ndebele men would be away, and that their
timing was deliberate. This inference has been drawn by several
historians, but it is unsupported by any direct evidence indicating
how the Griqua planned their attack.[85] In the absence of such
evidence we must allow that their arrival at that fortuitous
moment was merely a coincidence.

Before continuing with the story of the Griqua attack on the
Ndebele, it is necessary to account for the absence of most of the
Ndebele armed forces.

In 1835 Andrew Smith learned from Ndebele informants that
the Sotho chief Ratsebe, whom Mzilikazi had captured by the
Vaal River twelve years before, bolted from the Ndebele about the
time of Barends' 1831 commando. It was pursuit of Ratsebe
which drew the Ndebele away from home just before the Griqua
arrived.

> At the time that the commando attacked the Matabeli, Calipi
> [Kaliphi] was absent with the *machaha* to retake cattle which Ratsipip
> [Ratsebe] had taken from Ramabutsetsi . . . Ratsipip fled as the
> Matabeli commando approached and left the cattle . . . They don't
> know where he is, but said he is far to the north.[86]

Griqua informants who participated in Barends' commando
confirmed this story, telling Smith that they had learned of the
campaign of the Ndebele men into Ngwato country from Ndebele
women they captured.[87] When Ratsebe reached Ngwato country
in early 1831 he caused so much trouble there that the Ngwato
sent to Mzilikazi for assistance.[88] Mzilikazi responded by sending
a large *impi* under the command of Kaliphi, but the Ngwato
regretted their request when the Ndebele also raided them.[89]

Before the Ndebele *impi* reached Ngwatoland Ratsebe fled
farther north. Kaliphi pursued him at least to the outskirts of
Shona territory, where he retook some of the cattle Ratsebe had
captured and raided additional cattle from Shona-speaking

Kalanga chiefdoms.[90] From the passage quoted above, it appears that Ratsebe himself eluded the Ndebele and continued north.[91]

Kaliphi's *impi* against Ratsebe is the earliest instance of Ndebele penetration into the future Matabeleland for which there is any clear record. Near-contemporary evidence hints of other such forays into present Rhodesia, but it is exceedingly vague.[92] Indeed, the whole question of early Ndebele penetration north of the Limpopo is a complex and a difficult one to resolve.

According to A. A. Campbell's version of Ndebele tradition, Robert Moffat advised Mzilikazi to migrate with his people north of the Limpopo at the time of his first visit to the Ndebele in 1829. Campbell relates that after Moffat left him, Mzilikazi sent off five 'regiments'

> to see whether the words of Mtshede [Moffat] were those of truth. We crossed the Limpopo and struck the Mzingwani river, up which we travelled. From there we passed through the Gwanda to the Tekwani river, and there attacked Mgibe, a Swina [Shona] chief, killed many of his people, and took all his cattle. We then returned the same way we had come, until we recrossed the Limpopo, when we went to Tshupula's, a Basuto chief, whom we killed with many of his people, seizing his flocks and herds.
>
> While we were there five messengers reached us from the king, telling us that the Boers [*i.e.*, Griqua] scattered all at home, and that we were to return at once.[93]

Although Campbell calls the invaders of Ndebele country 'Boers', the context of this passage makes it clear that his informants were alluding to the Griqua and that the events he describes occurred in 1831. A greater problem in Campbell's evidence is that he associates the trans-Limpopo campaign with the 'Moffat Myth'—the popular Ndebele belief that Moffat advised the Ndebele to migrate north . As I shall show in Chapter 5, Moffat almost certainly never gave Mzilikazi any such advice. Even allowing for the possibility that he did so, however, circumstances point to his 1835 visit—*after* the Barends commando—as the moment he would have suggested migrating. These are problems to be explored more thoroughly in the chapter on the Ndebele migration to Matabeleland. For now they need only be mentioned to point up the difficulty of interpreting traditional evidence on this subject. In this latter regard it is worth commenting on how other historians have distorted Campbells's evidence on the question of Ndebele raids into Shona country from the Transvaal.

A. T. Bryant describes the Ndebele campaign against 'Mgibe', but he merely borrows from Campbell's 1905 article on Ndebele history.[94] Unfortunately, he muddles his chronological associations badly, making it appear that the Ndebele spent years fighting the Shona. For no apparent reason he dates the Mgibe campaign to the time of Mzilikazi's arrival in the central Transvaal (which he gives as 1826) *and* with the moment of the first Zulu invasion (which he incorrectly dates to 1830, not 1832). He correctly dates Barends' invasion to 1831, but he fails to acknowledge that this is the only event which Campbell associates with the moment of the actual Ndebele campaign into Shona country.[95] Bryant's errors are not in themselves important since virtually all early writings on Ndebele are permeated with similar errors. However, Bryant has been regarded as such a reliable authority that his statements have profoundly influenced the conclusions of later historians. A recent account of Ndebele history, which has been called the most authoritative yet written on early Ndebele settlements, draws on *both* Bryant and Campbell to suggest that the Ndebele raided the Shona *three times* from the Transvaal during this period.[96] It should therefore be reiterated that Campbell is the sole authority for Ndebele tradition on this subject, that he alludes to a single raid, and that the raid he alludes to occurred when the Griqua were invading the Ndebele in 1831.

The Griqua invasion

With most of his fighting men off in the north, Mzilikazi waited at home, ignorant of the impending Griqua attack forming to his southwest. Meanwhile, the invaders covered the distance between the Makwassi River and the Magaliesbergs at a rate of about fifty miles per day.[97] Ndebele border patrols either failed to sight the advancing enemy, or could not move fast enough to warn Mzilikazi that horsemen were coming.

As the Griqua force reached the Magaliesbergs, they easily swept through Ndebele cattle posts.[98] Dividing into smaller parties, they penetrated perhaps as far as the Aapies River before turning back to regroup.[99] Mzilikazi himself retreated into the mountains and the Griqua captured cattle and some women without further opposition.[100] With his manpower severely depleted, Mzilikazi probably recognized the futility of fighting the

Griqua in open field actions.[101]

Barends had instructed his men to capture only enough cattle to tempt Mzilikazi to pursue them into a pre-arranged trap, perhaps back at his own position on the Makwassi.[102] However, they ignored his plan and instead accumulated such a large booty that they had difficulty moving.[103] These operations took a single day.[104]

Slowed by their captured livestock, the Griqua crept back towards the Magaliesbergs, requiring two full days to reach just west of the Hex River where they regrouped.[105] The second night they feasted on their captured oxen until late in the evening and then slept without troubling to set a watch.[106]

While the triumphant Griqua dallied, Mzilikazi assembled his reserve of veteran soldiers for a counter-attack.[107] Mzilikazi stayed at the Aapies River headquarters town while his men set off in pursuit of the invaders.

As in 1828, captured Ndebele women warned the Griqua to expect a retaliatory night attack, but again their advice was ignored.

> The women told that two months ago the young men [*majaha*] were away to the Bamangwato; that the old men were only at home. The latter fought in the day, the others in the night [*sic*; just the opposite is intended] because they are weaker. They said, 'Those are the night fighters. Most are at home, therefore you must take care they fight only in the night. . . .'
> Where they halted was an open level place away from hills. After they got the cattle all together the people formed round, then kindled fires and killed to eat. After that Gert Hooyman the chief came round and asked some what they thought; he, before anyone answered, said, 'I expect the Caffers to-night.' Then said one of the Hemraad, Jan Pinnear [Pienaar], 'Answer, how shall the Caffers come; the Caffers do not fight, how then shall they come tonight?' Nothing more was said and then they went to sleep, not one placed to watch.
> The order of the chief Barend was if they took cattle that they were to make fires round them, and then the people to saddle up and leave the place till daybreak, but that was disregarded.[108]

Accounts taken from Griqua survivors hold that they were awakened in the night to find themselves completely surrounded by a circle (or double circle) of Ndebele men.[109] Their accounts suggest that they had been grouped in a compact encampment. However, this conclusion does not tally with Ndebele-derived accounts, which are likely to have been more accurate. The perspectives of individual participants in any battle are generally narrow; they often produce wildly distorted pictures of a battle as a whole. The perceptions of the Griqua must have been especially limited: awakened suddenly in the dark, they could not have known very clearly what was going on around them. This point is worth some attention, as Griqua-derived accounts have contributed greatly to European perceptions of Ndebele military tactics in these affairs. On this occasion, at least, the Ndebele counter-attack was more complicated than a simple encirclement.[110] It appears that the Griqua were actually dispersed in small groups, surrounding the livestock they had captured. The Ndebele rushed into the men and into the cattle shortly before dawn, throwing everything into unimaginable confusion.[111]

In 1835 Ndebele informants told Andrew Smith, then near the actual scene of the battle, that the Griqua had crowded the cattle along a ridge, where

> the Griqua commando was divided into small portions and encircling the cattle; . . . When the attack commenced, they were all divided. Their loss was very great, arising in various ways. The greatest number were trampled by the cattle, which scampered off in all directions. as soon as the Matabeli commenced. Others were killed by the Griquas themselves, who fired without showing consideration, and others were killed by the Matabeli. The horses were tied fast and almost all of them were killed.[112]

The Tswana allies, who had been camped nearby, also rushed into the melée, adding to the confusion.[113] Many Griqua died in their sleep. Some Ndebele women whom the Griqua had captured were killed accidently, but most returned home safely.[114] There are no estimates of the numbers of Ndebele killed; circumstances suggest that their casualties must have been high. All the cattle were retaken.[115]

At least 300 Griqua/Korana, and perhaps an equal number of Tswana lost their lives.[116] Some sources estimated the Griqua casualties in terms of the number of survivors, which they placed variously at less than a half dozen.[117] However, these extreme figures disagree with other estimates and must be regarded simply as wild rumours current immediately after news of the Griqua disaster became known. An indication that a significant number of Griqua did escape is the report that an Ndebele commander had to flee from Mzilikazi's wrath for his failure to annihilate the Griqua.[118]

The guns of the invaders were worse than useless to them, for they carelessly shot each other in the dark.[119] This time their horses were also useless. When the battle was over, the Ndebele found most horses still tied up in neat rows; they killed all but a few and then burned everything left on the battlefield.[120] As many as 250 horse carcasses and 300 abandoned firearms may have gone up in flames that day.[121]

Aftermath of Griqua commando, late 1831: disenchantment with firearms

Mzilikazi's decisive repulse of Barends' commando destroyed his respect for firearms. Briefly, at least, he scoffed at the power of both Europeans and Griqua. In November 1831 the Hurutshe sub-chief Moilwe told a French missionary that

> Although Motselekatse has hitherto shown himself so well disposed towards you, his attitude has now completely altered. Since his defeat of the Griquas and their fire-arms, he considers himself the master of the world. He proudly declares that there can be but two lords in the universe, one to rule the heavens and the other to reign on earth; that he holds absolute sway below; that he will soon come to visit the white king [i.e., Governor of the Cape] and to teach him that he fears neither his muskets nor his bullets; that the latter's grapeshot could give his warriors naught but the pox and that he longs to know of what stuff those great bullets are made, concerning which such wonders are told. Moreover . . . Motselekatse has ceased to draw any distinction between Europeans and Griquas; he accuses the former of supplying the latter with arms against him . . . .[122]

Subsequent events and Mzilikazi's considerate treatment of European traders present in Ndebele country at the time of Barends' attack prove that Moilwe exaggerated the depth of his ill-feelings towards Europeans at this date.[123] Nevertheless, Moilwe's contention that Mzilikazi no longer feared guns stands up.[124] Mzilikazi clearly realized the nature of his tactical advantage in situations in which he could surprise his enemies at night:

> Mussalakatze says guns would be very good things if they did not require to be reloaded, but if those that came against him armed with guns are not mounted and cannot run away from his men, he does not care for them.[125]

In spite of his new contempt for firearms, Mzilikazi did keep many which he had captured from Bloem and Barends. He also continued to trade for ammunition with Europeans, who visited him regularly through the early 1830s.[126] These weapons may have been used mainly for ceremonial purposes, however.[127]

Supply, logistics, and tactical considerations were all problems which mitigated against the Ndebele adopting guns on any significant scale. Even if they had wanted guns badly, they could not have gotten sufficient weapons and ammunition to equip more than a small fraction of their men. In order to use firearms effectively they would have had to establish specialized units. However, there was never any effort to create such units and the weapons which the Ndebele did have were distributed more or less randomly throughout the army. Hence, there was no coherent system of training gunmen and there were no channels of supply. European visitors had to be recruited to clean and to repair the Ndebele guns and most visitors commented upon their sorry condition. The Ndebele seemed to be more interested in the prestige of ownership than in the practical use of guns.

The primary orientation of the Ndebele army was towards aggressive warfare. Campaigns on foot were conducted over long distances. The Ndebele travelled without riding- or pack-animals. Young boys were employed as porters on campaigns, but for the most part soldiers carried their own gear. The addition of heavy guns and their essential paraphernalia would have imposed a severe strain on their carrying capacity, thereby reducing their mobility. This limitation further discouraged the adoption of guns.

Perhaps the Ndebele might have used firearms defensively against invaders, but it did not occur to them to train themselves to do so. In their wars against the Griqua they found that their strategy of retreat, cautious pursuit, and surprise counter-attack worked on almost every occasion.[128] The aggressive spirit of the nation probably also mitigated against the adoption of any conscious defensive training.[129]

Conceivably the Ndebele might have used the horses captured from the Griqua to give them the mobility and carrying power required to use firearms more effectively. However, horses presented even greater obstacles to adoption. They were faster, more intelligent, and more delicate than any animals which the Ndebele domesticated; hence they required new and difficult skills in care and handling. And the Ndebele lacked even the experience of using oxen for riding or for packing.[130] For them to have mastered horsemanship would have required a jump in aptitude for which they were quite unprepared. Furthermore, they could not have counted on anyone to assist them.

More basic, however, was the extreme sensitivity to disease of horses in southern Africa. In addition to the usual diseases which ravaged livestock, the horses easily succumbed to a form of distemper known, appropriately, as 'horse sickness'. The horses which the Ndebele had captured died off quickly; by 1836 not one remained alive.[131] The difficulties of keeping horses alive would have been aggravated by the hazards of taking them into different regions on raids or during migrations. The conditions necessary to keep horses healthy varied radically, even within limited geographical regions. A mobile society such as that of the Ndebele would have taken generations to master the care and use of horses.[132]

Even after several clashes with Griqua gunmen, Ndebele experience against firearms in combat was limited. The Griqua were fine horsemen and excellent marksmen in open, moving battles. However, their foolishness in allowing themselves to be surprised in situations in which they lost all their advantages gave the Ndebele a misleading impression of the potential of firearms. Against such stupid enemies, Mzilikazi's scepticism about the value of guns was well-founded. Furthermore, in the early 1830s he faced no other military problems in which guns would have given him a significant advantage. His misfortune was that his attitude did not change until he met the far more resourceful Voortrekker gunmen in 1836.

The Ndebele prepare to migrate west, 1831-32

Although the decisive Ndebele victory over Barends' commando effectively destroyed the possibility of further serious trouble with the Griqua, Mzilikazi was still anxious to end the petty harrassment of cattle raiders. He attempted to negotiate with Barends, but the old Griqua chief persisted in his delusion that he would yet conquer the Ndebele.[133] However, Barends' now meagre following soon received an unexpected blow when they were hit hard by smallpox. Barends never again troubled Mzilikazi.[134]

From 1825 to 1831 Mzilikazi had regarded the Griqua and

Korana as his most dangerous enemies. During Shaka's lifetime the Zulu remained only a potential threat to the Ndebele because Shaka was caught up in his wars with other coastal peoples. However, after Mzilikazi learned of Dingane's succession to the Zulu kingship in 1828 his fear of a Zulu attack heightened.[135] And now that the Griqua threat was gone in late 1831, he apparently decided to prepare to move farther west. The change in his attitude was well expressed in 1835, when Moffat wrote of Mzilikazi that

> the only enemy he feared was Dingaan . . . He pointed to the south and west, and said that the Griquas and Bastards and Corannas were troublesome, like the wolves. They were only a parcel of thieves, and destitute of courage, for in no instance had they ever stood, or could stand the brunt of battle. He had always destroyed and driven them with a handful of men and the mere striplings of his army.[136]

Before 1831, with the Griqua to the southwest, and the Zulu to the southeast, Mzilikazi's only safe avenue of escape was farther to the north—a direction which he clearly did not want to go.[137] Shortly after the war with Barends Mzilikazi began to clear the path to the west by attacking Tswana groups which had aided Barends. The Hurutshe chief Moilwe complained in November that

> since the recent affair between Barend and Motselekatse, it was impossible to trust the latter . . . he had already destroyed a large number of towns around them and . . . most probably the turn of the Bahurutsi would soon follow, for they were the only tribe which had hitherto been spared . . .[138]

For the moment the Hurutshe, who had not supported Barends, were spared. But Mzilikazi hit other Tswana very hard. He ordered that the towns of his vassal Pilane be destroyed, his cattle appropriated, and young Kgatla men incorporated into the Ndebele army. Pilane himself fled north, and his half-brother Molefi remained to regroup the Kgatla survivors under Mzilikazi's rule.[139]

Mzilikazi did not feel an immediacy in the Zulu threat, as he clearly took his time in preparations for migration. In addition to softening up the Tswana, Mzilikazi extended his diplomatic contacts. He encouraged the French missionaries to open a chain of stations between himself and Kuruman. Some messengers he had once sent to Kuruman had been murdered by Tswana along the way.[140] He hoped that a series of mission stations would end such harrassment, as well as establish a safe escape route west in an emergency.[141]

In March 1832 Mzilikazi ordered the French missionaries, then getting started among the Hurutshe, to send him one of their number for a personal visit. Jean-Pierre Pellissier thus became the third missionary to meet Mzilikazi.[142] The two men cordially discussed the possibility of a mission station among the Ndebele, but Pellissier recognized that Mzilikazi's interest in such a project was not at all spiritual. Mzilikazi detained Pellissier long enough to have the latter's men repair and clean Ndebele guns, so Pellissier concluded that Mzilikazi was only interested in missionaries as military instructors. Although Mzilikazi naturally wanted to use the guns he owned, his real interest in the missionaries was their potential value as diplomatic go-betweens.

Despite their scepticism about Mzilikazi's sincerity, the missionaries were anxious to cultivate his friendship in order to expand their work. But before they could fulfill his request, the Zulu of Dingane intervened to upset everyone's plans.

The Zulu-Ndebele war of 1832

The Ndebele and the Zulu fought two major wars in the Transvaal during the 1830s. Dingane sent large forces against Mzilikazi in the central Transvaal in 1832 and then in the western Transvaal in 1837. These were the only wars Mzilikazi fought with the Zulu after he fled Zululand.[143] Before reconstructing the history of the 1832 Zulu war, it is necessary once and for all to dispose of a pervasive chronological error which has found its way into the literature dealing with Zulu-Ndebele relations. And that is the frequently-made assertion that the Zulu attacked the Ndebele in 1830.[144] No such war was fought during that year. Some historians who recognize that the Zulu attacked the Ndebele in 1832—the correct year—have evidently been troubled by the number of authorities who mention an 1830 war; they attempt to reconcile the apparent contradiction in dates by holding that the Zulu and Ndebele fought in *both* years. Not surprisingly, their accounts of the second, non-existent war tend to be terribly vague.[145]

The date of 1830 for the Zulu attack derives from errors in two

independent sources. The first error lay in the faulty recollection
of Henry Francis Fynn, an English trader who worked among the
Zulu and their neighbours during this period. The second error lay
in interpretations of the chronologically ambiguous tradition
recorded by A. A. Campbell. Virtually all modern authorities
draw upon one or both of these sources, directly or indirectly.

Fynn was one of the few Europeans who knew both Shaka and
Dingane intimately. His writings are a seminal source for early
Zulu history and his evidence has long been regarded as definitive
on many points. At the time of Dingane's 1832 attack on
Mzilikazi Fynn himself was trading among the Mpondo, but he
was fully aware of the war going on.[146] He kept a diary during
these years, but it was later buried in his brother's grave by the
Zulu. The 'diary' he composed for publication was thus written
from memory years later.[147] In those later memoirs he gave the
date of the Zulu-Ndebele war as 1830.[148] This must have been a
simple lapse in memory, for he says nothing about a war in 1832,
and no other contemporary source mentions any war before 1832.
Indeed, there is explicit evidence that Dingane attacked Mzilikazi
only once before 1837.[149] That Dingane attacked Mzilikazi in mid
1832 is proven by the testimony of an impressive number of
contemporary sources, on both the Ndebele and the Zulu sides.[150]
However, most later historians seem to have drawn only on
Fynn's memoirs.[151]

Campbell's elusive 1905 newspaper article, previously discussed
in many contexts, added additional weight to the date of 1830.
Campbell assigns no dates in his rendition of Ndebele history, but
he places the context of the Zulu attack immediately *between*
Robert Moffat's first visit (datable to 1829) and Barends'
commando (datable to 1831). In 1912 D. F. Ellenberger
interpreted Campbell's evidence as a corroboration of Fynn's
date, and then (1929) A. T. Bryant drew on both Fynn and
Ellenberger to reaffirm 1830 as the date of the Zulu war.[152] The
combined authority of these two prestigious writers persuaded
subsequent historians to accept their faulty chronology.

The results of this false chronology have been almost too
bewildering to describe. One could adduce examples of false
associations between almost every possible combination of
unrelated events between 1828 and 1832. Untold violence has been
done to the correct sequence of events, making intelligent
interpretation almost impossible. Correction of the date to 1832

should lay many such problems to rest permanently. We can now turn our attention to the war itself.

After Dingane succeeded Shaka as Zulu king, he responded to popular sentiment by curtailing the constant and exhausting wars waged by his predecessor. His pacific policy worked for several years, but he eventually found that the military system built by Shaka geared Zulu society for regular warfare and that his soldiers demanded action.[153] He seems then to have concluded that a big campaign would satisfy his troops, while temporarily removing them as opponents to his authority at home. There were no external threats looming over Zululand, so it was safe for him to send his men quite far away. The Ndebele, then more than 300 miles inland from the Zulu, were a likely target. Dingane wanted a large haul in cattle, and the Ndebele herds were attractively large.[154] It has been suggested that Dingane had personal reasons for wanting to defeat Mzilikazi,[155] but he was more likely simply interested in getting the latter's cattle.[156]

Dingane evidently decided to attack the Ndebele after he learned of Barends' commando of 1831. The first news to reach Zululand of the affair indicated that the Griqua had carried off all the Ndebele cattle, but subsequent reports must have corrected that mis-impression, otherwise the Zulu would not have bothered to attack the Ndebele.[157] Dingane may have surmised that the initial success against the Ndebele which had been enjoyed by the Griqua commando revealed Mzilikazi's weakness against attack, concluding that his own men would finish the job the Griqua had begun. His later behaviour clearly shows that when he sent his men off he expected a major triumph.

Despite Mzilikazi's long-standing fear of being attacked by the Zulu, he was ill-prepared for the invasion when it actually came. The Zulu appear to have fallen upon the Ndebele completely by surprise. Since the Zulu foot soldiers could not have advanced against the Ndebele outposts as swiftly as the Griqua horsemen had done the previous year, it is difficult to understand why the Ndebele totally failed to detect their approach. Once again the main Ndebele military forces appear to have been campaigning elsewhere, but in this instance there is little evidence to indicate where they were.[158]

Observers in Zululand recorded that the Zulu army began its march inland at the end of the 1832 harvest season, which would have been around late June or early July. Since the *impi* returned to Zululand by late August, we can surmise that its outward march covered the 300 miles to the Oori River in something under a single month.[159] The Zulu commander was named Ndlela; the number of men he commanded was not recorded, but was apparently quite large.[160] He reinforced his Zulu troops along the way by recruiting Sotho enemies of the Ndebele.[161]

Confused testimony about the war itself reflects the classic difficulty of interpreting evidence from battle participants. The perceptions of individual combatants about what is going on around them are universally untrustworthy because they generally have extremely limited perspectives. Accounts taken from participants in this war differ so markedly that most of their details must simply be rejected altogether.[162] Modern historians have generally failed to compare accounts from both Zulu and Ndebele participants; the result has been a greatly exaggerated picture of Zulu success.[163] Although the actual outcome undeniably had a significant impact on the Ndebele, the war itself might best be described as indecisive; both sides seem to have suffered equally.

Traditional evidence pertaining to the war is marred by apparently deliberate falsification. As in Ndebele traditions of Mzilikazi's defeat by the Zulu at Nthumbane Hill eleven years earlier (see Chapter 1), the theme of betrayal is invoked to explain Mzilikazi's initial setbacks. According to Campbell, just before the Zulu army arrived in the Magaliesbergs an important Ndebele commander defected to the enemy. This man, Nhalanganiso, is said to have

> met a Zulu impi sent by Dingaan and acted as guide, and at night they attacked the Ndinanene and Nkungweni kraals, killing most. One man brought the news to Mzil[ikazi], who ordered out and led his regiments and fought the Zulu at the Ndinanene kraals, and, after varying success—beat them inflicting heavy loss.[164]

The credibility of this account is lessened by the fact that the Zulu commander should not have required a special Ndebele guide to find the Ndebele towns when he was passing through a region full of neighbours hostile to Mzilikazi.[165]

Despite the discussed objections, Campbell's version of the war is roughly accurate. Drawing upon his evidence and upon various near-contemporary sources which derived from both the Zulu and Ndebele sides, we can reconstruct the war in outline.

The Zulu attacked the Ndebele from the southeast, storming

several towns around the upper reaches of the Oori tributaries before meeting significant resistance.[166] After these initial successes, however, the Zulu hesitated indecisively.[167] This pause gave Mzilikazi the chance to mount a counter-offensive. Ndebele troops then moved south from unscathed centres to meet the Zulu in an open-field battle near the source of the Sand River.[168]

Of the battle itself, little can confidently be said, except that both sides took a beating and withdrew before anything was decided.[169] At some point during the conflict a group of older Ndebele men broke ranks and fled, only to be punished later by Mzilikazi.[170] The Ndebele were evidently not fighting at their full strength, but the Zulu had the disadvantage of having to fight in unfamiliar terrain after a long march. The suffering on both sides must have been great. Three years later Mncumbathe described the battle to Andrew Smith:

> Many were killed on both sides so that they could not number them. Most of those killed were *machaka* [*sic*]. The *tuna* [*induna*] was also killed. Also many of the ring-kops [*madoda*, or married men] were killed, and two of their *tunas* carried off half the cattle they first took.[171]

The indecisive nature of the encounter is reflected in the ambiguous claims made by representatives of both sides as to who had 'won'.[172] The Zulu carried away some Ndebele cattle, but Dingane reportedly was so dissatisfied with the amount that he executed several officers.[173] An entire Zulu 'regiment' was said to have deserted Dingane for Mzilikazi in order to escape a similar retribution for. failure.[174] These were hardly the reactions of a victorious army.

The notion that the Zulu defeated the Ndebele has undoubtedly arisen, in part, from the fact that shortly after the Zulu withdrew from the central Transvaal, Mzilikazi directed a wholesale migration to the Marico River, one hundred miles farther west. Fear of further Zulu attacks may have triggered this action, but—as we have seen—it was a move which had been planned for perhaps a year before the Zulu ever arrived.[175] The apparently direct connection between the Zulu attack and Mzilikazi's abrupt move to the west was given further weight by A. A. Campbell's 1905 newspaper article, which introduced a major error into the literature. This error is worth discussing in some detail, both for its intrinsic importance and for its value as an example of how a subtle misreading of tradition can lead to major misinterpretations.

To re-iterate, we know that from the central Transvaal Mzilikazi moved *west* to the Marico River in mid-1832.[176] However, we read in Campbell's account of the Zulu war (quoted in part above) that after the Zulu retreated, 'Mzil[ikazi] thought it wise to trek *north*, and they did so and built their kraals at the *Mlulu* mountains.' The only mountains in the Transvaal to which this passage could refer are the Lulu, or Leolu, Mountains of Pediland—about 150 miles *northeast* of Mzilikazi's position in mid-1832. Indeed, it was towards Pediland that Campbell's earliest disciple D. F. Ellenberger specifies that Mzilikazi fled.[177] As we shall see, Ellenberger drew the correct geographical inference; it was Campbell's chronology that was in error.

Later historians were evidently troubled by the contradiction between the well-established fact that Mzilikazi migrated west and Campbell and Ellenberger's reference to the 'Mlulu Mountains'. Those who have addressed themselves to this issue at all have adopted Ellenberger's assertion that Mzilikazi fled to a 'stronghold' in the Mlulus, but they have remained silent on the embarrassing question of *where* these mountains were.[178] This unsatisfactory compromise has helped to portray Mzilikazi as a desperate refugee, forced to flee in panic before an overwhelming Zulu onslaught before he was able to regroup his people for their eventual migration west.

While Ellenberger was passing on this new fallacy, Campbell himself was having second thoughts about his geography on this point. He knew that the Ndebele moved west after the Zulu war, but he evidently had no idea where the Mlulu Mountains were, for he nowhere mentions Pediland in his writings. In his book, *Mlimo* (originally written before 1911), his narrator says that

> our king, knowing by bitter experience the ever likely wrath of the Zuly kings, feared what Dingaan might further do, so our things were packed and we journeyed *west*, as far as the Mlulu Mountains, where we built our kraals.[179]

This is nonsense, of course. There are no 'Mlulu' Mountains in the western Transvaal. Campbell revised his version of this incident to reconcile what he knew to be the facts of Mzilikazi's movements in 1832 with an Ndebele tradition pertaining to events ten years earlier of which he was only partly aware.

The key to Campbell's confusion about the Mlulu Mountains lies in the fact that nowhere does he mention that Mzilikazi ever invaded Pediland. He evidently collected a tradition alluding to

Mzilikazi's original *northward* flight from Zululand which resulted in the temporary Ndebele occupation of the Lulu Mountains in Pediland (see Chapter 2). Not recognizing the correct context of the tradition, he mistakenly associated it with Mzilikazi's war against the Zulu in 1832. This explains why his original account stresses that Mzilikazi had to flee *north* from the Zulu and why the Mlulu Mountains figure into it. Seen in its correct context, the tradition is merely a minor confirmation of what other sources document in detail, *i.e.*, that Mzilikazi fled from Zululand to Pediland in the early 1820s. Removed from the context of the 1832 Zulu-Ndebele war, this tradition takes with it the implication that the Zulu reduced Mzilikazi to a desperate refugee in 1832.

The Zulu war was the last episode in the central Transvaal phase of Ndebele history and it thus closes the narrative portion of this chapter. The migration to the western Transvaal will be discussed in the next chapter. To conclude this chapter I shall summarize what is known about the Ndebele population, settlements, and livelihood in the central Transvaal.

The Ndebele population in 1832

Demographic data for the Ndebele during their residence in the central Transvaal are very limited. The Methodist missionary James Archbell was the only visitor to estimate their total numbers, but his figure of about 60,000 to 80,000 is almost certainly far too large.[180] Other than Archbell's estimate, we have only scraps of data: a few estimates of the sizes of towns or of *impis*, and a sort of vague impression of the relationship between the Ndebele population to the populations of other peoples with whom they came into contact. We have somewhat better data for the next period in Ndebele history when Mzilikazi was living by the Marico River. Figures from this later period help to illuminate the central Transvaal period.

One would expect that due to the expansive nature of the Ndebele state, its population should have grown at a steady rate. This tendency was at work throughout the Transvaal years, but during the 1830s two epidemics struck the Ndebele and thereby reduced their numbers by an indeterminate, but possibly significant amount.[181] In 1832 smallpox swept through the interior of South Africa, and this disease appears to have reached the Ndebele.[182] In 1834 and 1835 smallpox again struck the Ndebele,[183] as well as an epidemic of what Dr Andrew Smith called bilious fever, which took a heavy toll.[184] The severity of this latter epidemic was expressed in the words of one Ndebele man who 'said that the Matabeli were almost extinct' in mid-1835.[185] Moffat also described the effects of this disease, but added that 'tho the number of the Matabele have been thereby reduced, yet the population is very considerable . . .'[186]

This evidence shows that any upward growth of the Ndebele population was offset by diseases. Although precise data are not available, it thus seems reasonable to conclude that the Ndebele population in 1832 roughly equalled that of 1835 or 1836. Hence, estimates of Ndebele population for these later years might be applied with approximately equal validity to the central Transvaal period. I shall discuss the actual data for the later period in more detail in later chapters; for now it is helpful to draw on some of this evidence to illuminate the present subject.

Andrew Smith's party saw more of the Ndebele settlements in 1835 than did any other literate visitors to the Ndebele during the entire Transvaal period. His own estimate of the size of Mzilikazi's military manpower was very conservative:

> If Masalacatze were called upon to muster every man he has in his country, he could not produce 4,000, a number which even the Griquas would laugh at. He is in the habit of concentrating his people wherever he may be himself, and under such circumstances strangers see them and infer his strength. At such times almost the entire of his country is without inhabitants, only a few old men and the women being dispersed here and there to take charge of the enormous herds of cattle.[187]

This estimate conforms with figures for the sizes of *impis*, which seem to have numbered in the hundreds, not in the thousands of men, on most occasions. Even so, several hundred well trained and tightly disciplined Ndebele were more than a match for Mzilikazi's Sotho/Tswana enemies on most occasions.[188] The record of Ndebele military achievements does not in itself indicate a large Ndebele population. Also, the limited size of the Ndebele army explains why Mzilikazi was left so vulnerably exposed when his troops were out of the country on truly large-scale campaigns.

A popular misconception which has contributed to the inflated estimates of Mzilikazi's manpower during this period was the so-called 'conquer or die' ethic he allegedly imposed on his soldiers:

On no account will Motselekatse tolerate flight in battle, and if his warriors yield to superior strength and numbers, or retire instead of exposing themselves to massacre, no sooner have th·y appeared before him than they are put to the sword. To die or to conquer, to triumph or to perish, such is his watchword.[189]

It is true that Ndebele men often fought with reckless disregard for their own lives, but Mzilikazi certainly did not have enough men to afford such an extravagant policy. This is proven by his reaction to a conflict with the Griqua when some married Ndebele men

> did not effect that destruction among the enemy the King considered they ought to have accomplished; and punished them in consequence; but the tribe being too weak to admit of the usual practice which chiefs who reason like Musulakatzi adopt, namely putting to death any person who manifests any want of courage, he preferred withholding their wives from them until they should wipe away the stain which at present disgraced their characters.[190]

Thus, in contrast to Shaka and Dingane—who used terror as an instrument of political power[191]—Mzilikazi had to use more positive inducements to command his men. Consequently, he was a better-liked ruler than the contemporary Zulu kings.[192]

In a special report to the Cape Colonial Governor Smith specified that his estimate of 4000 armed Ndebele men applied to 'the male population between the ages of 15 and 60'.[193] These must have constituted nearly all the adult men. Assuming Smith's estimate to be approximately correct, what does this figure for adult males imply for the Ndebele population as a whole? This is a very difficult question to answer because of the abnormal age and sex structure of the population. Many observers commented on the high proportion of women and the low proportion of children among the Ndebele.[194] Normally, one would expect a roughly equal number of males and females, and, in a society with high infant mortality, a child/adult split at about age 15. Hence, an adult male population of c. 4000 would imply a total population of (4 × 4000) or about 16,000 people. However, all of these proportions are uncertain. Nevertheless, the *order of magnitude* should not have been substantially different from the approximation of 16,000. The Ndebele probably never numbered more than 20,000 persons during the 1830s (exclusive of non-Ndebele who resided among them). This figure is offered only as an order of magnitude, but one which was necessarily a fraction of Archbell's estimate of 60,000 to 80,000.[195]

This downward-revised population estimate has two important implications. First, it shows that what success Mzilikazi achieved in the Transvaal was not won simply by sheer strength of numbers. Intelligent planning, training, discipline, and leadership all contributed to Ndebele power.

Secondly, it implies that the better-documented Ndebele population size of *c.* 100,000 for the 1890s resulted from a more rapid increase after 1840 than has hitherto been realized.[196]

Ndebele settlements, 1827–1832

All Europeans who visited Mzilikazi during this period met him at a town near the source of the Aapies River which Moffat called Mzilikazi's 'capital'.[197] We should not read too much into Moffat's designation, however, because of Mzilikazi's known proclivity for moving about between many of his towns.[198] Nevertheless, it is clear that the region around the upper Aapies and upper Oori Rivers was the centre of the most important Ndebele towns. This is where Mzilikazi himself mostly stayed, as well as some of his leading officials, such as Kaliphi and Gwabalanda.[199] Most other Ndebele towns appear to have been along the northern slopes of the Magaliesbergs between the Oori and Elands Rivers.[200]

There is no first-hand account of Ndebele towns very far north of the Magaliesbergs. Smith and W. C. Harris, who travelled around the Oori River in 1835 and 1836 respectively, confirm the impression that most of the Ndebele had lived just north of this mountain range. One suspects that Ndebele informants may have exaggerated the northern extent of their country to earlier visitors in order to give a misleading impression of their power.[201] In any case, the tsetse fly belt just north of the Pienaars River probably limited Ndebele expansion in that direction.[202]

South of the Magaliesbergs Mzilikazi cleared the country of all human settlement, evidently in order to maintain a buffer zone through which his enemies would have trouble moving.[203] And, as emphasized previously, the Ndebele were continuing to expand towards the west during this entire period.

Some non-Ndebele towns subject to Mzilikazi were interspersed among Ndebele settlements; others were dotted around the periphery of the Ndebele from the northeast to the west.[204] The presence of non-Ndebele peoples among the Ndebele probably contributed to the exaggerated estimates of the numbers of Ndebele. These other peoples cannot properly be counted as Ndebele, as they could not be relied upon in military emergencies. Although they grudgingly tended Ndebele cattle and paid Mzilikazi taxes, they often fled the country to avoid wholesale conscription into his *impis*.[205]

In summary, the Ndebele occupied an area about one hundred miles wide from east to west, and perhaps fifty miles long from north to south, with their main concentration in the southeast.

The curious fact that no European who visited Mzilikazi in the central Transvaal recorded the name of any of his towns makes it difficult to correlate the places they visited with places named in Ndebele traditions and elsewhere. Nevertheless, it is reasonable to guess that the 'capital' town visited by Europeans was called *Mhlahlandlela*, a name mentioned in its Sotho form, *Motlatlantsela*, as Mzilikazi's residence by Arbousset and Daumas in 1842.[206] Campbell gives us some other town names; we can infer that these were also near the sources of the Oori because he associates these with the 1832 Zulu invasion which we know was centred there.[207]

The names of these towns are not intrinsically important. However, modern authorities have tended to push their locations farther and farther north as successive writers have compounded geographical errors. The result is an altogether misleading picture of Ndebele settlement, stretched by one historian as far north as the Limpopo![208] Such errors support the exaggerated notions of the size of Ndebele population. Furthermore they reinforce the picture of a major Zulu victory over the Ndebele in 1832 by implying that the Zulu ravaged more than 150 miles of Ndebele territory between the Magaliesbergs and the Limpopo.[209]

Revision of the picture of Ndebele settlements conforms with such population data as we have, and it places the settlements of this period more logically into the historical sequence of compact settlements between the Vaal River and Southern Rhodesia between 1823 and 1893.

The central Transvaal period is the first for which we have first-hand descriptions of the Ndebele way of life, but the data available give us only the most superficial picture. As one would expect, cattle played a prominent role in Ndebele life. Ndebele settlements then, as later, were organized largely around the needs of cattle, which may well have outnumbered people. Cattle had to be distributed rather widely to equalize pressure on pasture land and water supplies. Hence, human settlements were also dispersed. A typical town comprised three to five thousand head of cattle and perhaps several hundred people of all ages.[210] In 1832 Pellissier described the settlements he saw:

> In comparison with the size of their population, the Matebele occupy a very large territory, Motselekatse owns so many herds of cattle that it is seldom possible to find more than two hundred souls in the same locality. They dispose their huts in the quaintest manner; their villages are invariably built in a circle of at least three hundred feet in diameter. This area is bounded by a barricade of brushwood within which the cattle are enclosed at night. It is around this fence that their huts are built; they are made of reeds and matting.[211]

The towns were normally built on elevated areas so that the cattle could be seen while they were grazing during the day.[212] This arrangement was also suited for sighting the approach of enemies, although one wonders from their experiences during this period whether this capability did the Ndebele any good.

Each time new cattle were captured Mzilikazi created a new town and assigned a body of men to guard it.[213] The relationship between this system and the growth of regimental towns is not clear at this stage. Towns comprising individual 'regiments' evidently existed by this time; however, no Europeans saw them and the brief references in traditions are not very informative.[214] For fuller information on such subjects we must look at later periods of settlement.

CHAPTER IV

DISASTER IN THE WESTERN TRANSVAAL, 1832–1837

In mid-1832 the Ndebele shifted their settlements from the Magaliesbergs to the Marico Valley of the western Transvaal, where they remained until the end of 1837. These last years south of the Limpopo are by far the best-documented in Ndebele history before the 1860s. In the western Transvaal the Ndebele were closer than ever before to the outposts of literate European missionaries and traders with whom they maintained regular communication throughout this period. Furthermore, European writers by then knew much more about the geography and peoples of the interior than they had previously; hence, their commentaries were better informed and more accurate than in prior years. We have no first-hand accounts of the Ndebele kingdom between early 1832 and 1835, but we have a steady and reasonably accurate second-hand record for these years. Most important, however, are the comparatively voluminous first-hand accounts written by the numerous European visitors to Mzilikazi during 1835–36.[1] These accounts give us almost continuous first-hand records for Ndebele activities between mid-1835 and early 1837, and they are also valuable because for information on earlier years. Finally, 1835 also saw the expansion of European settlement north of the Orange River in the mass movement known as the 'Great Trek'. The ensuing Ndebele-Afrikaner wars attracted considerable attention towards the Ndebele which helped to produce further documentation with which we can round out the record of Ndebele history south of the Limpopo.

It will be seen that contemporary and near-contemporary European documentation is crucial to reconstructing this phase of Ndebele settlements, for it is a period poorly remembered in Ndebele tradition. Once again, however, the recorded oral accounts of non-Ndebele informants provide invaluable insights into Ndebele relations with their neighbours, and such evidence is drawn upon extensively in this chapter.

This chapter treats the final sub-Limpopo phase of Ndebele history in far greater detail than does any previous account, but it presents no major revisions. Such errors as exist in the earlier literature are pointed out, but these are mostly minor. Generally, the chapter refines chronological details, establishes significant connections between events, and elaborates on episodes previously overlooked or underplayed by historians.

Removal to the Marico Valley, August-September 1832

As I showed in the previous chapter, the Ndebele began preparations to remove to the western Transvaal months before the Zulu invaded the Magaliesbergs. The Zulu attack in August 1832 merely realized long-standing Ndebele fears and made their subsequent removal from the region appear more precipitous than it actually was. The actual move differed from previous migrations in that it was a shift of settlements within an already established Ndebele domain. Most of the Sotho/Tswana peoples to the west had already been conquered and were ill-prepared to resist further.

Almost immediately upon the withdrawal of the Zulu forces from the Magaliesbergs Mzilikazi launched three Ndebele forces against the Kwena, Ngwaketse, and Rolong.[2] These attacks commenced in early August.[3] One of the first forces fell upon the Rolong of Tawana at Khunwana, just south of the upper Molopo River. The Ndebele devastated the Rolong town, killing many people and driving the remainder south.[4] Mzilikazi later justified his destruction of Khunwana as an act of revenge, because the Rolong had participated in Barend Barends' commando, and because chief Tawana had had several Ndebele messengers killed while en route to Kuruman the previous year.[5]

At the same moment another Ndebele force attacked the Ngwaketse, who were then apparently at Kanye. Alone among the Tswana, the Ngwaketse resisted. However, the Ndebele surrounded their town at night and then routed them at daybreak. Most of the surviving Ngwaketse fled into the Kalahari Desert under Sebego, who had earlier usurped the Ngwaketse chiefship.[6]

The third Ndebele force attacked a branch of the Kwena ruled by Kgama, who lived near the confluence of the Marico and Oori

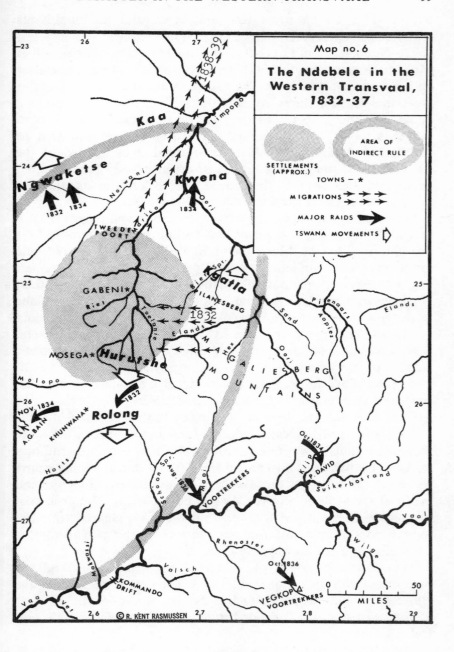

Rivers. The Kwena town was destroyed, and its inhabitants scattered or captured.[7]

The Ndebele did not have to attack the Hurutshe of Mokgatlha. Mokgatlha was already Mzilikazi's acknowledged vassal, and he had not participated in the Barends commando the year before. Nevertheless, the flurry of Ndebele military activity created a panic on the upper Marico. In early August the French missionaries at Mosega abandoned their station and fled to Kuruman.[8] And when the Hurutshe themselves learned of the destruction of the Rolong shortly afterwards, they too lost their nerve and fled south. The Ndebele were left the uncontested masters of the entire Marico Valley by September.[9]

Mzilikazi's personal role in the invasion campaigns is not recorded. However, it appears that he himself soon removed his headquarters to the Marico and that the shifting of Ndebele settlements was completed in a short period of time.[10]

Very early reports out of Ndebele-occupied territory tell of Ndebele settlements over the whole of the former Hurutshe territory—a region which seems to have remained the core Ndebele territory over the next five years.[11] Except for a gradual westward encroachment into Ngwaketse territory,[12] the basic pattern of Ndebele settlement appears not to have altered until late 1836. Thus, the comparatively extensive evidence on Ndebele settlements collected by Europeans in 1835-36 probably pertains with equal validity to the years leading up to their visits.

As in earlier settlements, Ndebele fears of external attack were directed primarily southwards. Many Ndebele towns and military posts were thus concentrated in the Mosega basin on the upper Marico.[13] There seem to have been no settlements of any kind south of the Molopo River.[14] As will be shown, the Ndebele kept the region between the Molopo and the Vaal cleared of other human populations, and they maintained regular patrols in that region in search of hostile interlopers.[15]

The westward extent of Ndebele settlement is difficult to determine with precision. Most Ndebele towns seem to have clustered around the Marico River and its tributaries, but at least a few cattle posts extended into the southeast of present Botswana.[16]

The northern extent of Ndebele settlement is less vague. In 1835 Andrew Smith travelled to the Tropic of Capricorn, describing settlements he observed on the way. His geographical references are not always clear, but it is evident that Ndebele towns extended at least to the confluence of the Marico and Oori Rivers—a point affirmed by a later traveller.[17]

In the east Ndebele cattle posts extended to within twenty-five miles of the upper Oori River, and to the Pilanesberg Mountains.[18] In the southeast a number of important towns lay beside the Toelanie River.[19]

Mzilikazi had no 'capital' town in the Western sense, but he frequently resided at a town called Gabeni (Kapain), just west of the Riet's confluence with Marico.[20] Gabeni was situated approximately at the centre of the kingdom's geographical expanse, but the bulk of the population seems to have resided to the south.[21] Gabeni may have been established as an administrative centre as early as 1832, but evidence for this is not conclusive.[22]

No precise reconstruction of the distribution of towns seems possible. Fortunately, however, Smith's general description conforms fairly well with the more random scraps of evidence recorded by him and other contemporary writers, and it is thus worth quoting at length.

> [Mzilikazi's] posts are placed with considerable regularity. His own kraal is nearly in the centre of his country, and then his principal soldiers are placed round him in posts not very distant from each other and no one of them more than an hour's walk from his kraal. At these posts his best cattle and those for breeding are kept; outside of those again are placed posts about nine in number in each direction where he fears the approach of any enemies. Thus in the direction of Kuruman he has eight or nine posts, in the direction in which the Griquas can approach him eight or ten, in the direction of Sabiqua [Sebego] a like number, and in the direction in which Dingan's commando approaches also a number. Each of these divisions have the different kraals so placed that they are within sight of each other. Between each of these posts in the openings he has small Buchuana [Tswana] kraals, but these are within the outer circle . . . At these outposts the worst cattle are kept. . . . The kraal in which his own cattle are kept is in one of the most secure parts of the country and scarcely any of the people are permitted to go near it, lest by their traces an enemy should discover it.[23]

In order to enhance observation of potential enemies, towns were generally built on hills and surrounding trees were cut down.[24] The towns themselves varied considerably in size and in composition of population, but they tended to be laid out according to the same plan: houses formed protective circles around interior cattle folds.[25] Individual towns contained from several dozen to more than a thousand people.[26] Cattle herds were distributed according to the principles alluded to by Smith above and according to the physical attributes of the land itself. The numbers of cattle tended by individual towns bore no necessary relationship to the numbers of people in the towns.[27]

Town populations also varied considerably in their age and sex structures. Militarily strategic towns contained from several dozen to several hundred men who were trained and ready to fight. These units were periodically shifted between locations, according to prevailing defensive considerations.[28] Many towns were made up principally of adult women occupied in food production.[29] Indeed, it was occasionally observed that females heavily outnumbered males throughout the kingdom.[30] The apparent predominance of females was, however, probably more characteristic of the central regions most frequently visited by outsiders; in the more remote regions cattle posts were occupied mainly by males below the fighting age.[31]

Ndebele impact upon the Tswana of the western Transvaal

The rapid Ndebele occupation of the western Transvaal devastated many Tswana chiefdoms, as we have seen. Some Tswana stayed at their homes and accepted Ndebele rule, but most communities were scattered until the Ndebele themselves left the Transvaal five years later. Ngwaketse who did not follow Sebego into the Kalahari joined the general Tswana exodus to the south. Many Rolong followed their chief Tawana to the Harts River, where they were soon joined by Mokgatlha, Moilwe and several hundred Hurutshe refugees.[32] These traditional rulers had difficulty holding their remnant followings together during the ensuing years. Kuruman attracted away from them many people who assumed, correctly, that Mzilikazi would not attack the mission station of his friend Robert Moffat.[33] Meanwhile, the Ndebele raided freely between Kuruman and Mosega, clearing the region of human settlement, and leaving the Tlhaping and their wards near Kuruman in a constant state of alert.[34] Some refugees at Kuruman came to distrust the Tlhaping chief Mahura, so they moved even farther south. Many of these people sought protection under the Griqua rulers at Griqua Town and Philippolis.[35] There they found safety from the Ndebele, who never mounted any major raids south of the depopulated zone.

The sudden concentration of thousands of refugees between Kuruman and the Orange River created an economic crisis in which many Tswana apparently died from starvation. To avert disaster some refugees, notably the Hurutshe, returned to their former homes in Ndebele-occupied territory to recapture stores of food. A missionary living among the refugees reported that 'hundreds of these unfortunate people were stabbed to death' in their attempts.[36] Undaunted, however, many Hurutshe and others remained just south of the Ndebele domain and continued to raid Ndebele cattle at every opportunity, as other refugees had done against Ndebele settlements in previous years.[37]

While it is clear that the Ndebele invasion of the Marico Valley drove many Tswana out of the region, it is also clear that many other Tswana elected to remain at their homes and to accept Ndebele rule. European travellers observed wholly or predominantly Tswana towns interspersed throughout the entire Ndebele kingdom.[38] Typically, residents of these towns had to work for the Ndebele. Some towns, for example, comprised mostly Tswana women engaged in agriculture.[39] Many, perhaps most, Tswana towns tended cattle regarded as Ndebele property. These arrangements seem to have worked satisfactorily, for the Ndebele entrusted cattle to very remote posts. Even among the Ngwaketse, who were never completely subjugated, local men were left in charge of Ndebele cattle posts.[40] In some cases, as among the Kgatla at the Pilanesberg Mountains, only one or two Ndebele men oversaw posts.[41] Beyond the range of Ndebele settlements to the north, Mzilikazi placed Ndebele cattle among the Kaa.[42] Occasionally he relocated subject communities into territories unfamiliar to them in order to maintain the security of his perimeter regions.[43] When subject chiefs treated livestock too much as their own, they were disciplined severely. In late 1834, for example, Mzilikazi had the Kwena chief Kgama killed for behaving too independently.[44] Similar punitive expeditions were undertaken periodically, but recalcitrant chiefs occasionally went into hiding and bided their time until Mzilikazi left the Transvaal.[45]

Subject chiefs paid taxes to Mzilikazi in various forms. Documentation on this subject is skimpy, but some explicit evidence exists. One Kwena chief was said to grow tobacco for the Ndebele.[46] The Hurutshe chief Moilwe—who later deserted Mzilikazi—provided 'skins and karosses'.[47] The Ngwato paid tribute in iron tools and weapons.[48]

Andrew Smith wrote that some Hurutshe were anxious to escape Ndebele domination, but they were 'afraid to fly in twos or threes, because unless the entire [sic] leave the kraal at the same time, those that remain are put to death.'[49] Elsewhere, however, he found at least one Tswana community in which the people 'seem quite satisfied with their present situation'.[50] Such contradictory evidence makes it difficult to assess the general attitudes of the conquered peoples towards the Ndebele; however, generally, they seem to have been passively content. It is significant that a Phiring group which fled Mzilikazi later returned and submitted to him. He in turn entrusted them with livestock to tend.[51]

As was the case throughout early Ndebele history, the kingdom depended upon partially incorporated peoples to provide a fully rounded society. Hence, it was observed that most of the women living in the Mosega Basin were Kwena and Hurutshe.[52] As we shall see, many such Tswana subjects deserted the Ndebele at the earliest opportunity five years later.

Jan Bloem returns, May 1834

Ndebele occupation of the Marico Valley was completed by the end of 1832; the following year was a peaceful one. The Ndebele kept busy by establishing new towns and cattle posts, organizing agricultural production, and bringing local peoples under administrative control. These tasks made major aggressive wars unnecessary and impractical, and the kingdom was not troubled by outside aggression.[53]

This comparative tranquility began to dissolve in January 1834 when an Ndebele patrol over-ran a Hurutshe refugee camp near the Harts River. A survivor of the attack communicated the news to Mokgatlha, who in turn appealed to the Korana for assistance against the Ndebele.[54] This incident appears to have sparked the new hostile phase in Ndebele relations with the Griqua/Korana.

As I showed in previous chapters, certain Griqua/Korana groups competed with the Ndebele as predators against other highveld communities. The rise of the Ndebele state in the Transvaal served effectively to consolidate many small Sotho/Tswana communities within this new single and powerful unit. And as the formerly dispersed, independent communities were scattered or absorbed by the expansionist Ndebele state, the Griqua/Korana had increasingly to confront this new power to compensate for their loss of easier prey. Mzilikazi's move to the western Transvaal aggravated their problem, for it thrust into their midst many Tswana refugees with whom they then had to compete for food and space. To Griqua/Korana predators the solution to their problems would have been the shattering of the Ndebele kingdom—a task which they attempted with foolhardy persistence.

The Ndebele defeat of Barend Barends' large commando in 1831 cut severely into Griqua/Korana manpower, but it did not still their desire to destroy Mzilikazi. Rumours that the Griqua/Korana were about to renew their war on Mzilikazi were widespread after 1831. The third major commando against him did not materialize until May 1834, but it appears that the Griqua/Korana continued their annual minor cattle raids against the Ndebele, as before 1831.[55] Meanwhile, the Griqua/Korana themselves feared that Mzilikazi was about to retaliate against them—an apprehension encouraged by the nervous new Tswana refugees among them.[56] The possibility of such an Ndebele attack was heightened, from the Griqua/Korana perspective, by the elimination of Sotho/Tswana settlements which had previously served as a 'buffer' zone.[57] Tension was further aggravated by the occasional presence deep in Griqua/Korana territory of Ndebele reconnaissance parties.[58] The Ndebele attack on the Hurutshe refugees in January 1834 appears to have set into motion a Griqua/Korana invasion which had been developing for three years.

Documentation for the 1834 Griqua/Korana commando is sparser than that for the 1831 commando. Specifics on the size and composition are unavailable; nevertheless, it clearly was a large force, comprising Griqua, Korana and Tswana men.[59] In 1834, as in 1828, the Korana chief Jan Bloem commanded the allies. Among the Tswana participants was the Hurutshe sub-chief Moilwe, who had only recently fled from Ndebele territory.[60]

This commando was remarkable in that it closely followed the pattern of the two previous major invasions. Once again the

Griqua/Korana force descended upon undefended Ndebele outposts while Mzilikazi prepared a counter-stroke. And once again the invaders retreated with their booty, only to be overtaken, surrounded, and defeated by an Ndebele force three days later. Apparently significant numbers of men on both sides were killed. Bloem himself barely escaped alive after his horse was killed from beneath him.[61] Moilwe was more successful; he escaped with several hundred cattle.[62]

This third fiasco added to the humiliation of the Griqua/Korana. Nevertheless, they continued to boast that they would soon renew the war against Mzilikazi, and even knowledgeable European observers believed them.[63] The Griqua/Korana did not, however, return in force until three years later, by which time the Ndebele had already been softened by other invaders.

The immediate effect of Bloem's 1834 commando on the Ndebele was probably a sharpened fear of outsiders. Over the next two years unannounced strangers were attacked without warning.

Campaigns and border incidents, 1834

During the years they occupied the Marico Valley the Ndebele waged fewer aggressive wars than they had from their earlier settlements. Campaigns such as those against the Kwena chief Kgama and the Hurutshe refugees were—from an Ndebele point of view—merely 'police actions' within an established sphere of influence. For the moment, the exploratory and expansionist phase in Ndebele history was over. Ndebele warfare then served two purposes: to defend against external aggressors, and to define political relationships with already subjugated peoples.

The Ngwaketse chief Sebego was the only remaining Tswana chief whom Mzilikazi wished to subjugate. In 1834 the Ndebele were in partial occupation of the Ngwaketse homeland and they received token tribute from Sebego; however, the Ngwaketse ruler stubbornly refused to make his final submission to Mzilikazi.[64] Mzilikazi regarded Sebego as his 'toughest' Tswana adversary, and the latter's continued defiance galled him.[65] For at least two reasons he wished to conquer the man. First, he would have wanted to set Sebego as an example of the futility of resistance;

secondly, he wanted to keep Ngwaketse territory open as a potential corridor for Ndebele migration.

Sometime in mid-1834 Mzilikazi launched his fifth campaign against Ngwaketse headquarters.[66] He evidently expected an easy victory, for he sent a force comprising only inexperienced youths after Sebego. He retained his older soldiers at home, apparently in anticipation of another Griqua/Korana invasion after the May commando.

The Ndebele youths marched deep into the Kalahari Desert, where they were weakened by the rigours of the terrain. Sebego defeated them easily and sent them limping back to Mzilikazi lacking any booty to show for their efforts.[67] Sebego still feared that Mzilikazi would send a major force against him, so he retreated farther inland. He resettled near Ghanzi in central Botswana, more than 350 miles northwest of the Marico River.[68] There he remained unmolested by the Ndebele until the latter had resettled north of the Limpopo.[69]

The first notable test of Mzilikazi's border policy came in October 1834. Early that month a party of Griqua hippopotamus hunters from Thaba Nchu advanced down the Wilge River towards the Vaal.[70] A man named Peter David led the hunters, some of whom had earlier been followers of the bandit leader Barend Barends. Tswana refugees living south of the Vaal communicated the news of the hunting party—including the identity of its members—to Mzilikazi.[71] Not knowing the full intentions of the hunters, Mzilikazi feared that their arrival portended the major invasion he had been awaiting since May.[72] He therefore sent an armed force 150 miles southeast to the Vaal.

On or about 8 October the Ndebele force found the Griqua divided into two hunting parties along the Vaal. Unprepared to defend themselves, both parties were quickly overwhelmed by the Ndebele. Using their horses to escape, the Griqua abandoned their wagons and equipment to the Ndebele.[73] The force returned to Mzilikazi's headquarters with seven wagons—the first to fall into Ndebele hands—oxen, some horses, and miscellaneous goods.[74]

In their rush to escape death the Griqua unintentionally left behind three children whom the Ndebele captured and took to Mzilikazi. These children were two daughters and a nephew of Peter David.[75] Capturing alien children was common in Ndebele warfare, but these particular children quickly assumed an enormous importance. Their release became a central issue in future Ndebele-Griqua peace negotiations. Furthermore, they later helped to feed rumours that the Ndebele were holding European children. These rumours—which were probably false—provided Afrikaner adventurers with a justification for waging war against the Ndebele as late as 1847.[76] As it developed, one child soon died; the other two were thoroughly incorporated into Ndebele society, demonstrating the breadth of its inclusiveness.[77]

Just over a month after the David incident there occurred another Ndebele-Griqua confrontation. This time the affair was complicated by the involvement of Andrew Geddes Bain, a white trader from Graaff Reinet. Bain had been commissioned to collect wildlife specimens for a museum, and was proceeding to the interior with the intention of obtaining Ndebele permission to hunt north of the Vaal. In Griqua territory he hired several men to assist him; unfortunately, he failed to demur when a few other men voluntarily attached themselves to his party.[78]

At the Mareetsane River, a tributary of the Molopo in the region depopulated by the Ndebele, Bain learned that some Hurutshe had just raided an Ndebele cattle post, killing an Ndebele herder. He expected soon to see an Ndebele punitive force, but he still hoped to meet with Mzilikazi. While he encamped to await developments, four Griqua quit his party to do some free-lance cattle rustling. Unbeknownst to Bain, Ndebele scouts reported all these developments to Mzilikazi.[79] Meanwhile, the Griqua attacked an Ndebele post in the Mosega Basin, where they killed several Ndebele and carried off the cattle. Mzilikazi, who happened to be residing nearby, immediately sent his *induna* Kaliphi in pursuit with about 200 men.[80]

The morning of 8 November the errant Griqua rushed into Bain's camp with the Ndebele close behind. After seizing another horse, the Griqua again fled, leaving the dumbfounded Bain and a few other men to defend themselves. When Kaliphi attempted to encircle the camp with his men, the remaining defenders also bolted on horseback, abandoning all their wagons and goods.[81] Kaliphi recaptured the livestock and returned to Mzilikazi with Bain's wagons; however, he was reprimanded for failing to overtake the cattle thieves themselves.[82]

Bain's experience alarmed Europeans in the Cape Colony, for it was the first hostile encounter between the Ndebele and whites.[83] However, Europeans knowledgeable about Mzilikazi refused to consider the incident indicative of his inherent hostility towards whites and they condoned his actions.[84] Even as Bain fled back to the Cape Colony, he met a trader on his way to Mzilikazi. This trader, named Gibson, ignored Bain's panicky warnings, and continued his journey to Ndebele country without incident.[85]

Mzilikazi himself later acknowledged that Bain was personally innocent of involvement in the Griqua cattle raid, but he still regarded Bain responsible for the actions of members of his party. Early the next year he communicated an open message to the Colony in which he 'regretted the circumstances of that attack . . . which was to be attributed to the extreme difficulty of distinguishing his friends from his foes' and he offered to return the wagons to Bain.[86] However, he steadfastly refused to do so unless Bain paid him some kind of compensation.[87] He later explained his position to Robert Moffat:

> When it was reported to me that he (Mr B[ain]) was stopping on the limits of my territories & was accompanied with Griquas I commanded a number of spies to watch his motions. These spies discovered by observation & information that these Griquas were in Mr B's services or were employed in shooting game for him. I gave the strictest orders that he should not be molested. My spies waited till they saw four men on horseback leave the wagons and make direct to the nearest outpost when they made a desperate attempt to take cattle. Could I act otherwise than I did with these things before my eyes? especially when I was informed that the wagons retired towards the west immediately after the horsemen left them.' The above agrees with what Mr B told me [i.e., Moffat] . . .[88]

In sum, the incident reaffirmed Mzilikazi's determination to defend his borders and it gave him new cause to distrust the Griqua. It also proved that he was anxious not to offend Europeans.

Expanding contacts with Europeans, 1832–36

In the previous chapter I showed how Mzilikazi wanted to establish a chain of mission stations between himself and Kuruman in order to maintain a safe communications corridor with the European Colony. The flight of the French missionaries from Mosega on the eve of the Ndebele occupation in August 1832 temporarily spoiled Mzilikazi's plans. Afterwards, he renewed his efforts to obtain missionaries for much the same reasons as before. Over the next three years he communicated regularly with Robert Moffat through messengers.[89] He never lost his enthusiasm for Kuruman and frequently expressed his desire to visit the station himself.[90] After resettling by the Marico he publicly reiterated his desire for missionaries to live among the Ndebele, and he let it be known that the French agents were welcome to return to Mosega.[91] The Frenchmen—Lemue, Pellissier, and Rolland—considered the invitation briefly, but then succumbed to their fear of the Ndebele and started a new mission at Mothetho, near Kuruman.[92] Their refusal to return disappointed Mzilikazi, who regarded missionaries as potential allies in his on-going rivalry with Dingane. He knew that Europeans lived among the Zulu, and felt that he was at a disadvantage so long as none lived among the Ndebele.[93]

Meanwhile, the American Board of Commissioners for Foreign Missions (ABC) had formed in Boston; its directors were seeking prospective mission fields. As the backers of the ABC shared the Congregational tenets of the London Missionary Society (LMS), they became the natural allies of the LMS in Southern Africa. John Philip, the South African superintendent of the LMS, encouraged the ABC directors to consider stations among the Ndebele and the Zulu, hoping thereby to widen Protestant influence in Southern Africa, while helping to quell intra-African wars.[94]

The ABC accepted Philip's challenge and prepared two groups of missionaries for the Ndebele and the Zulu.[95] In the meantime an unrelated development within South Africa was occurring which led directly to the implanting of the American mission among the Ndebele and to greatly expanding Ndebele contacts with the European world.

In mid-1833 Dr Andrew Smith, founder of the South African Museum in Cape Town, organized the 'Association for the Exploration of Central South Africa' for the purpose of collecting scientific specimens and data in the regions between the Orange River and the Tropic of Capricorn which were largely unknown to Europeans. With the support of the Cape Colonial government, which wished to establish informal diplomatic ties with northern rulers, Smith assembled about fifty men, including twenty Europeans.[96] In August 1834 his expedition crossed the Orange River.[97]

Smith slowly travelled through present Lesotho, whence he

turned southwest, then north, reaching Kuruman in late January 1835. During this journey he viewed Moshweshwe, Sekonyela, Peter David, and other Sotho/Tswana and Griqua/Korana leaders. From these people, especially Moshweshwe, he heard terrible accounts of Mzilikazi's alleged treachery to strangers.[98] He became worried, but felt it was crucial his expedition pass through Ndebele territory. At Kuruman he begged Robert Moffat to accompany him to Mzilikazi. Moffat recognized the diplomatic possibilities deriving from the expedition, so he joined it. He was especially interested in seizing the opportunity to confer with Mzilikazi about the American missionaries, who were then on their way to South Africa.[99]

The combined Smith/Moffat expedition reached the Molopo River in late May. There it was met by cordial Ndebele officials, who quickly ushered the visitors into Mzilikazi's presence at Mosega. Moffat himself remained with Mzilikazi in the Mosega basin until early August, while Smith's party explored Ndebele territory and the regions to the north.

Although the previous year's border incidents had left the Ndebele extra-cautious about strangers, Mzilikazi welcomed Smith enthusiastically, trusting in Moffat's association with the expedition. The way in which he responded to the expedition's approach is instructive, in view of his difficulties with unannounced visitors.

> They are so many; but nevertheless I wish to see them. I am confident their hearts are white and they will not injure me. I have heard much of the awful things (meaning cannon) with which the white people are supplied to destroy other people and have been told by one of my own subjects who visited Graham's Town that there are more white people than Zoolas and that their soldiers never sleep either by day or by night. Yet I am without fear because had they any intention of injuring me they would not have sent me word they were coming.[100]

When Moffat raised the subject of the American mission, he easily obtained Mzilikazi's promise of full support of a station among the Ndebele.[101] Moffat and Mzilikazi separated in a spirit of mutual good will, not guessing that their next meeting would occur almost twenty years later.[102] Soon after Moffat left Mosega, his fellow missionaries from Kuruman paid Mzilikazi a brief visit for the purpose of obtaining building timber.[103]

The cordiality with which Mzilikazi entertained Smith's expedition swiftly altered Smith's image of the Ndebele ruler.

Smith dropped his conception of Mzilikazi as a bloodthirsty despot; he now saw him as the wounded party in Ndebele dealings with the Griqua/Korana. Smith determined to use his own influence to effect a general peace settlement. A week after his arrival in Mosega he wrote to the chief of Griqua Town, Andries Waterboer, to moot the subject of Griqua-Ndebele peace negotiations.[104]

As explained in the previous chapter, Mzilikazi's own earlier peace initiatives to the Griqua/Korana had been ignored.[105] Waterboer, however, was a much different character from such leaders as Barend Barends and Jan Bloem. He was a peaceful, Western-oriented ruler, closely identified with the interests of the LMS. Mzilikazi knew of Waterboer's association with Moffat's missionary society, and of Waterboer's influence among. the surrounding Tswana peoples; he professed to admire him greatly.[106] Waterboer's stature in the interior was greatly enhanced by a visit he made to Cape Town early in 1835, when he signed a treaty of friendship with the British governor. When he returned to Griqua Town he was visited by many neighbouring chiefs. Afterwards he planned a major diplomatic journey to repay all their visits in an effort to build a general peace. He was especially anxious to meet Mzilikazi to settle the long-standing Ndebele-Griqua/Korana problem. However, Smith's letter urged him to postpone his trip until after Smith concluded his own stay in Ndebele country.[107] Mzilikazi also wanted to meet with Waterboer, but their proposed meeting was repeatedly delayed and never took place.[108] Among the issues thus left unresolved was the question of Mzilikazi's releasing Peter David's wagons and the captured children. We can only speculate on the wider significance of this lost opportunity to stabilize political relationships in the interior.

Before Smith's expedition left Cape Town, Smith was delegated by the Colonial government to establish semi-official diplomatic links with chiefs north of the Orange River. He bestowed gifts and symbols of friendship upon various chiefs, eventually making the same gestures to Mzilikazi at Mosega. He asked Mzilikazi a prescribed set of questions: did he want alliance with whites? did he want white traders in his country? did he want missionaries, and would he support them? and so on. Mzilikazi readily answered 'yes' to all these questions and was rewarded with a medal as a token of friendship. He also received 'two ornamented cloaks and two looking-glasses, large size'.

In common with the other interior chiefs, Mzilikazi seemed to interpret Smith's diplomatic gestures a good deal more seriously than the Colonial government had intended. According to Smith, these chiefs felt they had 'actually consummated treaties, and most of them immediately declared they were . . . "white people", and under the "white king" '.[109]

In contrast to the other chiefs, Mzilikazi further responded to Smith with a diplomatic initiative of his own. Within a month of the expedition's arrival, he suggested sending an embassy of his own to the governor at Cape Town to cement his developing alliance with the Europeans. He especially wanted to obtain white assistance against the Griqua/Korana, and he seems to have had some idea of buying firearms in Cape Town.[110] The resulting embassy is one of the earliest examples in Southern African history of an African delegation's visiting a European power centre.

After Smith's expedition completed its explorations towards the Tropic of Capricorn it was joined by the Ndebele envoys. Mzilikazi delegated Mncumbathe, who had visited Kuruman for him in 1829, to head the embassy, which included one other *induna*, an interpreter, and two servants. These men took with them twenty head of cattle with which to make purchases in the Colony.[111] They accompanied the scientific expedition to Graaff Reinet, where it was disbanded, and then continued with Smith to Port Elizabeth. From there they travelled by sea to Cape Town, arriving in late January 1836.

While on the road Smith endeavoured to prevent his Ndebele companions from learning about the Xhosa Frontier War, which was then just ending.[112] However, his efforts were useless. The circumstances of the war had become common knowledge among the Ndebele even before he left Mzilikazi. The Ndebele were very concerned about the Frontier War for two reasons. They feared that the Xhosa, if defeated, might be driven into Ndebele territory, and they wondered if the Cape Colony had territorial ambitions north of the Vaal.[113] Hence, an underlying motive of Mzilikazi's embassy might have been to forestall a potential Colonial-Ndebele war.

Mncumbathe's delegation spent six weeks in Cape Town. During this time the Cape government made every effort to impress upon the Ndebele the full might of Europeans. The

Ndebele were taken to a military review and demonstration and were generally encouraged to find wonderment in all that they saw in the Colony's premier city.[114]

The climax of the embassy's trip came on 3 March when Mncumbathe and Governor Benhamin D'Urban signed a treaty of general friendship.[115] As Mzilikazi's representative Mncumbathe promised that his king would 'be a faithful friend and ally of the colony'; that he would preserve the peace, except in self-defence; that he would protect white visitors to his country, especially missionaries and traders; and that he would generally behave in a non-belligerent and co-operative manner. In return, the governor promised to treat Mzilikazi and his subjects as friends. In contrast to the promise made on behalf of Mzilikazi, the governor did not pledge to be the 'ally' of the Ndebele. By the terms of the treaty, the governor sent a number of gifts to Mzilikazi and promised that additional gifts would be forthcoming.[116] The governor also promised to 'consider' sending a government agent—probably a missionary—to live among the Ndebele.[117]

The terms of the treaty were too general for it to carry weight through any sort of crisis; however, this shortcoming proved irrelevant, as neither party ever attempted formally to invoke them.[118]

Mncumbathe left Cape Town shortly after signing the treaty and reached Griqua Town early in May. There Andries Waterboer assisted the Ndebele in getting their new wagon across a river, and he provided them with additional provisions and some guides. Waterboer and Mncumbathe discussed the possibility of Waterboer's serving as a referee in Peter David's claims against Mzilikazi. Although Mzilikazi later sent a letter of thanks to Waterboer for his assistance, nothing ever came of the latter's diplomatic gesture.[119]

At Kuruman the Ndebele were joined by members of the American missionary party, which had already begun to establish a station at Mosega, and the whole party reported to Mzilikazi in June.[120]

Mzilikazi's success in hosting many European visitors during 1835 elated him, so he let it be known that more would be welcome.[121] He was also anxious to see the American missionaries, who had reached Griqua Town while Moffat was with him at Mosega. The LMS agents at Kuruman urged the Americans to send at least one of their number to Mzilikazi immediately in order to capitalize upon Moffat's influential presence. However, the Americans were tired of travelling. They preferred to adjust to life in the interior and to study languages before proceeding further.[122] Their delay proved a costly mistake, for Mzilikazi's enthusiasm to meet them waned considerably after Moffat left him.

Eventually, two of the missionaries, Daniel Lindley and Henry Venable, arrived in the Mosega Basin in early February 1836 to prepare the way for the rest of the party. Meanwhile, their families waited at Kuruman with the third missionary, Dr A. E. Wilson, and his family.[123] At Mosega Lindley and Venable were received cordially by Kaliphi, who assisted them to establish their residence. Over the next two months they rebuilt the house abandoned by the French missionaries in 1832. Mzilikazi was then residing at Gabeni, fifty miles to the north, and he largely ignored the Americans until they paid him a brief visit. Afterwards they rejoined their families at Kuruman.

In June most of the Americans returned to Mosega with Mncumbathe's embassy; the rest followed a month later.[124] The missionary families settled down in their large shared house and attempted to commence their work. Meanwhile, Mzilikazi received Mncumbathe's report on the embassy. In July Wilson responded to Mzilikazi's request to draft a letter to the Cape governor by paying his first visit to the king. At Gabeni he helped Mzilikazi to open the parcels from the governor. He returned to Mosega sensing that somehow he and his fellows were being 'used' by the Ndebele.[125]

The letter Mzilikazi dictated to Wilson is a curious document, worthy of some comment—especially since it is the only extant piece of correspondence known to have been composed by Mzilikazi himself.[126] In it Mzilikazi thanked D'Urban for the various gifts, and he described himself as now being 'English'. He then went on to enumerate additional articles he wanted from the governor.[127] Most importantly, he invited colonial subjects to visit him, but specified 'that the people to south, east of this must not come [sic].' This was a clear reference to his insistence that all visitors approach him from the direction of Kuruman if they were not to be mistaken as hostile. Just over a month later this policy was again tested, with profound consequences.

The Americans found their position at Mosega increasingly difficult. Mzilikazi remained aloof from them; his people tolerated their presence, but did little actively to support them. All attempts to proselytize were futile.[128] Worse, almost all of them soon became seriously ill. When Lindley and Venable had refurbished their house during their first visit, they made the mistake of shutting it tight with wet plaster inside. The house was still damp when they returned, apparently causing them to contract 'rheumatic' fever. By mid September Wilson's wife was dead; the others were struggling merely to survive. Their pitiful condition made them unimpressive proponents of the Christian diety; their influence among the Ndebele was thereafter minimal. Finally, the climacteric events developing around them occupied the full attention of their hosts, completing the reduction of the missionaries to little more than passive—but per-ceptive—observers.[129]

The coming of the Voortrekkers, 1836

The Ndebele should have had many reasons to regard 1835 as a particularly successful and promising year, and 1836 opened with even greater promise.[130] Their herds of livestock were large and they enjoyed an agricultural abundance.[131] They had entertained many visitors from the Cape Colony, and relations with their immediate neighbours appeared stabilized. The year 1836 opened with the successful diplomatic mission to Cape Town and the arrival of the first permanent white residents, whose presence seemed to promise many benefits. The Ndebele therefore must have felt they were on the threshold of an era of peaceful and increasingly prosperous contacts with the European world. Unknown to the Ndebele, however, an unprecedentedly large European migration was then developing in the Cape Colony. This was, of course, the emigration of thousands of Afrikaner families which became known as the 'Great Trek'.

The comparatively sudden migration of Afrikaners out of the Colony was the culmination of Afrikaner dissatisfaction with British colonial rule, under which they had lived since 1806.[132] The key to Afrikaner bitterness lay in the government's failure to stabilize the eastern frontier of the Colony where white and Southern Nguni expansion overlapped. To the white farmers of the eastern Cape the government demanded too much and provided too little security in return. Many farmers who fought in the 1834-35 Frontier War resented the government's failure to impose a sufficiently harsh settlement on their enemies. To them this was the final grievance in a history of misrule, so they determined to quit the Colony in order to form their own sovereign domains in the north. In late 1835 Afrikaner families began to cross the Orange River in ever-increasing numbers. The participants in this migration became known as 'Voortrekkers'.

The Voortrekkers were a rugged lot. They were accustomed to frontier conditions and were capable of living largely independently of European centres. Many of the men were expert horsemen and fine marksmen. Experienced in fighting Africans, they were highly self-confident. They entered the South African interior with a determination and sense of historical mission perhaps matched only by the earlier Nguni migrants, such as Mzilikazi's original band.

To Africans the Afrikaner Voortrekkers resembled the Griqua, whom they already knew. Indeed, the two peoples are consistently confused in Ndebele tradition. However, the Voortrekkers differed from the Griqua in several decisive characteristics. The failure of the Ndebele to perceive these differences quickly helped to create a confrontation which soon became irreconcilable. The Voortrekkers were unique among whites and Griqua in that they moved into the deep interior in large numbers, taking with them their entire families and all their worldly goods. They carried with them a strong impulse for self-survival, reinforced by their feelings of alienation from the Africans whom they encountered on the way. Unlike the Griqua, they confronted their common enemies with a degree of discipline and social order which transcended their own factional disputes in every crisis.

The Voortrekker migration was never a single, coherently planned population movement. Families grouped together in bands of from two or three to several hundred; alignments among different bands changed constantly. The migrants' only shared plans were the common decision to quit the Colony and the vague intention of resettling somewhere in Natal or around the Vaal River. As various bands grouped together, they elected leaders, but these were only temporary commanders. Generally, the tendency towards social fission remained paramount and individual families often went their own way.

In early 1836 two of the largest Voortrekker parties to leave the eastern Cape Colony crossed the Orange into the present Free

State. They were led by Andries Hendrik Potgieter and Sarel
Cilliers, who joined forces to create a composite band of about
two hundred people. This band momentarily stalled, undecided
over the direction to pursue. In May the party encamped by the
Sand River while Potgieter, Cilliers and a few other men separated
to explore the northern Transvaal. With their leaders gone, the
members of the camp gradually dispersed along the southern
banks of the Vaal.[133]

Between May and August of 1836 the Ndebele appear to have
been remarkably ignorant of the presence of the Voortrekkers
south of the Vaal and of the exploratory bands off to the
northeast. It should be emphasized that there is no convincing
evidence that the Ndebele knew anything about the Voortrekkers
before August. Ndebele tradition has surprisingly little to say
about the Voortrekkers.[134] Stranger, however, is the silence of
contemporary literate commentators on this issue, especially in
view of their prolific comments about later developments.[135]

In early August a few detached Voortrekker bands crossed the
Vaal just above its confluence with the Mooi River (near present
Potchefstroom). About 'the same time, non-Voortrekker
Afrikaners from the Cape Colony crossed the Vaal nearby to
hunt. Some of these hunters, led by Stephanus Erasmus, ventured
deep into the Transvaal.[136]

Finally, information on Afrikaner movements reached
Mzilikazi. On 15 August he sent an *impi* of anout 500 men to the
Vaal, just as he had done against Peter David two years before.[137]
On about the 21st the Ndebele force fell upon Erasmus' base
camp and nearly destroyed it.[138] Erasmus returned to his camp
during the battle, but he and his sons were unable to help their
besieged friends and relatives, so they rode off to obtain help
from Voortrekker camps. The Ndebele force then divided; part of
its members returned to Mzilikazi with captured livestock and
wagons, while the others marched up the right bank of the Vaal.
A few miles upstream they found a Voortrekker camp,
comprising mostly members of a family named Liebenberg. This
camp, too, was wiped out.[139]

Erasmus returned to the Vaal with twelve more men on
horseback whom the Ndebele engaged in a prolonged but
indecisive battle. As was typical in fights between African foot
soldiers and mounted gun-men, even overwhelming numbers of
Ndebele could not easily prevail against skilled opponents in an

open-field battle. At the end of the day all Ndebele withdrew, leaving several wrecked Afrikaner camps by the Vaal. Including stragglers, as many as fifty whites may have been killed, plus an unknown number of nonwhite servants.[140] The Ndebele seem to have lost about the same number of people.[141] The *impi* returned to Mosega with five wagons, several dozen horses, several teams of oxen, and more than a thousand cattle.[142] The whole campaign lasted two weeks.[143] The Afrikaners fell back as well, regrouping south of the Vaal.

Whatever Mzilikazi's reasons for attacking the Afrikaners, they could not have included any general ill-feeling towards whites. For, through these and later Ndebele-Afrikaner hostilities white missionaries and hunters worked and travelled freely within his kingdom.[144] Nor could he have felt any special hostility towards the Afrikaners, since he seems to have known nothing about who they were before August.[145] He simply regarded all who entered his territory from the southeast as enemies. This is an aspect of his foreign policy which white observers stressed. Mzilikazi insisted that friendly visitors first obtain clearance from Robert Moffat at Kuruman, and that they then approach his kingdom from the southwest.[146] According to a British army officer who hunted in Ndebele territory in August:

[Mzilikazi's] late attack on the Boers was owing, I think, to their having entered his country by the Vaal River, from which direction he is constantly annoyed by the inroads of the Griquas & Korannas. He told me himself that all who went to visit him must travel the proper road, meaning the one by Kuruman. I was in Moselekatse's country when the Commando collected, they told me without hesitation where they were going & for what purpose. In the event, they said, of the waggons belonging to Griquas, all were to be destroyed, but if they were white people they were to be brought to him/Moselekatse/ without injury to person or property. Why such slaughter took place I can't imagine, it will in my opinion annoy Moselekatse.[147]

The question of whether or not these Ndebele attacks on the Afrikaner camps were justified remains a live issue in modern South African historiography. While it is clear that the Afrikaners engaged in no overtly hostile behaviour towards the Ndebele, it is also clear that they did not bother to obtain Mzilikazi's permission to cross the Vaal, even though they had been warned by others to do so.[148] Hence, it seems fair to say that these conflicts grew out of mutual misunderstandings. Unfortunately, neither side was inclined to compromise and the hostilities soon grew worse.[149]

Vegkop, October 1836

Shortly after the first Ndebele-Afrikaner clashes, Potgieter and Cilliers returned from their exploratory journey to the north. They quickly realized that the still-scattered Voortrekker parties might be in danger, so they regrouped all their followers by the upper Rhenoster River. Determined to continue their northward trek, the Voortrekkers evidently were attempting to improve their defensive situation while they watched for further developments from the Ndebele side. They waited for Mzilikazi to make the first peace initiative.[150]

We can only surmise what Mzilikazi was thinking through the next six weeks. Thus far, his encounter with the Voortrekkers had been a mixed success. His August *impi* had easily overrun several Voortrekker camps and captured considerable livestock, but he had lost fifty men in the process. The Afrikaners had done nothing overtly hostile beyond trespassing into his domain, but they remained massed south of the Vaal as though they meant to try again. Furthermore, their immense herds of livestock must have presented a tempting prize.

If Voortrekker intentions were strictly peaceful, Mzilikazi apparently intended to let them prove it.[151] Through September, however, neither side moved to negotiate. On 9 October Mzilikazi sent most of his soldiers against the Voortrekker camp and he designated Kaliphi as his commander.[152] This *impi* comprised about three thousand men, a third of whom were non-Nguni servants and camp-followers.[153] The *impi* marched southwest about 175 miles, arriving at the Rhenoster River in a week.[154]

The Voortrekkers meanwhile had stayed close together while their scouts patrolled the region. Several days before Kaliphi appeared indigent Tswana warned the Voortrekkers of his approach.[155] By this time a few Voortrekker families had fled south for safety, leaving behind thirty to forty families, which included about thirty-five adult men with about fifty ox wagons.[156] Under the command of Potgieter and Cilliers these families formed their wagons into a defensive *laager* at the foot of the hill later called *Vegkop*, 'the hill of the fight'.[157] The *laager* was a formidable barricade in which the wagons were tightly lashed together and reinforced with strong thorny branches in all the links. A secondary barrier was made in the centre of the ring to serve as a refuge for non-combatants. Oxen, cattle, sheep and goats were so numerous that they were left outside the *laager*, but horses were kept inside. Part of the *laager* could be opened to permit the passage in and out of horsemen. As a whole, these arrangements marked an advance in the design of wagon *laagers* by the Afrikaners, who had earlier used simpler versions in the Southern Nguni frontier wars.[158] The new design created a stronghold largely impenetrable even to the militarily more sophisticated Northern Nguni over the next several years.

When Kaliphi's *impi* approached to within about ten miles of the *laager* most of the Afrikaner men rode out to greet it. The Afrikaners took with them an African interpreter and signalled their desire to parley.[159] Unfortunately, we have no way of knowing what, if any, instructions Mzilikazi had issued to Kaliphi to meet such a situation. Most Voortrekker accounts insist that the Ndebele reacted to their peace gesture only by rising to attack; however, the situation was probably more complex. According to the hitherto overlooked testimony of one Afrikaner participant in this meeting, a nervous Voortrekker fired his gun into the Ndebele ranks before negotiations could commence; only then did the Ndebele rise to charge.[160] It may be that Kaliphi had been prepared to talk peace, for many years later Mzilikazi told an Afrikaner hunter, 'with the Boers I was prepared to make peace. But they gave me no chance.'[161] Regardless of what actually transpired by the Rhenoster, the battle had begun.

From their horses the Voortrekkers repeatedly fired their guns into the Ndebele who unsuccessfully attempted to surround them. The Ndebele pursued the Voortrekkers for several hours until the latter reached the *laager*. Many Ndebele were left dead on the field, but not a single Voortrekker was killed. Once again, the combination of foot soldiers with hand spears against mounted gun-men was grossly unequal in an open field confrontation.[162] Only the urgent necessity of defending their families in the *laager* prevented the Afrikaners from exploiting their advantage to a greater extent. After the horsemen withdrew into the *laager*, the Ndebele halted—out of gunshot range—to eat, rest, and regroup.[163]

This respite gave the Afrikaners valuable extra hours in which to clean their weapons and to make final preparations for the impending assault on the *laager*. Women continued to cast lead bullets and to sew bullet-bags, which were fired from larger guns. The scatter-fire from these guns was ideally suited for the close-range shooting in which the men were about to engage.

Finally, Kaliphi divided his men into two wings which charged the *laager* from opposite sides, the men yelling and pounding on their shields as they advanced. The ensuing battle lasted only about fifteen minutes, but its effect on the Ndebele was devastating.[164] As the Afrikaners fired their bullet-bags into the densely-packed attackers the fallen Ndebele quickly grew into a heap of bodies around the *laager*. The rising mound of dead and wounded demoralized the remaining Ndebele and inhibited their very movement. Not a single man penetrated the *laager*. In frustration, the Ndebele showered their ill-suited hand spears over the barricades and then withdrew.[165]

The Ndebele had apparently not been ordered to destroy the Voortrekker camp completely, so they turned their attention to rounding up undefended livestock. They gathered about 6,000 head of cattle, more than 40,000 sheep, and all the Voortrekkers' wagon oxen.[166]

As the Ndebele marched away, Afrikaner horsemen again emerged from their *laager*, this time to attempt recapture of their stock. They killed some stragglers, but failed to retake any of their property.[167] Within two weeks the exhausted Ndebele force returned to Mzilikazi. Never again did the Ndebele fight south of the Vaal River.

Kaliphi himself was wounded in his knee, but he managed to make it home. Many other soldiers died along the way. About 150 men had been killed during the assault on the *laager*. Perhaps three times that number died altogether, including those killed in the initial skirmish and those who died on the return march.[168] The Afrikaners suffered only two killed, and about a dozen wounded.[169]

It is fruitless to attempt naming a 'victor' of the battle at Vegkop. The Ndebele captured the whole of the Afrikaners' livestock, but they lost a significant number of men without inflicting serious damage on the Afrikaners themselves. On the other hand, the Afrikaners waged a brilliant defence, but they were left stranded and almost helpless after the battle. The Ndebele could probably have wiped them out, had they had the patience or the inclination to mount a prolonged siege. However, the longterm consequences of such a result would probably have been the same. For at that moment hundreds more Voortrekkers were gathering by the Modder River; the loss of thirty-five adult men at Vegkop would have made little difference to the large forces the Voortrekkers were soon to muster. Indeed, the Ndebele attacks on the first Voortrekker parties gave other Voortrekkers a greater unity of purpose than they might otherwise have achieved. Over the next year, humbling Mzilikazi was one of the few issues on which all Voortrekkers agreed.

The Voortrekkers' successful defence at Vegkop had more subtle effects. It gave all Voortrekkers greater confidence in their fighting abilities against Northern Nguni forces, and it contributed to their belief that they were divinely protected. The survival of more than thirty men at Vegkop also gave them a nucleus of warriors with first-hand knowledge of the Ndebele. And the survival of Hendrik Potgieter left them with an implacable and vigorously aggressive anti-Ndebele leader. He personally directed the retaliatory effort which ensued.

Voortrekker retaliation: Mosega, January 1837

After the Ndebele withdrew from Vegkop, the stranded Voortrekkers sent a messenger south to obtain help to evacuate the camp's wagons. At Thaba Nchu the messenger secured the assistance of the Methodist missionary James Archbell and the Rolong chief Moroka, who provided teams of oxen and men to move the wagons. By early November the whole party was safely re-encamped by the Modder River, where new Voortrekker bands were continuously arriving from the Cape Colony.[170]

Potgieter and Gert Maritz—a new arrival—became the acknowledged leaders at the Modder River, and they soon started to organize a retaliatory strike against Mzilikazi.[171] They enlisted Afrikaner volunteers and solicited the participation of various enemies of the Ndebele who had resettled in that region. December 20th was set as the departure date for a commando, but bad weather forced postponement until January.[172]

Once again, we know little about what the Ndebele were thinking during this period. It is clear, however, that they were not anticipating an immediate Voortrekker attack. They knew that they had left Potgieter and Cilliers' party helpless at Vegkop, and they probably knew little about the numbers of new Voortrekkers massing to the south. Furthermore, they had never experienced a major invasion during the summer months, and their very reaction to the forthcoming attack proved their unpreparedness.[173]

The loss of so many men at Vegkop had a depressing effect on Ndebele morale, as described by Dr Wilson:

> When the army of the Zoolahs returned, there was nothing but lamentation heard in the land for weeks on account of those slain in battle. A good many of those with whom we were acquainted, from the neighboring towns, were killed; numbers returned home wounded; some applied to me for surgical aid.[174]

By January Mzilikazi himself was back in residence at Gabeni. Few soldiers were left in the Mosega Basin, and no special defensive preparations were made.[175]

By the end of December the Voortrekkers had assembled a commando at Thaba Nchu. It comprised 107 Afrikaner men, who served under Potgieter and Maritz' split command; about forty-five Griqua and Korana; and more than sixty Tswana, mostly Rolong. The Afrikaners, Griqua, and Korana were all mounted and armed with firearms. All but a few of the Tswana lacked firearms and marched on foot.[176] The Griqua were commanded by Peter David.[177] The Rolong represented all four divisions which earlier had been driven from the southwestern Transvaal by the Ndebele. Chief Matlabe—formerly a captive of Mzilikazi at the Marico River—served as the commando's main guide.[178] He led some of his own clansmen, and was accompanied by his fellow chiefs, Tawana and Gontse, and some of their people.[179] Only about six Korana participated, led by Gert Taaibosch.[180] At the last moment the Tlokwa chief Sekonyela joined with a few men.[181] There may have been additional Tswana participants, but evidence on this point is inconclusive.[182]

The motives behind the allied commando were complex. The Voortrekkers, who clearly dominated the affair, were then *already* contemplating a second and more powerful strike against Mzilikazi. Their immediate objectives were to retake all the livestock they could handle and to impress the Ndebele with a setback in their own territory. If 'conquest' were possible, it was to come later.[183]

Rolong motives for participation were deeper-rooted. They

wished to resettle in their former homelands—the vacated region between the Molopo and Vaal Rivers—but they recognized their own weakness in any head-on confrontation with the Ndebele. Alliance with the Voortrekkers gave them an unprecedented opportunity to retake their own land. Rolong participants were careful to spell out their own objectives in their arrangements with the Voortrekker leaders.[184] To the Voortrekkers, however, the Rolong were not full partners in the commando, but merely guides and tenders of livestock. The gap in Rolong and Voortrekker views later led to serious problems.

Peter David's band probably wahted mainly to recoup David's losses at the hands of the Ndebele in 1834. The handful of Korana and Tlokwa participants could not have had major grievances against the Ndebele, so they probably joined largely in the hope of getting a share of the expected booty.

Contemporary Afrikaner records for this period are poor, considering the numbers of literate people involved. Little is known about the details of how the commando was organized and led. Potgieter and Maritz seem to have acted as semi-autonomous leaders; the degree to which they controlled the non-Afrikaner participants is unclear. Maritz' section left Thaba Nchu first, on 3 January 1837; Potgieter's section followed the next day.[185] On 13 January the two sections joined at 'Kommando Drift', a crossing point on the Vaal River just above the Makwassi confluence. There they left their wagons and began a more rapid march towards the upper Harts River, from which they turned towards the Mosega Basin. This course put them on the 'Kuruman road'—the direction from which the Ndebele least expected to be attacked.[186]

On the night of the 16th the commando encamped just outside the basin. As dawn broke on the 17th the horsemen stormed the Ndebele towns, shooting down almost everyone in their path. The American missionaries who were on the scene described the massacre.

> Sometime before sunrise, we were aroused by the startling cry, A commando! a commando! In half a minute after this alarming cry a brisk fire commenced on a kraal of people a few hundred yards from our house. The fire of one followed that of another in quick succession . . . In a few minutes we were in the midst of a slaughter. The people fled toward our house . . . Those who fled were pursued by the Boers with a determination to avenge themselves for the injury they had received. . . . Several balls passed over our house, some

struck it, and one passed through Brother Venable's chamber window . . . The Boers attacked and destroyed thirteen, some say fifteen, kraals. Few of the men belonging to them escaped, and many of the women were either shot down or killed with assegais.

We have no means of ascertaining how many lives were destroyed. We suppose from two to four hundred.[187]

A running battle continued—apparently much as the missionaries described it—about six hours. The terrain in the basin was relatively open, giving the horsemen an ideal field in which to rout their unprepared enemies.

By the middle of the day about four to five hundred Ndebele were killed.[188] Some had attempted to resist the onslaught, but their efforts were futile.[189] No coherent defence was ever organized, possibly because the district chief Kaliphi was then in Gabeni with Mzilikazi.[190]

The Afrikaners and Griqua suffered no casualties at all.[191] The Afrikaners seem to have carried the brunt of the allies' fighting. The Griqua somehow got separated from the main force, so their actual contribution to the destruction is unclear.[192] The Rolong tended livestock as it was captured and ran down Ndebele stragglers. One Rolong killed by the Ndebele and another accidentally shot by horsemen constituted the only allied casualties.[193]

The allies collected about six to seven thousand head of cattle—all they could manage easily—and returned south by the route they had followed coming in.[194] Most Ndebele started fleeing north, and no attempt was made to pursue the invaders as on former occasions.

About this same time Jan Bloem and Moilwe entered the country with an independent commando of Korana and Hurutshe. They apparently found the Ndebele already in such disarray that they could not inflict much further damage or capture much livestock.[195]

Meanwhile, the allied commando recrossed the Vaal and divided up their captured cattle. Some of the participants of this affair who testified upon it many years later disagree on the question of whether the Rolong shared in the booty. This was an important point, in view of Rolong claims that they had participated in the commando only to regain their lost territory.[196] The Voortrekker commanders, Potgieter and Maritz, argued whether the cattle should be distributed amongst the

Afrikaners strictly on the basis of their contributions to the commando, or on the basis of losses which some of them had suffered the previous year. Potgieter, who naturally argued the latter point, prevailed in the dispute, but a permanent rift was created in the Voortrekker leadership which soon became aggravated by other issues.[197] This rift in Voortrekker leadership had an important bearing on subsequent Ndebele-Afrikaner hostilities.

Shortly after the allied commando struck the Mosega Basin Potgieter informed the American missionaries of his intentions against the Ndebele, and he advised them to quit their station and to return to Thaba Nchu with his men. He stressed that as the Voortrekkers would soon mount an even larger commando against the Ndebele, Mzilikazi's kingdom was about to be destroyed and there therefore would not be any mission field left.[198] Since the missionaries had failed to establish a true rapport with their hosts, they naturally feared what might happen to them if they chose to remain in the wake of the white-led massacre. Consequently, they elected to accompany the commando when it left at midday.

It is questionable whether the missionaries' lives would have been in danger among the Ndebele, had they decided to stay. Shortly after they had left, Mzilikazi in fact voiced his regret over their decision.[199] The missionaries themselves justified their leaving by emphasizing their belief that Mzilikazi's end was near.

> We did not like the idea of leaving him so abruptly and with a company of men who had shed the blood of so many of his people, lest our so doing might put an insuperable barrier in the way of other missionaries who might possibly wish hereafter to approach him for the purpose of giving instruction. Yet we thought the possibility of our doing mischief in this way very small as the time of his overthrow, we fully believed, had come. It is not possible for him to stand against the incensed Boers . . .[200]

The missionaries were only partly correct in their predictions. Though it was true that the Afrikaners were to contribute to the driving of the Ndebele from the Transvaal—a development which probably would have ended the missionaries' work—it was not true that the missionaries' actions would have no impact on later mission efforts. Suspicion that there was a connection between the founding of missions and white invasion remained ingrained in Ndebele attitudes for decades. Hence, attempts to open a mission station in the new Ndebele territory north of the Limpopo thirty years later were resisted, in part, because of the example set by the Americans. It was only Robert Moffat's continued personal influence with Mzilikazi which made a new mission possible.[201]

Although the American missionaries' separation from the Ndebele was permanent, their connection with Ndebele history was not yet ended. For they soon joined their ABC counterparts in Zululand where they reported on the last Zulu-Ndebele war. Early the following year, when war broke out between the Zulu and the Voortrekkers, the missionaries found themselves in a situation similar to that they had experienced at Mosega. For the second time they let pass the opportunity to become Christian martyrs and left their mission station as quickly as possible.[202]

The last Zulu-Ndebele war, June 1837

Until the arrival of the Voortrekkers on the highveld, the Ndebele regarded the Zulu as their most dangerous enemies.[203] Fear of the Zulu had caused the Ndebele to plan moving away from the Magaliesbergs even before the Zulu attack in 1832. This fear remained strong after the Ndebele resettled by the Marico River. Each year false reports of approaching Zulu *impis* alarmed the Ndebele.[204] By late 1836 the Ndebele were shifting their settlements northward gradually to get still farther from the Zulu.[205] The allied commando of January 1837 accelerated this northward movement and virtually emptied the Mosega Basin of human settlements, reconcentrating the population along the lower Marico.[206] We can only guess at how far north the Ndebele intended to resettle at this time. For before the year was out, three additional invasions forced them to withdraw completely from the Transvaal. The scale of the ensuing migration should have required careful planning; it is unlikely that Ndebele leaders waited until the final disaster of 1837 to make the necessary decisions.[207]

During the four years after the indecisive Zulu-Ndebele encounter of 1832 Dingane intended to renew his war against Mzilikazi, but did not act.[208] Early in 1837, however, he learned of Mzilikazi's defeat by the allies and he decided it was an opportune moment to level a decisive blow against the Ndebele.[209] In late May he organized a large *impi* under the command of Ndlela and secretly sent it inland.[210]

Evidence for the route followed by Ndlela's army is vague. The Zulu appear to have been uncertain about Mzilikazi's whereabouts and to have passed through his former territory by the Magaliesbergs before turning towards the Mosega Basin—a journey which took them about 350 miles.[211] The winter on the highveld was unusually harsh that year. Severe cold and scarcity of water cut into the Zulu ranks and left the survivors too weak to fight at their best when they reached the Ndebele.[212]

When the Zulu entered the Mosega Basin, probably in late June, they found that all the Ndebele had already left the region.[213] The Zulu followed the emigrants' trail north and evidently found some people still in the process of migrating.[214] At some point the Zulu force separated into two parties; one section rounded up Ndebele cattle, while the other sought out Mzilikazi.[215]

In the ensuing conflict at least one pitched battle was fought, on or near the Pilanesberg Mountains.[216] It resulted in another stand-off in which both sides suffered heavy losses.[217] Meanwhile, the other section of the Zulu army rounded up several thousand head of cattle and numerous sheep before the whole force withdrew.[218] The Ndebele pursued the Zulu and recaptured some livestock, but the invaders still delivered to Dingane the greatest booty of his reign.[219]

On the return march the Zulu army suffered more than it had on the outward march. Europeans who witnessed the arrival of the army in Zululand in early September estimated that of more than a thousand men who failed to return, most had succumbed to the rigours of the march.[220] Many of the captured animals, especially the sheep, also died on the march.

Dingane was negotiating with Voortrekkers a possible land concession when his army returned. He assumed that much of the captured stock had originally belonged to the Voortrekkers attacked by Mzilikazi the previous year. However, the Voortrekker commander Piet Retief inspected the captured animals and concluded that such was not the case.[221]

Mzilikazi's encounters with the Voortrekkers had left his cattle herds at about their previous levels, while reducing his manpower by perhaps 900 people. In contrast, the Zulu invasion brought a net reduction of several thousand cattle and cost the Ndebele perhaps several hundred more men.[222] Before the Ndebele could recover from these setbacks, more were to come.

The final Griqua invasion, August 1837

While the Ndebele were having their troubles with the
Voortrekkers and Zulu, their various Griqua/Korana enemies
were planning new attacks on them. At least as early as February
Barend Barends publicly attempted to organize a new commando.
However, his efforts were spoiled by Andries Waterboer, who
used all his influence to discourage Griqua and Tswana chiefs
from assisting him.[223]

The Griqua at Philippolis ignored Waterboer. They regretted
not having joined the January allied commando, so they began to
organize a new one of their own in June.[224] These Griqua justified
their aggression by claiming they wished merely to recover Peter
David's lost children; however, David himself was not associated
with them, and he continued to identify with Voortrekker
interests.[225]

In late July or early August a large force of Griqua left
Philippolis under the command of Jan Isaac.[226] They rode to
Hebron on the Vaal River, where they were joined by Jan Bloem
and a number of other Korana—whose own January commando
had failed.[227] At Taung, on the Harts River, they were joined by
Bloem's former Hurutshe ally Moilwe.[228] Finally, at the
Mareetsane River they were joined by the Tlhaping chief Mahura.
Mahura himself dropped out the next day, but some of his people
remained with the commando.[229]

From the Mareetsane the commando apparently advanced
north into Ngwaketse territory which was still occupied by
Ndebele, and fell upon several Ndebele cattle posts.[230] Accounts
of what then transpired differ greatly, but it appears the Griqua-
led force met little Ndebele resistance and carried off several herds
of cattle.[231] About one hundred Ndebele were killed in the confrontation.[232] By late September the Griqua and their allies were
safely back at their own homes.[233]

Ndebele-derived sources are largely silent on this episode, lost
as it was in memories of a very confusing year, but the attack
appears to have had the effect of forcing a further contraction of
Ndebele settlement around the lower Marico River.[234]

Final disaster: the Voortrekkers return, November 1837

When the Voortrekkers invaded the Mosega Basin in January, they were already planning to return against the Ndebele in a matter of weeks. However, once they returned to their base by the Modder River, rifts in their leadership made renewed action temporarily impossible.[235] Potgieter himself turned his attention to organizing permanent Afrikaner settlements in the northern part of the present Orange Free State, which was now considered safe from Ndebele attacks. Soon, however, he was trying to revive Voortrekker interest in a new anti-Ndebele commando. In May and June serious attempts were made to launch such a commando, but each effort had to be postponed.[236] Later, when the Philippolis Griqua commando passed through the Voortrekker camps, the Griqua tried to enlist the aid of the Voortrekkers, but were turned down. Meanwhile, the Voortrekkers talked about demanding reparations from Mzilikazi to effect a peaceful Afrikaner-Ndebele settlement. Whether an attempt was ever made actually to open negotiations is not clear.[237]

The Voortrekkers camping in the Free State elected as their supreme governor Piet Retief, a prominent ex-colonial official. Retief wanted to direct all Voortrekker energies towards Natal, so he discouraged plans for new fighting in the Transvaal. By October, however, he was away to the coast, so he lost control over dissident Afrikaner factions. Potgieter seized the opportunity provided by Retief's absence to mount his long-delayed commando. This time he was joined by Pieter Uys, another recent emigrant from the Cape Colony. Potgieter and Uys organized 360 Afrikaner men in two semi-autonomous forces.[238] Potgieter again appealed to Moroka for assistance and was provided with about two dozen Rolong men, led by Mongala.[239]

This time Potgieter and Uys made every preparation for a truly major offensive thrust against the Ndebele. At the end of October their commando departed from the Suikerbosrand, in the southern-central Transvaal, with a train of horse-drawn wagons which proceeded west.[240] The commando encamped just outside the Mosega Basin, where the wagons were left under a thirty man guard. On 2 November the main body of men entered Mosega, which they naturally found deserted. Following the pattern of the earlier Zulu *impi*, the commando advanced north in search of the

Ndebele. This time they moved slowly, intending to conserve their energy for a decisive confrontation.

On 4 November the Voortrekkers found the Ndebele about fifty miles northeast of Mosega at a place they later called 'Maaierskop'. At that point began a running battle said to have lasted nine days.[241] The Afrikaner horsemen scattered each concentration of Ndebele soldiers they met, and gradually pushed the entire Ndebele population still farther north. On 12 November they turned back from Tweedepoort Rand—about twenty-five miles north of Mzilikazi's former residence at Gabeni.

As the commando withdrew, the Ndebele overtook the Rolong men who were herding captured cattle, routing them and retaking part of their livestock.[242] Since none of the Voortrekkers was killed, the commando was otherwise an unqualified success. The Voortrekkers were convinced that it was through their efforts alone that the Ndebele had been driven from their homes, and they soon claimed an enormous region north of the Vaal as theirs by right of conquest.[243]

There is simply not enough evidence from the Ndebele side on this particular confrontation to assess its specific impact on Mzilikazi's already disrupted kingdom. The Voortrekkers claimed to have killed at least 3,000 of his people, but this figure is almost certainly exaggerated.[244] The Voortrekkers probably spent more time collecting Ndebele livestock than they did actually fighting.[245] Ndebele resolve to defend their territory must have been already shattered. By November they were on the threshhold of leaving the Transvaal anyway, so it seems unlikely they would have risked further losses of men in what they must have recognized as a futile resistance.

Although the particulars of this last Ndebele war in the Transvaal are difficult to recontruct, the war undoubtedly proved to the Ndebele that their security south of the Limpopo was irretrievably lost. This last blow simply made it impossible to postpone migration until preparations were completed. How that migration was conducted is the subject of the next chapter.

CHAPTER V

MIGRATION TO MATABELELAND, 1838–1839

This chapter completes discussion of the first phase of Ndebele history by following the Ndebele migration out of the Transvaal to the point when Mzilikazi himself halted in present Matabeleland. As Mzilikazi was among the last migrants to reach Matabeleland, his arrival there can be said to mark the end of the migration and, hence, the end of the migratory era. Thereafter the centres of Ndebele settlement never shifted significantly from the region of modern Bulawayo and the history of the Ndebele developed along new lines.[1]

The chapter opens with a discussion of what happened in the western Transvaal immediately after the Ndebele left, followed by an assessment of the identity and numbers of people who went north with Mzilikazi. The balance of the chapter deals with the migration itself.

When the Ndebele crossed the Limpopo at the end of 1837 they entered what might be called the 'dark age' of their historiography. Between 1837 and 1854 they were out of direct contact with literate observers. Events of this period must be reconstructed largely through subsequently recorded oral accounts and traditions.[2] Evidence for the migration itself presents special problems. The migration is perhaps the best-remembered event in traditions of early Ndebele history, but traditional authorities disagree on many important points. Material written down during the mid-nineteenth century contains scattered pieces of first-hand testimony which help to correct traditions; however, a fully satisfactory reconstruction of the migration may be beyond recovery. For this reason the problems of evidence are discussed in somewhat greater depth here than has been the case in previous chapters.

A peculiar aspect of much of the traditional evidence for the migration is a pervasive emphasis on the missionary Robert Moffat, even though it can be shown that he had virtually nothing to do with the migration. He is variously credited with having warned Mzilikazi of the coming of the Voortrekker wars; having advised Mzilikazi to move north; having met Mzilikazi somewhere in Botswana; and having given the Ndebele directions on how to reach a particular hill near present Bulawayo. These elements—some of which can be seen to be mutually exclusive—constitute what I call the 'Moffat Myth', a subject worth discussing in some detail. Analysis of this myth illuminates many of the difficult problems pertaining to the migration and thus provides some clues in reconstructing the migration. Furthermore, this myth is an interesting case study in the rapid development of mythic elements in traditions.

The present reconstruction of the migration makes no claims of being 'definitive', but it does offer several solutions to outstanding problems connected with this epic. First, it shows that the Ndebele migrants separated into divisions north of the Limpopo rather than south of that river, as is commonly believed. Secondly, it identifies the leader of one division of migrants—who has only been known to history by the name Gundwane—as the military commander Kaliphi, and it attempts to demonstrate the significance of this finding. Thirdly, it refutes the widely-held notion that the Ndebele brushed with the Kololo of Sebitwane by the Zambezi River during the migration. Finally, arguments are advanced for refining and tightening up the entire chronology of the migration, and it is concluded that the migration to Matabeleland was completed by about mid-1839—a year or two earlier than has hitherto been supposed.

Ndebele aftermath: the western Transvaal after 1837

The western Transvaal was the fourth region occupied and then abandoned by the Ndebele south of the Limpopo. Of the four regions it suffered the most profound consequences. The Ndebele state reached its apogee of power while in the western Transvaal, and it was there that it caused the greatest social dislocation among Sotho/Tswana communities. And, in contrast to the other regions of former Ndebele occupation, the peoples of the western Transvaal had little time to recover between the departure of the Ndebele and the arrival, in force, of Afrikaner settlers.

The social and political disorders of the South African *Difaqane* had given rise to other state-builders besides Mzilikazi.[3] Mzilikazi's uniqueness lay in his being the only Nguni ruler to build a state system on the highveld among predominantly Sotho/Tswana-speaking peoples. There were other state-builders on the highveld during this period, but these were Sotho/Tswana chiefs, such as Moshweshwe, Sekonyela, Sekwati, and others, who worked among closely related peoples in or near their own homelands. Had Mzilikazi not appeared on the highveld in the early 1820s, it is possible that one or more Sotho/Tswana state-builders would have arisen in the regions he himself consolidated.

When Mzilikazi left the eastern Transvaal his place was effectively taken by the Pedi chief Sekwati, whom he had originally driven out of the region. In the western Transvaal Mzilikazi drove out a number of potential statebuilders, including Sebitwane and Molitsane. Unlike Sekwati, however, neither of these two men ever returned to the western Transvaal, though each would have liked to remain there. Sebitwane instead went on to establish his Kololo state in present Zambia, while Molitsane eventually became a protégé of Moshweshwe in Lesotho.[4]

After the Ndebele left the western Transvaal, the Voortrekkers arrived to take their place; there was not time for a major new Tswana paramountcy to develop.[5] Instead, the Voortrekkers claimed the western Transvaal—indeed, the *entire* Transvaal—by right of conquest over Mzilikazi; they used this claim to dispute the rights of refugee communities to their original homelands.[6] For many years there were too few Afrikaner settlers effectively to occupy the territory; however, the combination of Afrikaner bravado and persisting refugee insecurity prevented the development of significant Tswana resistance against Afrikaner encroachments.

As soon as the Ndebele began crossing the Limpopo to the north at the end of 1837, Sotho/Tswana refugees started returning to their former homes. The first refugees to do so were Mzilikazi's former subjects, many of whom—as will be discussed in the next section—deserted him during his crisis. Other refugees were people who had never been under Ndebele rule, but who had fled their homes to escape Ndebele raids as early as ten years before.

During 1838 the Voortrekkers were busy fighting the Zulu and founding settlements far to the east. They occupied the western

Transvaal slowly; however, Tswana reoccupation was also slow. Mosegâ, for example, remained largely deserted through 1839. The Hurutshe did not begin to return there in force until about 1846.[7] Meanwhile, the Ngwaketse regrouped by their former headquarters,[8] and some Rolong returned to the Molopo River region from Thaba Nchu.[9] Shifts among other societies also took place, but fear of the Ndebele persisted into the 1840s, discouraging many communities from taking up the tasks of rebuilding in earnest.[10] Such fears were partly justified. Two years after Mzilikazi arrived in Matabeleland, he turned his attention back to the south and sent *impis* into southeastern Botswana and the western Transvaal to collect people and livestock he had reluctantly left behind.[11]

The Ndebele population on the eve of migration

In order to assess the Ndebele achievement in migrating from the Transvaal to Matabeleland, where they rebuilt their kingdom on a larger scale, accurate data on the numbers of people who went north would be invaluable. Unfortunately, such data is unobtainable. In Chapter Three I showed why our best estimate of Mzilikazi's subject population in the Transvaal—a figure of about 20,000 people—represents only an order of magnitude.[12] Through the 1830s the population was in constant flux. Wars and disease periodically cut into the population, but such losses were compensated for, to an unknown degree, through forced recruitment of new subjects and natural increase.

When the Ndebele moved into the Marico district in 1832 they continued their pattern of steady expansion into neighbouring Sotho/Tswana communities, so their population likewise must have continued to grow. However, in 1834–35 a bilious fever epidemic killed more than a thousand people.[13] In late 1836 the Ndebele entered into a period of successive major wars in which they lost well over a thousand more people. They appear to have suffered a net population drop during their last few years in the Transvaal, but we can only guess at its actual magnitude.

When the Ndebele commenced their northward migration, they experienced further population losses as a result of many Sotho/Tswana-derived subjects' electing to remain behind. According to Robert Moffat, writing in 1842, Mzilikazi allowed all the captive Bahurutsi, Bakhatla, and other neighbouring tribes, to return to their own land. This was a measure which astonished the natives, who have since congregated on the ancient domains of their forefathers . . .[14]

Moffat's claim that 'all' subject Tswana were thus released is a gross exaggeration, since it is clear that many such people followed Mzilikazi to Matabeleland. Furthermore, Mzilikazi's ostensible willingness to let some of these people remain behind was more a consequence of his difficult circumstances than of his desire to 'liberate' anyone. Years later Moffat himself wrote that 'Moselekatse is ever alive to increase the number of his people instead of diminishing them; therefore his extreme reluctance to part with a captive from a neighbouring tribe.'[15]

A more accurate picture of how Tswana separated from Mzilikazi was written still later by Thomas Morgan Thomas:

Many of the Bechuana captives, taking advantage of the disturbed state of the country, and sheltered by the thick forests through which their victors now had to pass, made good their escape, and took with them large numbers of horned cattle and flocks.[16]

Thomas's view is supported by the testimonies of several former subjects of Mzilikazi who effected their escape during the confusion of late 1837 and early 1838.[17] Other Sotho/Tswana also deserted Mzilikazi during this period, but we have no data on how many did so.[18] It should be emphasized that many of those who remained behind had had fairly strong ties with the Ndebele state; some had fought for Mzilikazi and had held minor positions of authority.[19]

The total number of Sotho/Tswana who deserted Mzilikazi at the outset of the migration could not have been great since many others accompanied him to Matabeleland. In 1835 Andrew Smith estimated that 'more than 2/3' of Mzilikazi's people were of local, Sotho/Tswana extraction, the remainder being coastal Nguni.[20] One hundred years later the Southern Rhodesian Native Affairs Department estimated that Sotho/Tswana-derived Ndebele still outnumbered Nguni-derived Ndebele by a similar proportion.[21] The remarkable similarity of these two estimates suggests that the ratio of Sotho/Tswana to Nguni in the Ndebele population did not change substantially during the Ndebele migration out of the Transvaal.

Sotho/Tswana subjects were not the only people to abandon Mzilikazi during his time of crisis. A number of his Nguni followers, including some of his own clansmen, remained behind in the Transvaal.[22]

In sum, what we can say about the Ndebele population at the beginning of 1838 is that it was probably reduced by several thousands of people from what may have been its peak size in about 1834. Assuming that Mzilikazi ruled about 20,000 people at that earlier date, it would follow that roughly 15,000 people accompanied him to Matabeleland. Some of these people died along the way; how many we do not know.[23]

Ndebele knowledge of the trans-Limpopo region before 1838

Among the many problems pertaining to the migration to Matabeleland is the question of what knowledge the Ndebele had of this region before they resettled there. In Chapter Three I examined evidence for early Ndebele penetration north of the Limpopo and showed that satisfactory evidence exists for only one major foray there. That was an *impi* which the *induna* Kaliphi commanded in 1831 in pursuit of Sotho who had deserted Mzilikazi and carried off Ndebele cattle from the Magaliesberg settlements. According to the evidence cited in that earlier chapter, Kaliphi's *impi* appears to have reached the future Matabeleland, penetrating perhaps as far north as the twentieth parallel of latitude. As I shall show below, Kaliphi himself commanded the first division of migrants to reach Matabeleland in 1838, while another division of migrants wandered far to the northwest. The fact that Kaliphi went more or less directly to the region he had visited before—while the other Ndebele migrants went in a completely different direction—suggests that the Ndebele knew little about the trans-Limpopo country before 1838, and that what little they knew derived largely from Kaliphi's 1831 *impi*.

The question immediately at hand is whether the Ndebele attempted any other reconnaissances of the trans-Limpopo between 1831 and 1838. The answer is that they may have done so in 1836, and possibly in 1837, but that, if they did so, they seem to have obtained little useful information from their efforts.

A. A. Campbell's post-1904 renderings of Ndebele tradition are among the major sources of evidence for the 1831 *impi* across the

Limpopo.[24] In 1898 he wrote a version of Ndebele tradition which places a similar trans-Limpopo *impi* clearly in the context of the 1836–37 Ndebele-Voortrekker wars:

> Umziligas sent an Impi to spy out the land up north. The impi fought their way up to Mangwe [River]. Seeing the Matopos they sent a part of their Impi through the hills to spy, they went as far as the n'gwy [*sic*; = Gwai?] River and then returned to the King, picking up the remainder of the Impi at Mangwe, and reported favourably on the country they had visited.

The account continues, telling how the soldiers returned to find that their homes had been attacked by the Voortrekkers during their absence (this would have been January 1837), and how Mzilikazi decided to start moving north, but was again attacked by the Voortrekkers (November) before the migration commenced in earnest.[25]

Comparison of the above story to the story Campbell wrote later about the 1831 *impi* (quoted in Chapter Three, above) reveals that both deal with the same events. This conclusion is supported by the fact that each of Campbell's separate renditions of Ndebele history gives but one version of the story. When he wrote his first account in 1898 he failed to recognize that the Ndebele called both the Griqua and the Afrikaners 'Boers' (*amaBhunu*); hence, he failed to recognize the correct context of the *impi* story.[26] This was an error he corrected in his later writings, though he retained the term 'Boers'.

The purpose of this somewhat lengthy digression is to illustrate the depth of the problem of interpreting Ndebele traditions for this period. Throughout this study I have stressed the ways in which traditions—and even firsthand authorities—mix up information about similar but distinct events. Here we have seen that not only are different Griqua attacks on the Ndebele confused in the evidence, but also that Griqua and Afrikaner attacks are confused with each other. Although I have just dismissed Campbell's story of an 1836/37 Ndebele foray across the Limpopo by showing that the story refers to events of 1831, it may in part allude to authentic events of 1836.

On 18 August 1836—immediately before the first Ndebele-Voortrekker clash—the American missionaries at Mosega wrote that it was 'rumored that there is a people far to the north, who have much cattle and a fine country; and that Moselekatsi has sent out his spies, with a view of attempting their conquest'.[27] No further contemporary documents illuminate what the outcome of this 'spying' was, but the above statement lends impressive support to Campbell's original story about spies to the north during this same period. It therefore seems reasonable to conclude that his traditional sources confused Kaliphi's apparently large-scale *impi* of 1831 with one or more minor reconnaissance expeditions into the same area during 1836. However, the associated implication that these 'spies' were sent north for the express purpose of finding a new home for the Ndebele at that point is probably based simply on hindsight. There is no convincing evidence that the Ndebele made any serious plans to migrate across the Limpopo before the disasters of 1837 forced them to leave the Transvaal.

Whatever information the Ndebele obtained about the trans-Limpopo before 1838 probably was not great. During the 1860s Mzilikazi is said to have told an Afrikaner hunter,

> When your people drove me out of Marico, I trekked north, and *knew nothing* of the country ahead, and we heard all manner of stories of strong nations of fighting men who lived underground or on the tops of high mountains. [my ital.][28]

Whether or not the above story is apocryphal, the fact remains that positive evidence for prior Ndebele knowledge of Matabeleland is not at all impressive. And, as I shall show in the next section, Ndebele ignorance of their future homeland is a premise of the mythic elements contained in their traditions of the migration.

The making of a myth: Robert Moffat and the Ndebele migration to Matabeleland (1)

A curious feature of Ndebele tradition which has been noted for over a hundred years is the widely-believed story that the missionary Robert Moffat warned Mzilikazi that war with the Voortrekkers was inevitable if the Ndebele remained in the Transvaal, and that he should avoid such a disaster by leading his people to the region which became the present Matabeleland.

> He had travelled far, this white man, and he told the king of a land far north, where food was plentiful and cattle throve, and where he would live in peace. His words were words of wisdom, for he foretold the coming of the Boers to yet again disturb us; and that so long as we remained in those parts it would always be so.[29]

Versions of the story vary in details, but they mostly emphasize
one or both of its two main elements: first, that Moffat foretold
the coming of the Voortrekker conflicts; second, that his personal
instructions guided the Ndebele to Matabeleland.[30] The greater
stress is generally upon the second element: ' "Our fathers add
that, if he [Moffat] had not directed them, they would have
perished in the desert." '[31] Such stories were being told by the
Ndebele at least as early as the 1870s and they are still believed by
many Ndebele and Europeans alike.[32] As I shall attempt to
demonstrate, all of these stories—which might collectively be
labelled the 'Moffat Myth'—serve one historical purpose: to
explain why the Ndebele left the Transvaal and how they got to
their present home. The Myth is such an integral part of traditions
about the migration to Matabeleland that it must be analysed in
detail in order to reconstruct the migration itself.

Many historians have treated the Moffat Myth sceptically, but
none has attempted to explain its significance.[33] The most obvious
objection to the Myth is that Moffat could not have advised the
Ndebele on how to get to Matabeleland since he himself never
crossed the Limpopo before 1854.[34] Hence, any claim that his
alleged advice was based upon his own experience in that region is
demonstrably false.

Other objections to the Myth were expressed by Moffat's son
John Smith Moffat during the latter's 1887 visit to Matabeleland:

> Indunas have all dwelt much on the statement that it was my father
> who advised Umzilegaas to migrate northwards to this country, as he
> would not be able to live at peace with the Boers so near to him. I am
> not aware that my father ever gave such advice; it is unlikely, as he
> would have known that it meant a continuation of the same career of
> conquest and extermination of peaceful tribes in an extended region
> northwards, which he had deplored as having taken place in what is
> now the Transvaal.[35]

In a letter which he wrote shortly after the above statement the
younger Moffat added that the story was also current among the
'common people', and that he himself did 'not recollect ever to
have seen a reference to it in his [father's] voluminous letters and
journals of the period in question.'[36]

In actual fact the elder Moffat did refer to his having advised
Mzilikazi to migrate north to avoid the Voortrekkers. In
Missionary Labours and Scenes, which he published in 1842, he
wrote, 'In the last conversation I had with him [Mzilikazi] I

warned him against a rupture with the farmers [*i.e.*, Voortrekkers] . . .'[37] And, in an anonymous letter eleven years later, he wrote:

> It has been stated on good authority that an individual in whom M.[zilikazi] placed almost unbounded confidence earnestly and repeatedly warned him by every means to avoid coming into collision with the Boers and rather retire into the interior than commence a warfare with the white man.

The unnamed 'individual' was, of course, Moffat himself.[38] Moffat's above two statements ostensibly support both elements of the Myth; however, it can be demonstrated that, intentionally or unintentionally, Moffat grossly distorts what he actually must have said to Mzilikazi in 1835.

A crucial aspect of this whole subject which has been overlooked even by critics of the Myth is that Moffat not only knew nothing of Matabeleland when he talked to Mzilikazi in 1835, he also could have known nothing about the Voortrekkers. The Voortrekker movement did not begin to take shape until *after* Moffat had left Mzilikazi. Nothing he wrote in 1835 indicated that he suspected Afrikaners would soon be moving into the interior, indeed, the trek movement took South Africa by surprise once it started. In mid-1835 most Afrikaner farmers were living south of the Orange River, far from the Ndebele. If, as Moffat later implied, he expected the Ndebele soon to clash with whites, the British Colonial government would have appeared a far more likely adversary.[39] Furthermore, everything we know about Moffat's behaviour through 1835 indicates that he wanted the Ndebele to remain where they were. He hoped that the Ndebele would be transformed into a major stabilizing force for peace on the highveld, and he worked to establish the American missionaries among them to help achieve this goal. Finally, when the Voortrekkers did appear on the scene in August 1836, their arrival surprised the Ndebele, the American missionaries, and Moffat himself.[40]

Given that Moffat could not have warned the Ndebele of the coming of the Voortrekkers, it remains to be explained why so many people—possibly including himself—later believed he had done so. Between 1839 and 1843 Moffat visited England and wrote his book on his missionary experiences. By this time the Afrikaner exodus from the Cape Colony was a well-known and controversial subject throughout the British Empire. Moffat was already growing prejudiced against the Voortrekkers because of their frequently rough dealings with African societies and their harmful effect upon missionary work. While he deplored the initial Ndebele attacks on Voortrekker camps of August 1836, he equally deplored the harsh Voortrekker retaliation, which resulted in the massacre of hundreds of people. His displeasure with what he observed of Voortrekker behaviour grew during the succeeding years and he expressed it in comments he wrote for publication.[41] Consciously or unconsciously, his changing perspectives on the Voortrekkers distorted his view of himself in relationship to the Ndebele, whom he regarded as victims of the trek movement. First he came to see himself as the proponent of peace who had warned the Ndebele not to fight the white men who were sure to come; later he saw himself as the person who advised the Ndebele to escape conflict by migrating north. In sum, he symbolized the efforts of Christian mission work to preserve peace in southern Africa.[42] Ironically, the Myth of Moffat as the Ndebele protector developed among the Ndebele partly for the same reasons he came to believe it himself.

As must be typical of all myths, kernels of truth lay behind the first element of the Moffat Myth. When Moffat visited Mzilikazi in 1835 he did warn the king about the dangers of continued warfare. However, what he feared was not the possibility of an Ndebele-white confrontation, but rather escalation of the recurring Ndebele wars with the Griqua/Korana. In 1835 Moffat particularly wanted to resolve Peter David's claims against Mzilikazi and he hoped that Andries Waterboer would act as a go-between, as discussed in the previous chapter. The fact that Ndebele-Griqua hostilities were uppermost in Moffat's mind is revealed in the very passage of his book in which he claims to have warned Mzilikazi against fighting whites. He seems to have inserted his reference to the Afrikaners as an afterthought—one which must have been based on his hindsight. When he had warned Mzilikazi against aggressive warfare he had been thinking mainly about the Griqua/Korana; he later saw the disastrous Ndebele confrontations with the Afrikaners as the fulfillment of his prophecy. From that perspective he probably re-interpreted what he had said as having been a specific warning not to fight the Afrikaners.

Over the ensuing years the Ndebele seem to have reinterpreted Moffat's warning of 1835 the same way he did. For the Ndebele this tendency towards re-interpretation was undoubtedly strengthened by their characteristically confusing Afrikaners and Griqua—a point which cannot be over-stressed. In 1835 Moffat warned the Ndebele against such practices as attacking Griqua hunting parties—as they had done the previous year—predicting that if they persisted, escalating warfare would lead to their eventual 'scattering'. The following year they ignored his advice by attacking Voortrekker parties by the Vaal in circumstances almost identical to the Peter David incident of 1834. It is not surprising that the Ndebele viewed the ensuing Afrikaner retaliation and their own disorderly flight from the Transvaal as the fulfillment of a prophecy by Moffat.[43]

The making of a myth: Robert Moffat and the Ndebele migration to Matabeleland (2)

The second element of the Moffat Myth, *i.e.*, the belief that Moffat both advised Mzilikazi to migrate north and instructed him on exactly where to go, is at once easier to dismiss and harder to explain than the first element of the Myth. The fact that Moffat never travelled north of the Limpopo before 1854, and that he therefore could not have described a place he had never seen requires no further comment. The question remains, then, whether Moffat simply advised Mzilikazi to go north. And if not, how did this idea become so firmly an entrenched aspect of the Myth?

If we accept the conclusion that Moffat did not anticipate the coming of the Voortrekker-Ndebele wars, then his primary reason for his advising the Ndebele to migrate out of the Transvaal disappears. In any case, the inherent improbability of his proposing that the Ndebele carry their wars into a new territory is well argued by his son in the quotation cited above; the point is supported by Moffat's own efforts to help establish the American mission station among the Ndebele at Mosega. Except for the single, anonymous letter Moffat wrote in 1853, there is no documentary evidence to support the Myth's contention that Moffat advised Mzilikazi to emigrate from the Marico District of the Transvaal. The basis for this element of the Myth must lie in Moffat's prediction that the Ndebele would be 'scattered' if they continued their aggressive wars.

Despite the impossibility of Moffat's having told the Ndebele how to reach Matabeleland, even traditional authorities which ignore the aspect of his predicting the coming of the Voortrekkers insist that he gave detailed instructions on the route to follow.

> Moffat, who was generally liked and trusted by the tribe, advised Mziligazi to leave for the country lying far north and now known as Southern Rhodesia. Moffat told the king that in order to reach this land, they must travel with the sun on their right cheeks in the morning and their left cheeks in the afternoon, their destination being what is now known as Ntabayezenduna; in other words, they were to travel due north from the Transvaal.[44]

Thabazinduna, the specified destination, is mentioned in many accounts. A prominent flat-topped hill near Bulawayo, it figures significantly in later Ndebele history and was a natural symbol to attach to the epic story of the migration to Matabeleland.[45]

The difference between Moffat's vague prediction of a scattering of the Ndebele and the claim that he gave detailed instructions on how to reach a specific hill in Matabeleland is a significant one which requires additional evidence to explain. The key lies in a major variation of the Myth which holds that Moffat met Mzilikazi somewhere in Botswana (typically, just north of Ngwato territory), and that it was there—not in the Transvaal—that he told him how to find Matabeleland.[46] According to one such tradition, after the Ndebele migrants had just passed through Ngwato territory,

> going north they met Mr Moffat, who was returning from a hunting expedition. . . . Mr Moffat asked Mziligazi where he was going.
> Mziligazi replied: 'I am running away from Shaka and the Amabuna [Boers].' He said he did not know where he was going.
> And Moffat said: 'You go on, and you will find a country with the hills on this side (pointing to his right) with thick bushes . . .'
> Moffat directed him along a road which led to Panda Matenga and told him to turn to the east when he got to Panda Matenga.[47]

The story continues to tell of how Mzilikazi followed the instructions, eventually arriving in present Matabeleland.

Such versions of the Myth appear incredibly inaccurate; for not only did Moffat not travel north of the Limpopo before 1854, he never in his career made an extended trip for the purpose of hunting. Paradoxically, this variation to the Myth helps to explain its origin. What seems actually to have happened was that at some point in his northward migration, Mzilikazi employed the services of a foreign guide who helped him to find Matabeleland after he had become separated from half of his people. Since the migration became regarded in tradition as a great national epic, the Ndebele were probably disinclined to attribute their eventual success to an outsider. However, the fact that an outsider had assisted Mzilikazi to complete his journey could not be suppressed; instead, credit for the stranger's contribution was assigned to Robert Moffat, whose prestige among the Ndebele was already great. Explanations of Moffat's role were thus invented to conform to what was otherwise true about his relation with the Ndebele. The various points on which traditional authorities differ—such as whether Moffat gave his advice north or south of the Limpopo—can mostly be explained by the obvious discrepancies between fact and invention. Hence, whereas one line of tradition simply substitutes Moffat for the unknown guide, another line of tradition acknowledges that Moffat did not meet Mzilikazi north of the Limpopo and therefore has him giving his instructions before the migration started.

Summers and Pagden have previously attempted to explain the second element of the Moffat Myth by proposing that someone other than Moffat guided Mzilikazi to Matabeleland. They suggest that a man with Moffat's Ndebele name, *Mtshete*, or perhaps a man with a flowing beard like Moffat's, simply became confused with Moffat in Ndebele memories. Unfortunately, they fail to adduce evidence that any such person actually existed.[48] Interesting though that argument is, it is probably irrelevant. It seems inherently unlikely that the Ndebele would have confused the well-known Moffat with an African simply on the basis of a similar name or superficial physical resemblance. Furthermore, they would have had a more compelling reason to submerge the identity of such an outsider into that of Moffat: they held other African peoples in contempt and would not have wished to glorify them.

Mzilikazi's actual guide to Matabeleland appears to have been a Tswana hunter, a man seen at Mzilikazi's court during the 1860s. Years later Jan Viljoen recalled how amazed he had been by the freedom of a Rolong man at the Ndebele court to 'stride up to Mzilikazi, jerk a calabash of beer from his mouth, insult the king, drain the beer, and then go off unpunished.' Mzilikazi explained the man's remarkable privileges as the reward for his guiding the Ndebele to Matabeleland. Mzilikazi recalled that during his north-ward migration he ' "was perplexed and in great uncertainty when one night this Barolong strayed into my camp and was brought before me.'' ' The unnamed Rolong described the future Matabeleland and promised to lead Mzilikazi there. The king accepted the offer, promising unlimited rewards for success, or a year of slow death for failure. The man succeeded, and became, in effect, the king's court jester—a role scarcely qualifying him to find an honoured place in Ndebele tradition.[49]

Part of the Moffat Myth probably derives from the story of the anonymous Rolong guide. The circumstances of his story are strikingly similar to traditional accounts of Moffat's meeting Mzilikazi somewhere in Botswana. Furthermore, the story of how Mzilikazi himself finally found Matabeleland fits into what we know about the course of the migration, as will be reconstructed below.

One final comment needs to be made about the origins of the Moffat Myth. I have argued that Moffat did not advise Mzilikazi to migrate north from the Transvaal. Even assuming these arguments are all valid, it remains quite possible that the Ndebele misunderstood something else that he said to them. Moffat communicated with Mzilikazi through interpreters; chances for mis-translation were always present. Therefore, Moffat might easily have intended one thing, while Mzilikazi thought he was saying something quite different. We know that Moffat said something to Mzilikazi about the possibility of the Ndebele being 'scattered'. The wars of 1836-7 and the subsequent migration created a period of enormous confusion in which memories could easily become unreliable. When Moffat revisited Mzilikazi in 1854 he became the first European to enter Matabeleland after the Ndebele had settled there. To some Ndebele this fact might have confirmed their notions that Moffat had possessed prior knowledge of, or experience in, the region. And, as we have seen, by 1854 Moffat himself seems to have believed that he was responsible for having recommended that the Ndebele migrate to their new region. He further enhanced his prestige among the Ndebele with additional visits to Mzilikazi in 1857 and 1859-60. By the time of Mzilikazi's death in 1868 Moffat's prestige was so great that it is not surprising that he came to share with the king an epic place in Ndebele history.[50]

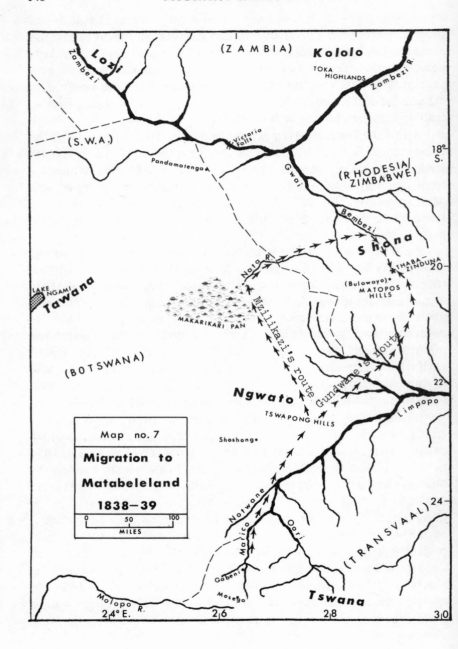

Map no. 7

**Migration to
Matabeleland
1838–39**

0　　　50　　　100
MILES

The migration starts, November 1837–January 1838

As we saw in the previous chapter, the successive invasions of 1837 forced a concentration of the Ndebele population around the lower Marico River. There the Ndebele planted crops during the spring season, evidently intending to remain in the region at least through the harvest season of the following year. Whether the Ndebele were contemplating a major migration to the north at that time is a matter of speculation. Whatever their prior plans had been, they decided to quit the Transvaal completely during or immediately after the second Voortrekker commando in November. As soon as the Voortrekkers withdrew from the lower Marico, the Ndebele began moving north. They abandoned their unripened crops and heavy possessions, taking with them only their remaining livestock.[51]

The migration began in a disorderly manner. Small bands of people and lone individuals fled north separately. Even Mzilikazi himself may have been a lone straggler briefly.[52] The confusion which obviously prevailed suggests that the migration began suddenly, without careful planning or leadership. The initial disorder accounts for the ease with which many Sotho/Tswana subjects broke away, as earlier discussed.

Most of the people appear to have marched northeast between the Marico and Notwane Rivers; they turned approximately due north at about the 27th line of eastern longitude.[53] Others may have initially gone northwest, turning east as they entered the fringes of the Kalahari Desert.[54] Whatever the exact routes of all the migrants, it is clear that all or most of them soon re-united in the Tswapong Hills, a spot in Ngwato territory about 200 miles north-northeast of Gabeni.[55]

About ten years before the arrival of the Ndebele in Ngwato territory, Sebitwane's Kololo had passed through and ravaged the region.[56] The Ngwato had required years to recover from that earlier blow; they were anxious not to repeat the experience with Mzilikazi's people, with whom their previous dealings had been unpleasant but remote. Hence, the Ngwato scattered before the new invaders, leaving their ripening crops for the Ndebele to harvest.[57] The Ndebele also helped themselves to Ngwato cattle, but were apparently unable to find many.[58]

During their brief stay in Ngwato territory the Ndebele celebrated an important set of religious festivals associated with the annual harvest: the *inxwala/ukucinsa* cycle.[59] These Nguni ceremonies involved elements of national reaffirmation of the king's power, expressions of devotion to ancestral spirits, and the king's ritual sanctifying of the year's harvest. The personal participation of the king was essential and the whole cycle had to be completed before new crops could be eaten. The cycle typically fell at the height of the rainy season, a moment which varied between late November and early February in that region. As I shall show below, the regular timing of this cycle provides valuable clues to the reconstruction of the migration's chronology.

The migrants divide into two parties, early 1838

The Ndebele probably completed their religious observances in about January 1838. Soon afterwards they separated into two large divisions to continue their migration in a more orderly fashion.[60] Traditions disagree somewhat on where the division was undertaken; however, there is virtual unanimity that such a two-fold division occurred early in the migration, and that one division went approximately north under Mzilikazi's personal leadership, while the other went more or less directly to central Matabeleland under an *induna* called 'Gundwane Ndiweni'.[61] As will be shown, that division almost certainly took place in Ngwato territory in eastern Botswana.

One line of Ndebele tradition holds that the Ndebele separated into divisions south of the Limpopo River—presumably immediately after the November 1837 Voortrekker invasion of the lower Marico.[62] Most modern historians who discuss the migration accept this incorrect assertion.[63] The notion of the sub-Limpopo division probably derived partly from confused memories of the first phase of the migration, during which it was true that the Ndebele crossed the Vaal in many small bands. However, it is clear—as we have seen—that most or all of the migrants soon regrouped in Ngwato territory after crossing the Limpopo. Had they not all regrouped under Mzilikazi they could not have celebrated the *inxwala/ukucinsa* cycle as a single nation. Such a circumstance would have produced a political crisis—as in fact occurred the following year—which would not have been overlooked in tradition. Hence, the conclusion that the division took place north of the Limpopo is dictated both implicitly by traditional references to a re-gathering north of the Limpopo and by the complete absence of evidence concerning difficulties over the *inxwala/ukucinsa* which would have attended any division of the migrations south of the Limpopo. Finally, an independent line of evidence affirms that the Ndebele divided into two groups north of the Limpopo and that this division occurred in Ngwato territory, where we would expect to find it. According to the missionary John Mackenzie, who worked among the Ngwato between 1862 and 1876,

> Old men have described to me how from the fastnesses of their hills they could see the Matabele pass in two divisions—one by the pass of Monakalonwe [Manakalongwe] leading to Lake N'gabi [Ngami], and the other on what is now the Matebele Road.[64]

This Ngwato description of the routes conforms fairly closely to what can be reconstructed of each Ndebele division's route.

That the Ndebele separated into two large divisions in eastern Botswana is certain; less clear are the reasons behind this separation. The division seems to have been deliberate and planned; however, some traditional authorities suggest that it was unintentional.[65] We can probably safely dismiss the notion that the Ndebele separated accidentally as merely another example of confusion with the earlier, disorderly phase of the migration out of the Transvaal. Assuming, then, that the separation was deliberate, it remains to be answered what its purpose was. What did the Ndebele know about the country north of the Limpopo? Did each of the migrant parties know where it was going? And—more basically—was the division undertaken with a view towards eventual reunification?

No easy answers are available for any of these questions. Given that as many as 15,000 people and an unknown quantity of livestock participated in the migration, compelling reasons for dividing into smaller groups immediately become evident. The problem of obtaining food and water for so many mouths would have made it impractical for the whole nation to travel in a single body. Yet if the Ndebele leadership had a good idea of where to resettle, more sensible plans for organizing the migration should have suggested themselves. For example, assume for the moment that early in 1838 the Ndebele agreed upon settling in present Matabeleland. Would it not have been logical for most of the people to remain where they were—in Ngwato territory—while advance parties prepared a route into the new country, and then to have moved the rest of the people there by stages? By contrast, what actually happened was that about half the nation marched directly to Matabeleland, while the other half advanced north. This scenario suggests either one of two reasons for the migrants' division. Either they separated with no intention of reuniting later, or they did not know where they would end up resettling, hoping in the meantime to cover as much territory as possible without becoming hopelessly fragmented into smaller parties in the process.[66]

The two divisions remained separated for over a year, during which Gundwane's party established settlements in Matabeleland. Meanwhile, Mzilikazi's division wandered off to the distant northwest. The reasons for this long separation are somewhat hazy. One gets the impression from traditional evidence that all parties had intended quickly to reunite in the new land, but that Mzilikazi's party simply got lost for a while.[67] By contrast, there are two strong arguments for concluding that the Ndebele had not intended to reunite, and that the fact that they eventually did so was the result of chance. First, Mzilikazi himself apparently wanted to cross the Zambezi River during his northward march, whereas the other migrants did not budge from Matabeleland once they reached it. Only when he was frustrated in his attempt to approach the Zambezi did Mzilikazi turn to find the rest of his people.[68] Second, Gundwane's group may not have expected to see Mzilikazi again, for when the time for the 1839 *inxwala/ukucinsa* festival came round, they installed his son as king in his place.[69]

Rather than attempt to resolve these questions at present, I shall allow the relevant evidence to emerge in my discussion of the courses of each division's movements below.

'Gundwane Ndiweni': Who was he?[70]

The commander of the division of migrants which marched from eastern Botswana to Matabeleland is named in tradition as 'Gundwane Ndiweni'. Since Mzilikazi himself commanded the other division of migrants, it would appear that Gundwane's position gave him a rank second only to that of the king—an impression supported by the traditions which identify him.[71]

Oddly, nothing seems to be known about Gundwane before 1838. Traditions identify him only in the context of the migration and its immediate aftermath and his name does not appear in any of the travellers' accounts of the 1830s. It seems incredible that a man with no known background could emerge with such great power so suddenly, yet hitherto no historian has commented on this paradox.

The key to the mystery of Gundwane's apparent anonymity before 1838 is that he was known to Europeans by another name. According to a grandson of Mzilikazi who was interviewed in the late 1930s, 'Nkalipi and Gundwana are one and the same man'. 'Gundwane' was the man's original, childhood name, and 'Kaliphi' was a praise-name given him during Mzilikazi's flight from the Zulu.[72] Etymological evidence supports this claim: - *gundwane* means 'mouse' or 'rat' in Sindebele, while -*kaliphi* means 'sharp, smart, masterful, bold, courageous', *etc.*[73] The former name can probably be attributed to some chance circumstance around the time of the man's birth; the latter name clearly conveys significant praises.[74]

Kaliphi has already been mentioned several times in this study. It is clear that he was a major figure in the kingdom through the 1830s and it makes a great deal of sense that someone of his stature was designated to command one division of migrants in 1838.[75] Furthermore, it is highly significant that it was he who commanded the *impi* which reached present Matabeleland in 1831. Since, as we have seen, the Ndebele appear to have had little first-hand knowledge of the trans-Limpopo region before migrating there, Kaliphi was probably chosen to lead his migratory division because of his prior experience in the region. In sum, he fits the description of a man whom we would expect to occupy 'Gundwane's' role during the migration.

The identification of Kaliphi as 'Gundwane' solves another puzzle as well, *viz.*, what happened to Kaliphi *after* 1837? Kaliphi seems to disappear from historical record just as quickly in 1837 as 'Gundwane' appears the following year.[76] Obviously the appearance of the latter name explains the disappearance of the former. Kaliphi was well known to European visitors during the 1830s. When Robert Moffat visited the Ndebele in Matabeleland in 1854 he asked Kaliphi's son Monyebe what had become of his father. Monyebe replied only that his 'father was a great warrior, and had died in battle, fighting to defend Moselekatse . . .'[77]

Significantly, Monyebe supplied no further details on his father's death. He was reticent because he wished to cover up the true circumstances of his father's death.

The circumstances of 'Gundwane's' death are well remembered in tradition, and they were not honourable. He was with the group that installed Mzilikazi's son as king after reaching Matabeleland. When Mzilikazi rejoined these people shortly afterwards, he executed the dissident *indunas*. Gundwane's complicity in the ostensible rebellion was apparently unconfirmed, nevertheless he was among the first to fall in the purge. Irrespective of his political motives in the affair, he was blameworthy for his failure to keep Mzilikazi's kingdom intact during the latter's absence. According to some traditional authorities he was falsely accused of treason by rivals; if so, his family would have cause to fear for their own safety later. In any case, his reputation was ruined and his passing was not the kind of subject a son would wish to discuss with a European. Assuming that Gundwane and Kaliphi were indeed the same person, it should be clear why the son, Monyebe, would lie to Moffat by saying his father had died in Mzilikazi's defence.

Monyebe's own fate lends further support to the conclusion that Kaliphi and Gundwane were one man. In 1862 he himself was executed by Mzilikazi in the midst of a political crisis. This is an issue on which we can at present only speculate, but it seems quite possible that Monyebe fell victim to the same kind of familial political rivalries which had earlier contributed to his father's execution, and that he had had good reason to be reticent in his conversation with Moffat in 1854.[78]

The first migrants reach Matabeleland, mid 1838

Assuming that the Ndebele divided into two approximately equal parties, it follows that Kaliphi/Gundwane's division contained about seven or eight thousand people.[79] Traditions record the names of the *amabutho* ('regiments') which travelled in each division. The names associated with Kaliphi/Gundwane's division include several closely identified with the Khumalo royal family. At least two of Mzilikazi's sons—Nkulumane, the heir-apparent, and Lobengula, the actual successor as king—and their mothers travelled in this division, as well as the hereditary Khumalo regent, Mncumbathe.[80] The presence of persons so closely associated with the Khumalo royal house in this party lends persuasive weight to the theory that the original division of migrants was planned amicably with the intention of eventual reunion.

It is occasionally asserted that Kaliphi/Gundwane's division contained most of the Ndebele women and children; however, this notion is not supported by any explicit evidence, and is in fact contradicted by evidence that whole families travelled with Mzilikazi's division.[81]

Kaliphi/Gundwane's division marched out of Ngwato territory in an east-northeasterly direction—roughly following the 'Matabele Road' mentioned by Mackenzie's Ngwato informants; they turned north in the Gwanda District of present Rhodesia. Passing along the eastern side of the Matopos Hills, they finally halted near the Malungwane Hills.[82] The spot where they stopped became the approximate centre of the Ndebele kingdom and remained so during the rest of the century.

It is difficult to pinpoint the time of the migrants' arrival. There is some indication that they arrived during the local harvest season. This would mean that they moved extremely rapidly from Ngwato territory, where they had just left after a harvest. Furthermore, traditional evidence seems to confuse the situation which Kaliphi/Gundwane's group found in Matabeleland with the situation found by Mzilikazi about a year later. What does seem clear is that Kaliphi/Gundwane arrived before the next rainy season, and therefore by mid-1838.[83] There is nothing in any evidence to suggest that his group dallied anywhere along the way.

Kaliphi/Gundwane's followers now found themselves in the midst of the Kalanga branch of the Shona-speaking peoples. Their new territory had only recently been the centre of a loose, but vast, empire ruled by a line of people known as the Rozvi.[84] Surprisingly, neither the Ndebele nor the Kalanga seem to remember very much about their very first contacts. Part of the reason lies in the fact that the Rozvi centres had been devastated by Ngoni migrant groups during the previous decade. The Kalanga were thus poorly prepared to resist the latest invaders. Many of them scattered—especially to the east—and the Ndebele occupied the region with little or no fighting.[85] The years of Ndebele-Shona wars were in the future.[86]

While Mzilikazi's division was still off to the northwest,

Kaliphi/Gundwane's people built towns and planted crops. Their first major settlement they named *Gibixegu*, apparently in honour of the Zulu town to which Mzilikazi had been attached during his service under Shaka.[87]

Mzilikazi's wanderings, 1838-1839

The route of Mzilikazi's division was longer and is more difficult to trace than that of Kaliphi/Gundwane's division. Traditional authorities stress the notion that Mzilikazi wandered aimlessly in and around northeastern Botswana, but the impression that he was 'lost' is probably exaggerated.[88] More nearly contemporary evidence suggests that Mzilikazi knew where he wanted to go, but that his path was hindered by physical obstacles.

The success of Kaliphi/Gundwane's division in rapidly locating and settling in what became the permanent Ndebele home contrasted with the experience of Mzilikazi's division. Mzilikazi arrived on the scene after settlement was an accomplished fact with nothing useful to show for his extended travels. His division had faced greater hardships than had the other. His people periodically had to divide into smaller groups to search for food and water over a wider area and, apparently, to get their bearings. One unit reached as far west as Lake Ngami, where it lost a significant number of men in a brush with the Tawana.[89] Additional parties fanned out in other directions, thus contributing to the impression in some traditions that Mzilikazi himself wandered over a wide area. A more accurate picture is given by a modern informant:

> Mziligazi lived on the land, capturing the cattle from the tribes all round. . . . The scouts went far and wide . . . and kept on coming back and reporting while Mziligazi remained behind. Sometimes when they found a good spot, Mziligazi would stop there four or five months, but all the time they were looking for the others [*i.e.*, other Ndebele].[90]

Mzilikazi remained with the main body of his division probably throughout his migration. One of the first stopping places for the division as a whole appears to have been the Makarikari Salt Pan, about 125 miles north-northwest of the Tswapong Hills.[91] It is difficult to say whether they deviated from a direct route in their march from Tswapong to Makarikari. According to A. A.

Campbell, they passed through the Bulalima District of Rhodesia on their way north; however, as this area would have been considerably out of the way, Campbell's informants probably were confusing this period of migration with a later period of Ndebele settlement in the same region.[92]

A curious problem to which I have already alluded is Mzilikazi's apparent desire to cross the Zambezi River during this migration despite his evident intentions to rejoin the rest of his people, who seem to have been uninterested in following him in that direction. It is possible that he conceived the plan to cross the Zambezi only after he had separated from Kaliphi/Gundwane's division in eastern Botswana. Perhaps he grew more interested in seeing the other side of the river as he approached it more closely and perceived its defensive possibilities against his perennial southern enemies.[93] Certainly the land he was traversing in north-eastern Botswana was relatively inhospitable. Since he seems to have known nothing about the territory settled by the rest of his people, he may have regarded the northern side of the Zambezi as his best hope for new settlements. His scouts reached the Victoria Falls, returning to report favourably to him.[94]

Unfortunately, as Mzilikazi advanced across the Nata River (which enters the Makarikari from the east), his cattle were devastated by parasite-carrying tsetse fly; he was then forced to turn away to the southeast. In 1854 he revisited the Nata River with Robert Moffat, who described Mzilikazi's prior experience there:

> He intended to have gone on to the other side of the Zambesi, but he had not gone far beyond where we now are before his progress was arrested by the fly, which compelled him to return and occupy the country in which he now lives. . . .
> He with his company and a great many cattle had no sooner entered the *tsetse* region when scores died. He instantly saw that advance without them, and of course without food, would be impossible, when he commenced a retreat in direct course to whereabout he now lives. From their ignorance of the locality of the tsetse, it was some days before they got out from among them. The cattle died so rapidly that their carcasses were lying within sight of each other along the course they had taken, and where they halted for the night, hundreds were left dead.[95]

The Nata River basin was as far north as Mzilikazi himself ever travelled; he never saw the Zambezi River.[96]

At this point it is necessary to elaborate on a subject which has been much misunderstood by modern historians, *viz.*, the misconception that the Ndebele brushed with the Kololo by the Zambezi during Mzilikazi's northward march.[97] A number of traditional authorities assert that the Ndebele fought the Kololo by the Zambezi *before* Mzilikazi reached Matabeleland;[98] however, such traditions confuse Mzilikazi's abortive initial approach to the Zambezi with a series of Ndebele-Kololo wars by the Zambezi which commenced several years later. Several lines of evidence can be adduced to prove that the Ndebele did not fight the Kololo at the time of the formers' migration.

Moffat's account (quoted above) of Mzilikazi's near-disaster by the Nata River rules out the possibility that any significant number of Ndebele men even reached the Zambezi River, and it is broadly corroborated by traditional sources. Furthermore, several Ndebele traditional authorities specifically deny that the Ndebele fought the Kololo at this time.[99]

Evidence from the Kololo side should be regarded as conclusive. For the Kololo recalled that they suffered their first attack from the Ndebele while they were living in the Toka highlands.[100] As the Toka highlands lie about 150 miles northeast of the Victoria Falls—which Ndebele scouts are known to have reached—the Kololo were almost certainly far out of reach of Ndebele arms in 1838. Even those sources which hold that Mzilikazi's whole division reached the Zambezi do not suggest that it ventured anywhere near the Toka highlands.[101]

The Ndebele later did mount several major attacks on the Kololo, but only *after* they were firmly established as a nation in Matabeleland.[102] The first *impi* found the Kololo in the Toka highlands. The attack was unsuccessful, but the new Ndebele threat persuaded the Kololo to remove their settlements to the more defensible riverain region of the Lozi people, northwest of the Victoria Falls. Subsequent Ndebele-Kololo wars were fought in and near Lozi territory.

The cycle of Ndebele-Kololo wars is an especially difficult one to unravel. Unlike the earlier cycles of Ndebele-Griqua wars, *etc.*, there is no contemporary documentation to assist in differentiating and dating separate, but ostensibly similar, events. The period of Mzilikazi's migration evidently later became confused in tradition with the cycle of Kololo wars because Ndebele remembered he had tried to cross the Zambezi, and because Ndebele reconnaissance at the Zambezi took place in the same region as several of the Kololo wars.

Reunion in Matabeleland and the end of
Ndebele migrations, c. mid-1839

Mzilikazi's personal arrival in Matabeleland ended the era of Ndebele migrations, and with them the subject of this study. In order to reconstruct the circumstances and dating of his arrival there some reference must be made to the political crisis which immediately ensued; however, no attempt will be made to analyse this later event in detail as it belongs more properly to the next phase of Ndebele history.

Mzilikazi's division of migrants entered present Rhodesia *via* the Nata River around the end of 1838 or early 1839. This dating can be inferred from the apparent fact that it was in this region that he celebrated the *inxwala/ukucinsa* festival, which would have fallen due about then.[103] Explicit evidence for his conducting the religious rites in northwestern Rhodesia is somewhat weak; however, it is not contradicted by any source, and it fits logically into the overall chronological pattern of the migration. Mzilikazi had to observe these rites at some point between the observances of early 1838 in eastern Botswana and the time he rejoined Kaliphi/Gundwane's party, since it is clear that the latter group conducted its own festival in his absence in Matabeleland during his absence.

After the .*inxwala* Mzilikazi continued as far east as the Bembezi River. There he established a temporary settlement remembered as Nkokolobeni, or Nkonkolombela.[104] Up to this point it appears that the two Ndebele divisions were unaware of each other's whereabouts. Exactly how contact was re-established between the two groups is a matter of controversy in traditional evidence: sources disagree on which party took the first initiative to find the other. It is an issue with obvious political implications, as it refelcts upon the loyalty to Mzilikazi of the people first to arrive in Matabeleland.

In addition to various claims as to which group sent out scouts to find the other, another current runs through the evidence, *viz.*, the impression that Mzilikazi came upon the Matabeleland settlers purely by chance. Yet another explanation is suggested by the Moffat Myth, variants of which hold that Mzilikazi encountered Robert Moffat near the Nata River, and that *there* Moffat told him how to find Matabeleland. Obviously Moffat did not do this, but it was possibly around the Nata that Mzilikazi met the Rolong hunter discussed above. Mzilikazi's actual circumstances appear to conform to the story of how the Rolong helped him out of his difficulty, and the whole scenario resembles many versions of the Moffat Myth. (One wonders what effect Moffat's 1854 trip to the Nata River with Mzilikazi had on the later development of the Myth. Did the Ndebele think Moffat had been to the same place before?) In sum, no definitive answer to the question of how Mzilikazi's and Kaliphi/Gundwane's divisions found each other appears attainable.

While the question of *how* Mzilikazi found the rest of his people remains unanswerable, there is no controversy about the situation he found when he arrived in Matabeleland: his son, Nkulumane, had been made king in his place.[105] During Mzilikazi's separation from these other people, they had faced the crisis of celebrating the annual *inxwala/ukucinsa* festival without a king:

> Rumours had reached this main body of the Matabele, that Mzilikazi and his company had all perished by the Salt Pans in the desert. The months passed and still no further news of him was forthcoming and the time of their annual tribal ceremony drew near. This ceremony, the inxwala . . . could not be celebrated without the presence of the king to officiate.[106]

Some of the leading men in Kaliphi/Gundwane's party resolved the problem by installing Nkulumane as king (or perhaps as acting king) to conduct the *inxwala*. Doubtlessly, the political motivations behind this act were more complex than are implied here.[107] The only point to be made here is that these things happened around late 1838 or early 1839, since this must have been the time a new *inxwala* was due. The *inxwala* celebrated in Matabeleland would thus have coincided with the same rites conducted by Mzilikazi when he was still in the northwest.

It is almost certain that Mzilikazi's party reached central Matabeleland by mid-1839. Traditional authorities indicate that he arrived there *shortly after* the other Ndebele had completed their *inxwala* observances.[108] The moment he arrived, the era of Ndebele migrations ended. Ndebele removal to Matabeleland was complete, and their area of settlement never again shifted significantly from where they stood in 1839.[109]

APPENDIX A

WHO WERE THE 'NDEBELE'?

Detailed examination of the social history of the Ndebele people is beyond the scope of this study. Nevertheless, it is useful to ask who were the 'Ndebele'? and how did they come into being as a people?

The term 'Ndebele' is used throughout this study primarily in a political sense. The Ndebele are thus regarded as those people who recognized Mzilikazi as their sovereign, and who possessed certain rights and responsibilities within the state system he created after he left Zululand in c. 1821. This definition excludes such people as were unwillingly held captive, or whose relationship to Mzilikazi was that of tributaries. The concept of the king's sovereignty naturally implies the existence of a kingdom. The kingdom founded by Mzilikazi ceased to exist in 1894, when his son and successor died. Afterwards the concept of Ndebelehood took on different kinds of meaning. In this study no attempt is made to define 'Ndebele' in non-political terms. The difficulty of doing so is manifest by the ethnic situation in present-day Rhodesia, where the question of who is 'an Ndebele' is still a live issue.[1]

The name 'Ndebele' is a good example of the almost universal tendency of peoples' receiving their names from outsiders. 'Ndebele' is an Anglicized form of the Nguni word *Amandebele*, which in turn derives from the Sotho word *Matebele*.[2] The original meaning of *Matebele* is obscure and controversial. Of the many definitions put forth, the most convincing is that which to the Sotho connoted 'strangers from the east'.[3] The Sotho, who lived in the central regions of South Africa, generally applied this name to the Nguni-speaking peoples of the eastern coast. Mzilikazi's people were given the name when they moved inland from Zululand. But his were not the only people to be called 'Matabele'. Other nineteenth century intrusive groups, including the Hlubi, Ngwane, and others, were all called 'Matabele' by the Sotho. Occasionally, even Sotho bands received the nickname; the important thing was that the peoples receiving this nickname were regarded essentially as strangers.[4] Gradually, however, most of these other intrusive groups either moved on, or they were absorbed by local communities. Eventually the name 'Matabele', or 'Ndebele' in its Anglo/Nguni form, came to apply only to Mzilikazi's people and to the 'Transvaal Ndebele'. These latter were the descendants of much earlier Nguni immigrants onto the highveld. Mzilikazi had dealings with some of these communities during the 1820s; however, his people and the Transvaal Ndebele are essentially unrelated.[5]

Mzilikazi and his people did not call themselves Matabele or Amandebele until much later in the nineteenth century. They preferred older Nguni names which emphasized their origins, such as Zulu and Mangoni.[6] Eventually, however, they came to see themselves as something greater and more heterogeneous than an Nguni tribe and they accepted the new name to stress their common identity.[7] Although Mzilikazi may never have called his people 'Ndebele' during his own time, in retrospect it is perhaps the most accurate name we can apply to them. It was always political rather than ethnic unity which gave his people a sense of commonality. His people deserve a national, rather than a tribal, name from the moment Mzilikazi became an independent ruler.[8]

SOURCES FOR EARLY NDEBELE HISTORY

All sources used in this study exist in published or unpublished written form, and are readily accessible in various libraries and archives. For the purpose of discussion, I classify these sources according to three temporal categories: contemporary, near-contemporary, and traditional. Each category can be further divided according to the perspectives of ultimate authorities for pieces of information. The most outstanding distinctions to be made are those separating first-hand from second- or third-hand observations, and Ndebele-derived from non-Ndebele-derived information. Obviously, these various categories are not always mutually exclusive. Travellers' books of the 1830s, for example, contain complex mixtures of first and second-hand observations, Ndebele and non-Ndebele derived information, and contemporary as well as non-contemporary data. I offer my categories merely to provide a framework against which individual sources can be measured. I would argue only that sources tend to be more reliable when they are closer to the events they describe, and that the possibility of bias or distortion behind any given statement must be understood. For these reasons I have attempted rigorously to examine the derivation of all sources used in this study, and I feel it is worthwhile to summarize my findings here.

Contemporary evidence

The most outstanding feature of contemporary written evidence for early Ndebele history is that none of it was penned by an Ndebele person. The Ndebele possessed no form of writing before they encountered European culture, and even then few Ndebele learned to write before the end of the nineteenth century. Furthermore, for the period studied here there are virtually no written documents even dictated by an Ndebele (a notable exception, Mzilikazi's letter to Governor D'Urban, is discussed in Chapter 4). Thus, such contemporary documents as do exist for this period contain largely the observations of outsiders, mostly Europeans. Visitors to the Ndebele recorded first-hand observations of Ndebele life, but they saw a limited range of Ndebele activities. There are no contemporary first-hand accounts of an Ndebele migration, and almost no such accounts of the Ndebele at war. For evidence on these subjects, we must rely upon contemporary second-hand documentation, and upon non-contemporary categories of evidence.

No literate person is known to have visited and to have reported on the Ndebele before 1829, when Mzilikazi was living near present Pretoria. However, when the Ndebele were moving through the eastern Transvaal, reports of their movements reached European ears and were recorded in missionaries' letters and colonial government reports as early as 1823. Scattered but very useful second-hand documentation of the period between 1823 and 1829 can thus be found in the files of Wesleyan Methodist and London Missionary Societies [WMMS & LMS, respectively] and in various official files of the Cape Archives [CA].

The first-hand record of Ndebele activities commenced in 1829 when traders reached Mzilikazi's court and publicized his interest in obtaining Christian missionaries to the Cape Colony. Soon thereafter James Archbell of the WMMS and Robert Moffat of the LMS visited Mzilikazi and wrote the first lengthy descriptions of the Ndebele. Additional literate Europeans visited the Ndebele in 1832, 1835, and 1836-7. Throughout this period, even during years when no Europeans visited him, Mzilikazi communicated regularly with Europeans, especially Robert Moffat. Hence information about Ndebele activities and intentions circulated widely among literate Europeans and was duly recorded in many places. Less formal, but equally valuable, information also circulated through other channels, as both African and non-African traders and hunters and political refugees moved about in the interior. In addition to the above named archives colonial newspapers—particularly the *Graham's Town Journal* [*GTJ*]—which was founded in December 1831—contain much second-hand and some first-hand evidence on Ndebele affairs. As one would expect, this information pertains mostly to the events of widest interest to the peoples of the interior: namely, wars and population movements.

The best and most voluminous first-hand observations of the Ndebele were recorded by Europeans who visited them in the western Transvaal in 1835, 1836, and early 1837. Moffat paid Mzilikazi a second and lengthier visit there in 1835; he also visited the Ndebele three times in the future Matabeleland during the 1850s. He recorded all these visits in long letters to his wife and to his mission directors. These letters have been published as his *Matabele Journals* (2 vols., London, 1945). His earliest visits are also described in his book, *Missionary Labours and Scenes in Southern Africa* (London, 1842). His career writings make him the uncontested leading European authority on the Ndebele during King Mzilikazi's long reign; however, the most informative writer on the Ndebele of the 1830s is another man, Dr Andrew Smith.

In 1835 Andrew Smith led a large scientific expedition through Ndebele territory. He maintained a voluminous diary of his trip as well as a volume of ethnographic notes. In addition he wrote an official *Report of the Expedition* (Cape Town, 1836) and he almost completed a two volume journal for publication. In contrast to men like Moffat, Smith was ignorant about African societies, but his ignorance actually increases the evidentiary value of his writings. Taking little for granted, he wrote down everything he observed, and he asked Africans questions which other travellers either did not trouble to ask or did not bother to record. His knowledge of African languages was nil and his orthography was incredibly inconsistent, but he tended to write down things as he heard them, and he often identified his informants. Consequently, his writings contain a wealth of detail and a variety of perspectives rare among travellers' accounts of his time.

Between early 1836 and January 1837 three American missionary families lived among the Ndebele. Their success as missionaries was slight, but their letters and journals contain among the most perceptive accounts of Ndebele affairs then written; they also provide the longest continuous chronicle of Ndebele activities through any part of the period under study (see American Board of Commissioners Archival material). Also during 1836 a British hunter, Captain W. C. Harris, travelled in Ndebele territory and wrote a lengthy account of his trip in *Wild*

Sports of Southern Africa (London, 1839). The significance of these particular records is magnified by the importance of the events occurring while they were written.

None of the various African peoples whom the Ndebele fought during the 1820s and 1830s were themselves literate, but many had literate Europeans living or travelling among them. These Europeans—mostly missionaries and traders—left invaluable records of Ndebele wars from their adversaries' perspectives. Particularly important are their descriptions of Griqua/Korana and Zulu conflicts with the Ndebele. These records are scattered through books, newspaper articles, and missionary and government files of the period.

Perhaps the climactic episode of Ndebele warfare south of the Limpopo was the encounter with Afrikaners (Boers) in 1836–7. Along with the Zulu and Griqua/Korana the Afrikaners helped to drive the Ndebele out of the Transvaal, and they were among the last people to see the Ndebele south of the Limpopo. Unfortunately, few Afrikaner participants in these wars were functionally literate. Hence, even this period of massive white confrontation with the Ndebele is documented largely by second-hand contemporary reports, and by memoirs recorded decades later.

A remarkable shortcoming of all contemporary evidence should be stressed. Although the total body of first-hand documents pertaining to the Ndebele would fill perhaps seven or eight printed books, none of this material contains a true eye-witness description of either an Ndebele migration or an Ndebele battle with non-Europeans. These records contain numerous descriptions of such events, but all such descriptions are second-hand accounts recorded far from the scene of the events themselves, or are translated paraphrases of first-hand accounts taken from informants long afterwards. This latter type of evidence is better regarded as 'near-contemporary' evidence.

Near-contemporary evidence

Throughout the main text I describe as 'near-contemporary' such evidence as was taken from both African and non-African participants in events well after those events occurred. This is the kind of evidence which would be called 'oral history', were it collected today from living informants. I am hesitant to use the term 'oral history' here, however, as it connotes more systematically collected data than that upon which I actually draw.

Relevant near-contemporary evidence can be found in most documents written by Europeans who travelled north of the Orange River after the early 1820s, when the Ndebele presence on the highveld began to be felt. Travellers and missionaries met displaced peoples, Ndebele enemies, and eventually the Ndebele themselves. They haphazardly interviewed these peoples about past events and recorded what they learned in bits and pieces throughout their various writings. Occasionally they identified their informants by name and attempted to record statements in the informants' own words—invariably translated, however—but typically they simply passed on information without revealing much about where and how they acquired it. Naturally, one must do the best one can to determine the ultimate provenance of their data.

The first missionaries to visit Mzilikazi in 1829 were also the first scribes to record summaries of earlier Ndebele history. Later visitors added fuller information on those and the succeeding years, and this practice continued well after the Ndebele had left the Transvaal. Again, the best source of Ndebele oral accounts up to 1835 is the collected writings of Andrew Smith. A particularly valuable source of such evidence from the later, Matabeleland period is the LMS missionary Thomas Morgan Thomas' book, *Eleven Years in Central South Africa* (London, 1871). Few Ndebele who had been with Mzilikazi south of the Limpopo survived beyond the 1870s; thereafter freshly-recorded evidence pertaining to the early years came mostly from transmitted traditions, rather than from first-hand memories.

One of the most valuable subcategories of evidence used in this study comprises the near-contemporary accounts of non-Ndebele people who fought against, or were associated with, the Ndebele state during the 1820s and 1830s. Many of these peoples had even closer contacts with literate Europeans than did the Ndebele themselves. This was especially true after the 1830s, when European activities north of the Orange River began to expand rapidly. The various writings of these Europeans provide many independent lines of evidence with which to reconstruct the history of Ndebele relations with their neighbours from opposing perspectives. This situation for the 1820s and 1830s contrasts favourably with the history of Ndebele relations with their neighbours later in the nineteenth century, when such trans-Limpopo adversaries as the Shona long remained out of touch with literate persons who might have recorded their points of view.

Compared to the generally haphazard manner in which oral evidence was collected from the Ndebele, some non-Ndebele-derived sources are quite good. And, while the Ndebele lost contact with the literate world through the 1840s and early 1850s, many of their former African adversaries were still telling their stories of the earlier years to missionaries, travellers, and even colonial government officials. There is little doubt but that much potential Ndebele evidence died out during this hiatus in communication. An example of the crucial importance of even casually-recorded evidence lies in the writings of the famous missionary/traveller, David Livingstone. Livingstone was the only literate person to meet the Kololo king Sebitwane. He just happened to meet and interview the man shortly before the latter's death in 1851; from him he obtained the most coherent account of Ndebele-Kololo conflicts ever recorded. Had Livingstone reached the Kololo just a few weeks later, reconstructions of the important cycle of Ndebele-Kololo wars would now be almost impossible.

A particularly outstanding source of non-Ndebele oral history is an official British commission report, *Evidence taken at Bloemhof . . .* (Cape Town, 1871). The *Bloemhof* blue book contains verbatim testimonies pertaining to the diamondfields territory dispute of 1871. More than twenty of the witnesses—including Sotho, Griqua, and Afrikaners—were men who had had first-hand dealings with the Ndebele during the 1820s and 1830s. Several of them had even lived under the aegis of the Ndebele state and had fought on its side in several wars; others had fought against the Ndebele, or had otherwise observed the Ndebele during those early years. Consequently, much of their testimony pertains directly to Ndebele history and contains a wealth of details and insights not found elsewhere.

As previously noted, the Afrikaners whom the Ndebele fought in the 1830s were only semi-literate. The most important Afrikaner-penned document contemporary to that period of conflict, *The Diary of Erasmus Smit* (trans., Cape Town, 1972) is actually a second-hand account, written far from the areas of fighting. Such first-person Afrikaner accounts as exist were recorded decades later; they must therefore be classified as near-contemporary evidence and treated with the same cautions relevant to recorded African testimonies. Afrikaner memoirs are collected in John Bird (ed.), *Annals of Natal* (2 vols., Pietermaritzburg, 1888), and in G. S. Preller (ed.), *Voortrekkermense* (4 vols., Kaapstad, 1920-5).

Traditional evidence

Traditional evidence is that which is collected from informants who got their information from members of prior generations. The oral transmission of memories between generations—not the manner in which they are eventually recorded—is what characterizes traditional evidence as a category. Nowadays we tend to think of traditional evidence as something necessarily collected and recorded scientifically; however, useful Ndebele traditions were being casually recorded almost as fast as they were being created in the mid-nineteenth century, as the first generation of Ndebele died out. The ever-increasing number of literate Europeans who visited Matabeleland through the rest of the century sprinkled traditional accounts of Ndebele history throughout their published and unpublished writings. Much information thus recorded is unobtainable elsewhere. One valuable early example of a statement of Ndebele tradition is in Alex Bailie's report to the Cape Colony government in 1876 (Cape Archives, GH 19/12).

More systematic recording of Ndebele tradition began in 1898, while the British were establishing colonial administration over Matabeleland. Native Commissioners working in different districts compiled detailed reports on Ndebele history. These are now available in two important files in the National Archives of Rhodesia [NAR] (see A 3/1/8/28 and NB 6/1/1).

One of these early Rhodesian Native Commissioners, A. A. Campbell, went on to write a full-length history of the Ndebele kingdom in 1911. Assuming the pen-name 'Mziki', he later published the book as *Mlimo: The Rise and Fall of the Matabele* (Pietermaritzburg, 1926). Campbell claimed the story was taken from a single informant, one Malida ka Mabuyu—whom he says accompanied Mzilikazi out of Zululand. However, it is clear that the early part of the book is actually based upon traditional evidence collected by Campbell and his fellow Native Commissioners, as well as some early written records.

Since it contains by far the fullest treatment of early Ndebele history based upon tradition, *Mlimo* reveals much about the limitations of traditional evidence for that period: chronological sequences are often confused and demonstrably inaccurate; the identities of Ndebele adversaries are often mixed up; and periods of comparative peace and stability are ignored in favour of dramatic events. An even greater problem in *Mlimo*—and in virtually all near-contemporary and traditional evidence—is the failure to differentiate clearly between similar-appearing, but chronologically separate, events, especially cycles of recurring wars with the Zulu, Griqua/Korana, Kololo, and others. Without existing contemporary evidence, it would be almost impossible to place many of these events in their correct contexts, and a misleading picture of the scale of Ndebele warfare would prevail.

Campbell's writings had a much more profound impact on modern Ndebele historiography than has been recognized. In about 1905 he wrote a draft article on Ndebele history containing all the essential points on the early years later incorporated in *Mlimo*. Although that article seems never to have been published, its conclusions found their way into two compendiums of South African traditional history which have had a clear and seminal influence on all subsequent literature on Ndebele history. First, D. F. Ellenberger read Campbell's draft article and based a chapter on the Ndebele upon it in his *History of the Basuto* (London, 1912). Later, A. T. Bryant drew upon Ellenberger's Ndebele material in his own monumental *Olden Times in Zululand and Natal* (London, 1929), a massive survey of Northern Nguni history. Recognizing neither the connection between Bryant and Ellenberger's information, nor their mutual dependence upon Campbell's obscure article, virtually all twentieth-century historians of the Ndebele have drawn heavily upon the first two historians' books. Ellenberger's and Bryant's presumed authority has thus helped to perpetuate significant errors originated by Campbell.

Meanwhile, amateur ethnological research became a popular pastime among Europeans in colonial Rhodesia who continued to collect Ndebele tradition after official government interest waned. A few, such as F. W. T. Posselt and Neville Jones, published books, but such material mostly appeared in the pages of the government-issued annual, *Nada* (1923–). This publication is a mine of historical data, and much of it is written in the exact—but translated—words of African informants. The largest single body of recorded traditions, however, is unpublished. During the late 1930s R. F. Windram conducted a series of lengthy interviews with members of the former Ndebele royal family. The English-language transcripts of his interviews extend to about 250 typed pages of apparently verbatim testimony (see NAR, WI 8/1). Windram directed his informants to testify about issues mainly relevant to the late nineteenth century, but the transcripts as a whole are nevertheless a rich source of information about the early years, particularly the period of migration to Matabeleland.

The inherent weaknesses of Ndebele traditions with respect to early history are at least partly the product of the historical experience itself. During their first two decades the Ndebele constituted not so much a nation as a loosely-knit aggregation of ethnically diverse peoples, held together mainly by their common search for collective strength under the leadership of Mzilikazi. Throughout those years his followers came and went constantly; few shared all his adventures; fewer still were able later to pass on coherent memories of those turbulent years to descendants. Mzilikazi migrated vast distances five separate times; his followers meanwhile fought almost constantly with their ever-changing neighbours. Frequent shifts of surroundings gave the early Ndebele little time to familiarize themselves with either landscapes or neighbours. Even in early near-contemporary evidence it is clear that living informants had trouble remembering exactly where they had been, and with whom they had fought. Obviously the memories contained in traditions can be no sharper than the recollections of their primary informants. As a result, traditions of the early years recall the names of only the most famous Ndebele adversaries, such as Zwide, Shaka, Moshweshwe, and a few others. Furthermore, they make hash of the geographical framework of the migrations; the chronological sequences of the period suffer just as badly.

Ndebele traditions should be, and apparently are, much better for the trans-Limpopo years. For north of the Limpopo the kingdom entered into a period of comparative stability; physical surroundings remained constant, and, for the most part, so did their neighbours. Furthermore, as the Ndebele gradually coalesced into something more like a true nation, with shared values and culture, they increasingly shared the same historical experiences, and hence the same traditions. New generations tended to see their national history largely in the context of their trans-Limpopo environment, against which the sub-Limpopo experiences of their predecessors must have seemed remote, vague, and scarcely relevant.

Although I would argue that Ndebele tradition is probably not a promising field for the early history of the kingdom, I would hasten to add that traditional evidence as a category is crucial to this study. For the short-comings of Ndebele tradition are partly corrected by non-Ndebele tradition, which is also more abundant. Mzilikazi's twenty-year passage through southern Africa is well remembered in the traditions of the peoples with whom he came into contact. For many the transit of the Ndebele state was a traumatic event, remembered in some detail in traditions. Such traditions are especially useful in reconstructing the geography of Ndebele movements and wars. Whereas the Ndebele kept moving until they got to Matabeleland, their neighbours mostly stayed in or near their ancestral homes where they retained tangible landmarks to which to affix traditional stories. For example, Ndebele-derived evidence generally is very weak on the geography of Mzilikazi's operations in the eastern Transvaal during the early 1820s; by contrast, numerous traditional sources of eastern Transvaal peoples enable us to reconstruct his movements there in some detail. Similar contributions to Ndebele history are made by non-Ndebele traditions in many other contexts.

The sources of non-Ndebele traditions used in this study are widely scattered, but a few published books pull considerable data together. The earliest was compiled by the British-administered Transvaal Native Affairs Department [TNAD] in *Short History of the Native Tribes of the Transvaal* (Pretoria, 1905; reprinted, 1968), a book containing summaries of field reports on local histories, arranged by ethnic groups. Read as whole, the volume gives an impressive picture of the depth of the Ndebele impact upon the peoples of the Transvaal. Twenty-five years later the Union government's Department of Native Affairs began issuing its Ethnological Publications. These form a series of regional and ethnographic surveys, many of which contain fresh traditional evidence. Several volumes, most notably those of P. L. Breutz and N. J. van Warmelo, contain considerable evidence pertaining to the Ndebele.

All the sources mentioned in this essay, as well as many others, are discussed in greater detail throughout the main text and footnotes of this book. References to some of the more important authorities can be found in the index.

NOTES

CHAPTER I

1. See, for example, Stanlake Samkange, *Origins of Rhodesia* (London, 1969), 11-13; and J. D. Omer-Cooper, *The Zulu Aftermath* (London, 1966), 131. Ironically, Mzilikazi's relationship with Shaka is cited as an especially clear case of a subject-master relationship by Gerhard Liesegang, 'Nguni migrations between Delagoa Bay and the Zambezi', *Afr. Hist. Studies*, III, 2 (1970), 324.

2. The argument that Shaka himself was largely responsible for introducing these innovations into Northern Nguni states is strongly expressed in John Omer-Cooper, 'Aspects of political change in the nineteenth-century Mfecane', in L. M. thompson (ed.), *African Societies in Southern Africa* (London, 1969), 207, 218ff. Interestingly, he explains the development of the Swazi state along quasi-Zulu lines as a case of emulation, since this state was forming *before* Shaka came to power. See also A. J. Wills, *An Introduction to the History of Central Africa* (2nd ed., London, 1967), 65.

3. Fynn, an English trader, was one of the first Europeans to visit Shaka and he became the latter's confidant. He kept a diary through the 1820s and 1830s, but it was lost so he later had to rewrite his material from memory. His 'diary' from the Shakan years was not published until 1950, but some of his historical notes were published in John Bird (ed.), *The Annals of Natal* (Pietermaritzburg, 1888), and were thus available to Bryant.

4. Bryant is responsible for the chronological framework followed in the present chapter; unfortunately, he does not explain how he has derived his dates. The subject is important and complex, worthy of a major reassessment.

5. Such comparisons are especially evident in Mziki, *Mlimo: The Rise and Fall of the Matabele* (Facsimile rep., Bulawayo, 1972; first publ., 1926), 41, 62, 142, etc.

6. On the location of Mzilikazi's birthplace, see Allen Gardiner, *Narrative of a Journey to the Zoolu Country* (London, 1836), 51; Bryant, *Olden times*, 419. Estimates of Mzilikazi's age made by Europeans who met him place his birthday between 1793 and 1799, inclusive. Estimates of his age include: James Archbell to Wesleyan Methodist Missionary Society [hereafter WMMS], Plaatberg, 31 Dec 1829 (WMMS Archives, London, S. Afr., box III, 1829, no. 37) —thirty years; W. C. Harris, *The Wild Sports of Southern Africa* (London, 1839), 123—forty years in 1836; T. M. Thomas, *Eleven Years in Central South Africa* (2nd ed., London, 1971; first publ., 1872), 159—twenty-seven years in c. 1822. Bryant, *Olden Times*, 421, calculates that Mzilikazi could not have been younger than thirty in 1823.

7. This account follows Bryant, *Olden Times*, 419-20. His description of Khumalo movements is partially corroborated in evidence collected from Ndebele informants by Andrew Smith in 1835. See Smith, 'Memoranda A; notes on Tswana, Sotho and Matabele tribes', pp. 106-7, in vol. XII of Andrew Smith Manuscripts [hereafter, Smith MSS] (South African Museum, Cape Town). See

also J. Y. Gibson, *The Story of the Zulus* (Facs rep, New York, 1971; first publ., 1903), 30.

Two sources name Mashobane's new towns. T. Arbousset and F. Daumas, *Narrative of an Exploratory Tour*, trans. from the French (Facs. rep., Cape Town, 1968; first publ. in English, Cape Town, 1846), 185, name *Umtulu*, said to be three days north of the Zulu king Dingane's capital, *Mgungunglove*. These writers do not identify the provenance of their information on this point. George Wilkerson, 'The Matabele Nation', p. 5 (National Archives of Rhodesia, Salisbury [hereafter, NAR], WI 1/1/1), names *Engumeni* and *Esigudeni*, said to be near Mt Ngome [ca. 27° 45′ So. lat., 31° 30′ E. long.]. Wilkerson was an artisan missionary for the London Missionary Society in Matabeleland around the turn of the century.

The relationship between Northern Nguni clans and chiefdoms is discussed by Monica Wilson, 'The Nguni people', in Wilson & L. M. Thompson (eds.), *The Oxford History of South Africa* (Oxford, 1969), I, 118; see also Bryant, *Olden Times*, 72ff.

8. This account follows Omer-Cooper, *Zulu Aftermath* Chap 2;, E. J. Krige, *The Social System of the Zulus* (3rd impression, Pietermaritzburg, 1965; first publ., 1936), Chap 1; and L. M. Thompson, 'Co-operation and conflict: the Zulu kingdom and Natal', in Wilson & Thompson (eds.), *Oxford History*, I, 334ff.

9. Samkange, *Origins*, 8-9.

10. Many published books identify 'Nompethu' as Mzilikazi's mother, but it is not clear whether they draw upon independent sources of information or upon each other. In chronological order of publication, some of the more important are: Gibson, *Story of the Zulus* (lst ed., Pietermaritzburg, 1903), 24; A. T. Bryant, *A Zulu-English Dictionary* (Pinetown, Natal, 1905), 52; Mhlagazanhlansi [Neville Jones], *My Friend Kumalo* (Bulawayo, c. 1946), 8; and P. S. Mahlangu, *Umthwakazi* (Cape Town, 1957), 4. Wilkerson, 'The Matabele Nation' (c. 1909), 5,gives her name as 'Lompetu'—a simple variant of 'Nompethu'.

11. In Robert Moffat's journals of his 1835 and 1854 visits to Mzilikazi he mentions having met or heard of several of Mashobane's surviving wives. These women were Mzilikazi's classificatory 'mothers', but Moffat specified that none was his physiological mother. See *Matabele Journals of Robert Moffat*, ed. by J. P. R. Wallis (London, 1945), I, 86, 113, 308.

12. The genealogies of Mzilikazi's sons were much discussed in Matabeleland after his death in 1868, and reference was frequently made to his marriage ties to the house of Zwide. See Thomas Baines, *The Northern Goldfields Diaries*, ed. by J. P. R. Wallis (London, (1946), I, 274 (Baines got his information from the trader Sam Edwards, who had first visited Mzilikazi in 1854); Henri Depelchin and Ch. Croonenberghs, *Trois Ans dans L'Afrique Australe; Le Pays des Matabélés* (Bruxelles, 1882), 211; Thomas, *Eleven Years*, 227.

13. This double connection is made explicit by Mtompe Kumalo, whose evidence is recorded in Mhlagazanhlansi, *My Friend Kumalo*, 8. According to Hilda Kuper, Northern Nguni custom regards as 'preferential' a marriage of a man to a woman of his own mother's patri-clan. See *An African Aristocracy* (London, 1961; first publ., 1947), 95-6.

Note that the designation of Mzilikazi's mother and wives as 'daughters' of Zwide applies in the classificatory sense, and that each of these women may or may not have been physiological daughters of Zwide.

14. Bryant, *Olden Times*, 420.

15. Indeed, this same custom was cited by Ndebele in 1869 as the explanation of the thirty-year disappearace from Matabeleland of Mzilikazi's heir-presumptive, Nkulumane. Disagreement among Ndebele factions as to whether Nkulumane was living in exile in Natal or had been killed in c. 1839 led to a political crisis over the succession to Mzilikazi's kingship. For general discussion of these issues, see L. F. Morrow, 'Pre-Mfecane carry-overs in subsequent Ndebele politics', in *Collected Seminar Papers . . .* (London, 1971-2), 85-95; and Richard Brown, *The Ndebele Succession Crisis, 1868-1877* (Rep., Salisbury, 1966; first publ., 1962).

16. Thomas, *Eleven Years*, 155.

17. Bryant, *Olden Times*, 172-3; Mahlangu, *Umthwakazi*, 4-5.

18. Andrew Smith, MSS, XII, 106-7; Daniel Lindley, *et al.*, to R. Anderson, Mosika, 18 Aug 1836 (American Board of Commissioners for Foreign Missions Archives, Cambridge, Mass [hereafter, ABC Arch]), reprinted in D. J. Kotzé (ed.), *Letters of the American Missionaries* (Cape Town, 1950), 132; S. N. G. Jackson, 'Statistical report for the year ending 31 March 1898', Belingwe (NAR, NB 6/1/1); Statement of Ginyalitsha, p. 3 in R. F. Windram Papers (NAR, WI 8/1); Alexander Bailie, 'Journal, 1876-1878', p. 42 (NAR, BA 10/2/1).

Other, implicit references to Zwide's having Mashobane killed are Moffat, *Matabele Jnls.*, I, 29; Harris, *Wild Sports*, 47; and Mziki, *Mlimo, 32*.

19. Bryant, *Olden Times*, 173, says that Zwide had Mashobane's body decapitated. According to Ginyalitsha (NAR, WI 8/1), Zwide had one of Mashobane's arms cut off.

20. Mziki, *Mlimo*, 32; Bryant, *Olden Times*, 173; and Mhlagazanhlansi, *My Friend Kumalo*, 7. Samkange, *Origins*, 10, follows Bryant on this episode, but he adds a twist which is corroborated by no other source. According to him, when Mzilikazi returned to his chiefdom from Ndwandwe country, he found a younger brother, Umvundhlela, usurping the chiefship. This brother fled on Mzilikazi's arrival, however.

21. Bryant, *Olden Times*, 173.

22. Statement of Ntabeni, pp. 49-50, in Windram Papers (NAR, WI 8/1).

23. The dates are Bryant's. For a broader perspective on the purely military aspects of these wars, see K. F. Otterbein, 'The evolution of Zulu warfare', reprinted in Paul Bohannon (ed.), *Law and Warfare* (Garden City, 1967), 351-7.

24. A fascinating, but probably partly apocryphal, account of this battle is given in E. A. Ritter, *Shaka Zulu* (London, 1971; first publ., 1955), 116ff. Ritter generally draws heavily on Bryant's *Olden Times*, but he adds numerous details for which he appears to be the sole authority. Born in 1890 and raised in Zululand, he claims to have gotten much of his information from Zulu informants, but he almost never identifies his sources.

There is no evidence to suggest that Mzilikazi participated in this battle. Peter Becker, author of the popular biography of Mzilikazi, *Path of Blood* (London, 1962), holds that Mzilikazi learned of the battle only after it was over (p. 17). Like Ritter, however, he cites no authority for this statement (none of his listed references support him on this point).

25. Bryant, *Olden times*, 209, holds that Zwide was attacked by the Pedi paramount chief Thulare near the Komati River, but that he was able to turn the tables so that Thulare ended up paying Zwide tribute. This episode provides a valuable chronological perspective on the Zulu-Ndwandwe wars since Thulare is known to have died in 1820. Both the dating of Thulare's death and the ultimate fate of the remnant Ndwandwe are discussed in the next chapter.

26. The subsequent careers of Zwangendaba and the Soshangane are traced in Omer-Cooper, *Zulu Aftermath*, Chaps 4-5; Bryant, *Olden Times, passim;* J. A. Barnes, *Politics in a Changing Society: A Political History of the Fort Jameson Ngoni* (Manchester, 1967; first publ., 1954), Chap 1; *etc.*

27. The vagueness of modern historians on this point is demonstrated in Omer-Cooper, *Zulu Aftermath*, 130-1; and W. F. Lye, 'The Ndebele kingdom south of the Limpopo River', *Jnl. of Afr. Hist.*, X, 1 (1969), 88.

28. That Mzilikazi joined Shaka *after* the second war is implied in Mziki, *Mlimo*, 32; and *The Diary of Henry Francis Fynn*, ed. by J. Stuart and D. M. Malcolm (Pietermaritzburg, 1969; first publ., 1950), 20-1.

29. Those sources which hold that Shaka conquered Mzilikazi are generally vague on this point. See Thomas, *Eleven Years*, 156; Bailie, 'Journal' (NAR, BA 10/2/1); Mhlagazanhlansi, *My Friend Kumalo*, 7; John Mackenzie, *Ten Years North of the Orange River* (Edinburgh, 1871), 307; Wilkerson, 'Matabele Nation', p. 5 (NAR, WI 1/1/1); Jackson, 'Statistical report' (NAR, NB 6/1/1).

30. Moffat, *Matabele Jnls.*, I, 29; A. Smith, MSS, XII, 44; Ginyalitsha, p. 3 (NAR, WI 8/1); Mahlangu, *Umthwakazi*, 4-5. Mzilikazi's hatred of Zwide is stressed in Thomas, *Eleven Years*, 227; and Bryant, *Olden Times*, 595.

31. Ritter, *Shaka*, 151-2. Ritter's evidence is discussed in detail below.

32. This conclusion is supported by Gibson, *Story of the Zulus* (2nd ed., 1911), 30, according to whom Mzilikazi joined Shaka 'about the time he obtained his *first victory* over Zwidi'. (my italics). Gibson's 1903 edition gives a somewhat different version (pp. 24-5).

My conclusion is given further support in A. Smith, MSS, XII, 106: 'Ziete [Zwide] attacked Chaka *after* Massalacatzie fled from him' (my italics).

33. Mtompe Kumalo, in Mhlagazanhlansi, *My Friend Kumalo*, 7.

34. Bryant's dates for these wars are approximate; however, we can be fairly confident that there was a one year gap between the two wars because major campaigns were typically waged during the dry winter months of mid-year. I shall return to the subject of winter warfare in later chapters. See *Olden Times*, 204ff.

36. Becker, *Path of Blood*, 20. Becker identifies his informants only as 'grey-beards'. It is not clear whether he refers to Ndebele or Zulu informants. Possibly he draws upon Ritter (see below).

36. Ritter, *Shaka*, 151-2, 163. Ritter identifies his informant as Signanda Cube, whom he says was a nine year old page in Shaka's service. He further describes Signanda as his 'one living link with Shaka'. Signanda died in 1906. Ritter would have had to interview him before he himself was sixteen, since he was born in 1890.

37. For examples, see footnotes 1 and 2, above. A more cautious view is expressed by A. J. B. Hughes and J. van Velsen, 'The Ndebele', in Hilda Kuper, Hughes and van Veslen, *The Shona and Ndebele of Southern Rhodesia* (London, 1955). 47n.

38. Mtompe Kumalo, in Mhlagazanhlansi, *My Friend Kumalo*, 7.

39. These examples are from A. Smith, MSS, XII, 44, and Thomas, *Eleven Years*, 156, respectively.

40. Harris, *Wild Sports*, 47; Bailie, 'Journal', p. 42 (NAR, BA 10/2/1); Wilkerson, 'Matabele Nation', p. 5 (NAR, WI 1/1/1).

41. Bryant, *Olden Times*, 595.

42. Statement of Ginyalitsha, p. 3 (NAR, WI 8/1).

43. Mzilikazi's position in this respect was far from unique. According to Max Gluckman, 'The rise of a Zulu empire', *Scientific American*, 202, 4 (1960), 166, Shaka 'built his kingdom so rapidly that he had to leave untouched those chiefs who surrendered to him voluntarily'.

44. Bryant, *Olden times*, 123.

45. Wilkerson, 'Matebele Nation', p. 5 (NAR, WI 1/1/1); Gibson, *Story of the Zulus* (1903 ed.), 25, (1911 ed.), 30; Mhlagazanhlansi, *My Friend Kumalo*, 7. See also Becker, *Path of Blood*, 21.

46. Trevor Cope (ed.), *Izibongo; Zulu Praise-Poems* (Oxford, 1968), 132 + n.3; Mahlangu, *Umthwakazi*, 5. This view receives significant support from evidence given to Andrew Smith in 1835 by a top Ndebele official, Mncumbathe, who said that Mzilikazi declined Shaka's invitation to live near him because he feared Shaka 'would kill him and take his people'. See *The Diary of Dr Andrew Smith*, ed. by P. R. Kirby (Cape Town, 1940), II, 260.

47. Bryant, *Olden Times*, 586; Ritter, *Shaka*, 196.

48. This inference is mostly strongly supported by Ritter, *Shaka*, 205.

49. Statement of Ginyalitsha, p. 3 (NAR, WI 8/1): 'Tshaka had given him [Mzilikazi] another part of the country'; Mziki, *Mlimo*, 32ff, implies that Mzilikazi had never left the Insikwebesi region; D. Lindley, *et al.*, Mosika, 18 Aug. 1836 (ABC Arch.), describe Mzilikazi's post as being on the 'frontier'.

W. C. Harris, *Wild Sports*, 47, describes Mzilikazi's location as 'an important military post'; however, this description contradicts a passage he wrote several years earlier which is otherwise identical to his passage in his book. He wrote an anonymous article, 'The emigrant farmers', appearing in the *Grahamstown Journal* [hereafter, *GTJ*] (20 April 1837) which describes Mzilikazi's post as merely a 'kraal or out-station'. Possibly when he wrote his book for publication, he changed his wording to magnify Mzilikazi's importance.

50. Thomas, *Eleven Years*, 156, implies this view. Much of the historical material in his book was first published in 'Mission to the Matebele [*sic*], *Missionary Magazine & Chronicle* (London, Oct. 1864), 281-9 (throughout this book *Eleven Years* is cited except in cases where the article differs). In modern literature the notion that Mzilikazi was a favourite of Shaka's is most strongly expressd in Ritter, *Shaka*, 125, *et passim*.

51. According to A. Smith, *Diary*, II, 172, Ndebele men were 'still sing[ing] songs about Chaka' in 1835. On comparisons between Mzilikazi and Shaka in Ndebele traditions, see fn 5, above.

52. Krige, *The Social System of the Zulus*, 13, summarizes: 'Between 1820 and 1823 Shaka's armies swept Natal clean.' See also Bryant, *Olden Times*, 217ff; and Omer-Cooper, *Zulu Aftermath*, 33ff.

53. Moffat, *Matabele Jnls.*, I, 29, and *Missionary Labours and Scenes in Southern Africa* (London, 1842), 544-5; Thomas, *Eleven Years*, 156-7; [Joseph Moss], 'The origin and rise of Matabeleland', *Diamond Fields Advertiser* (Kimberley, 12 June 1880), p. 3; H. H. Methuen, *Life in the Wilderness* (London, 1846), 89 (Methuen got his information from Moffat personally in 1844, and it contains a number of points not written anywhere by Moffat himself); Vere Stent, *A Personal Record of Some Incidents in the Life of Cecil Rhodes* (Facs. rep., Bulawayo, 1970; first publ., Cape Town, 1925), 39-40. (Stent's account of Rhodes' meeting with rebel Ndebele leaders in 1896 contains Somabulane's recitation of the history of the kingdom); Statement of Ginyalitsha, p. 3 (NAR, WI 8/1). Other important sources on this campaign are cited below.

54. Bryant, *Olden Times*, 422. The geographical reference is Bryant's, but the story of the campaign itself is not original to his book. His *Zulu-English Dictionary* (publ., 1905) gives a much briefer version of the story, minus the identity of the Sotho chief (p. 52). For his fuller story in *Olden Times* (publ., 1929) he draws upon D. Fred Ellenberger, *History of the Basuto* (London, 1912), 203–4. Ellenberger in turn got his information from a draft article on Ndebele history written by A. A. Campbell in about 1905. Detailed notes from Campbell's article—recorded by J. M. Orpen—were found in Ellenberger's collected papers in Lesotho by W. F. Lye, who has generously given me a copy of his transcript of those notes. It is clear from this instance, and many others discussed in this study that Campbell's obscure article (which seems never to have been published) deeply influenced both Ellenberger's and Bryant's treatments of Ndebele history. For further comments on this article, see Lye, 'Ndebele kingdom', 92, n.26.

According to Orpen's notes of Campbell's article, Mzilikazi 'asked leave of Tshaka to attack a Basuto chief named Somnisi (?Ra Mnisi).' '(?Ra Mnisi)' was probably inserted by Orpen or Ellenberger (the transcript I have seen is typed, so I cannot compare handwritings), for in his book *Mlimo* (publ., 1926) Campbell gives only the form 'Somnisi' (p. 33). Ellenberger gives the name as 'Ra'nisi' (the substitution of an apostrophe for an *m-* prefix is common in such early Southern Bantu orthographies); Bryant gives the name simply as 'Ranisi', There can be no doubt about the interconnections between these three authorities.

55. Ritter, *Shaka*, 203ff, gives many details, but his account is inherently implausible.

56. A few sources hint at earlier raids, but give no specifics: Moffat, *Matabele Jnls.*, I, 29; Alexander Bailie to Chief Clerk, Bulawayo, 31 Dec. 1876 (Cape Archives, Cape Town [hereafter, CA], GH 19/12). Bailie's letter contains a long summary of Ndebele history based upon apparently fresh information he collected in Matabeleland while investigating labour recruitment for the Diamondfields. His correspondence from his 1876 trip is published in British Parliamentary Paper C.2220 (1879).

57. Mziki, *Mlimo*, 33. I know of no other source which confirms that Mzilikazi was circumcized then, or at any other time.

58. On the Ndebele in the 1830s, see A. Smith, MSS, XII, 106; on the dying-out of circumcision among the Northern Nguni generally, see Bryant, *Olden Times*, 98–9; Wilson, 'The Nguni', 125; and Hughes and van Velsen, 'The Ndebele', 66–7.

Before the nineteenth century Nguni circumcision had been associated with the organization of males into age-sets, or circumcision schools known as *amabutho* (sing., *ibutho*). As circumcision died out, these age-sets increasingly took on militaristic functions and they came to be known as 'regiments' to Europeans. This process was taking place among the Ndebele during the period studied in this book, but it is far too poorly documented to analyze meaningfully. Fortunately, evidence from the late nineteenth century is vastly superior on this subject. For a masterful analysis based largely on this later data, see Julian Cobbing, 'The evolution of Ndebele Amabutho', *Jnl. of Afr. Hist.*, XV, 4 (1974), 607–31. See also p. 237, n. 109, below.

59. If Campbell's assertion that Mzilikazi was circumcized very shortly before he left Zululand is correct, it follows that he could not have married into the house of Zwide until he reached the Transvaal. I shall return to this point in the next chapter.

60. 'The reminiscences of Ivon Fry', told to R. F. Windram, 1938, p. 85 (NAR,

FR 2/2/1). Fry visited Lobengula in 1887 and 1888. During the 1880s circumcision was said to be practiced only among the 'royal family'. See J. G. Wood, Unpublished journal 1887–1888, p. 75 (NAR, WO 1/4/1).

61. Peter Nielsen, *The Matabele at Home* (Bulawayo, 1913), 6.

62. I should add, however, that I am sceptical of the possibility that significant new evidence on this subject will ever be found.

63. A. Smith, *Diary*, II, 260–1; Mziki, *Mlimo*, 33; and Ritter, *Shaka*, 206, all agree on the geographical points.

64. In his draft article Campbell identifies the man as Qozo. See also Mziki, *Mlimo*, 33.

65. See, *e.g.*, Moffat, *Matabele Jnls.*, I, 29; Thomas, *Eleven Years*, 157; Methuen, *Life in the Wilderness*, 89; Statement of Ginyalitsha, p. 3 (NAR, WI 8/1); Wilkerson, 'Matabele Nation', p. 5 (NAR, WI 1/1/1).

66. Mziki, *Mlimo*, 34–5. Campbell gives essentially the same story in his 1905 article; his introduction of a first-person narrator in his book is merely a fictive device.

67. Shaka's anger is stressed by Moffat, *Matabele Jnls.*, I, 29; Statement of Ginyalitsha, p. 3 (NAR, WI 8/1); and Mhlagazanhlansi, *My Friend Kumalo*, 7.

68. This impression is conveyed in Ritter, *Shaka*, 203ff, who suggests that most of Shaka's armed forces were then engaged in wars to the south, thus leaving him short-handed at his headquarters.

69. Campbell identifies the hill and gives other important details in his 1905 article and in *Mlimo*. Ellenberger, *History of the Basuto*, 204, draws upon Campbell's article; Bryant, *Olden Times*, 422–3, follows Campbell closely, even on details omitted in Ellenberger. One wonders if he had access to Ellenberger's papers, which included notes from the Campbell article?

Other sources which corroborate points in Campbell's account include: Moffat, *Matabele Jnls.*, I, 29; Statement of Ginyalitsha, p. 3 (NAR, WI 8/1); A. Smith, *Diary*, II, 260–1; and Jackson, 'Statistical report', 1898 (NAR, NB 6/1/1). Methuen, *Life in the Wilderness*, 89–90, generally follows Moffat—from whom he personally got his information—but he adds that 'Moselekatze . . . only escaped under cover of darkness, he himself hiding in a tree. At daybreak he rallied his men . . .'

70. A. Bailie, 31 Dec. 1876 (CA, GH 19/12); Moss, 'Origin and rise'; Statement of Mkulani, in Donald Moodie, 'Matopo-Mawabeni: Statistical report', 11 April 1898 (NAR, NB 6/1/1). Bryant, *Zulu-English Dict.*, 52, has the fighting take place in the Drakensbergs, but these mountains are not mentioned in this context in his *Olden Times*. Presumably he altered his account after seeing Campbell's material.

71. A. Smith, MSS, XII, 197, and *Report of the Expedition* (Cape Town, 1836), 27. Moffat, *Matabele Jnls.*, I, 25, suggests he lost 'most' of his cattle.

72. The latter point is stressed in: Moffat, *Matabele Jnls.*, I, 29; A. Smith, *Diary*, II, 261; D. Lindley, *et al.*, 18 Aug. 1836 (ABC Arch.); Mziki, *Mlimo*, 43; Moss, 'Origin and rise'; and G. W. Stow, 'The intrusion of the stronger Bantu races, continued', ts., p. 171 (South African Library, Cape Town). Other sources which merely stress the total losses are: Bailie, 31 Dec. 1876 (CA, GH 19/12); Statement of Mkulani, in Moodie, 11 April 1898 (NAR, NB 6/1/1); and Jackson, 'Statistical report', 1898 (NAR, NB 6/1/1).

73. It is perhaps significant that when the Ndebele and Zulu next fought, in 1832, the fighting again took place in mountainous terrain. This may have added to the

confusion in traditions of the escape from Zululand. The reverse is certainly true, for it is clear that at least one element from the earlier episode found its way into traditions of the 1832 war (see section on the Mlulu Mts. on pp. 90-1, below).

74. This is explicit in A. Smith, MSS, XII, 107; and Mziki, *Mlimo*, 43-4. 'Unyoga' is also mentioned in Thomas, *Eleven Years*, 159, 204. Campbell identifies Nyoka in his 1905 article, which is followed by Ellenberger, *History of the Basuto*, 204, and Bryant, *Olden Times*, 423. Bryant adds more information on Nyoka's identity and location.

75. Moffat, *Matabele Jnls.*, I, 29.

76. Lindley, *et al.*, 18 Aug. 1836 (ABC Arch.). This letter is printed, in a slightly altered form, in Kotzé (ed.), *Letters*, 124-42.

77. This idea is most strongly expressed in Moss, 'Origin and rise'. See also Statement of Mkulani, in Moodie, 11 April 1898 (NAR, NB 6/1/1); Mhlagazanhlansi, *My Friend Kumalo*, 7; and Somabulane's açcount in Stent, *A Personal Record*, 40 (Somabulane incorrectly gives Dingane's name in place of Shaka's, but the context is unmistakable.)

78. Mziki, *Mlimo*, 41.

79. Letter of P. Lemue, Mothetho, 1 Jan. 1833, in R. C. Germond (ed.), *Chronicles of Basutoland* (Morija, 1967), 110. Lemue was one of three French missionaries who worked at Mosega on the eve of the Ndebele occupation of the western Transvaal in mid-1832. One of these men, Jean-Pierre Pellissier, visited Mzilikazi in the central Transvaal early in 1832. Ndebele soldiers and other of Mzilikazi's subjects visited Mosega frequently while the French missionaries were there. It may have been from such people, or from Pellissier, that Lemue got his information.

80. According to Fynn, *Diary*, 20-1, Mzilikazi, Beje and Mlotsha joined Shaka at the same time. On the resistance of the last two to full incorporation, see Bryant, *Olden Times*, 595ff. According to Bryant, Beje finally succumbed to Dingane in about 1830, Mlotsha to Mpande in 1840.

81. This estimate is explained in Chap. 3, below.

82. Fynn, *Diary*, 21, and in Bird (ed.), *Annals of Natal*, I, 68. Curiously, Fynn did not estimate *when* Mzilikazi left. I interpret his silence on this point as an indication that Mzilikazi had left Zululand more than one or two years before Fynn arrived there in 1824.

83. Bryant, *Olden Times*, 81-2.

84. *Ibid*, 70ff; Wilson, 'The Nguni', 116ff.

85. Lindley, *et al.*, 18 Aug. 1836 (ABC Arch.); Statement of Ginyalitsha, p. 3 (NAR, WI (NAR, WI 8/1); Mhlagazanhlansi, *My Friend Kumalo*, 7; W. A. Elliott, *Gold from the Quartz* (London, 1910), 32 (Elliott was an LMS agent in Matabeleland from 1888 to 1892); and Ritter, *Shaka*, 135.

86. Bailie, 'Journal', p. 42 (NAR, BA 10/2/1).

CHAPTER II

1. Ndansi Kumalo, 'The story of Ndansi Kumalo of the Matabele tribe, Southern Rhodesia', recorded by J. W. Posselt & M. Perham, in *Ten Africans*, ed. by M. Perham (London, 1936), 64. Ndansi got his story from his father, who accompanied Mzilikazi through this period.

2. See, for example, Somabulane's account in Stent, *Some Incidents*, 39-40;

David Carnegie, *Among the Matabele* (London, 1894), 15; Mahlangu, *Umthwakazi*, ch. 4; Mhlagazanhlansi, *My Friend Kumalo*, 7; Hughes & van Velsen, 'The Ndebele', 48; *etc*.

More recently, A. J. Wills, *An Introduction to the History of Central Africa* (2nd ed., London, 1967), 63-4, not only has Mzilikazi reaching the Transvaal via the Orange Free State, but he also has him crossing the Orange River on the way.

3. My use of this term is discussed in an appendix at the end of this book. Broadly, I argue that 'an Ndebele' was any person who recognized Mzilikazi as his sovereign.

4.See, *e.g.*, L. M. Thompson, 'Co-operation and conflict: the high veld', 403-4, which cites 'Ndebele tradition' respecting an Ndebele defeat by the Pedi as an example of a trustworthy tradition. Thompson draws on Bryant, but Bryant actually got his information from non-Ndebele sources. This case is discussed at length in the section on Ndebele-Pedi conflicts below.

5. The relationship between Bryant and Campbell's writings is discussed at greater length in an appendix to this study. Arbousset and Daumas' book was translated into English and published as *Narrative of an Exploratory Tour. . .* (Cape Town, 1846).

6. Bryant, *Olden Times*, 422-32; cf., Lye, 'Ndebele kingdom', 88-93; Omer-Cooper, *Zulu Aftermath*, 131-41; and Becker, *Path of Blood*, Part I.

7. Bryant, *Olden Times*, 424, 427. A map of the eastern Transvaal showing the various places historians have placed *ekuPumuleni* can be found in R. K. Rasmussen, 'Mzilikazi's migrations south of the Limpopo, c. 1821-27: a reassessment', *Trans-African Jnl. of Hist.*, V, 1 (1976), 52-74.

Bryant first mentioned *ekuPumuleni* in *Zulu-English Dict.* (1905), 52. This seems to have been the source of the claim that *ekuPumuleni* was 'not far from the Vaal River' in W. A. Elliott, *Gold from the Quartz* (London, 1910), 32. Elliott—formerly an LMS agent in Matabeleland—undoubtedly read Bryant's Zulu dictionary in the course of preparing his own dictionary of the Sindebele language.

Pelling, *Practical Ndebele Dict.*, 125, affirms Bryant's definition of *ekuPumuleni* as the 'place of rest'.

8.Lye, 'Ndebele kingdom', 88-9; Omer-Cooper, *Zulu Aftermath*, 131-3. Both of these authorities are otherwise generally accurate in their reconstructions of the complex relations among *Difaqane* peoples.

9. Moss, 'The origin and rise of Matabeleland'. Sobhuza's willingness to allow a Zulu enemy to pass through his country was proven earlier when he allowed Zwide to enter Swaziland after Shaka crushed the Ndwandwe. See Bryant, *Olden Times*, 320.

10. Msebenzi, *History of Matiwane and the Amangwane Tribe*, ed. by N. J. van Warmelo (Pretoria, 1938), 82; Philip Bonner, personal communication, Johannesburg, July 1972.

On Sobhuza's career, see Bryant, *Olden Times*, 318ff.; Kuper, *An African Aristocracy*, 12-14; Omer-Cooper, *Zulu Aftermath*, 49ff.

11. Andrew Smith, MS., XII, 107; Mziki, *Mlimo*, 45ff.

12. James C. Macgregor, *Basuto Traditions* (Cape Town, 1905), 43. Ellenberger, *History of the Basuto*, 139, holds that the Phuthing were driven west by the Ngwane of Matiwane. There is, however, strong evidence that Mzilikazi preceded Matiwane onto the highveld. See 'Statement drawn up at the request of the Chief Molitsane', n.d. [1852], in G. M. Theal (ed), *Basutoland Records* (Cape Town, 1883), I, 517; A. Smith, *Diary*, II, 391; R. Moffat, *Missionary*

Labours, 372; R. Moffat to parents, Griqua Town, 23 July 1823 (LMS, SA, 9/1/C).

13. Mziki, *Mlimo*, 45-50. Campbell gives essentially the same account in his unpublished 1905 article.

14. This chiefdom was named after its founding chief; later in the nineteenth century it was also known by the name of its current chief, Maboko (or Mapoch). For summaries of Ndzundza history, see N. J. van Warmelo, *Transvaal Ndebele Texts* (Pretoria, 1930); and Hermanus M. Fouries, *Amandebele van Fene Mahlangu* (Zwolle, 1921).

15. Mziki, *Mlimo*, 51; Ellenberger, *History*, 205; Arbousset & Daumas, *Narrative*, 294; Bryant, *Olden Times*, 424.

16. van Warmelo, *Transvaal Ndebele Texts*, 13.

17. Mahlangu, *Umthwakazi*, Chap. 3.

18. A. A. Campbell to C. N. C., Insiza, 1 April 1898 (NAR, NB 6/1/1). Cf., Mziki, *Mlimo*, 51ff.; Ellenberger, *History*, 205; and Bryant, *Olden Times*, 424.

19. Mziki, *Mlimo*, 54-5. The Ndebele were said during the 1830s occasionally to execute their own criminals by impalement, but this is the only case I have seen in which a defeated enemy was said to have been killed thus.

20. Transvaal Native Affairs Department [hereafter, TNAD], *Short History of the Native Tribes of the Transvaal* (Facs. rep., Pretoria, 1968; first pub., 1905), 55; van Warmelo, *Transvaal Ndebele Texts*, 10.

21. van Warmelo, *ibid.*, 17, 19, 80; T. M. Thomas, *Eleven Years*, 159; Mhlagazanhlansi, *My Friend Kumalo*, 8.

22. Arbousset & Daumas, *Narrative*, 294.

23. G. W. Stow, 'Intrusion of the stronger Bantu races', ts., 174. On this point Stow cites ' "Memoir of the Rev. H. Moore Dyke" who gives the date as 1828?' I can trace neither Moore Dyke nor the 'Memoir'.

24. Perhaps the most famous example in African history is the tradition of the Ngoni chief Zwangendaba's crossing the Zambezi River on the day of an eclipse in 1835. See Omer-Cooper, *Zulu Aftermath*, 65-7. Another example, the death of the Pedi ruler Thulare on the day of an eclipse, is discussed below.

25. Richard Gray, 'Eclipse maps', *Jnl. of Afr. Hist.*, VI, 3 (1965), 260, and 'Annular eclipse maps', *Jnl. of Afr. Hist.*, IX, 1 (1968), 153.

26. W. G. Moore, *A Dictionary of Geography* (Baltimore, 1966), 149, states: 'The upper parts of a river are situated near its source . . .'. On the interpretations of other historians, see fn. 7, above.

27. Bryant, *Olden Times*, 427; cf., p. 424.

28. *Ibid.*, 425. According to Bryant, Mzilikazi called out 'rainmakers' to end the drought; however, the Ndebele official Mncumbathe told Andrew Smith that he himself had never seen rainmakers before he visited Hurutshe country in 1829. See Smith MS, XII, 106.

29. Smith, *Diary*, II, 101.

30. [Alexander Merensky], 'Beiträge zur Geschichte der Bapeli [*sic*]', *Berliner Missionsberichte*, 20 (1862), 330-1; D. R. Hunt, 'An account of the Bapedi', *Bantu Studies*, V, 4 (1931), 283-4; H. O. Mönning, *The Pedi* (Pretoria, 1967), 22; C. Schulyer to Capt. M. Clarke, Fort Weeber, 31 May 1879: Report on the history of the tribes in the district (Pretoria Archives, Secretary for Native Affairs [hereafter, PA, SN], 1A). I am indebted to Philip Kennedy for providing me with a photocopy of Shulyer's very useful report.

31. TNAD, *Short History*, 31; Merensky, 'Beiträge', 332ff.; Hunt, 'Account', 285; Schulyer, 31 May 1879 (PA, SN 1A).

32. TNAD, *Short History*, 31, is apparently the earliest authority to associate Thulare's death with an eclipse, but it errs in assigning the eclipse to 1824. An annular eclipse occurred over South Africa in 1824, but it appears to have passed over a route too far from Pediland to have made much of an impression on the Pedi. See Gray, 'Annular eclipse maps', 153. Furthermore, it will be shown below that the Ndebele must have reached Pediland *before* 1824. Thulare was certainly dead before they arrived.

Merensky, 'Beiträge', 331, does not mention any eclipse, but he estimates the date of Thulare's death as 1824 for other, unspecified reasons. He reaffirms this date in an article published in a Natal newspaper article, reprinted in Parliamentary Paper, C.1748 (London, 1877), 143. Merensky worked as a missionary among the Pedi during the early 1860s.

33. Gray, *ibid*. In the previous chapter I called attention to Bryant's assertion that Thulare clashed with the Ndwandwe king Zwide at the Komati River after the latter fled Zululand (see *Olden Times*, 209). Assuming that Thulare did die on or very near to the date of the 1820 eclipse, we can safely conclude that the last war between Zwide and Shaka was fought in or before 1819. This conclusion conforms with the chronology of Mzilikazi's early career presented in the first chapter.

34. Hunt, 'Account', 285; Mönning, *The Pedi*, 22. Interestingly, Arbousset & Daumas, *Narrative*, 185, specify 1822 as the date of Mzilikazi's invasion of Pediland, although their chronology of subsequent events is unsatisfactory—as will be discussed below.

35. This version originated in Arbousset & Daumas, *Narrative*, 178; cf., Ellenberger, *History*, 205; Bryant, *Olden Times*, 427; and Lye, 'Ndebele kingdom', 89.

36. Merensky, 'Beiträge', *passim*; C.1748, p. 143; Hunt, 'Account', 285ff; TNAD, *Short History*, 31 (this source appears to draw upon Merensky); N. J. van Warmelo, *A Genealogy of the House of Sekhukhune* (Pretoria, 1944), 47; and J. A. Winter, 'The tradition of Ra'lolo', in *Report of the Tenth Annual Meeting of the South African Association for the Advancement of Science* (Cape Town, 1913), 98ff.

Winter describes his informant Ralolo as a Pedi 'induna' about fifty years old; the latter's account is given in an apparently paraphrased first-person form.

37. Several Ndebele-derived sources allude to the encounter with the Pedi: Thomas, *Eleven Years*, 159, 204, includes the name 'Utulwane' in his lists of chiefs whom Mzilikazi conquered in the Transvaal. Utulwane is the Nguni form of Thulare (see Bryant, *Olden Times*, 209), and it evidently represents an anachronistic reference to Mzilikazi's conquest of Thulare's successors. Robert Moffat, *Matabele Jnls.*, I, 87, mentions the Ndebele conquest of a 'Mokone' (*i.e.*, Sotho) town named *Marematsane*. This was probably the Pedi town of *Marema* mentioned by Arbousset & Daumas, *Narrative*, 185.

A. A. Campbell nowhere explicitly mentions the Pedi in his renditions of Ndebele tradition. He does, however, refer to Mzilikazi's flight to the Mlulu Mountains' in the context of an 1832 war between the Ndebele and the Zulu (see *Mlimo*, 59-60). In the next chapter I shall show how his statement is actually an anachronistic reference to Mzilikazi's 'flight' from the Zulu to the Leolu (or Mlulu) Mountains of Pediland in 1821-22. He evidently simply failed to recognize the correct context of his traditional evidence on this subject.

38. Mahlangu, *Umthwakazi*, 11, describes this period as a time when Mzilikazi

'was starving'.

39. Merensky, 'Beiträge', 333; Hunt, 'Account', 286; TNAD, *Short History*, 31; Winter, 'Tradition of Ralolo', 98; Schulyer, 31 May 1879 (PA, SN 1A).

40. Merensky, *ibid.*; Winter, *ibid.*

41. Merensky, *ibid.*; Winter, *ibid.*; TNAD, *Short History*, 31; van Warmelo, *Genealogy*, 47; Schulyer, 31 May 1879 (PA, SN 1A).

Arbousset & Daumas, *Narrative*, 178, hold that Mzilikazi killed Malekutu—Thulare's first successor as paramount chief—however, the various Pedi-derived sources cited throughout this section agree that Malekutu was actually killed by Phethedi and his other brothers.

42. Winter, 'Tradition of Ralolo', 98; Hunt, 'Account', 286; Schulyer, *ibid.*

43. Merensky, 'Beiträge', 333, 335-6; C.1748, 143; Schulyer, *ibid.*; Winter, *ibid.*, and 'The history of Sekwati', in *Report of the Tenth Annual Meeting . . .* (Cape Town, 1913), 329; van Warmelo, *Genealogy*, 47.

44. Winter, *ibid.*, and Hunt, 'Account', 286, specify a single year; cf., Merensky, 'Beiträge', 333, which states that Mzilikazi 'sich nicht weiter um das Land bekummert zu haben.'

45. Winter, *ibid.*; Hunt, *ibid.*

46. Winter, *ibid.*

47. Hunt, 'Account', 286.

48. *Ibid.*; Merensky, 'Beiträge', 333-4; Schulyer, 31 May 1879 (PA, SN 1A). A. Merensky, 'Esquisse geographique et naturelle du Sud-Est de L'Afrique', trans. by F. Polchet, in *Bulletin Société Belge de Geographie*, 2 (1878), 464, adds that Mzilikazi denuded Pediland of livestock, bringing on the tsetse infestation.

49. *Narrative*, 185-6.

50. Some of these historians are cited in fn. 35, above.

51. Winter, 'Tradition of Ralolo', 98.

52. Gerhard Liesegang, 'Nguni migrations between Delagoa Bay and the Zambezi River, 1821-1839' *African Hist. Studies*, III, 2 (1970), 324-5. Nqaba's career is also discussed in Bryant, *Olden Times*, 460ff., and Omer-Cooper, *Zulu Aftermath*, 57-8, *et. passim.*

53. *Olden Times*, 461; cf. p. 424 and *Zulu-English Dict.*, 52. Pedi-derived sources do not mention Nqaba by name; however, Merensky, 'Beiträge', 333, alludes to a band of 'Kaffern' (perhaps meaning Nguni in this context) under a chieftainess named Matyatye, or Ssete, who may have clashed with Mzilikazi around this time.

54. Bryant, *Olden Times*, 424, 461; cf., Liesegang, 'Nguni migrations', 320.

55. Bryant's account of Ndebele history gives only a bare hint of his having ever done field-work among the Ndebele (see, *e.g.*, reference to modern Matabeleland in *Olden Times*, 425). Furthermore, he could not have done field-work among Nqaba's people since they were scattered in western Zambia around 1840. On the break-up of Nqaba's band, see Mutumba Mainga, *Bulozi Under the Luyana Kings* (London, 1973), 75.

56. Arbousset & Daumas, like many European writers of their time, indiscriminately interchange terms such as 'Zulu' and 'Matabele' with reference to all the Nguni groups they discuss. See, *e.g.*, *Narrative*, 33, 75-7 , 133ff.

57. Just as the Pedi seem to have remembered Nqaba as connected with the Gaza kingdom of Soshangane, so may have the Ndebele. Thomas' list of Mzilikazi's conquests in the Transvaal includes the name Umzila (*Eleven Years*. 159. 204). Mzila was the name of the Gaza king at the time Thomas wrote. As the Gaza are

not known to have fought the Ndebele, perhaps Thomas' evidence is another anachronistic transference of Nqaba's identity.

58. By contrast, Arbousset & Daumas' assertion that Mzilikazi's troops returned against the Pedi in the year 1827 is more difficult to explain. No other independent authority suggest that the Ndebele attacked the Pedi after they themselves had left the eastern Transvaal.

59. Bryant, *Zulu-English Dict.*, 52, states: 'for some reason or other the two parties fought . . . ' *Olden Times* does not clarify this issue. Since Bryant is so vague on all specifics, including the geography and relative chronology of this encounter, he may simply have been wrong in asserting that the Ndebele and Ngoni of Nqaba fought each other.

60. One such example—that of the Hlubi chief Mehlomakhulu—is discussed below in the section on the expansion of Ndebele society.

61. See Omer-Cooper, *Zulu Aftermath, passim*.

62. Bryant, *Olden Times*, 425-6; Ellenberger, *History*, 205; Lye, 'Ndebele kingdom', 89; L. M. Thompson, 'Co-operation and Conflict: the high veld', 404.

Omer-Cooper, *Zulu Aftermath*, 133, alludes to an intermediary settlement between *ekuPumuleni* and Pretoria which he says was 'near the junction[?] of the Apies and Vaal Rivers'. The Aapies and Vaal Rivers are unconnected. Omer-Cooper's map (p. 132) does not clarify his statement.

63. Merensky, 'Esquisse geographique', 464. Cf. Map of tsetse belts in Wilson & Thompson (eds.), *Oxford History of South Africa*, I, 138. As will be shown in later chapters, tsetse fly seem to have halted Mzilikazi's northward migrations on two other occasions—in c.1827 and in c.1839.

64. Philip to LMS, Cape Town, 7 March 1833 (LMS, SA 13/3/B). See also, Philip to J. B. Purney, Cape Town, May 1833, in D. J. Kotzé (ed.), *Letters of the American Missionaries* (Cape Town, 1950), 33.

65. P. Lemue, 1 Jan. 1833; Lemue, March 1832; and J. Pellissier, 12 May 1832, in Robert C. Germond (ed.), *Chronicles of Basutoland* (Morija, 1967), 110-1, 87, 95, respectively.

66. Robert Moffat alludes to the Ndebele having been defeated by some unnamed people 'far into the tropics'. See *Matabele Jnls.*, I, 18, *Missionary Labours*, 545.

67. It should be borne in mind that the missionaries' references to Portuguese territory must be interpreted loosely in view of the tenuous hold the Portuguese had on the coastal region during this period.

68. Perhaps the Ndebele learned of the regions to the west from the Pedi. Shortly before the Ndebele invaded Pediland, the then-paramount chief of the Pedi, Malekutu, had commanded a major cattle-raiding expedition deep into the western Transvaal. See Merensky, 'Beiträge, 331-2; Hunt, 'Account', 284; TNAD, *Short History*, 31; and P. L. Breutz, *The Tribes of Rustenburg and Pilansberg Districts* (Pretoria, 1953), 63, 87-8, 181, 328. Breutz' account draws upon the traditions of the various western Transvaal peoples whom Malekutu fought.

69. TNAD, *Short History*, 55.

70. *Ibid.*, 42. Both the Khudu and 'Matabele' are named in a list of tribes living around the Makwassi River region in 1824; see Samuel Broadbent to WMMS, Maquassi, 31 March 1824 (WMMS, SA, II, 1824, no. 23).

71. Thomas Morgan Thomas, Jr., Untitled paper on Ndebele history, n.d. [1910?], in J. M. Orpen Papers (CA, Acc. 302, vol. 24, pt. 2). Thomas was an

N.C. in Southern Rhodesia at the time he wrote this paper. His remarks on the Khudu are similar—but not identical—to those in TNAD, *Short History*. The two accounts are clearly related, but the direction of influence is unclear.

72. On the battle and the circumstances surrounding it, see Robert Moffat, *Apprenticeship at Kuruman*, ed. by I. Schapera (London, 1951), 91-5, *Missionary Labours*, 354ff; William F. Lye, 'The Difaqane: the Mfecane in the southern Sotho area, 1822-24', *Jnl. of Afr. Hist.*, VIII, I (1967), 107ff.

73. R. Moffat to parents, Griqua Town, 23 July 1823 (LMS, SA 9/1/C). Cf., Moffat to brother, 23 July 1823 (NAR, MO 5/1/1), folio 562); *Apprenticeship*, 101. Moffat himself seems later to have concluded that these 'Matabele' were the Ndebele of Mzilikazi; see *Missionary Labours*, 372. See also A. Smith, *Diary*, II, 391.

74. J. Melville to A. Stockenstrom, Griqua Town, 1 Oct. 1823, encl. in Stockenstrom to Lt. Col. Bird, Graaff Reinet, 16 Oct. 1823 (CA, CO 2649, no. 161).

75. Moffat, *Matabele Jnls.*, I, 15-16. Moffat's Ndebele guide during his 1829 visit to Mzilikazi was one of the 'Mantatees' whom Mzilikazi captured in 1823. See *Matabele Jnls.*, I, 9; *Missionary Labours*, 525.

'Mantatee'—like 'Matabele'—was a widely used term for the predatory bands of the period. 'Yellow ' was an early European name for the Vaal River; the word 'Vaal' itself derives from the Dutch for 'tawny ' or 'faded', referring to the murky colour of the river's water. See Charles Pettman, *South African Place Names* (Queenstown, 1931), 89.

76. Ellenberger, *History*, 205-6.

77. A. Smith, *Diary*, I, 266; II, 117, 119-20, and MS, XII, 90. Ratsebe's desertion of Mzilikazi in 1831 is discussed in the next chapter.

78. This estimated date is simply the midway point between the battle at Dithakong (June 26) when the Sotho refugees must have started to move east, and the date of the colonial report of their collision with the Ndebele (Oct. 1).

79. See Samuel Broadbent, *A Narrative of the First Introduction of Christianity Amongst the Barolong* (London, 1865). Broadbent writes about his own experiences in the interior and he also draws heavily upon the writings of his associates, particularly Thomas Hodgson and James Archbell. Most of the original documents used by Broadbent can still be seen in the archives of the Wesleyan Methodist Missionary Society in London.

80. *Ibid.*, 93. See also R. Hamilton to Melville, New Lattakoo, 5 Aug. 1824, copy in Ed. Edwards to WMMS, Griqualand, 8 Jan. 1825 (WMMS, SA, III, 1825, no. 2).

81. These were the Kwena of Lettoyane; see TNAD, *Short History*, 21. Unfortunately, the chronological sequence in this account presents major problems, as it places Mzilikazi's outster of the Kwena after events which must have occurred several years after his arrival by the Vaal.

82. The Ndebele lived in the central Transvaal about five years (c.1827-1832), and in the western Transvaal just over five years (mid-1832 to late 1837).

83. See his unpublished 1905 article, and *Mlimo*, 62. Ironically, a newly-drawn map in the 1972 reprint edition of *Mlimo* shows an Ndebele migration route which does not even approach the Vaal River, even though the map faces the very passage referring their crossing the Vaal.

84. Some adherents to the Bryant version are cited in fn. 62, above.

85. *Matabele Jnls.*, I, 17.

86. *Ibid.*, I, 124. *Likwa* (Lekue, Liqua, *etc.*) was an Nguni name for the Vaal

River; see Pettman, *Place Names*, 156.

87. Smith, *Diary*, II, 261-2. For other explicit references to Ndebele occupation of the Vaal, see *ibid.*, II, 74, 98; Smith, MS, XI, 2, and XII, 107; Moffat, *Matabele Jnls.*, I, 89, and *Missionary Labours*, 511; Henry H. Methuen, *Life in the Wilderness* (London, 1846), 90. Methuen got his information from Moffat in 1844.

88. Eugene Marais, 'The blood trail in the Transvaal; tales of the Matabele recalled by a man who may be the last survivor of those who saw them . . . ', in *The Star* (Johannesburg, 17 Oct. 1925), p. 5.

89. The Ndebele were also credited in both African and European traditions with the building of stone structures in the western Transvaal which had been observed by the missionary/traveller John Campbell in 1821—eleven years before the Ndebele even arrived in the western Transvaal. See P. L. Breutz, *The Tribes of the Marico District* (Pretoria, 1953), 15. Moffat, *Matabele Jnls.*, I, 100, suggests that the organic building materials actually used by the Ndebele in the western Transvaal were unlikely to leave traces very long after the Ndebele left.

90. W. C. Scully, 'Fragments of native history', in *The State*, II (Johannesburg, Nov. 1909), 595-603; Ellenberger, *History*, 154-5; Bryant, Olden Times, 153; Omer-Cooper, *Zulu Aftermath*, 90.

91. Scully, *ibid.*, 596. J. N. Pelling, *Practical Ndebele Dict.*, 84, confirms the meaning of the town's name.

92. Scully, *ibid.*, 599.

93. TNAD, *Short History*, 17; Breutz, *Tribes of Rustenburg*, 88, 164, 182, 291.

94. The western extent of Ndebele settlements fell somewhere east of the Schoonspruit, according to Moroka, a Rolong chief. See Evidence of Moroko [*sic*], in Cape of Good Hope blue book, *Evidence taken at Bloemhof before the Commission appointed to investigate the claims of the South African Republic . . .* (Cape Town, 1871), 138. [This important document is hereafter cited as *Bloemhof.*]

95. E. Marais, 'The blood trail'. Marais implies that the hunter was Jan Viljoen (1811-1891), who knew Mzilikazi well during the 1860s. For other examples of Ndebele justifications of their raiding, see A. Smith, *Diary*, II, 169, 243-4, 252; Mahlangu, *Umthwakazi*, 7.

96. In addition to specific cases documented throughout this section, see Ellenberger, *History*, 199; Arbousset & Daumas, *Narrative*, 234; Mziki, *Mlimo*, 55.

97. See fn. 80, above.

98. On the Rolong, see Evidence of Moroko, in *Bloemhof*, 137; Jnl. of R. Moffat, 8 April 1826, in *Apprenticeship*, 215-16. The Ngwaketse campaign is discussed below.

99. Campbell to C.N.C., Insiza, 1 April 1898 (NAR, NB 6/1/1).

100. Cf., Mziki, *Mlimo*, 55, in which only a brief reference to Molitsane is made. 'Manyoba' is not mentioned until a chapter dealing with Ndebele raids into the Transvaal from Matabeleland (*i.e.*, after 1839); see pp. 96-7. Campbell's unpublished 1905 article is substantially the same on these points.

101. The distance was about 150 miles. Even this distance is only about half the distance implied by historians who suggest that the Ndebele raided the Ngwaketse from a settlement in the eastern Transvaal.

102. Isaac Schapera, 'A short history of the Bangwaketse', *African Studies*, I, I (1942), 4, and *Praise-Poems of Tswana Chiefs* (Oxford, 1965), 147; George W.

Stow, *The Native Races of South Africa* (London, 1905), 460ff.

103. Thomas Hodgson to WMMS, Vaal River, 12 Nov. 1825 (WMMS, SA, IV, 1825, no. 61).

104. J. Tom Brown, *Among the Bantu Nomads* (London, 1926), 254–5; Edwin Lloyd, *Three Great African Chiefs* (London, 1895), 146-8. Motswasele II was the father of Sechele I, whom Mzilikazi later attacked despite Kwena aid against the Ngwaketse (see next chapter). On Kwena genealogy, see Schapera, *Praise-Poems*, 122.

105. Brown, *ibid.*, 255; Lloyd, *ibid.*, 145–6. These two sources of Ngwaketse tradition, as well as Hodgson's letter of 12 Nov. 1825 (WMMS, SA, IV, 1825, no. 61), all assign responsibility for Makaba's death to the Ndebele in this attack. Thomas, *Eleven Years*, 159, 204, includes Makaba in his list of chiefs whom Mzilikazi conquered while in the Transvaal, but—as we have seen—his list is characterized by anachronistic references to famous rulers. His reference to Makaba is a clear indication that the Ndebele defeated the Ngwaketse, but it might be interpreted as a reference to a war which occurred after Makaba's death. Makaba's death is generally attributed to Sebitwane, who raided the Ngwaketse around this time. David Livingstone, *Missionary Correspondence*, ed. by I. Schapera (London, 1961), 175, 180, seems to have originated this idea; however, it is not clear whether Sebitwane (or other Kololo) told him this, or he inferred this conclusion from circumstantial evidence. Cf., Livingstone, *Missionary Travels and Researches in South Africa* (25th ed., New York, 1859), 98–9, *Missionary Correspondence*, 89, and Moffat, *Missionary Labours*, 434, for a broader perspective on this question.

The 'Manyoba' mentioned by Campbell in the quotation given on the previous page was probably an Ndebele name either for Makaba himself, or for the Ngwaketse generally. The Ngwaketse are rarely mentioned by name in Ndebele tradition, but the name Manyoba appears frequently in contexts which very likely pertain to the Ngwaketse. See, *e.g.*, Mhlagazanhlanzi, *My Friend Kumalo*, 9; Statement of Mkulani, in D. Moodie, 'Matopo-Mawabeni; statistical report', 11 April 1898 (NAR, NB 6/1/1).

106. Brown, *ibid.*, 255; Lloyd, *ibid.*, 148; Smith, *Diary*, II, 205. An Ngwaketse woman apparently seized in this raid is mentioned below in the section on the expansion of Ndebele society.

107. The connection between these two events is based on the assumption that the Manyoba campaign mentioned by Campbell above was indeed against the Ngwaketse.

108. Thomas Hodgson to WMMS, Plat Berg, 23 June 1827 (WMMS, SA, IV, 1827, no. 21, pt. 47), gives a first-hand description of Molitsane's band in March 1826. On Molitsane's career, see 'Evidence of Maletzame [Molitsane], taken at Colberg, 23 July 1830, before Commission of Inquiry into reports of cruelties against native tribes beyond the Orange River', (CA, Lt. Governor's file [hereafter, LG] 9, pp. 64-5); 'Statement drawn up at the request of the Chief Molitsane', in Theal (ed.), *Basutoland Records*, I, 517ff; William F. Lye, 'The Sotho wars in the interior of South Africa, 1822-1837', Ph.D. Thesis (UCLA, 1969), 105-10.

109. See J. A. Engelbrecht, *The Korana* (Cape Town, 1936). The Khoikhoi are better known in European writings as 'Hottentots'. The latter term is best avoided because of its pejorative connotations (see any edition of the Oxford dictionary).

110. Lye, *ibid.*, 111ff; J. S. Marais, *The Cape Coloured People* (Johannesburg, 1962; first pub., 1939), 32ff.

111. A. Smith, *Diary*, II, 261-2 (quoted above in section on Vaal settlements); Moffat, *Matabele Jnls.*, I, 89-90; Mziki, *Mlimo*, 55.

112. 'Statement of Molitsane', in Theal (ed.), *Basutoland Records*, I, 517; A. Smith, MS, XII, 129. Smith got his information from Hodgson (see fn. 108, above).

113. Livingstone, *Travels*, 98ff. (see also Livingstone's various volumes of published letters, *passim*). The best available summary of Sebitwane's career is Edwin W. Smith, 'Sebetwane and the Makololo', in *Great Lion of Bechuanaland* (London, 1957), 367ff. See also Omer-Cooper, *Zulu Aftermath*, 115ff.

114. 'Statement of Molitsane', in Theal (ed.), *Basutoland Records*, I, 517; E. Smith, *ibid.*, 377; Ellenberger, *History*, 308; Eugene Casalis, *The Basutos* (London, 1861; first pub. in French, 1859), 73.

115. Livingstone, *Travels*, 99.

116. A. Smith, *Diary*, II, 205, seems to allude to the Ndebele taking cattle from Sebitwane.

117. The decade of the 1840s is outside the scope of this study, but the problem of dating Ndebele-Kololo wars during that period is discussed in Chapter 5, below. See also R. K. Rasmussen, *Mzilikazi of the Ndebele* (London, 1977), Chapter 5.

118. See especially Omer-Cooper, *Zulu Aftermath*, *passim*.

119. Mziki, *Mlimo*, 52. The notion that 'dilution' of the original Nguni stock of the Ndebele contributed to the downfall of the kingdom is stressed throughout Campbell's book (see, *e.g*, p. 81).

120. van Warmelo, *Transvaal Ndebele Texts*, 15-16, gives three Transvaal Ndebele clan names (Mabhena, Msumanga, and Mahlangu) which appear in Mtompe Kumalo's list of *Enhla* (*i.e.*, Sotho-derived) clan names among the Rhodesian Ndebele; see Mhlagazanhlansi, *My Friend Kumalo*, 53. Very likely, members of these three clans were taken from the Transvaal Ndebele by Mzilikazi.

The *Enhla* are one of three ethnic divisions into which the Ndebele are said to be divided. The other divisions are the *Zansi* (Nguni-derived) and *Holi*, or *Tjabi* (mainly Shona-derived after 1839). The question of whether these three divisions made up a 'caste' system is an important and controversial one. Unfortunately, there is so little evidence pertaining to this subject for the period treated in the present study that I feel it is prudent not to enter the debate. For comments on the concept of 'caste' among the Ndebele, see Thomas, *Eleven Years*, 153-4; E. A. Maund, in Parliamentary Paper C.4643 (London 1886), 113; Mziki, *Mlimo*, 80, *et passim*; Hughes and Van Velsen, 'The Ndebele', 73-4; Lye, 'Ndebele kingdom', 100-101; *etc.*

121. Winter, 'Tradition of Ralolo', 98; Hunt, 'Account', 286. Merensky, 'Beiträge', 333, says that many of the Koni ruled by the Pedi chief Makopole 'submitted' to Mzilikazi, but he does not specify that any Pedi did so.

122. T. M. Thomas, Jr., Unpub. MS., p. 3.

123. Note, *e.g.*, Madubangwe's reference to receiving an Ngwaketse wife, below.

124. *Olden Times*, 425. Bryant makes this statement with reference to what he calls the *ekuPumuleni* period, which he dates to 1825 or 1826 (compare pp. 425-6). Hence, the period to which he refers overlaps the period of Ndebele settlements by the Vaal.

125. See Hughes and van Velsen, 'The Ndebele', 44, *et passim*.

126. Mhlagazanhlansi, *My Friend Kumalo*, 53, lists a total of 107 Ndebele clan names (*isibongo*), of which 63, or 59%, are Nguni-derived (*zansi*). On the limited role of the clans in Ndebele social organization, see Hughes & van Velsen, 'The Ndebele', 85; and A. J. B. Hughes, 'The restructuring of Ndebele society under European control', unpublished ts., n.d. [c. 1956], p. 337.

127. Hughes, *ibid*. I have seen no evidence which contradicts this conclusion.

128. Bryant, *Olden Times*, 425. A few exceptions to this generalization are mentioned in later chapters of this study.

129. Stow, 'Intrusion', ts., p. 173. The 'Gozane' named in this passage appears to have joined Mzilikazi in 1831 or 1832 (see next chapter).

130. Their careers are discussed in Lye, 'Sotho wars', 54ff; Omer-Cooper, *Zulu Aftermath*, 86ff; and Bryant, *Olden Times*, 135ff.

131. See fn. 90, above.

132. Bryant, *Olden Times*, 153, places Mzilikazi at the Aapies River during this episode; however, Madubangwe clearly refers to the Vaal settlements.

133. Scully, 'Fragments', 597-8.

134. *Ibid*., 599. The Kroonstad District and the Vaal River are about twenty miles apart at their closest points.

135. *Ibid*., 599-600; Bryant, *Olden Times*, 154; Ellenberger, *History*, 180.

136. Scully, 'Fragments', 600.

137. Ellenberger, *History*, 180.

138. See, *e.g.*, Omer-Cooper, *Zulu Aftermath*, 91 + n.

139. Campbell, 1 April 1898 (NAR, NB 6/1/1); A. Smith, MS, XII, 47.

140. The relevant contemporary documents are printed in Msebenzi, *History of Matiwane*, 239ff. See also Lye, 'Difaqane', 121-2, and 'Sotho wars', 64ff. Bryant, *Olden Times*, 143, and Ellenberger, *History*, 185, both attribute an Ndebele attack on the Ngwane as Matiwane's reason for crossing the Orange River.

141. Smith, MS, XII, 47. Matiwane himself submitted to the new Zulu king Dingane, but was soon executed by the latter.

142. Bryant, *Olden Times*, 424, 209. On the chronology of Ndwandwe movements, see fn. 33, above.

143. Fynn, *Diary*, 118.

144. *Ibid*., 122-9; Bryant, *Olden Times*, 586-94. Fynn was an eye-witness to this battle.

145. *Olden Times*, 425. Bryant seems to have gotten his information from Henry Fynn. See Fynn, *Diary*, 21; the same information was published in John Bird (ed.), *Annals of Natal* (Pietermaritzburg, 1887), I, 68.

The Ndebele appear to have puzzled over the fate of Sikhunyane and the other surviving Ndwandwe; see Thomas Baines, *Northern Goldfields Diaries*, ed. by J. P. R. Wallis (London, 1946), I, 274. Baines got his information from the trader Samuel Edwards—one of the first Europeans to visit the Ndebele in Matabeleland—who in turn got his information from the *induna* Mbigo.

146. In the previous chapter the subject of Mzilikazi's marriages to two of Zwide's daughters was discussed. In view of the isolation of the Ndwandwe from the Khumalo after Zwide fled Zululand (c. 1819), and taking into account the likelihood that Mzilikazi could not have married any woman until after he was circumcized (c.1821), it is reasonable to conclude that Mzilikazi met and married Zwide's daughters was discussed. In view of the isolation of the Ndwandwe from

147. Lye, 'Ndebele kingdom', 89, makes a similar argument with respect to the influence which Nqaba's arrival in the eastern Transvaal had on Mzilikazi's decision to move west. The persisting Ndebele fear of the Zulu is discussed at length in the next two chapters.

148. Smith, *Diary*, II, 262.

149. Peter Wright to LMS, Griquatown, 10 Sept. 1828 (LMS, SA 11/2/B); R. Moffat & R. Hamilton to LMS, New Lattakoo, 6 March 1829 (LMS, SA 11/3/B); W. van Ryneweld to Lt. Col. Bell, Graaff Reinet, 18 Sept. 1828, copy in Letters from Civil Commissioner, Graaff Reinet (CA, LG 2, no. 40).

150. This conclusion is reinforced by the impression given by the first European visitors to Mzilikazi in 1829 that the Ndebele had been living in the region for more than a year. See the account of the traders Schoon and McLuckie in J. C. Chase, 'Substance of the journal of two trading travellers . . . ', *South African Quarterly Jnl.*, I, 4 (1830), 402–7; Jnl. of R. Moffat's first visit to Mzilikazi, in *Matabele Jnls.*, I, 3–31; and James Archbell to WMMS, Plaat Berg, 31 Dec. 1829 (WMMS, SA, III, 1829, no. 37).

CHAPTER III

1. The basis for this date is discussed in the previous chapter. On the direction of the migration through the mountains, see TNAD, *Short History*, 17; Breutz, *Rustenburg*, 88, 164, 182, 291.

2. Traditional evidence for these prior invasions is presented in Breutz, *Rustenburg*, 430 *et passim*.

3. Moffat, *Matabele Jnls.*, I, 6ff; Lye, 'Sotho wars', 88.

4. Among the resistors were the Kwena of chief Mogopa and the Fokeng of Noge. See Breutz, *Rustenburg*, 64, 88; TNAD, *Short History*, 17. Some of these people might have been the followers of the 'chief of the Blue Cattle', whose crushing defeat by the Ndebele was described to Moffat by an Ndebele man of Sotho origin. See *Matabele Jnls.*, I, 9–10.

5. Smith, *Diary*, II, 175; Breutz, *Rustenburg*, 90, 257, 291; TNAD, *Short History*, 43.

   By 1832 Mzilikazi was estimated to have had thirty-two subject chiefs under him. See Statement of J. Philip, copy in W. van Ryneweld, Graaff Reinet, 3 Jan. 1833 (CA, CO 2743, no. 2). Philip got his information from various LMS missionaries in the interior with whom he corresponded.

6. Among those Sotho chiefs who fled north were the Kgatla chief Pilane: see Smith, *Diary*, II, 175 *et passim*; J. Tom Brown, *Among the Bantu Nomads* (London, 1926), 268; and the Kgatla chief Motsepe: see TNAD, *Short History*, 29. Those who scattered or fled in other directions included the Bahwaduba branch of the Transvaal Ndebele: see N. J. van Warmelo, The *Bahwaduba* (Pretoria, 1944), 25; Khosane's Taung: see TNAD, *ibid.*, 39; Breutz, *Rustenburg*, 164; and the Po of Mogale: see Breutz, *ibid.*, 176–7. The Kwena of Thebenare attempted to reach the Kwena of Sechele, but were intercepted by the Ndebele: see Breutz, *ibid.*, 148.

   Many refugees fled south of the Vaal River into the present Orange Free State Province. See TNAD, *Short History*, 41; Breutz, *Rustenburg*, 111, 125, 198.

7. These resistors included the 'Kwena' of Kubung: see TNAD, *Short History*, 15; and the people of 'Magah': see Eugene Marais, 'Blood trail'.

8. This conclusion is inferred from the traditions of Makau's Kgatla. See

TNAD, *Short History*, 29.

9. Smith, *Diary*, II, 117, 185.

10. On the Kgatla and Kwena living near the Pienaars River, see Breutz, *Rustenburg*, 90, 257; on the Hurutshe of Mokgatlha, see Samuel Rolland, letter of July 1831, in Germond (ed.), *Chronicles of Basutoland*, 80.

W. A. Elliott, *Handbooks to Our Mission Fields: South Africa* (London, 1913), 105, gives 1830 as the date of Mzilikazi's reduction of the Ngwato to tributary status. I have not been able to corroborate this assertion with contemporary evidence; however, Elliott's material seems to be based on archival research and is otherwise generally reliable.

11. Smith, *Diary*, II, 175-6, and MSS, XII, 120; Breutz, *Rustenburg*, 182, 219.

12. Smith, *Diary*, II, 251; TNAD, *Short History*, 39, 41; Breutz, *Rustenburg*, 88, 111.

13. Smith, *Report of the Expedition* (Cape Town, 1836), 25; and *Diary*, II, 98; W. C. Harris, *Wild Sports*, 189; James Archbell to WMMS, Plaat Berg, 31 Dec. 1829 (WMMS, SA, III, 1829, no. 37).

14. Archbell, *ibid*. Archbell was the only European to approach the Ndebele settlements in the central Transvaal from the south who left any description of his route.

15. Statement of Molitsane, in Theal (ed.), *Basutoland Records*, I, 517; Smith, *Diary*, II, 262.

16. Smith, MSS, XI, 2, and *Diary*, I, 158. Smith got his information from the Korana chief Haip, who was an ally of Molitsane. The chronology proposed here is extrapolated back from the firmer dates of subsequent events.

17. This figure is estimated from reports of casualties, the numbers of cattle taken, and the general impression derived from all available accounts. A ceiling on the number of Griqua/Korana who might have participated in the commando is suggested by the estimate of a Cape Colonial agent that the *total* number of 'Bergenaars' living north of the colony who had guns and horses was only 600. See M. van Ryneweld, Graaf Reinet, 18 Sept. 1828, copy in Letters from Civil Commissioner, Graaff Reinet (CA, LG 2).

18. Peter Wright to LMS, Griquatown, 10 Sept. 1828 (LMS, SA 11/2/B), is the best authority for this date. R. Moffat and R. Hamilton to LMS, New Lattakoo, 6 March 1829 (LMS, SA 11/3/B), interviewed Bloem himself, and they confirm 1828 as the year of his commando.

19. J. C. Chase, 'Substance of the journal of two trading travellers [Schoon and McLuckie], and of the communications of a missionary [Archbell] . . . ', *South African Quarterly Jnl.*, I, 4 (July-Sept., 1830), 406.

All citations of Chase's article given here pertain to Schoon and McLuckie's journal. The section of the article based on Archbell is merely an extract of his letter to the WMMS of 31 Dec. 1829, which I cite from the original copy.

20. *Ibid.*, 406, confirms both points. R. Moffat to brother, Lattakoo, 30 Dec. 1828, in *Apprenticeship at Kuruman*, 289, confirms date of the Ndebele attack on the Ngwaketse. See also Evid. of Moilo [Moilwe] and Magala, in *Bloemhof*, 315, 327. Magala was an Hurutshe who claimed to have particpated in the Ndebele campaign against the Ngwaketse.

21. Evid. of Magala, in *Bloemhof*, 327.

22. Smith, MSS, XI, 2ff. This passage is also summarized in Smith, *Diary*, I, 158 ff. Note that most accounts of Griqua/Korana attacks on the Ndebele such as Haip's tend to confuse the details of attacks occurring in 1828, 1831, 1834, and (occasionally) 1837.

23. Moffat & Hamilton, 6 March 1829 (LMS, SA 11/3/B), got this figure from Bloem.

24. Smith, MSS, XI, 3.

25. See, for example, Becker, *Path of Blood*, 89; and Omer-Cooper, *Zulu Aftermath*, 138. Omer-Cooper also errs in dating *both* Bloem's commando and the Ndebele pursuit of Molitsane to 1829. Lye, 'Sotho wars', 157, seems to imply that the Ndebele did not pursue the Taung beyond the Vaal River.

26. Evid. of J. H. Visser, in *Bloemhof*, 249. *Trekboers* were independent Afrikaner farmers who lived well beyond the centres of European settlements before the exodus of Afrikaner farmers from the Colony during the so-called Great Trek of the mid-1830s.

27. Chase, 'Substance', 406; Smith, *Diary*, I, 266, and MSS, XII, 90. Smith got his information from the trader Schoon, whom he met at Kuruman in Feb. 1835.

In his *Diary* (I, 378) Smith apparently inferred from Schoon's information that the Bloem invasion and the Ndebele campaign against Molitsane both occurred in 1829. Smith's error in this regard may be the basis for Omer-Cooper's identical mistake (see fn. 25).

28. Chase, *ibid.*; Smith, *Diary*, I, 266.

29. Evid. of Matlabi [Matlabe], in *Bloemhof*, 262. Matlabe's evidence is confirmed by Rolong traditions in TNAD, *Short History*, 8.

Note that Matlabe's account does not even hint that he joined Molitsane in attacking Mzilikazi. This is an important omission on his part, for G. W. Stow, *Native races of South Africa*, ed. by G. M. Theal (London, 1905), 515–6, holds that it was Matlabe himself who initiated the whole anti-Ndebele campaign. Stow further holds that in the course of the Ndebele pursuit of Molitsane's Taung *and* Matlabe's Rolong, Matlabe quarrelled with Molitsane and then defected to Mzilikazi's side. Lye, 'Sotho wars', 109, follows Stow's account.

Smith, *Diary*, I, 381. names Molitsane, Matlabe and Tawana (another Rolong chief) as allies of the Griqua in Barend Barends' 1831 commando against the Ndebele (discussed below). Since it is clear that Molitsane did not participate in that particular commando, it is possible that Smith was actually referring to Bloem's 1828 commando. If so, then Smith's evidence provides the only corroboration that Matlabe aided in attacking Mzilikazi in 1828.

Stow's account of Matlabe's participation in the 1828 commando is inherently suspect: why would Mzilikazi have tolerated Matlabe's submission so quickly after the latter had attacked him? Stow's failure to cite his evidence, the tenuousness of Smith's evidence, cited just above, and the apparent silence of Rolong traditions on this issue are all good reasons to reject Stow's conclusions here. Matlabe almost certainly submitted to Mzilikazi's rule *before* Bloem's commando.

30. Evid. of Magala [variously spelled Magaal, *etc.*], in *Bloemhof*, 326–8. Magala's evidence may be self-contradictory; he seems also to claim that he was a member of the Ndebele *impi* against the Ngwaketse which he dates to the same moment. However, since he calls that *impi* 'the first commando against' the Ngwaketse, he may actually be referring to an earlier campaign in which he participated. Such an error in his testimony would not be surprising in view of the long gap between these events and the time of his appearance before the Bloemhof Commission (1871).

Evid. of Visser, in *Bloemhof*, 249, confirms the bloodiness of the Ndebele-Taung battle: 'I examined hundreds of bodies, all of which had been killed by assegais . . . I saw no bodies of Moselikatse's people.'

31. Evid. of Matlabi, in *Bloemhof*, 262.

32. Evid. of Jan Pienaar, in *Bloemhof*, 347; Evid. of Maletzame [Molitsane], taken at Colberg, 23 July 1830, before Commission of Inquiry into Reports of Cruelties against Native Tribes beyond the Orange River, pp. 64-5 (CA, LG 9); Statement of Molitsane, in Theal (ed.), *Basutoland Records*, I, 517; Eugene Casalis, *The Basutos* (London, 1861; first pub. in French, Paris, 1859), 'Sotho wars', 212-13.

33. Archbell, 31 Dec. 1829 (WMMS, SA, III, 1829).

34. Moffat, *Matabele Jnls.*, I, 4.

35. Moffat's visits to the Ndebele and his own writings are discussed in the Appendix to this study (see p. 165). See also his two most important biographies: John Smith Moffat [his son], *The Lives of Robert and Mary Moffat* (2nd. ed., London 1885), and Cecil Northcott, *Robert Moffat: Pioneer in Africa* (London, 1961). The former work contains lengthy quotations from letters of Moffat and his wife some of which have not been published elsewhere.
    In his introduction to his edition of *Apprenticeship at Kuruman; being the Journals and Letters of Robert Moffat, 1820-1828*, I. Schapera makes an observation about Moffat's interest in the Tswana which would apply equally to his interest in the Ndebele: 'He was apparently interested in the BaTlhaping, not as people with lives of their own, but merely as souls to be saved.' (p. xxvi).

36. George Thompson, *Travels and Adventures in Southern Africa*, 2 vols. (London, 1827), I, 232ff.; Moffatt, *Apprenticeship at Kuruman*, 91-5. Thompson and Moffat left the only eye-witness accounts of the battle.

37. Livingstone, *Missionary Correspondence*, 174-5, 180. Livingstone got his information from the Kololo king Sebitwane, a participant in the battle on the Sotho side.

38. Lye, 'Sotho wars', 220ff.

39. See fns. 19 and 27 above, on the traders' evidence.

40. Mzilikazi also expressed interest in obtaining a cannon. See Smith, *Diary*, I, 263.

41. Archbell's letter to the WMMS of 31 Dec. 1829 (WMMS, SA, III, 1829) seems to be his only extant account of this visit. A severely edited version of this letter appeared in the Methodist *Missionary Notices*, VI, 355ff. This edited version was reprinted in Andrew Steedman, *Wanderings and Adventures in the Interior of Southern Africa*, 2 vols. (Facs. rep., Cape Town, 1966; first pub., London, 1835), II, 31ff. Extracts were also reprinted in Chase, 'Substance', 407ff.
    The original letter is difficult to read because of the heavy black editorial slashes drawn through parts of it. An example of one important editorial deletion is mentioned below in fn. 45.

42. Moffat, *Matabele Jnls.*, I, 4.

43. Mncumbathe (variously spelled as Nombati, Ukumbaze, *etc.*) appears to have held a position in the Ndebele equivalent to the highest ranking non-military officer, except for Mzilikazi. Little is known about his origins or how he attained his rank. He appears to have left Zululand with Mzilikazi and to have held the post of hereditary regent in the original Khumalo chiefdom. He left behind a son in Zululand named Khokhela, whom Henry Fynn described as 'a man of high rank' in the Zulu kingdom. See Fynn, *Diary*, 191; Bryant *Olden Times*, 277-8.
    Bryant, *ibid.*, 427, implies that Mncumbathe joined Mzilikazi after the latter was established in the Transvaal but no other authority corrobates this assertion. Summers and Pagden, *The Warriors*, 60, seem to draw upon Bryant's statement

in their assertion that Mncumbathe joined Mzilikazi in 1829—a conclusion which is certainly incorrect.

44. Mzilikazi's apparent coolness towards Archbell might have been partly due to the latter's indiscretion in allowing the Griqua chief Barend Barends to enter Ndebele territory in his company (Barends is discussed below).

45. Moffat, *Matabele Jnls.*, I, 27-8, 30; Archbell, 31 Dec. 1829 (WMMS, SA, III, 1829). Archbell's original letter contains the statement that Mzilikazi wanted white men to 'bring horses & guns'. The editor of the Methodist journal *Missionary Notices* (see fn. 41, above) appears to have been responsible for crossing out 'guns' in the letter and substituting '&c.' The edited version is that published by Steedman and others.

46. Mzilikazi frequently expressed his desire to visit Kuruman personally in later years, but he pointed out that the retinue he would have to take with him might cause a panic among the Tswana to his southwest. See Smith, MSS XI, 173; Moffat, *Matabele Jnls.*, I, 74.

47. Moffat, *ibid.*, I, 31.

48. Moffat, *Missionary Labours*, 278.

49. Prosper Lemue, [27] Nov. 1830, in Germond (ed.), *Chronicles*, 76, states that the Hurutshe were conquered by Mzilikazi 'a few years ago and became his tributaries.'
    Note that Magala's account, cited above, refers to Hurutshe participation in Ndebele campaigns against the Ngwaketse at least as early as 1828.

50. Samuel Rolland, July 1831, in Germond, *ibid.*, 80. R. Hamilton to Moffat, [Kuruman], 19 Nov. 1830 (NAR, MO 5/1/1, folios 878-9), specifies that the Hurutshe paid their tribute in 'corn'.

51. Lemue, Nov. 1830, in Germond, *ibid.*, 76; Hamilton, *ibid.*; John Baillie, New Lattakoo, 25 Aug. 1831, extract in *Evangelical Magazine & Missionary Chronicle* (April 1832), 163-4.

52. Hamilton, *ibid.*

53. Peter Wright to LMS, Griqua Town, 3 Nov. 1831 (LMS, SA 12/4/D).

54. Arbousset & Daumas, *Narrative*, 312, give us the date. All later authorities appear to draw upon them for the date, adding details from the longer account of the conflict in Casalis, *The Basutos*.

55. Bryant, *Olden Times*, 431-2, is an exception; he associates this campaign with the moment of Barend Barends' commando against the Ndebele. However, Bryant dates the campaign to March 1831—which may be correct—but Barends' commando can be firmly dated to the following July, as will be shown below. Lye, 'Ndebele kingdom', 92, appears to draw upon Bryant in associating these two events, but he gives only the year 1831 as their date. Lye also holds that part of the Ndebele men were then campaigning north of the Limpopo River—a problem discussed below.

56. Arbousset & Daumas, *Narrative*, 312, say that the *impi* was 'divided into five small battalions'. L. M. Thompson, 'The high veld', 400, calls the force 'a powerful Ndebele impi'. This assertion is highly speculative and seems to be made to help forward the author's argument that it was an important event in Moshweshwe's career.

57. *Ibid.* names 'the Lighoyas' and 'the Mantetis' [Tlokwa] as among the chiefdoms attacked by the Ndebele. Ellenberger, *History of the Basuto*, 208, names the 'Lihoya, the Baramokhele, the Batlhokoa [Tlokwa], and Bamokoteli.'

58. Smith, *Diary*, I, 143. Smith got his information at Sekonyela's own town in 1834. Ellenberger, *History*, 208, confirms Smith's evidence with what must have been independent sources.

59. Casalis, *The Basutos*, 22-3. Smith, *Diary*, I, 143. says that the Ndebele surrounded the hill for three days.

60. Casalis, *ibid.* See Peter Becker, *Hill of Destiny: The Life and Times of Moshesh* (London, 1969), xxii-xxiii, for maps of Lesotho and Thaba Bosiu.

There is some disagreement among near-contemporary authorities about the number of places on the mountain which the Ndebele assaulted; however, authorities agree that the Sotho repelled the attackers by hurling stones down upon them. See Arbousset & Daumas, *Narrative*, 312; Mtompe Kumalo's account in Mhlagazanhlansi, *My Friend Kumalo*, 7; Somabulane's account in Stent, *Some Incidents*, 40; and Alexander Bailie to Chief Clerk, Bulawayo, 31 Dec. 1876 (CA, GH 19/12). Bailie's account, however, may have borrowed from Casalis' book.

Another Ndebele traditional authority, Mkulani, alludes only to the Ndebele having been beaten by Moshweshwe in mountains. See Statement of Mkulani, in Donald Moodie, 11 April 1898, 'Matopo-Mawabeni: statistical report' (NAR, NB 6/1/1).

Casalis, *The Basutos*, 329-30, gives the praise-poem of one Goloane, whom he calls the Sotho commander against the Ndebele during this battle. Unfortunately, the poem adds no insights on the event itself.

61. Casalis, *ibid.*, 23. Casalis seems to have gotten his information from both Ndebele and southern Sotho informants. He was a missionary in Lesotho from 1833, and he met Ndebele envoys at Cape Town in 1836 (this embassy is discussed at length in the next chapter). Mhlagazanhlansi, *My Friend Kumalo*, 7, confirms the outline of Casalis' account, but adds the incorrect point that Mzilikazi himself fought at Thaba Bosiu.

62. Arbousset and Daumas, *Narrative*, 312. Arbousset and Casalis entered Lesotho together in mid-1833. They probably both had access to the same Sotho informants. In 1836, however, Arbousset was joined by Daumas in an exploratory tour of the northern Orange Free State region, where they collected information from other informants. Casalis, as was mentioned, visited Cape Town in 1836 where he met Ndebele informants.

The only other near-contemporary authority to comment on this event was Andrew Smith, but he mentions neither the cattle gift nor the burning of the fields. See his *Diary*, I, 143.

63. See, *e.g.*, John Widdicombe, *Fourteen Years in Basutoland* (London, 1891), 30; W. A. Elliott, *Gold From the Quartz*, 33-4; Omer-Cooper, *Zulu Aftermath*, 102-3; Becker *Hill of Destiny*, 89; L M. Thompson, 'Zulu kingdom', 400.

It should be stressed that no authority claims that the Ndebele attacked Moshweshwe more than once; several authorities specify that they did so only once. See Smith, *Diary*, I, 113; Casalis, *The Basutos*, 24.

Occasionally it is implied that Mzilikazi himself participated in the Ndebele assault on Thaba Bosiu, but there is no foundation for this belief. See, *e.g.*, Mhlagazanhlansi, *My Friend Kumalo*, 7; Hughes and van Velsen, 'The Ndebele', 48. Peter Abrahams takes this idea further in his highly romantic historical novel, *Wild Conquest* (Harmondsworth, 1966; first pub., 1950), 282-8. Abrahams has Mzilikazi leading the assault as a general of the Zulu king Shaka; he concludes the episode by having Mzilikazi and Moshweshwe meet face-to-face on friendly terms.

64. Omer-Cooper, *Zulu Aftermath*, 98, 140, mistakenly connects the campaign

against Moshweshwe with the Ndebele pursuit of Molitsane—which actually occurred in 1829, as has been shown. His error lies in his associating Molitsane with Barend Barends' 1831 commando against the Ndebele. As we have seen, Andrew Smith's remarks on the Griqua/Korana commandos often confuse details of different events. Possibly Omer-Cooper drew his conclusions from Smith; however, his linking of these other events with the campaign against Moshweshwe appears to be his own invention.

65. Ironically, although Peter Sanders' perceptive little book, *Moshweshwe of Lesotho* (London, 1971), expresses the same conclusion (p.13), the author of its back-cover blurb implies that the Ndebele were among Moshweshwe's most dangerous adversaries. Legends do not die easily.

66. No authority seems to specify that the campaign emanated from the central Transvaal settlements; however, Casalis, *The Basutos*, 22, estimates that the Ndebele had to march over 300 miles to reach Thaba Bosiu, thereby implying that the attack had to have been launched after the Ndebele moved north from the Vaal River in mid-1827, since the Vaal is only about 150 miles from Thaba Bosiu. In 1828 the Ndebele were busy fighting off Bloem's commando; in 1829 they chased Molitsane deep into the Orange Free State; in 1830 they were fighting the Ngwaketse and other Tswana chiefdoms to their west; in 1831 (as will be discussed) they fought off Barends' commando and campaigned north of the Limpopo; in 1832 they fought off a Zulu invasion and then migrated west. Finally, the French missionaries reached Lesotho in 1833; they would not likely have erred in dating the Ndebele attack to before the year of their own arrival.

67. Smith, *Diary*, I, 384-5; Hamilton, 19 Nov. 1830 (NAR MO 5/1/1); Evid. of Molema, in *Bloemhof*, 143. Whether each of these authorities alludes to the same incident or to different incidents is unclear.

68. Hamilton, *ibid.* .

69. Peter Wright to A. Stockenstrom, Griqua Town, 10 Oct. 1837 (CA, LG 495, no. 65), summarizes Barends' career. Wright was the LMS agent at Griqua Town, which was ruled by Andries Waterboer—one of Barends' rivals. Additional details on Barends may be found in Thomas Hodgson and James Archbell to WMMS, Plat Berg, 22 Oct. 1827 (WMMS, SA, IV, 1827, no. 37).

70. George Thompson, *Travels*, I, 232.

71. Moffat, *Missionary Labours*, 529; Bryant, *Olden Times*, 430.

72. Hamilton, 19 Nov. 1830 (NAR, MO 5/1/1); A. Kolbe to A. Berrange, Philippolis, 7 Oct. 1831 (CA, GR 10/35); Peter Wright, information given to Steedman, in Steedman, *Wanderings*, II, 29-30. P. Lemue, 27 Nov. 1830, in Germond (ed.), *Chronicles*, 76, adds that the Tlhaping chief Mahure planned to join the commando; however, Mahure seems later to have changed his mind.

73. Moffat, *Missionary Labours*, 566.

74. Kolbe, 7 Oct. 1831 (CA, GR 10/35). In assessing the responsibility of Griqua factions in these affairs, one must take into account that the evidence of Christian missionaries was occasionally coloured by the political affilliations of different missionary societies with individual communities. Thus, while the WMMS superintendent W. Shaw blamed Hendriks—whose town of Philippolis was served by LMS agents—for instigating the commando, the LMS agent P. Wright blamed another WMMS agent for misguiding Barends. See W. Shaw to Philip, n.d., in John Philip Papers (LMS, 'Odds, Africa', 3/1/C); Wright to Philip, Griqua Town, 9 Nov. 1832 (*ibid.* , 3/1/B).

75. Smith, *Diary*, I, 382; Methuen, *Life in the Wilderness*, 79; Breutz, *Rustenburg*, 257. These sources all agree that Pilane invited Barends to mount

the commando for this reason. Methuen got his information from a Griqua participant in the commando whom he met in 1844.

76. J. Archbell to WMMS, Plaat Berg, 28 Aug. 1831 (WMMS, SA, V, 1831, no. 29), names Sebego in this context. Rolong participation is described in Evid. of Baikhaki, in *Bloemhof*, 143; R. Moffat to W. Ellis, Kuruman, 10 Jan. 1833 (LMS, SA 13/4/E); Statement of J. Philip, copy in W. van Ryneweld to Chief Sec., Graaff Reinet (CA, CO 2743, no. 2); Mary Moffat to father, Lattakoo, 15 Sept. 1831, in J. S. Moffat, *Lives*, 172-3.

The participation of other Tswana chiefs is described or alluded to in: Kolbe, 7 Oct. 1831 (CA, LG 3); Kolbe, Extracts of Jnl. for 1828-31 and Jnl. for 1831, Philippolis (LMS, SA Jnls., IV, no. 102).

77. Statement of J. Philip, *ibid.* A similar sentiment was expressed by a Griqua participant: Evid. of J. Pienaar, in *Bloemhof*, 19.

78. See anonymous letter, dd. 15 Dec. 1831, in *Grahams Town Jnl.* [GTJ] (6 Jan. 1832).

79. Moffat, *Missionary Labours*, 567, expresses this view. Moffat's opinion on this issue is especially valuable since he personally knew most of the principal figures involved, and he had ten years to reflect on the matter before recording his view. Smith appears to confirm Barends' sincerity, for he says that Barends applied to the Governor of the Cape Colony for aid in Pilane's behalf (*Diary*, I, 382).

In 1829 Barends was described as 'quite deaf . . . his voice being almost gone', and as on the verge of death. See Thomas Hodgson to WMMS, Buchaap [Boetsap], 7 June 1830 (WMMS, SA, V [Albany], 1830, no. 22).

80. Moffat, *Missionary Labours*, 566. Among the modern proponents of this theory are Becker, *Path of Blood*, 140; and Lye, 'Ndebele kingdom', 89.

81. Smith, *Diary*, I, 383. Smith got his information from Griqua informants in 1834.

82. The chronological evidence for this affair is comparatively good. Some European traders encountered the commando just north of the Vaal River, and then wrote immediately to Peter Wright to tell him about it. James Archbell arrived in Boetsap shortly after the commando had left. See Archbell, 28 Aug. 1831 (WMMS, SA, V, 1831, no. 29). Wright's evidence is cited below.

83. Various authorities estimated the following ratios of horsemen/footmen: Smith, *Diary*, I, 381—300 horsemen/plus Tswana (no number given); Harris, *Wild Sports*, 233—1000/(no number given); P. Wright, in Steedman, *Wanderings*, II, 29—300/1000; anon., in *GTJ* (6 Jan. 1832)—450/150 (some of latter were said to have ridden on oxen).

Harris and the *GTJ* got their figures from Hendrik Hendriks; Harris got his information from a Griqua named David Berghover ('Doud'); Wright got his information from the unnamed European traders.

These figures may be compared to the estimates of casualties in fn. 116, below.

84. Harris, *Wild Sports*, 234, affirms that Barends remained at the base camp. Wright, in Steedman, *Wanderings*, II, 29, and Methuen, *Life*, 79, give the location of the camp. Wright also gives the dates, based on the letter he received from the traders. One of these traders may have been Aaron Josephs, who is known to have been in the region. See Baillie to LMS, 25 Aug. 1831, in *Evangelical Mag. & Miss. Chron.* (April 1832), 164.

Andrew Smith names Hooyman as the Griqua commander, but he may have erred (*Diary*, I, 384). Evid. of Jan Pienaar, in *Bloemhof*, 19, names Goliath

Jaagers as 'provisional captain' of Adam Kok whom Barends had sent with the commando. Kolbe, 7 Oct. 1831 (CA, LG 3), names A.[dam] Kruger as the chief of the Korana participants in this commando. References to these other men as commanders may reflect the inherent divisions within the commando.

85. Stow, *Native Races*, 389-90, implies hat the Griqua attacked at that moment *because* the Ndebele men were far off in the north. Becker, *Path of Blood*, 141, and Bryant, *Olden Times*, 430-1, both suggest that Barends sent spies into Ndebele territory, and that these spies discovered the absence of the men.

86. Smith, *Diary*, II, 117, 119-20. Breutz, *Rustenburg*, 9, 181, 364, identifies Ramabusetsa as a Tlhakwane chief living near the confluence of the Marico and Oori Rivers.

87. Smith, *ibid.*, I, 383.

88. Smith, MSS, XII, 116.

89. Smith, *Diary*, II, 292. Moffat, *Matabele Jnls.*, I, 17-18, 87, mentions other early Ndebele raids against the Ngwato. See also fn. 10, above.

90. Smith, *Diary*, II, 222.

91. Traditions collected in the Tegwane region of Rhodesia recall the invasion of Ratsebe ('Sipipi'), who was said to have been 'driven out by the Matabele.' See W. E. Thomas to CNC, Tegwani, 5 March 1906 (NAR, A 3/18/28). Thomas does not name his informants, but the context of his statements suggests that they were Kalanga.

92. According to Moffat, *Missionary Labours*, 545, Mzilikazi 'had carried his arms far into the tropics, where, however, he had more than once met with his equal . . . ' During 1835 Andrew Smith travelled as far north as the Oori/ Marico confluence, where he wrote that a chief named Mapeli 'of the Balaka . . . far to the north . . . defeated the commando of Mas. [Mzilikazi] . . . ' (*Diary*, II, 190). Elsewhere he makes it clear that the 'Balaka' he mentions above were 'Bakalaka' or 'Mashoona', and thus most probably Kalanga-speaking Shona.

93. Mziki, *Mlimo*, 63-4. Campbell gives essentially the same passage in his unpublished 1905 article.

I have been unable to identify 'Mgibe', the chief Campbell names in this passage. David Beach, personal letter, 26 Oct. 1973, comments that he also cannot identify Mgibe, but that the man might have been a minor chief of the Kalanga. He points out that known Shona chiefs with similar names, such as Chivi (Chibi) and Mugabe, lived too far to the east to fit Campbell's geographical references. T. M. Thomas, *Eleven Years*, 159-60, 204, lists fourteen chiefs whom Mzilikazi conquered during his years in the Transvaal. To his first rendition of the list he adds the comment that 'Whilst the Amandebele army was engaged with one of these chieftains [unnamed], a strong force of Griquas' captured Ndebele cattle, and so forth. This statement appears to allude to the moment of Barends' 1831 commando. I believe that the name from his list to which Thomas alludes might be 'Umjipa', and that 'Umjipa' is either a severe corruption of 'Mgibe' or that both are corruptions of a third form of the name. I must add, however, that Christopher Ehret (personal communication, 1974) feels the forms of the names are too dissimilar to be related.

94. Bryant, *Olden Times*, 429. Cf. Ellenberger, *History,* 207. I discuss the connections between these three authorities at greater length in my article, 'Mzilikazi's migrations south of the Limpopo, c. 1821-27: a reassessment', *Trans-African Jnl. of History*, V, 1 (1976), 52-74.

95. Bryant, *Olden Times*, 426, 429, 431.

96. Lye, 'Ndebele history', 90-2. Lye recognizes the connections between Campbell, Ellenberger, and Bryant (indeed, I am indebted to him both for pointing these connections out to me and for lending me his notes of Campbell's article); however, he fails to perceive that all of Bryant's references to raids against the Shona launched from the Transvaal derive from Campbell's single statement about one raid. Consequently, he accepts Bryant's assertion that the Ndebele were fighting the Shona shortly after their arrival by the Oori River *and* during the time of the Zulu invasion (which Lye correctly dates to 1832), *and* he follows Campbell in dating an Ndebele raid on the Shona to the time of Barends' commando in 1831.

97. Wright, in Steedman, *Wanderings*, II, 29.

98. Baillie, 25 Aug. 1831, in *Evangelical Mag. & Miss. Chron.*; Mary Moffat, 15 Sept. 1831, in J. S. Moffat, *Lives*, 171-2; Peter Wright, 3 Nov. 1831 (LMS, SA 12/4/D); Hamilton, Moffat, *et al.*, 26 Dec. 1831 (LMS, SA 12/4/D).

99. Mary Moffat, *ibid*,; Smith, *Diary*, I, 384; anon. letter in *GTJ* (6 Jan. 1832). Mziki, *Mlimo*, 64, names the 'the three [*sic*] military kraals, Mzinyati, Nloezi, Ngondweni and Nkenenkene' which the Griqua stripped of cattle. No other source gives the location of these particular towns.

100. Wright, 3 Nov. 1831 (LMS, SA 12/4/D); Smith, *Diary*, I, 383; Bryant, *Olden Times*, 431; Harris, *Wild Sports*, 233.

101. Smith, *Diary*, I, 144, suggests that Mzilikazi's actions were part of his normal strategy against invaders, and thus that he planned from the onset of the invasion to retake his cattle by catching the Griqua off-guard. Archbell, 28 Aug. 1831 (WMMS, SA [Albany], V, 1831) corroborates Smith. Smith drew this conclusion on the basis of evidence he got from Griqua informants as his expedition moved into the South African interior in 1834. He appears to have altered his views after visiting the Ndebele themselves in 1835, for in *Report*, 27, he wrote:

> It is reported that during the early movements of the Griquas, the king was in a most desponding state, and cried like a child, seeing no prospect of ever again recovering his property, but every chance of being left with a ruined tribe, as occurred when he fled from Chaka.

102. Methuen, *Life*, 79, Methuen got his information from a Griqua participant named David Berghover.

103. Contemporary and near-contemporary estimates of the number of cattle captured are as follows: Methuen, *ibid.*—'near 4,000 head'; Smith, *Diary*, I, 383—'nearly 4,000 cattle'; anon. letter in *GTJ* (6 Jan. 1832)—c. 6,000 head; Smith, *Report*, 26—'the whole of the Matabele cattle'; Wright, in Steedman, *Wanderings*, II, 30—'the whole of their cattle'; Wright, 3 Nov. 1831 (LMS, SA 12/4/D)—c.20,000 head; Harris, *Wild Sports*, 234—'vast herds'. Moffat, *Missionary Labours*, 566, says only that the Griqua took too many cattle to move out easily.

104. This is the dominant impression I have inferred from the evidence as a whole. Some sources suggest that a running battle lasting up to three days was fought; however, the figure of three days may merely derive from the fact that the Ndebele caught up with the retreating commando on the third day of its retreat, as will be shown.

105. The battle was fought near a hill now known as Moordkop ('Hill of the Killing'), located at 27° 23′ E. long., 25° 26′ E. lat. See government map, South Africa 1:500,000, Johannesburg SE 27/26 (Pretoria, 1958).
Smith's expedition approached Moordkop in 1835, and one member of the

expedition, John Burrow, actually visited it. See Smith, *Report*, 26, and *Diary*, II, 115-6. W. C. Harris visited the hill in 1836. See *Wild Sports*, 233.

Summers and Pagden, *The Warriors*, 61 + fn. 7, mention a still-living farmer who claims that the bones from this battle are still to be seen on his property; however, they place the location of his farm about 50 miles southeast of Moordkop.

106. Wright, in Steedman, *Wanderings*, II, 29-30; Smith, *Diary*, I, 382; Archbell, 28 Aug. 1831 (WMMS, SA [Albany], V, 1831); Kolbe, 7 Oct. 1831 (CA, LG 3), all agree on the timing.

Methuen, *Life*, 79-80; Smith, *Report*, 27, and *Diary*, II, 116, affirm that no watch was set by the sleeping commando.

107. That they were the older men is specified by Smith, *Diary*, II, 262, and Moffat, *Missionary Labours*, 567. Campbell, unpub. 1905 article, and Mziki, *Mlimo*, 64, name the veteran Mhlope *ibutho* (or 'regiment'). Wright, in Steedman, *Wanderings*, II, 30, calls them an 'army of reserve'. In contrast to the above authorities, Harris, *Wild Sports*, 234, calls them 'a band of unpracticed soldiers, who had been hastily called together to meet the emergency'. Possibly Harris confuses this incident with elements of yet another Griqua/Korana commando in 1834, when, it appears, untrained youths actually did defeat the invaders (see Chapter 4, fn. 61, below).

108. Smith, *Diary*, I, 383-4. Jan Pienaar's own account was recorded at Bloemhof in 1871.

109. Methuen, *Life*, 80; Kolbe, Jnl. for 1831 (LMS, SA Jnls., IV, no. 102); Archbell, 28 Aug. 1831 (WMMS, SA [Albany], V, 1831).

110. Statement of J. Philip (CA, CO 2743, no. 2) exemplifies the stress of Europeans upon the Ndebele mode of fighting.

111. No authority suggests that the Ndebele counter-attack did not occur in darkness; most specify it occurred shortly before dawn. See Smith, *Diary*, I, 384, and *Report*, 27; Harris, *Wild Sports*, 233; Methuen, *Life*, 80.

112. Smith, *Diary*, II, 115-6. John Burrow, *Travels in the Wilds of Africa*, ed. by P. R. Kirby (Cape Town, 1971), 58, confirms the point about the cattle.

113. Smith, *Diary*, I, 290, 384; Kolbe, Jnl. for 1831 (LMS, SA Jnls., IV, no. 102).

114. Mziki, *Mlimo*, 64.

115. This point is made by almost all sources.

116. Estimates of the number of Griqua/Korana killed: Wright, in Steedman, *Wanderings*, II, 30—400 men; Kolbe, Jnl. for 1831 (LMS, SA Jnls., IV)—80 Griqua & 100 Korana killed, 100 men missing; Evid. of Pienaar, in *Bloemhof*, 19—600 men; A. Berrange to Acting Civil Commissioner, Graaff Reinet, 1 Sept. 1831 (CA, LG 3)—300 men; anon. letter in *GTJ* (6 Jan. 1832)—100+ Griqua, 100's of Tswana; Methuen, *Life* 78—400 men.

Estimates of the number of survivors: Berrange, *ibid.*—five to six men; Harris, *Wild Sports*, 234—two men; Bryant, *Olden Times*, 431—three men. These figures are stated explicitly in their respective sources. If we subtract the numbers of men said to have been killed from the numbers said to have participated in the commando in other sources, we get these estimates of the number of survivors: Evid of Pienaar, *ibid.*—300 men; Methuen, *ibid.*—400 men. Most other sources only specify that 'a few' Griqua survived the commando.

Those sources which state that only two or three men survived must grossly exaggerate the Griqua casualties. Besides Barends himself, the names of at least three other survivors have already been mentioned in the present study: Jan

Pienaar, David Berghover, and Hendrik Hendriks. Careful perusal of the documents cited here would no doubt reveal the names of many other individual survivors.

The above estimates of Griqua/Korana casualties should be compared to the estimates of the size of the original commando listed in fn. 83, above.

117. The accounts of Tswana participants are not as numerous as those of the Griqua/Korana. At least one Tswana participant, however, told his story to the Bloemhof Commission in 1871. See Evid. of Baikhaki [a Rolong man], in *Bloemhof*, 142-3.

118. Letter of H. Fynn to *GTJ*, dd. 21 Feb. 1832, reprinted, in Fynn, *Diary*,

119. Smith, *Report*, 27, and Methuen, *Life* 80, both estimate that more half the Griqua losses might have been self-inflicted.

120. Burrow visited the battlefield four years later and reported to Andrew Smith that all the horse carcasses were left in a straight line, indicating that they had been killed while still tethered together. See Smith, *Diary*, II, 116. Wright, in Steedman, *Wanderings*, II, 30, mentions that the horses were burned.

121. Archbell, 28 Aug. 1831 (WMMS, SA [Albany], V, 1831), estimates that the Griqua lost 200 horses and 100 muskets. Wright, in Steedman, *Wanderings*, II, 30, estimates that 250 horses and 300 guns were lost. Methuen, *Life*, 80, adds that when the Ndebele burned the captured weapons, more than 100 pounds of gunpowder and several loaded guns exploded. It is not, however, clear how Methuen's Griqua informant, David Berghover, would have known this fact.

122. Samuel Rolland, letter of 5 Dec. 1831, in Germond (ed.), *Chronicles*, 84.

123. Mary Moffat, 15 Sept. 1831, in J. S. Moffat, *Lives,* 173; Baillie, 25 Aug. 1831, in *Evangelical Mag. & Miss. Chron.* (April 1832), 164; Smith, *Diary*, I, 289-90.

124. See also, Harris, *Wild Sports*, 234; Smith, *Report*, 27.

125. Statement of J. Philip (CA, CO 2743, no. 2).

126. *Ibid*. estimates that Mzilikazi owned 400 guns and 300, and asserts that he was trading for ammunition. Robert Moffat to Richard Moffat, Kuruman, 15 Aug. 1832 (NAR, MO 5/1/1), estimates that Mzilikazi had more than 50 guns, and that he was attempting to get ammunition through missionaries. Jean Pellissier, Mosega, 12 May 1832, in Germond (ed.), *Chronicles*, 93-4, visited Mzilikazi early in 1832 and estimated that he had about 60 'rifles'.

On the identity of various traders who visited the Ndebele through this period, see E. C. Tabler, *The Far Interior* (Cape Town, 1955), 189. See also Ngwabi M. B. Bhebe, 'Ndebele trade in the nineteenth century', *Jnl. of African Studies*, I, 1 (1974), 87ff.

127. See, *e.g.*, David Lindley to Anderson, Mosika, 29 Aug. 1836 (ABC Arch.).

128. Smith, *Diary*, I, 144.

129. See, *e.g.*, John Mackenzie, *Ten Years North of the Orange River* (Edinburgh, 1871), 311.

130. Moffat, *Matabele Jnls.*, I, 30 n.3. For examples of the use of riding oxen among other southern African societies, see Monica Wilson, 'The Nguni people', 108, and the illustrations throughout Wilson and Thompson's *Oxford History of South Africa*, vol. I.

T. V. Bulpin, *Lost Trails of the Transvaal* (Johannesburg, 1965), 62, describes a battle between the Ndebele and the Voortrekkers (Boers) in 1837 in which the Ndebele are said to have ridden into combat on oxen with sharpened horns. Bulpin does not cite his sources, and I know of no corroboration for this somewhat fantastic story.

Harris, *Wild Sports*, 166, tells of how he and his companion attempted to teach some Ndebele men to ride horses, but they found that the Ndebele 'tumbled off the horse as fast as they ascended'. The Ndebele were evidently quite inexperienced in dealing with riding animals, but a few individuals did learn to ride horses during the 1830s. For an interesting description of attempts to teach the Ndebele to ride horses in the late 1880s, see Frank Johnson, *Great Days* (London, 1940), 43-4.

131. Burrow, *Travels*, 63, and Moffat, *Matabele Jnls.*, I, 125, found only one Ndebele horse still alive in 1835. Harris, *Wild Sports*, 166, found none alive in 1836.

132. The Ndebele thus contrasted with the basically sedentary Southern Sotho of Moshweshwe who became adept with both horses and guns.

133. Smith, *Diary*, II, 64-5. See also *Diary*, I, 231, on Mzilikazi's reconnaissance parties to Boetsap several years later.

More nearly contemporary observers give a somewhat different picture of Ndebele threats against the Griqua in late 1831. Andrew Steedman visited Griqua Town in October 1831, when he noted that people there daily expected an Ndebele attack (*Wanderings*, II, 25ff). See also Wright, in *ibid.*, II, 30-31.

134. Smith, *Diary*, II, 39; Hamilton, Moffat, *et al.*, 26 Dec. 1831 (LMS, SA 12/4/D).

135. Moffat, *Matabele Jnls.*, I, 28.

136. *Ibid.*, I, 128. The comment about 'striplings' refers to an Ndebele-Griqua/Korana encounter in 1834.

137. As was mentioned earlier in this chapter, tsetse fly lay to the north—a direction in which the Ndebele seem never, or rarely, to have raided.

138. Rolland, 5 Dec. 1831, in Germond (ed.), *Chronicles*, 84. For this time the Fench missionaries are the best European chroniclers of Ndebele affairs. They were then attempting to start a mission among the Hurutshe by the Marico River, where they frequently met Ndebele envoys. They corresponded regularly with other missionaries, and much of their information was passed on to the LMS and to the Colonial government by John Philip, the South African superintendent of the LMS.

139. Breutz, *Rustenburg*, 257; J. T. Brown, *Nomads*, 268; Smith, *Diary*, II, 152, 154-5, 165, 175, 186, 190, 218.

When Pilane returned to the Elands River in 1838, Molefi quietly abdicated in his favour.

140. Mary Moffat, 15 Sept. 1831, in J. S. Moffat, *Lives*, 173, and letter to father, Lattakoo, 8 May 1832 (NAR, MO 5/1/1, folios 906-7).

141. P. Lemue, Mosega, March 1832, in Germond (ed.), *Chronicles*, 87. Lemue drew this inference from information given him by Ndebele messengers to Mosega.

142. J. Pellissier, Mosega, 12 May 1832, in Germond (ed.), *Chronicles*, 90-7.

143. Contemporary documents contain a number of vague allusions to Zulu-Ndebele clashes through the 1830s. Most of these were probably merely rumours, but some might well refer to minor, chance encounters between small parties of men.

144. G. W. Stow, 'The intrusion of the stronger Bantu races', ts., p. 180; Ellenberger, *History*, 207; Bryant, *Olden Times*, 429-30; L. M. Thompson, 'The high veld', 404; Cope, *Izibongo*, 8; Summers and Pagden, *The Warriors*, 60.

145. Perhaps the worst offender is Peter Becker who uses the better part of two

chapters to discuss the two purported wars in each of two books: *Path of Blood* [re Mzilikazi], 131–4, 150–1; *Rule of Fear* [re Dingane] (London, 1964), 100–4, 143–4.

Other$ who accept the two-war theory are Omer-Cooper, *Zulu Aftermath*, 138–9, 142; D J. Kotzé, 'Die eerste Amerikaanse sendelinge onder die Matebeles', in *Argiefjaarboek vir Suid-Afrikaanse Geskiedenis*, 13de jaargang, deel I (Pretoria, 1950), 199–200; Bulpin, *Lost Trails*, 35–6.

Others who hold that the Ndebele and Zulu fought more than one war before 1837, but who are vaguer than the above named authorities in their dating, include: Preller, *Lobengula*, 28; Hughes and van Velsen, 'The Ndebele', 48; Posselt, *Fact & Fiction*, 164, Oliver Ransford, *The Rulers of Rhodesia* (London, 1968), 89.

146. H. Fynn to anon., n.d., in *GTJ* (21 Sept. 1832); Fynn, letter dd. Aug. 1832, in *GTJ*, reprinted in Fynn, *Diary,* 213, 218.

147. Editors' introduction, in Fynn, *Diary*, xii.

148. Bird (ed.), *Annals of Natal*, I, 68; Fynn, *Diary, 21*.

149. Smith, *Diary*, II, 261, and MSS, XII, 107 (both written in 1835); Campbell, unpub. article; Mziki, *Mlimo*, 58–9.

150. Zulu-derived evidence: H. Fynn (see fn. 146, above); C. J. Pickham to B. Norden, Amapondo Land, 19 Sept. 1832, in *GTJ* (12 Oct. 1832); James Cawood to B. Norden, Port Natal, 10 Sept. 1832, in *GTJ* (22 Nov. 1832); Samuel Young to James Townley, Wesleyville, 25 Sept. 1832 (WMMS, SA [Albany], V, 1832, no. 30).

Ndebele-derived evidence: S. Rolland, 25 Sept. 1832, in Germond (ed.), *Chronicles*, 103; John Baillie to LMS, Kuruman, 3 Jan. 1833 (LMS, SA 13/4/E); R. Moffat to W. Ellis, Kuruman, 10 Jan. 1833 (LMS, SA 13/4/E).

151. W. A. Elliott, *South Africa*, 105, is an exception. Elliott evidently studied LMS archival records to obtain the correct date.

152. Bryant, *Olden Times*, 429–30.

153. L. M. Thompson, 'Zulu kingdom', 351. On the impetus to wage war among the Ndebele at a later period, see Moffat, *Matabele Jnls.*, I, 322; Mackenzie, *Ten Years*, 310–11; Elliott, *Gold From the Quartz*, 74; Thomas Leask, *Southern African Diaries . . . 1865–1870*, ed. by J. P. R. Wallis (London, 1954), 71.

154. Andrew Smith visited Dingane in April 1832. He wrote nothing about any Zulu preparations for war, but he did mention that the Zulu were aware of Mzilikazi's prosperity at that date. See *Andrew Smith and Natal*, ed. by P. R. Kirby (Cape Town, 1955), 86-7.

155. See, *e.g.*, Bryant, *Olden Times*, 429, 595–603; Ritter, *Shaka Zulu*, 152. Somabulane, in Stent, *Some Incidents*, 40, alludes to Dingane's jealousy of Mzilikazi; however, the context of his remarks suggest that he was talking about Shaka, not Dingane.

156. Allen F. Gardiner, *Narrative of a Journey to the Zoolu Country* (London, 1836), 48–50; Bryant, *Olden Times*, 429-30; Cope, *Izibongo*, 178–80.

157. H. Fynn, letter dd. 21 Feb. 1832, in *GTJ*, reprinted in *Diary*, 218.

158. Pickham, 19 Sept. 1832, in *GTJ* (12 Oct. 1832), suggests that the Zulu force 'did not encounter the main army' of Mzilikazi. Smith, *Diary*, II, 78, notes that the Ndebele who fought the Zulu were all 'men', as opposed to youths (*majaha*) who were normally the first-line forces. Moffat, *Matabele Jnls.*, I, 69, corroborates Smith. By contrast, J. Baillie, 3 Jan. 1833 (LMS, SA 13/4/E), says it was the 'young soldiers' who made the counter-counter-attack against the Zulu.

159. Fynn, letter of Aug. 1832, in *Diary*, 218.

160. Arbousset and Daumas, *Narrative*, 186, give the Zulu commander's name as Omthlela, which Bryant, *Olden Times*, 429, corrects to Ndlela. Bryant further identifies Ndlela as the son of Sompisi and as 'the newly-installed Zulu generalissimo'. He names one Nzobo as Ndelela's 'lieutenant-general'. Stow, 'Intrusion', ms., p. 242 (the ts. contains an error here) calls Ndlela the commander of the 'noted Omobapankue regiment'. Gardiner, *Narrative*, 48, names a 'Georgo' as the commander who fought Mzilikazi. Since this name is clearly an altered form of the name of the British king, 'Georgo' might well have been Ndlela himself.

The impression that the force was large derives from reports of casualties which circulated in Zululand immediately after its return.

161. Smith, *Diary*, II, 74-5, names the 'Matok' as a Sotho group which joined the Zulu *impi*. The Matok were possibly a branch of the Tlokwa; however, Smith specifies that they were not associated with Sekonyela's Tlokwa. According to Breutz, *Rustenburg*, 90, some Kwena fought on the Ndebele side during this war.

162. Cf. Bryant, *Olden Times*, 429-30; Arbousset and Daumas, *Narrative*, 186; and account of Madubangwe, in W. C. Scully, 'Fragments', 598. According to Arbousset and Daumas, Ndlela freed Pedi 'slaves' whom Mzilikazi had forced to build his stockades at Mhlahlandlela; however, no other source corroborates them.

Unfortunately the difficulty of interpreting evidence dealing with this war is enhanced by the tendency of later informants to confuse aspects of it with those of the 1837 Zulu-Ndebele war. See, *e.g.*, Evid. of Magala and Gatsietsoe, in *Bloemhof*, 327-8, 188-90.

163. See, *e.g.*, Lye, 'Ndebele kingdom', 92; Bryant, *Olden Times*, 430; Summers and Pagden, *The Warriors*, 60.

164. Campbell, unpub. article. This same account is elaborated somewhat in Mziki, *Mlimo*, 58-9. Ellenberger, Bryant, and Lye all follow Campbell.

165. Despite these objections, the tradition may be based upon an actual incident. Fynn, letter of 21 Feb. 1832, in *Diary*, 218, mentions that a high Ndebele commander (unnamed) deserted to Dingane after having failed to annihilate Barends' whole force in 1831. However, Fynn further states that this same man returned to Mzilikazi. Since Fynn was writing in Feb. 1832, the unnamed man could not have guided the Zulu *impi* against the Ndebele; however, his disappearance shortly before the Zulu invasion may have contributed to later suspicions that he was responsible for the attackers finding the Ndebele.

166. Rolland, 25 Sept. 1832, in Germond (ed.), *Chronicles*, 103; Statement of J. Philip (CA, CO 2743, no. 2); Stow, 'Intrusion', ts., p. 180.

There is some uncertainty as to whether or not the Zulu burned the Ndebele towns they sacked. Andrew Smith visited some of these places three years later, but he was not sure whether the towns had been burned by the Zulu or by the Ndebele themselves when the latter moved out of the region shortly after the war. See *Diary*, II, 112-3, 120. Bryant, *Olden Times*, 425-6, implies that it was customary for the Ndebele to burn their houses when they moved.

167. Gardiner, *Narrative*, 143-4. Gardiner dates this war to c. 1834, but his context makes it clear that it is to the 1832 Zulu-Ndebele war that he refers.

168. There is some minor disagreement among near-contemporary sources, but the general location is clear. See Smith, *Report*, 26, and *Diary*, II, 101; Harris, *Wild Sports*, folding-map; David Hume, letter, n.d., in *GTJ* (30 June 1836); Breutz, *Rustenburg*, 90; Bryant, *Olden Times*, 429.

169. Smith, *Diary*, II, 78.

170. *Ibid.*, II, 38-9; Moffat, *Matabele Jnls.*, I, 69. Both of these accounts appear to have derived from the same informants.

171. Smith *Diary*, II, 262.

172. The first reports of the war to reach Zululand said that three entire Zulu 'regiments' had been destroyed; then came word that no Zulu at all had been killed. See S. Young, 25 Sept. 1832 (WMMS, SA [Albany], V, 1832); Cawood, 10 Sept. 1832, in *GTJ* (22 Nov. 1832). Mziki, *Mlimo*, 59, describes a major Ndebele victory celebration.

173. Cawood, *ibid*, reports the executions. Pickham, 19 Sept. 1832, in *GTJ* (12 Oct. 1832), gives 140 as the number of cattle the *impi* brought back to Zululand. Gardiner, *Narrative*, 48, 143-4, stresses Dingane's anger. Fynn, *Diary*, 174, describes Dingane's wars against Mzilikazi as uniformly unsuccessful.

174. W. B. Boyce to anon., Umgazi, 8 Nov. 1832, in *GTJ* (22 Nov. 1832). Boyce got his information from Fynn; his letter is reprinted in the latter's *Diary*, 219.

There is no specific corroboration from the Ndebele side that Zulu soldiers defected to Mzilikazi at this time; however, it is possible that they never reached Ndebele territory.

175. On fear of Zulu, see Smith, *Report*, 25, and *Diary*, II, 98; Harris, *Wild Sports*, 189.

176. The migration itself is discussed in the next chapter. Throughout the rest of the present section I have added italics to compass points in both my text and quoted material.

177. Ellenberger, *History*, 207. Mönning, *The Pedi*, 3, gives 'Lulu' as variant spelling of Leolu Mountains.

Ellenberger also follows Arbousset and Daumas in holding that the Zulu freed Pedi 'slaves' from the Ndebele (see fn. 162, above). He thus places Mzilikazi in the uncomfortable position of seeking refuge in the very place to which these alleged slaves were returning. Neither Ellenberger nor any of his own followers notice, however, that Arbousset and Daumas themselves specify that as the Pedi returned to their own homes, Mzilikazi went directly *west* to the Marico River.

178. Bryant, *Olden Times*, 430; Summers and Pagden, *The Warriors*, 60; Lye, 'Ndebele kingdom', 92.

An exception is Preller, *Lobengula*, 29, who confidently asserts that Mzilikazi fled *east* to hide in the Drakensberg Mountains until the Zulu threat subsided. This would have required him to flee in approximately the same direction followed by the retreating Zulu.

179. Mziki, *Mlimo*, 59-60.

180. Archbell, 31 Dec. 1829 (WMMS, SA, III, 1829). Lye, 'Ndebele kingdom', 96-7, accepts this estimate. It should be noted that Lye's documentation is somewhat misleading; he cites both Archbell's letter and Chase, 'Substance', but the latter is merely a reprint of the former.

W. B. Boyce to WMMS, Faku's Tribe, 26 Nov. 1832 (WMMS, SA [Albany], V, 1832, no. 37), estimates that the Zulu and the Ndebele were equally numerous in 1832 and that each society contained about 200,000 people—a vastly inflated figure. He apparently drew this conclusion on the basis of information he got from Henry Fynn. The latter probably inferred that the Ndebele and Zulu were equally strong because of their stand-off war.

181. In 1859 Mzilikazi told Robert Moffat that his people had not experienced any major medical problems since they had left the Transvaal, apparently implying that things had been worse south of the Limpopo. See Moffat, to LMS,

Nyate [Inyati], 26 Dec. 1859 (LMS, MM 1/1/B).

182. Hamilton, Moffat, *et al.*, 26 Dec. 1831 (LMS, SA 12/4/D); Statement of A. Kolbe, encl. in T. Perry to Civil Commr., Graaff Reinet, April 1832 (CA, GR 10/16); P. L. Breutz, *Tribes of Marico District* (Pretoria, 1953), 9.

183. Breutz, *Marico*, 9.

184. A. Smith to B. D'Urban, Black River, 15 Dec. 1835 (CA, GH 19/4); Moffat, *Matabele Jnls.*, I, 74, 81, 96.

185. Smith, *Diary*, II, 150; see also his p. 152.

186. R. Moffat to Ellis, Kuruman, 17 Sept. 1835 (LMS, MM 1/1/A).

187. Smith, 15 Dec. 1835 (CA, GH 19/4). Harris, *Wild Sports,* 168, estimated that Mzilikazi commanded about 5000 fighting men in 1836.

188. See, *e.g.*, Moffat, *Missionary Labours,* 545, which mentions an *impi* of 600 men sent far to the north; P. Lemue, Nov. 1830, in Germond (ed.), *Chronicles,* 76, which mentions an *impi* of 400 Ndebele men sent against the Ngwaketse during 1830; Smith, *Diary*, II, 202, which suggests that an *impi* of only 39 men caused the Kaa to flee their homes.

189. Pellissier, 12 May 1832, in Germond (ed.), *Chronicles*, 95. J. Philip to J. B. Purney, Cape Town, May 1833, in Kotzé (ed.), *Letters of the American Missionaries,* 32, echoes Pellissier's words on this subject. Moffat, *Matabele Jnls.*, I, 85, expresses the same ethic with respect to an elite Ndebele unit which fought only when victory was assured.

In later years Mzilikazi was said to have executed the few survivors of a disastrous campaign against Sebitwane's Kololo in about 1850. See Moffat, *Matabele Jnls.*, I, 240; Statement of Ginyalitsha, in Windram Papers (NAR, WI 8/1).

190. Smith, MSS, XI, 217-8. See also his *Diary*, II, 38-9. Cf. Moffat, *Matabele Jnls.*, I, 69.

Many Europeans also commented on Mzilikazi's advocacy of celibacy as a means of improving military discipline. See Pellissier, 12 May 1832, in Germond (ed.), *Chronicles*, 95; Moffat, *ibid*, I, 26; Moffat, 17 Sept. 1835 (LMS, MM 1/1/A).

191. E. V. Walter, *Terror and Resistance: A Study of Political Violence* (New York, 1969), esp. Chapters 6-10, is a persuasive study of the use of terror as an administrative and political tool in the Zulu kingdom and it contains many comments on the Ndebele kingdom as well.

192. Moffat, *Matabele Jnls.*, I, 137, quotes Smith, who visited both Dingane and Mzilikazi: 'the Matabele, or Zulus, here seem much more cheerful and happy than under Dingaan.'

193. [Smith] to D'Urban, n.d. [13 April 1836?], untitled military intelligence report (CA, GH 19/4).

194. Moffat, *Matabele Jnls.*, I, 99; Smith, *Diary*, II, 56-7.

195. Lye, 'Ndebele kingdom', 96-7, also accepts Smith's figures on the size of the Ndebele 'army', but he does not attempt to explain the large disproportion between this number and Archbell's estimate of 60-80,000 total people. In fairness to Lye, it must be added that he applies the latter estimate to include 'all these elements, Nguni and Sotho, military and subjugated, tributary and vassal'. The problem with this all-inclusive definition of the society is that it sets no meaningful boundaries. It will be recalled that the Ndebele 'tributaries' included such distant peoples as the Ngwato as early as 1830. Surely Lye would not have wished to include such tenuously affiliated communities in his estimate.

196. Hughes and van Velsen, 'The Ndebele', 45, comment that 'there are no accurate data on population for the Ndebele', and that this problem is partly due to the subjective nature of definitions of *who* 'the Ndebele' were at any given time (see my discussion of this problem in the Appendix, below). Most estimates made of the Ndebele population in the late 1880s—when there were many literate people in Matabeleland—placed their total numbers at over 100,000 people, and the size of their 'army' at about 15,000-20,000 men. Taking these figures only as orders of magnitude, it follows that the ratio of total population to soliders was something between 10:1 and 5:1 (my intuitive impression from all available evidence favours the latter figure). Presumably the age/sex structure of the Ndebele was closer to 'normal' then than it had been in the 1830s, when there seem to have been more Ndebele women than men. Therefore we might expect that the ratio of total population to soldiers would have been higher in the 1830s than in the 1880s-90s.

For estimates of the Ndebele population after 1885, see E. A. Maund, 'Matabeleland', in British Parliamentary Paper C.4643, 113; Evid. of J. W. Colenbrander, 25 Oct. 1894, in C.8130; 12, Archibald Colquhoun, *The Renascence of South Africa* (London, 1900), 180.

197. Moffat, *Missionary Labours*, 530, and *Matabele Jnls.*, I, 13; Chase, 'Substance', 405-6; Smith, *Diary*, II, 98.

198. Pellissier, 12 May 1832, in Germond (ed.), *Chronicles*, 94. European visitors to Mzilikazi at his later settlements comment on his tendency to move about in considerable detail. His ability to move about his domain was greatly enhanced after he acquired ox wagons, and his son Lobengula followed the same practice.

199. Smith, *Diary*, II, 112.

200. *Ibid.*, I, 266, II, 120 *et passim*; Chase, 'Substance', 406; Moffat, *Matabele Jnls.*, I, 7-13.

201. Archbell, 31 Dec. 1829 (WMMS, SA, III, 1829), described Ndebele settlements as 'densely scattered [*sic*] over a country 200 miles in extent'.

202. Smith, *Diary*, II, 117, 185.

203. Archbell, 31 Dec. 1829 (WMMS, SA, III, 1829).

204. Breutz, *Rustenburg*, 182.

205. *Ibid.*, 90, names Motsielwe, chief of the Mogopa Kwena, as an example of a leader who resisted conscription. His people were said to have been brutally punished for their insubordination.

206. Arbousset and Daumas, *Narrative*, 186.

207. Mziki, *Mlimo*, 58-9, 64, names *Ndinaneni* and *Nkungwini* in the context of the Zulu invasion of 1832, and *Mzinyati, Nloezi, Ngondweni,* and *Nkenenkene* in the context of Barends' 1831 invasion. Campbell mentioned the first two of these names in his unpub. 1905 article. Ellenberger, *History*, 207, and Bryant, *Olden Times*, 426, both draw upon Campbell's article for these names and then go on to add geographic details which must be largely speculative.

208. Ellenberger, *History*, 205, places *Motlatlantsela* 'on the right bank of the Ntsa-bohloko (Apis [Aapies] River), not far from its confluence with the Limpopo.' This description is confusing, as the Aapies joins the Oori River at 25° 05′ S. lat., and the Oori becomes the Limpopo at 24° 15′ S. lat. Which confluence does he mean?

Bryant, *Olden Times*, 426, alters this town's name to its Nguni form, *Mhlahlandlela*, and follows Ellenberger's geographical description.

Lye, 'Ndebele kingdom', 89-90 (including map) moves *Mhlahlandlela* to the Oori/Marico confluence, about 75 miles farther northwest than the above two authors place it. This results in the preposterous conclusion that Mzilikazi's headquarters town up to mid-1832 was almost due north of his subsequent settlements along the Marico River. This situation, along with the notion that Mzilikazi fled to the Mlulu Mountains after the Zulu war (see fns. 177-8, above) and the fact that he ended up by the upper Marico River in 1832, all suggest that he must have done considerable travelling during 1832 if my own conclusions are incorrect.

209. Arbousset and Daumas, *Narrative,* 186, stress that the Zulu burned '*Motlatlantsela*'. If so, the town must have been located somewhere around the upper tributaries of the Oori River, where the Zulu and Ndebele are known to have fought.

210. Moffat, *Matabele Jnls.*, I, 25, 30. Moffat estimated that one town held 6,000 head of cattle. Schoon and McLuckie, in Chase, 'Substance', 406, estimated there were 3,000 cattle in the first Ndebele town they entered while approaching Mzilikazi from the west. I calculate that the town to which they referred was somewhere around the vicinity of present Rustenburg.

211. Pellissier, 12 May 1832, in Germond (ed.), *Chronicles*, 96. Pellissier's description conforms closely to descriptions recorded at later Ndebele settlements. Cf., Henry Venable, 9 Feb., in Jnl. for 1836 (ABC Arch.).

A. E. Wilson, one of the ABCFM missionaries who went to Zululand after abandoning Mzilikazi in early 1837, thought that by that date Mzilikazi 'owned' more cattle than Dingane. See entry for 4 Sept. 1837, in 'Jnl. of A. E. Wilson', Ginani, Sept. 1837 (ABC Arch.).

212. Smith, *Diary*, II, 120, makes this observation with respect to former Ndebele towns around the Oori River, which he visited in 1835.

213. *Ibid.*, I, 270.

214. *Ibid.*, I, 264. Smith got his information from Robert Moffat.

CHAPTER IV

1. Most of these sources have already been cited many times previously. See especially Andrew Smith, *Diary*, MSS, and letters; Robert Moffat, *Matabele Jnls.*, *Missionary Labours,* and letters; W. C. Harris, *Wild Sports*: John Burrow, *Travels*; and the letters and jnls. of the American missionaries.

2. S. Rolland, 25 Sept. 1832, in Germond (ed.), *Chronicles*, 103.

3. Smith, *Diary*, I, 401, gives the date as 'early in August 1832'. He got his information from the French missionaries who had been at Mosega shortly before the invasion began. His evidence conforms with the consensus of contemporary documents which holds that the attacks were concurrent with the Zulu attack on the Ndebele. The Zulu are known to have returned to Zululand by late August. See Henry Fynn, letter of Aug. 1832, in *Diary*, 218.

4. S. Rolland, 25 Sept. 1832, in Germond (ed.), *Chronicles*, 104-5; Smith, *Diary*, I, 401-2; R. Moffat to father, Kuruman, 6 Dec. 1832 (NAR, WO 5/1/1); R. Moffat to Ellis, Kuruman, 10 Jan. 1833 (LMS, SA 13/4/E); P. Lemue to J. Philip, Vall [*sic*] River, 26 Jan. 1833, copy (LMS, SA 13/3/A).

5. Evid. of Moilo [Moilwe], in *Bloemhof*, 316; Smith, *Diary*, I, 401-2; Moffat to Ellis, *ibid*.

The messengers were killed shortly after the Barends commando, *i.e.*, in about

Sept. 1831. See Mary Moffat to father, Lattakoo, 15 Sept. 1831, in J. S. Moffat, *Lives*, 173.

6. Smith, *ibiḍ.*, Evid. of Gatsietsoe [Gaseitsiwe], in Bloemhof, 189; S. Rolland, in Germond (ed.), *Chronicles*, 103; P. Lemue, 1 Jan. 1833, in *ibid.*, 105; Lemue to Philip, 26 Jan. 1833, copy (LMS, SA 13/3/A).

Sebego survived this attack by about twelve years, but was falsely reported killed in some contemporary accounts, *e.g.*, R. Moffat to brother, Lattakoo, 10 Jan. 1833 (NAR, MO 5/1/1, f.939); J. Baillie to For. Sec., Kuruman, 3 Jan. 1833 (LMS, SA 13/4/E).

7. Rolland, *ibid.*; Lemue to Philip, *ibid.* Smith, *Diary*, I, 350 identified the chiefdom as a branch which had separated from Sechele's branch some time before.

8. R. Moffat to brother, Kuruman, 15 Aug. 1832 (NAR, MO 5/1/1, f.923-4); Baillie to For. Sec. 3 Jan. 1833 (LMS, SA 13/4/E).

9. Evid. of Moilo, *Bloemhof*, 316; J. Baillie, *ibid.*; R. Moffat to father, Kuruman, 6 Dec. 1832 (NAR, MO 5/1/1, f.935); Lemue to Philip, 26 Jan. 1833, copy (LMS, SA 13/3/A).

Breutz, *Marico*, 58, claims that a sub-chiefdom of the Hurutshe resisted the Ndebele at the Toelanie River.

10. P. Lemue, Mothetho, 1 Jan. 1833, in Germond (ed.), *Chronicles*, 111; J. Baillie, *ibid.*

11. Lemue, *ibid.*; Baillie, *ibid.*

12. Schapera, 'Short history of the Bangwaketse', 8-9.

13. Harris, *Wild Sports*, 86; Smith, *Diary*, II, 56, and MSS, XI, 235; R. Moffat, *Matabele Jnls.*, I, 65, 110, *et passim*; D. Lindley, *et al.*, to Anderson, Mosika, 18 Aug. 1836 (ABC Arch.), reprinted in Kotzé (ed.), *Letters*, 128.

14. Moffat, *Matabele Jnls.*, I, 125; Smith, *Diary*, II, 98.

15. Harris, *Wild Sports*, 351; Smith, *ibid*, and MSS, XI, 235.

16. Evid. of Moilo, in *Bloemhof*, 316; Smith, *Diary*, I, 335, II, 98; Schapera, 'Short history', 8.

17. Smith, *Diary*, II, 166, 207, 242, and *Report*, 29; Harris, *Wild Sports*, 218.

18. Smith, *Diary*, II, 118, 121, 124; Harris, *Wild Sports*, 249-50. Breutz, *Rustenburg*, 457, describes a remnant Ndebele community still living in this region into the 1950s.

19. Smith, *Diary*, II, 148; Harris, *Wild Sports,* 161; Breutz, *Rustenburg*, 14.

20. Smith, *Diary*, II, 240; Harris, *Wild Sports*, 120ff.; Breutz, *Marico*, 8-9.

21. Smith, *Diary*, I, 293.

22. I base this inference on the following statment from J. Baillie's letter to the LMS of 3 Jan. 1833:

'I have just heard from a traveller, who has come from Moselekatze, that the latter is residing 5 days journey from the Baharootzeland [an apparent reference to the Mosega Basin], but that his principal forces are stationed there.'

See also fn. 10, above.

23. Smith, *Diary*, I, 293-4. For another general description of the country, see Lindley, *et al.*, 18 Aug. 1836, in Kotzé (ed.), *Letters*, 127.

24. Burrow, *Travels*, 71; Smith, MSS, XI, 233-4.

25. Harris, *Wild Sports*, III; Burrow, *Travels*, 48, 71 (includes sketch of a town); Smith, *Diary*, I, 293 (includes sketch); Jnl. of H. Venable for 22 Jan.-18

May 1836, p. 22 (ABC Arch.); Lindley, *et al.*, in Kotzé (ed.), *Letters*, 128. See also Summers and Pagden, *The Warriors*, 36-9, for detailed discussion.

26. Harris, *ibid.*; Venable, *ibid.*, p. 23.

27. Burrow, *Travels*, 63.

28. Smith, *Diary*, II, 246, and MSS, XI, 235, 237. See also Julian Cobbing, 'The evolutionof Ndebele Amabutho', *passim*.

29. Smith, *Diary*, II, 78-9, 121, 124, 243; Burrow, *Travels*, 70; Moffat, *Matabele Jnls.*, I, 69.

30. Harris, *Wild Sports*, 168.

31. Smith, *Diary*, II, 148; Burrow, *Travels,* 48, 59.

32. Evid. of Moilo, in *Bloemhof*, 316; Lemue to Philip, 26 Jan. 1833, copy (LMS, SA 13/3/A); TNAD, *Short History*, 12; Rolland, in Germond (ed.), *Chronicles*, 104-5; R. Moffat to brother, 10 Jan. 1833 (NAR, MO 5/1/1, f. 939); R. Moffat to father, 6 Dec. 1832 (NAR, MO 5/1/1, f.935).

33. Lemue, *ibid.*; Smith, *Diary*, I, 402.

34. J. Baillie, 3 Jan. 1833 (LMS, SA 13/4/E); Lemue in Germond (ed.), *Chronicles*, 111; 'The native tribes, beyond the Colony to the north', in *GTJ* (16 May 1833); J. Philip to Purney, Cape Town, May 1833, in Kotzé (ed.), *Letters*, 32; Lindley, *et al.*, in *ibid.*, 126, 137; Smith, *Report*, 22.

35. Statement of J. Philip (CA, CO 2743, no. 2); 'Investigatus', 'The tribes to the northward', in *GTJ* (13 June 1833), and letter, dd. 27 May 1833, in *GTJ* (15 Aug. 1833); R. Moffat to brother, 10 Jan. 1833 (NAR, MO 5/1/1, f.939).

36. Lemue, in Germond (ed.), *Chronicles*, 107, Lemue to Philip, 26 Jan. 1833, copy (LMS, SA 13/3/A).

37. Smith, *Diary*, I, 322, II, 37, 151-2, 175. On at least one occasion the Tlhaping—who were not directly affected by the Ndebele occupation—raided Ndebele cattle. However, they became so fearful of Ndebele retribution, that they gave the cattle to Europeans to return to Mzilikazi in 1835. See Moffat, *Matabele Jnls.*, I, 135, *et passim*; Burrow, *Travels*, 39, 42, 76-7; Smith, MSS, XI, 182-3, 190, 195.

A specific example of Hurutshe cattle raids on the Ndebele is discussed in the section on A. G. Bain, pp. 108-9, below.

The Ndebele were also troubled by neighbours' cattle raids after they resettled north of the Limpopo. See D. N. Beach, 'Ndebele raiders and Shona power', *Jnl. Afr. Hist.*, XV, 4 (1974), 633ff.

38. Moffat, *Missionary Labours*, 583, and *Matabele Jnls.*, I, 70; Smith, *Report*, 29, and *Diary*, II, 134, 147, 160, 167, 239, 247ff.; Burrow, *Travels*, 72; Harris, *Wild Sports*, 243; Breutz, *Marico*, 97; TNAD, *Short History*, 12.

39. Smith, *Diary*, II, 147.

40. *Ibid.*, I, 335.

41. *Ibid.*, II, 57, 152.

42. *Ibid.*, II, 175-6.

43. *Ibid.*, II, 173, 249.

44. *Ibid.*, II, 168-9, 188-9, 225; Smith, *Report*, 29-30, and MSS, XII, 78; Burrow, *Travels*, 63-4; Harris, *Wild Sports*, 244-5.

The killing of Kgama appears to have occasioned the flight of the future Kwena chief Sechele from the Transvaal in late 1834. Smith, *Diary*, II, 177.

45. Examples were the Kaa chief Suwe, who seems to have rebelled in about 1834, and the Kgatla chief Pilane, whom Mzilikazi never caught. Smith, *Diary*, II, 42, 186, 190, 202, 215-6, and *Report*, 32. According to Breutz, *Rustenburg*,

364, the Ndebele killed a Tlokwa chief named Base in 1835.

46. Smith, *Diary*, II, 102.

47. Evid. of Moilo, in *Bloemhof*, 316.

48. Declaration of Cilika [Seleka], 13 Sept. 1888, in British Parliamentary Papers, C.5918, p. 170; Elliott, *South Africa*, 105; Stow, *Native Races*, 532. According to Lobengula, the Ngwato chief 'Chuwe' tended Mzilikazi's cattle. Lobengula to Chas. Warren, 28 June 1885, in C.4643, p. 99. Lobengula was probably actually referring to the Kaa chief Suwe (see fn. 45, above).

49. Smith, *Diary*, II, 249; see also, II, 167, and MSS, XI, 290-1.

50. Smith, *Diary*, II, 239.

51. Breutz, *Rustenburg*, 219.

52. Smith, *Diary*, II, 56-7.

53. The only campaign which can be firmly dated to 1833 was a punitive expedition against the Kwena chief Kgama in January. *Ibid*, I, 350.

54. Lemue, 28 Feb. 1834, in Germond (ed.), *Chronicles*, 113-4.

55. Smith, *Diary*, I, 327; A. G. Bain, in Steedman, *Wanderings*, II, 234.

56. Steedman, *Wanderings*, II, 25ff., 30-1; Statement of J. Philip, (CA, CO 2743, no. 2); John Edwards to WMMS, Buchaap, 27 March 1833 (WMMS, SA [Albany], V, 1833, no. 9).

57. Lemue to Philip, Graaf Reinet, 17 Feb. 1833, copy (LMS, SA 13/3/A).

58. Smith, *Diary*, I, 231.

59. Lemue, 1 June 1834, in Germond (ed.), *Chronicles*, 113.

60. Evid. of Jan Pienaar and Magala, in *Bloemhof*, 19, 326. Pienaar was a son-in-law of Bloem; Magala was a Hurutshe who was under Mzilikazi in 1834.

61. Lemue, in Germond (ed.), *Chronicles*, 113; Smith, *Diary*, II, 262; R. Hamilton, R. Moffat, and Edwards to Ellis, Lattakoo, 3 Sept. 1834 (LMS, SA 14/2/F); 'The native tribes', extract from anon. letter dd. Philippolis, 10 July 1834, in *GTJ* (31 July 1834); R. Moffat to brother, Kuruman, 28 July 1834 (NAR, MO 5/1/1), reprinted in J. S. Moffat, *Lives*, 181.

Moffat, *Matabele Jnls.*, I, 111, credits the children of incorporated Sotho/Tswana with having won the battle for the Ndebele.

62. Evid. of Magala, in *Bloemhof*, 326.

63. Smith, MSS, XI, 46; Moffat to Ellis, Kuruman, 30 Oct. 1834 (LMS, SA 14/2/F); Extract of letter from G. A. Kolbe, Philippolis, 14 July 1834 (CA, GH 19/4).

64. Smith, MSS, XI, 78.

65. Smith, *Diary*, II, 255. Smith attributes this description of Sebego only to 'M.'. The editor of his diary holds that 'M' was the Rolong chief Molema; however, the context of the passage suggests that 'M.' was actually Mzilikazi. On Sebego, see also Smith, *Diary*, II, 164.

66. It is clear that this campaign occurred in 1834. As will be shown, it seems to have occurred *after* Bloem's May attack. Hence, it was probably a winter campaign. Earlier Ndebele campaigns against the Ngwaketse were waged in 1825, 1828, 1830, and 1832.

67. Smith, *Diary*, I, 353; II, 165, 255; Evid. of Moilo, in *Bloemhof*, 315; Livingstone, *Travels*, 59-60.

Schapera, 'Short history', 8, cites the evidence of two Ngwaketse informants (Mathibe and Gasietsiwe) at Bloemhof regarding this event; however, their evidence so thoroughly confuses the whole cycle of Ndebele-Ngwaketse conflicts as to render their testimony useless in reconstructing the 1834 campaign.

68. A. G. Bain to J. C. Chase, Graaff Reinet, 18 Dec. 1834, in Steedman, *Wanderings*, II, 233; Schapera, *ibid.*; Lindley, *et. al.*, 18 Aug. 1836 (ABC Arch.), reprinted in Kotzé (ed.), *Letters*, 138.

69. Schapera, 'Short history', 10.

70. Smith, MSS, X, 159. Smith gives the name of this river as the 'Namahari'. It was also known as the 'Donkin'. See folding maps in Harris, *Wild Sports*, and Arbousset and Daumas, *Narrative*; and Pettman, *South African Place Names*, 103.

On the event itself, see Smith, *Diary,* I, 109; 'Investigatus', letter dd. Caledon River, 22 Oct. 1834, in *GTJ* (18 Dec. 1834). Note that Smith was entering Lesotho at the time of the Ndebele-Griqua confrontation, and that he later received accounts of it from both Griqua and Ndebele participants.

71. Smith, MSS, XI, 281, describes these Tswana as 'some paupers of the Mantatee tribe', thereby implying that they were Tlokwa connected with Sekonyela.

72. *Ibid.*, X, 161; XI, 177, 279; Moffat, *Matabele Jnls.*, I, 133-4.

73. Smith, *Diary*, I, 123, and MSS, X, 159ff.; Mziki, *Mlimo*, 65ff.; 'Investigatus', in *GTJ* (18 Dec. 1834).

74. *Ibid.*; Moffat, *Matabele Jnls.*, I, 134.

75. Mziki, *Mlimo*, 66; P. Wright to B. D'Urban, Griqua Town, 31 May 1836, in Parliamentary Paper 503, *Caffre War . . .* (n.l. [London], 1837), 352.

76. This myth seems to have arisen among both Africans and whites for two reasons. First, Africans—including Ndebele—who saw the captured Griqua children among the Ndebele regarded them as 'Europeans'; secondly, during the first Ndebele-Afrikaner clashes of August 1836 (discussed below) several children in a family named Liebenberg could not be found and were consequently believed captured by the Ndebele. There are numerous examples of contemporary and modern authorities who believed that the Ndebele captured the Afrikaner children. See, *e.g.*, Evid. of Cobejaan, in *Bloemhof*, 318; Paul Kruger, *Memoirs,* trans. by A. Teixeira de Mattos (New York, 1902), 8; E. Walker, *The Great Trek* (5th ed., London, 1965), 122; Bryant, *Olden Times*, 433; *etc.*

For connections between this myth and the 1847 Afrikaner attack on the Ndebele, see, Evid. of H. J. van der Merwe, in *Bloemhof*, 197; 'Herinneringe van A. H. en W. J. Potgieter', in G. S. Preller (ed.), *Voortrekkermense* (Kaapstad, 1920-25), III, 5; H. M. G. Jackson, 'A Boer invasion of Rhodesia', *Nada*, 2 (1924), 58-60.

77. David's daughter Truey was finally released by Mzilikazi into the custody of Robert Moffat exactly twenty years after she was captured. See Moffat, *Matabele Jnls.*, I, 328-9.

David's nephew Willem (known to the Ndebele as Velani) soon served Mzilikazi as an interpreter. He later served as a soldier, rising to a command position by the 1850s. Unhappily, he became involved in 'some crime over cattle', and was executed in 1859. See Jnl. of H. Venable, 22 Jan. to 18 May 1836, p. 39 (ABC Arch.); Moffat, *Matabele Jnls.*, I, 225, 232-4, 294; II, 220-1, 246; Moffat to Tidman, 26 Dec. 1859 (LMS, MM 1/1/B); Mziki, *Mlimo*, 67; A. Campbell to C. N. C., Insiza, 1 Apr. 1898, p. 8 (NAR, NB 6/1/1).

78. Bain recounted the entire affair in his letter to J. C. Chase, 18 Dec. 1834, reprinted in Steedman, *Wanderings*, II, 225ff. Note that the version of the letter printed in Margaret Lister (ed.), *Jnls. of Andrew Geddes Bain* (Cape Town, 1949), 141-5, is taken directly from Steedman's book. Bain elaborated somewhat on his story in 'The Tribes to the northward', in *GTJ* (2 Jan. 1835).

79. Moffat to Philip, Kuruman, 18 Sept. 1835 (LMS, MM 1/1/A).

80. Smith, *Diary*, I, 335; II, 263; Bain, in Steedman, *Wanderings*, II, 234ff. The offending Griqua were Hans and Piet Barends and two unnamed 'lads'. Burrow, *Travels*, 47, gives us Kaliphi's name.

81. Smith, *Diary*, II, 38; Bain, in Steedman, *Wanderings*, II, 238. Anon., in *GTJ* (2 Jan. 1835), gives 200 as the number of Ndebele involved.

82. Smith, MSS, XII, 77; Moffat, *Matabele Jnls.*, I, 134.

83. See, *e.g.*, Burrow, *Travels*, 15, in which he reports that some missionaries had 'heard the frightful stories of Masalikatsi's preferring the skins of white men for milk bags . . . '

84. R. Moffat to brother, Moselekatse's country, 12 June 1835 (NAR, MO 5/1/1, f. 1086); D. Lindley to Anderson, Cape Town, 12 March 1835 (ABC Arch.).

85. Bain, in Steedman, *Wanderings*, II, 242; Smith, MSS, XII, 77.

86. 'Tribes to the northward', in *GTJ* (13 Mar. 1835).

87. Smith, MSS, XI, 278–9; Moffat, *Matabele Jnls.*, I, 134.

88. Moffat to Philip, Kuruman, 18 Sept. 1835 (LMS, MM 1/1/A).

89. Moffat, *Missionary Labours*, 578; Moffat to Ellis, Kuruman, 3 Feb. 1834 (LMS, SA 14/2/F).

90. Moffat, *Matabele Jnls.*, I, 74, 96; Smith, MSS, XI, 173.

91. J. Baillie to For. Sec., Kuruman, 3 Jan. 1833 (LMS, SA 13/4/E); Moffat to Ellis, Kuruman, 17 Sept. 1835 (LMS, MM 1/1/A); letters of French missionaries, in Germond (ed.), *Chronicles*, 116ff. On Mzilikazi's general interest in obtaining missionaries, see Lindley to Anderson, Cape Town, 12 Mar. 1835 (ABC Arch.); Jnl. of H. J. Venable, 22 Jan. to 18 May 1836 (ABC Arch.).

92. Moffat to brother, Lattakoo, 10 Jan. 1833 (NAR, MO 5/1/1, f. 939); Moffat to John Smith, Kuruman, 26 Feb. 1834 (NAR, MO 5/1/1, f. 1008); Germond (ed.), *Chronicles*, 106, 151, 440.

93. Lemue to Philip, Graaff Reinet, 17 Feb. 1833, copy (LMS, SA 13/3/A).

94. Philip to J. B. Purney, Cape Town, May 1833, in Kotzé (ed.), *Letters*, 28ff.

95. D. J. Kotzé covers the history of this mission effort very thoroughly in his *Letters of the American Missionaries*, which has already been extensively cited here, and in his thesis, 'Die eerste Amerikaanse sendelinge onder die Matabeles', 129–318. The best account in English is in Edwin W. Smith, *The Life and Times of Daniel Lindley* (London, 1949), Chapters 3–4.

Note that Kotzé's edition of the missionaries' letters draws upon the edited letters printed in the ABC organ, *The Missionary Herald*, and not upon the original letters, which can be found in the ABC Arch. in the Houghton Library at Cambridge, Mass. For this study I have drawn upon a microfilm copy of the ABC Arch. material (seen at the Cape Archives). I have attempted also to cite such of this material as can be found in Kotzé's volume.

96. Burrow, *Travels*, 10, gives a complete list of the expedition's members.

97. This is, of course, the expedition which produced the documentation so extensively drawn upon in this study. For a concise account of the expedition—which includes lengthy quotations from Smith's hitherto unpublished journals, see P. R. Kirby, *Sir Andrew Smith* (Cape Town, 1965), 128–202. William F. Lye has just completed an edition of Smith's journals, which also incorporates considerable material from the latter's ethnographic notes (vol. XII of his MSS), to be published by A. A. Balkema in mid-1975.

98. Smith, MSS, X, 121, 149–50, 220.

99. R. Edwards to Ellis, Kuruman, 1 May 1835 (LMS, SA 14/5/D).

100. Smith, MSS, XI, 175. The Ndebele man who visited Grahamstown did so in the company of the English trader named Gibson. See Bain, in Steedman, *Wanderings*, 242.

101. Moffat, *Matabele Jnls.*, I, 86-7, 115, 127.

102. In 1854 Moffat became the first European to visit the Ndebele peacefully in their new home in present Matabeleland. See *Matabele Jnls.*, I, 139-382. For a general account of white penetration into Matabeleland, see Tabler, *The Far Interior*, esp., pp. 212ff.

103. R. Hamilton to Ellis, Kuruman, 12 July 1836 (LMS, SA 15/2/D).

104. Smith to Waterboer, 10 June 1835, copy, in Wright to Philip, Griqua Town, 15 July 1835, copy (LMS, SA 14/4/C); Wright to Ellis, Griqua Town, 5 Oct. 1835 (LMS, SA 14/4/E).

105. See, *e.g.*, Smith, Diary, II, 64; Moffat, *Matabele Jnls.*, 134.

106. Jnl. of Venable, 22 Jan. to 18 May 1836, p. 44 (ABC Arch.); Lindley, *et al.*, to Anderson, Mosika, 18 Aug. 1836 (ABC Arch.), reprinted in Kotzé (ed.), *Letters*, 137; Wright to D'Urban, Griqua Town, 10 Oct. 1836, Durban Papers (CA, Acc. 519, vol. 5, f. 136).

107. Smith to Waterboer, 10 June 1835 (LMS, SA 14/4/C); Moffat, *Matabele Jnls.*, I, 123.

108. Wright to Philip, Griqua Town, 17 Aug. 1835, copy (LMS, SA 14/4/C); Wright to D'Urban, Griqua Town, 31 May 1836, in Parlia. Paper 503, p. 352; Jnl. of Venable, p. 44 (ABC Arch.).

109. A. Smith, memo, in Parlia. Paper 503, p. 349.

110. Moffat, *Matabele Jnls.*, I, 96; Moffat to Ellis, Kuruman, 17 Sept. 1835 (LMS, MM 1/1/A); Burrow, *Travels*, 75.

The reference to Mzilikazi's desiring guns is somewhat enigmatic since, as was discussed in the previous chapter, he apparently regarded firearms as feeble weapons after his successes against the Griqua commandoes. Perhaps what he wanted was a cannon—a weapon of which he was known to be aware. In any case, his emissaries apparently did not obtain any kind of firearms during their trip.

111. Burrow, *ibid.*; A. Smith to D'Urban, Black River, 15 Dec. 1835 (CA, GH 19/4); Jnl. of Venable, 31 May to 2 Aug. 1836, p. 1 (ABC Arch.). The interpreter, Monaheng, was probably of Tswana extraction.

112. Smith to D'Urban, *ibid.*

113. Smith [to D'Urban], Port Elizabeth, 16 Jan. 1836 (CA, GH 19/4); Smith, MSS, XI, 271, 275, and *Diary*, II, 66. Note that Lye, 'Ndebele kingdom', 101, incorrectly inferred from Smith's texts that representatives from the Xhosa visited Mzilikazi in 1835. Smith's wording is tricky, but it certainly does not support Lye's conclusion—a point Dr Lye has granted in a personal communication (June 1972). There is some indication, however, that Southern Nguni refugees from the Frontier War fled to the Ndebele as the war was ending. See 'Investigatus', letter, dd. Bechuanaland, 1 Nov. 1836, in *GTJ* (29 Dec. 1836); Paul Kruger, *Memoirs*, 11.

114. A. Smith to Mrs [Mary] Moffat, Cape Town, 16 Feb. 1836, photocopy in Kirby Papers, envelope no. 9 (South African Museum, Cape Town). S. Cloete, *African Portraits* (Cape Town, 1969), 57-8, gives many interesting details about this visit which I have not been able to substantiate in any primary source. For example, Cloete says that after Mncumbathe saw a British regiment in review, Smith asked him what the Ndebele would do in a confrontation with such

troops. Mncumbathe is said to have answered, ' "We should just wait till we got them on difficult ground and then rush in from all sides and stab them, every man, before he could reload his musket." ' Unfortunately for the Ndebele, when their first confrontation with regular European troops occurred in 1893, the British were armed with repeating rifles and not inhibited by the need to reload.

115. The signed treaty is found in file GH 19/5 of the Cape Archives when it is not on display in the Archives museum. Most published copies of the treaty are taken from a draft version, which differed somewhat, in file GH 19/4. The complete treaty is to be printed in Lye's forthcoming edition of Andrew Smith's journals.

I know of no evidence to indicate that a second copy of the treaty was given to the Ndebele.

116. The total cost of the gifts was computed at £79 6s 1½d; the cost of transporting and housing the emissaries was figured to be £34 13s 3d. See, 'Memorandum of expenses . . . ', signed by Wm. Smith, 11 April 1836 (CA, GH 19/4). This memo was apparently separated from Andrew Smith's statement on expenses, in Smith to D'Urban, Cape Town, 21 Mar. 1836 (CA, CO 455, no. 26).

117. At that time Peter Wright, an LMS agent, was serving as a government agent at Griqua Town.

118. In his letter to Mary Moffat, Smith alluded to Governor D'Urban's expectation that Mzilikazi should be required to return the captives and goods taken from Peter David in 1834 as a condition of the treaty (see fn. 114, above). However, no such requirement was included in the treaty. This seems to have been an oversight, as it should have been known to Smith and D'Urban that Mzilikazi had been openly searching for some kind of *quid pro quo* to justify releasing David's property. See also, Lindley, *et al.*, 18 Aug. 1836 (ABC Arch.), reprinted in Kotzé (ed.), *Letters*, 136.

119. Wright to D'Urban, Griqua Town, 31 May 1836, in Parlia. Paper 503, p. 351; same to same, 10 Oct. 1836 (CA, Acc. 519, vol. 5, ff. 130-1, 136).

120. Jnl. of Venable, 31 May to 2 Aug. 1836, p. 1 (ABC Arch.).

121. 'Discovery to the north and east', in *GTJ* (18 Feb. 1836). This report was apparently based upon information obtained from the trader David Hume.

122. Mary Moffat to father, Lattakoo, 15 Sept. 1835 (NAR, MO 5/1/1, f. 1098).

123. Lindley to Anderson, Mosika, 29 Aug. 1836 (ABC Arch.); Jnl. of Venable, 22 Jan. to 18 May 1836 (ABC Arch.).

124. Jnl. of A. E. Wilson, 15 June to 30 July 1836 (ABC Arch.).

125. *Ibid.*; Capt. Sutton to D'Urban, Grahamstown, 7 Nov. 1836 (CA, Acc. 519, vol. 5, ff. 197-8). Sutton and another British officer were then hunting in Ndebele country and they witnessed Wilson's visit to Mzilikazi.

126. [Mzilikazi] to D'Urban, Kapeng [Gabeni], 18 July 1836 (CA, Acc. 519, vol. 5, ff. 208-10). A photograph of the first page of this letter can be seen in Kotzé, 'Die eerste Amerikaanse', facing p. 237. It is odd that Wilson sent the letter in the form he did, as it was left unfinished, unsigned and rife with solecisms and spelling errors.

127. In requesting additional gifts so quickly Mzilikazi fulfilled the British Foreign Secretary's fear that the Mzilikazi-D'Urban treaty would 'excite expectations which it might be dangerous to disappoint and inconvenient to gratify.' Glenelg to D'Urban, Downing St., 3 Sept. 1836 (CA, GH 1/23, no. 1649). Mzilikazi's requests seem to have been ignored.

128. Harris, *Wild Sports*, 87, 91; Kotzé, 'Die eerste Amerikaanse', hoofstukke

V-VII, and *Letters, passim*. See esp., Lindley, *et al.*, 18 Aug. 1836 (ABC Arch.), reprinted in Kotzé (ed.), *Letters*, 140. For an amusing view of the Americans' image among later missionaries in this part of Southern Africa, see David Livingstone's 1849 letter to his brother, in *Family Letters, 1841–1856*, ed. by I. Schapera (London, 1959), II, 54.

129. The missionaries described their medical problems in many letters to their directors some of which are reprinted in Kotzé; see *Letters*, 151ff., 162ff.; 'Die eerste Amerikaanse', 243ff.

130. This is not to suggest that the Ndebele actually viewed the passage of time in exactly these terms.

131. On Ndebele livestock, see, Lindley, *et al.*, 18 Aug. 1836 (ABC Arch.), reprinted in Kotzé (ed.), *Letters*, 128; Burrow, *Travels*, 59, 62–3; Harris, *Wild Sports*, 138-9; Jnl. of A. E. Wilson, 4 Sept. 1837 (ABC Arch.). After having spent time among both the Ndebele and the Zulu, Wilson estimated that the former owned more cattle.

On Ndebele agriculture, see Smith, *Diary*, II, 124, 52; Moffat, *Matabele Jnls.*, I, 68, 85; Jnl. of Venable, 31 May to 2 Aug. 1836, p. 8 (ABC Arch.).

132. There are many histories of the 'Great Trek' in Afrikaans and English. The views expressed here draw especially upon Eric Walker, *The Great Trek*; Manfred Nathan, *The Voortrekkers of South Africa* (South Africa & London, 1937); and Carel Potgieter & N. H. Theunissen, *Kommandant-Generaal Hendrik Potgieter* (Johannesburg, 1938).

Contemporary and near-contemporary Afrikaner evidence and perspectives can be found in Gustav S. Preller (ed.), *Voortrekkermense . . . Dokumente oor die Geskiedenis van die Voortrek*, 4 vols. (Kaapstad, 1920-25); J. C. Chase, *Natal, a Re-Print of all the Authentic Notices . . .* (facs. rep., Cape Town, 1955; first publ., 1843); and John Bird (ed.), *The Annals of Natal* (Pietermaritzburg, 1888), vol. I. Preller's volumes are the standard source-books for the Great Trek, but most of the memoirs were taken from people who either were children during the trek period, or were not first-hand witnesses in Afrikaner-Ndebele conflicts. The closest thing we have to an Ndebele perspective of the period is an appendix chapter (written sometime before Nov. 1837) in Harris, *Wild Sports*, 344-64.

133. Walker, *Great Trek*, 113 ff.; Potgieter & Theunissen, *Potgieter*, hoofstuk 5; Preller, *Voortrekkermense, passim*.

134. Most traditional commentaries contain only such generalities as 'the Boers drove Mzilikazi from the Transvaal'. The most detailed traditional commentary on this period is Campbell's book, *Mlimo*, but even it jumps directly from the 1834 clashes with the Griqua to the battle of Vegkop in Oct. 1836. The earlier Ndebele clashes with the Afrikaners are evidently confused with Ndebele-Griqua confrontations. The confusion of Griqua and Afrikaners was probably caused by the rush of events in 1837, during which Griqua and Afrikaners fought both together and independently against the Ndebele.

135. In June 1835 Smith alluded to Ndebele fears of white immigration (*Diary*, II, 66), but these fears were directed against the British, not the Afrikaners, whose emigration from the Colony did not commence in earnest until the end of that year. Oddly, the belief that Robert Moffat, during his mid-1835 visit to the Ndebele, warned Mzilikazi against clashing with Afrikaners was widespread among the Ndebele through the nineteenth century, even though Moffat could not have known anything about the impending trekker movement at the time of his visit. There is nothing in Moffat's 1835 writings to support this belief; however, he himself claimed to have predicted the Ndebele-Afrikaner clashes in

his later writings, *e.g.*, *Missionary Labours*, 587. Richard Brown, 'The external relations of the Ndebele kingdom', in L. M. Thompson (ed.), *African Societies in Southern Africa* (London, 1969), 264-5, cites an anonymous letter Moffat wrote in 1853 making this claim; however, Brown overlooks the implicit chronological discrepancies. Moffat made other references to this claim in the journal of his 1854 visit to Mzilikazi (*Matabele Jnls.*, I, 195, 328, 365). I believe that all of Moffat's later statements were either conscious or unconscious distortions of what he really said to Mzilikazi in 1835: a *general* warning against fighting strangers (especially Griqua). I discuss this subject more thoroughly in the next chapter, which treats the question of whether Moffat advised Mzilikazi to migrate north of the Limpopo.

Further evidence that Mzilikazi knew nothing about the Voortrekker movement before August 1835 is offered in fn. 145, below.

136. Erasmus's account of the whole episode is given in his letter to Col. Somerset, Somerset, Cry River, 9 Sept. 1836, copy encl. in Stockenstrom to D'Urban, Cradock, 1 Oct. 183 (CA, GH 18/1, no. 17). See also 'Herin. van A. H. [Jr.] en W. J. Potgieter', in Preller (ed.), *Voortrekkermense*, III, 3; 'Herin. van Hermanus Jacobus Potgieter', in *ibid.*, III, 38; A. E. Wilson, *et al.*, to Anderson, Grahamstown, 3 May 1837 (ABC Arch.), reprinted in Kotzé (ed.), *Letters*, 164 (see esp., fn. 3); Evid .of J. G. J. van Vuuren, in *Bloemhof*, 256; Evid. of D. F. Kruger, in *Bloemhof*, 218.

Bird, *Annals*, I, 231n., and other authorities claim that the attacks occurred south of the Vaal, but the evidence cited above leave no doubts of the falsity of this claim.

137. The date is from Wilson's letter cited above.

138. The date of August 21st can be extrapolated from other dates given in Erasmus's letter (see fn. 136). Kotzé, *Letters*, 153 n.4, arrives at the same date by interpolating from the dates of the *impi's* departure from, and return to, Mosega, as given in American missionary documents. Evid. of D. F. Kruger, in *Bloemhof*, 218, states that all these battles occurred on a single day, but other sources suggest they may have occurred over two days.

139. Erasmus to Col. Somerset (CA, GH 18/1); Wilson, *et al.*, 3 May 1837 (ABC Arch.); Harris, *Wild Sports*, 353; 'Herin. van M. J. Minnaar', in Preller (ed.), *Voortrekkermense*, IV, 134ff., *et passim*. See map in Potgieter & Theunissen, *Potgieter*, 50.

140. Nathan, *Voortrekkers*, 145, discusses the basis of this estimate. A more conservative estimate is given in Piet Retief to Dingaan, Port Natal, 8 Nov. 1837, in H. S. Pretorius and D. W. Kruger (eds.), *Voortrekker-Argiefstukke, 1829-1849* (Pretoria, 1937), 23. Figures given in contemporary documents vary greatly.

The Liebenberg family was the one commonly believed to have lost white children to the Ndebele (see fn. 76, above). It is interesting that in the American missionaries' account of these clashes (Wilson, *et al.*, 3 May 1837 [ABC Arch.]) they wrote that three 'Hottentots' were taken prisoner. Unlike the Ndebele, the Americans would not have confused whites with 'non-whites', so perhaps their letter helps to explain the basis of the myth of the captive white children.

141. Wilson, *et al.*, *ibid.*; Kotzé, *Letters*, 165.

142. Sources vary on details, but they are in general agreement on the orders of magnitude of these figures. Wilson, *et. al.*, *ibid.*; Erasmus to Col. Somerset (CA, GH 18/1); P. Wright to D'Urban, Griqua Town, 10 Oct. 1836 (CA, Acc. 519, vol. 5, ff. 135-6); J. Archbell to D. Campbell, Thaba Unchu, 4 Sept. 1836, copy encl. in Stockenstrom to D'Urban, Cradock, 27 Sept. 1836 (CA, GH 8/1,

no. 15); P. Retief to Dingaan, in Pretorius & Kruger (eds.), *Voortrekker-Argiefstukke*, 24 (see also fn. 166, below).

143. Wilson, *et al.*, *ibid.*; Wright to D'Urban, *ibid.*

144. Mzilikazi's good-will towards white travellers is demonstrated by his concern for the trader Gibson, who disappeared north of Ndebele territory after Mzilikazi had advised him not to go there. Gibson evidently died from a fever, and Mzilikazi sent out an expedition to bring back Gibson's servant 'in order that by his testimony he might clear himself [*i.e.*, clear Mzilikazi] from all suspicion of murder'. The servant was located, but was unintentionally killed because of a misunderstanding. See Harris, *Wild Sports*, 163-4.

145. Ndebele distrust of Afrikaners as a people was a phenomenon which developed *after* these events. For examples of later Ndebele attitudes towards Afrikaners, see Moffat, *Matabele Jnls.*, I, 372-3; C .H. S. Stabb, 'Notes and other papers', [1875] (NAR, ST 12/4/2), reprinted in *Africana Notes & News*, 17, 4 (1966) [I have not seen the latter ref.]. Rumours of impending Afrikaner invasions of Matabeleland were as common during the 1860s as rumours of Zulu invasion had been during the 1830s.

I believe it is significant that when a rumour of an impending commando attack (which did not occur) swept Ndebele country in June 1836, no one suggested that the enemies might be whites although the Afrikaners were at that moment massed just south of the Vaal. See Jnl. of Venable, 19 June 1836 (ABC Arch.).

146. Harris, *Wild Sports*, 350-2; Moffat, *Missionary Labours*, 586-7; 'Tribes to the northward' [information from Capt. Sutton], in *GTJ* (10 Nov. 1836); *etc.* For a defence of the Ndebele action with respect to Mzilikazi's treaty with the Colony, see Posselt, *Fact & Fiction*, 169-170.

147. Sutton to D'Urban, Grahamstown, 7 Nov. 1836 (CA, Acc. 519, vol. 5, ff. 198-9). Wilson, *et al.*, 3 May 1837 (ABC Arch.), affirm that this was indeed Mzilikazi's stated reason for his *impi*, but they suspected avarice was the underlying motive.

148. Evid. of Moroko, in *Bloemhof*, 137; Montsiowa [Montshiwa] to P. Wodehouse, Kalagari Moshaneng, 28 Aug. 1868, in *ibid.*, 154.

149. Harris, *Wild Sports*, 354, comments on failure of Afrikaners to negotiate. 'Tribes to the northward', in *GTJ* (10 Nov. 1836), suggests that Mzilikazi indicated his willingness to allow the Voortrekkers to pass through his country.

150. Unfortunately, none of the Afrikaner participants in these events seems to have kept anything like a diary during this period. The present account therefore draws upon evidence of contemporary second-hand informants who remained in the Ndebele towns or main Voortrekker camps.

151. Wilson, *et al.*, 3 May 1837 (ABC Arch.) stress Mzilikazi's reticence to discuss his own intentions.

152. *Ibid.* gives us the date. Harris met the *impi* on its return march, and he names its commander (*Wild Sports*, 112, 136, 176, 181, 356). Mziki, *Mlimo*, 70ff., names Kaliphi as the *impi's* commander and 'Gundwane' as its sub-commander. The next chapter argues that Kaliphi and Gundwane were actually the same man. The description of the battle of Vegkop in *Mlimo* betrays the author's reliance on at least some non-Ndebele sources, for it generally smacks of a white perspective by emphasizing the awe in which the Afrikaners are supposed to have been held by the Ndebele.

153. Wilson, *et al.*, 3 May 1837 (ABC Arch.), give us this figure. Voortrekker estimates were much higher—about five to six thousand Ndebele. The

Voortrekkers no doubt exaggerated the number of Ndebele because of their limited perspective of the situation and because of the natural desire to magnify their achievements. The Americans' figure is the more credible because they knew something of the numbers of Ndebele soldiers available to Mzilikazi, they saw the *impi* before and after the battle, and they had the opportunity to hear the Voortrekkers' side of the story. See also Harris, *Wild Sports*, 111-12, 355; Evid. of Cobejaan, in *Bloemhof*, 318 (Cobejaan fought on the Ndebele side in the battle).

154. Published estimates of the date of the ensuing battle have varied from 2 to 29 Oct.; however, it is clear that the battle occurred midway between these two extremes. The *impi* departed from Ndebele country on 9 Oct., and Mzilikazi received his first reports on the battle on 25 Oct. Wilson, *et al.*, 3 May 1837 (ABC Arch.).

A traveller who met the Voortrekkers soon after the battle give 'Monday, the 17th' as the date when the Afrikaners first learned the Ndebele *impi* was approaching (Letter from 'Investigatus', dd. Bechuanaland, 1 Nov. 1836, in *GTJ* [29 Dec. 1836]). Since most accounts agree that the Voortrekkers had several days to prepare between that point and the actual battle, it would follow that the battle occurred around 19 Oct. Kotzé, *Letters*, 153 n.5, also arrives at 19 Oct. as the battle's date by interpolating through the dates of the impi's departure from, and return to, Mosega.

Part of the existing errors in dating this battle might derive from the first Voortrekker account of the battle to be printed: 'Statement of J. G S. Bronkhurst',·n.d., in *GTJ* (30 Mar. 1837; reprinted from *Zuid-Afrikan*, 3 Mar. 1837), gives 29 Oct. as the date of the battle. As the 29th is clearly the incorrect date, one wonders if it were not a simple misprint for '19'. Harris seems to have read Bronkhurst's statement in the *GTJ*, for in *Wild Sports* he gives 29 Oct. as the date of the battle in his appendix on Ndebele-Afrikaner hostilities (p. 356), even though his main text—which apparently draws on his own diary—gives 25 Oct. the moment he first learned the battle was over (p. 136).

For further discussion of the dating of this battle, see Preller, *Voortrekkermense*, I, 129n., in which a case is made for dating the battle to 16 Oct.

155. These people were variously described as 'Mantatees' or 'Bushman Bechuanas'. See 'Statement of Bronkhurst', in *GTJ* (30 Mar. 1837); Evid. of D. F. Kruger, in *Bloemhof*, 218; Mziki, *Mlimo*, 70; Wilson, *et al.*, 3 May 1837 (ABC Arch.).

156. Wilson, *et al.*, *ibid.*; 'Investigatus', in *GTJ* (29 Dec. 1836); Preller, *Voortrekkermense, passim*; Erasmus Smit, *Diary*, ed. by H. F. Schoon, trans. by W. G. A. Mears (Cape Town, 1972), 2-3; 'Jnl. of the late Charl Celliers [*sic*]', in Bird (ed.), I, 238ff.

Smit never saw the Ndebele himself, but his diary is the most important contemporary Voortrekker record of this period. Sarel Cilliers' jnl. is the best first-hand Voortrekker account, but it was actually recorded many years later.

157. Useful plans of the Voortrekker camp and the surrounding countryside are in Nathan, *Voortrekkers*, facing p. 146, and Theunissen and Potgieter, *Potgieter*, 50.

158. Nathan, *Voortrekkers*, 146.

159. 'Statement of Bronkhurst', in *GTJ* (30 Mar. 1837); Cilliers, in Bird (ed.), *Annals*, I, 238-9; 'Herin. van J. H. Hatting', in Preller (ed.), *Voortrekkermense*, I, 125; 'Herin. van A. H. Potgieter, Jr.', in *ibid.*, III, 19.

160. Evid. of D. F. Kruger, in *Bloemhof*, 218, names 'John Robbertse' as the

offender. Kruger's evidence covers the entire period of Afrikaner-Ndebele conflicts and appears generally credible otherwise.

161. Eugene Marais, 'The blood trail in the Transvaal', *The Star* (17 Oc. 1925), 5.

162. The best example of this kind of fighting in South African history was the battle at Dithakong in 1823 in which about one hundred Griqua horsemen turned back a body of *Difaqane* refugees estimated to number 40,000. See William F. Lye, 'The Difaqane', 111ff.

163. There is some problem in reconstructing the exact sequence of these events and determining whether the Voortrekkers sallied forth from their *laager* more than once, but the present reconstruction should be approximately correct.

164. Fifteen minutes is the figure given by both Harris, *Wild Sports*, 356; and 'Investigatus', in *GTJ* (29 Dec. 1836); however, Harris may have drawn upon the latter source. No near-contemporary source suggests the battle lasted any longer, and Wilson, *et al.*, 3 May 1837 (ABC Arch.), say that it lasted only two to three minutes!

165. Descriptions of the battle broadly agree. See especially, Cilliers, in Bird (ed.), *Annals* 239-40. One of the few Ndebele traditional authorities to allude to this particular battle is Mkulani, whose statement is found in D. Moodie, 'Matopo-Mawabeni' statistical report', 11 April 1898 (NAR, NB 6/1/1). Many contemporary reports comment on the Voortrekkers' collecting more than a thousand Ndebele spears after the battle.

The disastrous effect of Afrikaner bullet-bags is revealed in the claim of one man to have killed nine Ndebele with a single shot (Smit, *Diary*, 2). For overviews of the battle, see G. Tylden, 'Vegkop, 2 October 1836 . . . ' *Afr. Notes & News*, 10, 4 (1953), 136-9; *ibid.*, 14, 5 (1961), 180-2.

166. These estimates are made by Bronkhurst, in *GTJ* (30 Mar. 1837); Wilson, *et al.*, 3 May 1837 (ABC Arch.); Harris, *Wild Sports*, 180, 356. Virtually all sources agree that the Ndebele captured the whole of the Voortrekkers' herds. P. Retief, in Pretorius and Kruger (eds.), *Voortrekker-Argiefstukke*, 24, gives the following statistics for Voortrekker losses during *all* their 1836 conflicts with the Ndebele: 51 saddle horses; 45 breeding horses; 945 draught oxen; 3,726 breeding cattle; 50,745 sheep and goats.

167. Contemporary sources disagree on whether the Voortrekker pursuit was mounted the same day as the main battle, the day after, or three days later. See Bronkhurst, in *GTJ* (30 Mar. 1837); 'Investigatus', in *GTJ* (29 Dec. 1836); Evid. of D. F. Kruger, in *Bloemhof*, 218; Harris, *Wild Sports*, 356.

168. Most contemporary or near-contemporary sources agree that about 150 Ndebele were killed in the *laager*. Later estimates are higher, probably because they do not differentiate between Ndebele losses at the *laager* and those which occurred elsewhere. For specific estimates, see 'Investigatus', in *GTJ* (29 Dec. 1836); Wilson, *et al.*, 3 May 1837 (ABC Arch.); Smit, *Diary*, 2; Cilliers, in Bird (ed.). *Annals*, I, 240.

169. All sources concur on this point.

170. Evid. of Moroko, Baikhaki, and J. G. J. van Vuuren, in *Bloemhof*, 137, 142, 256; Cilliers, in Bird (ed.), *Annals*, I, 240; Harris, *Wild Sports*, 354 ff. For a modern Rolong view of these events which emphasizes Rolong participation, see S. M. Molema, *Chief Moroka* (Cape Town, 1951), 47ff.

171. Wm. Gilfillan to A. Stockenstrom, Cradock, 15 Nov. 1836, encl. in Stockenstrom to D'Urban, Graham's Town, 15 Dec. 1836 (CA, GH 8/1, no. 62). Gilfillan also alludes to the prospective participation of Moshweshwe and

Barend Barends in this commando; however, neither actually joined it. For general accounts of Voortrekker activities through this period, see Walker, *Great Trek*, 126-9; Nathan, *Voortrekkers*, 151-61; Potgieter and Theunissen, *Potgieter*, 68-74; H. B. Thom, *Die Lewe van Gert Maritz* (Kaapstad, 1965), 122ff.

172. Smit, *Diary*, 12, 15.

173. On problems of summer warfare, see Smith, *Diary*, I, 143; Cope, *Izibongo*, 94; Statement of Ginyalitsha, p. 26, in Windram Papers (NAR, WI 8/1). E. Smith, *Lindley*, 110, suggests that the Voortrekkers expected the swollen Vaal River to inhibit any Ndebele pursuit during their own retreat.

174. Wilson to Anderson, 17 April 1837 [not on ABC microfilm], in Kotzé (ed.), *Letters*, 154. The American missionaries were the last friendly literate observers in Ndebele country.

175. Moffat, *Missionary Labours*, 587; Harris, *Wild Sports*, 359. Some Voortrekker accounts, which were recorded much later, refer to their finding Mzilikazi 'at Mosega'. These statements were merely symbolic.

176. Wilson, *et al.*, 3 May 1837 (ABC Arch.); 'An Inhabitant', letter, dd. Graaf-Reinet, 9 Mar. 1837, in *GTJ* (23 Mar. 1837); Evid. of van Vuuren, in *Bloemhof*, 256; Harris, *Wild Sports*, 357. Virtually all Voortrekker sources support these figures.

177. Van Vuuren, *ibid.*; Evid. of Matlabi, in *Bloemhof*, 264; Peter Wright to Mrs Philip, Philippolis, 1 Feb. 1837 (LMS, SA 15/3/A); Evid. of Moroko, in *Bloemhof*, 137.

The fact that some of David's followers were associated with Barend Barends' Griqua caused some remote observers falsely to report that Barends himself participated in the commando; *e.g.*, Hamilton, *et al.*, to Ellis, Kuruman, 15 June 1837 (LMS, SA 15/4/D).

178. Evid. of D. F. Kruger, van Vuuren, and Matlabi, in *Bloemhof*, 219, 256, 262. Matlabe had deserted Mzilikazi some time before January 1834, when he arrived at Thaba Nchu and requested sanctuary. See J. Archbell to WMMS, Thaba Unchu, 17 Jan. 1834 (WMMS, SA [Albany], VII, 1834).

The Voortrekkers may also have employed an Ndebele captured at Vegkop as a guide. See Harris, *Wild Sports*, 357-8.

179. Evid. of Moroko, Mongala, Baikhaki, and Molema, in *Bloemhof*, 139, 140, 142, 144; Extracts of letter from Mrs Smit, dd. 5 Jan. 1837, in *GTJ* (9 Mar. 1837); S. M. Molema, *Moroka*, 50.

180. Evid. of Moroko, D. F. Kruger, and Matlabi, in *Bloemhof*, 137, 219, 264.

181. Evid. of Kruger and Matlabi, in *Bloemhof*, 218, 264.

182. As is typical with so many of the events covered in this study, recorded oral accounts of this January commando frequently confuse it with the Voortrekkers' second commando in November. According to Breutz, both Hurutshe (*Marico*, 98) and Kwena (*Rustenburg*, 91, 112) participated in the January commando.

183. Wilson to Anderson, 17 April 1837, in Kotzé (ed.), *Letters*, 155; Wilson, *et al.*, 3 May 1837 (ABC Arch.), reprinted in Kotzé (ed.), *Letters*, 170; Extracts from letter of Gert Maritz, dd. Thaba Unchu, 7 March 1837, in *GTJ* (20 April 1837).

There is no basis for the popularly-held belief that the Voortrekkers hoped completely to defeat the Ndebele in January, but were prevented from carrying out their plans because their horses were exhausted.

184. The Rolong informants who testified at Bloemhof in 1870 provide invaluable evidence on this issue, but their testimony must be interpreted in the

context of the land dispute upon which they were then testifying. See esp. Evid. of Moroko and of Molema, in *Bloemhof*, 137, 144; Montsioa Toane to Wodehouse, 28 Aug. 1868, in *Bloemhof*, 154.

185. Smit, *Diary*, 15; Maritz, in *GTJ* (20 April 1837).

186. Evid. of Matlabe, in *Bloemhof*, 262; Harris, *Wild Sports*, 357 and folding map.

187. Wilson, *et al.*, 3 May 1837 (ABC Arch.), reprinted in Kotzé (ed.), *Letters*, 168-9. Campbell's book, *Mlimo*, contains nothing which can be firmly connected with the January commando, but he gives a somewhat vague story of an Afrikaner attack on Ndebele towns in which the Afrikaners are said to have carefully avoided shooting women (pp. 75-6). This is further evidence of the non-authenticity of parts of his book.

188. Smit, *Diary*, 20; 'An Inhabitant', in *GTJ* (23 Mar. 1837); Maritz, in *GTJ* (20 April 1837); Harris, *Wild Sports*, 358.

189. 'An Inhabitant', *ibid.*; Harris, *ibid.*

190. Harris, *Wild Sports*, 359.

191. All sources agree.

192. Evid. of D. F. Kruger, in *Bloemhof*, 219.

193. Evid. of Matlabi, in *Bloemhof*, 262; Smit, *Diary*, 20; Wilson, *et al.*, 3 May 1837 (ABC Arch.). See also S. M. Molema, *Moroka*, 50-2.

194. Most sources agree on these figures. On the commando's retreat, see esp. Evid. of Kruger, in *Bloemhof*, 219.

195. Evidence for this other commando is skimpy, and it is confused in oral accounts with evidence for other Griqua commandoes. Nevertheless, the fact that such an independent commando entered Ndebele country at this time seems certain. See D. Lindley to Anderson, Port Natal, 1 Dec. 1837, in Kotzé (ed.), *Letters*, 214; Evid. of Moilo, in *Bloemhof*, 316-7. According to Lindley, Mzilikazi was attacked four times during 1837 (he had not yet received news of the November Afrikaner commando, which would have been the fifth attack); the four assailants named were the Voortrekkers, Zulu, Jan Bloem, and the Philippolis Griqua (the Zulu and Philippolis Griqua attacks are discussed below). Moilwe's evidence makes it clear that Potgieter and Bloem's commandoes were both concurrent and unrelated.

196. According to Kruger and Matlabe, in *Bloemhof*, 219, 262, the Rolong received some cattle. According to Moroka, Baikhaki, and Montshiwa, in *Bloemhof*, 137, 142, 154, the Rolong got no cattle.

197. Maritz, in *GTJ* (20 April 1837); Evid. of Kruger, in *Bloemhof*, 219; Walker, *Great Trek*, 128-9.

198. According to Kruger, *ibid.*, it was Potgieter who advised the missionaries to leave. See also Wilson, *et al.*, 3 May 1837, and Wilson, 17 April 1837 (ABC Arch.).

199. R. Moffat to father-in-law, [April 1838], in J. S. Moffat, *Lives*, 217. Moffat got his information from some Tswana men from Kuruman who had worked for the Americans at Mosega. After the commando attack the Tswana remained with the Ndebele for several weeks and were 'kindly treated by them'.

200. Letter of D. Lindley [n.d.], quoted in E. Smith, *Lindley*, 106.

201. Moffat, *Matabele Jnls.*, II, 224; J. Mackenzie, *Ten Years North of the Orange River*, 315. Ironically, Mackenzie blamed the American missionaries for instilling in the Ndebele the idea that missionary stations preceded white invasions, but he himself later advocated a British take-over of the Ndebele state

in order to facilitate mission work. See W. Douglas Mackenzie, *John Mackenzie: South African Missionary and Statesman* (London, 1902), 175-6.

202. H. Venable to Anderson, Ginani, 24 Aug. 1837 (ABC Arch.) [not in Kotzé, *Letters*]; George Champion to Anderson, Ginani, 10 Aug. 1837 (ABC Arch.), reprinted in Kotzé (ed.), *Letters*, 191ff.; Kotzé, 'Die eerste Amerikanse', 277ff.

Dingane at first was reluctant to let missionaries from Mzilikazi's kingdom live among the Zulu, but he seems to have changed his mind when he learned that Wilson was a medical doctor. See Aldin Grout to Anderson, Ginani, 24 June 1837, and N. Adams to Anderson, Ginani, 22 Aug. 1837 (ABC Arch.).

203. This point is documented in the previous chapter. When Mzilikazi saw Moffat off in August 1835, he expressed his fear of the Zulu. Moffat, *Matabele Jnls.*, I, 128.

204. P. Lemue, [1] Jan. 1833, in Germond (ed.). *Chronicles*, 111; Moffat to Ellis, Kuruman, 10 Jan. 1833 (LMS, SA 13/4/E); 'The native tribes', in *GTJ* (16 May 1833); 'Port Natal', [information from John Cane], in *GTJ* (5 June 1834); Andries Waterboer to W. C. van Ryneveld, Griqua Town, 9 July 1834, trans. copy encl. in van Ryneveld to Col. Off., Graaff Reinet, 14 Aug. 1834 (CA, CO 2750, no. 58); Smith, *Diary*, II, 245 (entry for 26 Sept. 1835), and MSS, XI, 315 (June 1835); 'Tribes to the northward', [information from Capt. Sutton], in *GTJ* (10 Nov. 1836).

205. Lindley, *et al.*, 18 Aug. 1836 (ABC Arch.), reprinted in Kotzé (ed.), *Letters*, 140; Sutton to D'Urban, 7 Nov. 1836 (CA, Acc. 519, vol. 5, f. 199). The Americans indicated that there were also Ndebele 'spies' exploring far to the north at this time. These 'spies' might well have been north of the Limpopo looking for a new territory for the Ndebele to settle—a possibility tenuously supported by Ndebele tradition. See Campbell to CNC, 1 April 1898 (NAR, NB 6/1/1). However, Harris, *Wild Sports*, 137, 165, 189, appears to contradict the notion that the Ndebele were moving in 1836.

206. This movement is impossible to reconstruct in any detail, as there were no literate observers in the country to describe it.

Contractions of Ndebele settlements were described in 1863 and early 1871. See Leask, *Southern African Diaries*, 221; J. B. Thomson to Mullens, Inyati, 16 Feb. 1871 (LMS, MM 1/2/D).

207. This subject is discussed and documented in the next chapter.

208. Despite the many rumours of impending Zulu attacks (see fn. 204, above), there seems to be no positive evidence that the Zulu and Ndebele fought between 1832 and mid-1837. Explicit evidence demonstrating that they did *not* fight during those years was presented in the previous chapter in the section on the dating of the 1832 war.

209. Harris, *Wild Sports*, 362, suggests such a connection between the Voortrekker and Zulu attacks; however, he does not indicate whether his point is his own deduction or is based upon some Zulu-derived source, such as he might have read in the *GTJ*. Jnl. of Venable, 1 Sept. 1837 (ABC Arch.), affirms Dingane's intention 'completely [to] destroy Maselekatsi'.

210. Champion to Anderson, Ginani, 2 Jan. 1838 (ABC Arch.); Lindley to Anderson, Port Natal, 21 Aug. 1837, in Kotzé (ed.), *Letters*, 195. Evidence from other sources affirms the general time period during which the *impi* was gone. Ndlela is identified by Francis Owen to P. Retief, Unkunglove, 31 Oct. 1837, in *GTJ* (28 Dec. 1837); Owen, *Diary*, ed. by G. E. Cory (Cape Town, 1926), 38. The point about secrecy is made in an untitled article in the *GTJ* (21 Sept. 1837), p. 2.

211. Evid. of Magala, in *Bloemhof*, 327; Jnl. of H. J. Venable, 1 Sept. 1837 (ABC Arch.).

212. Harris, *Wild Sports*, 362. Other sources stress that the weather devastated the Zulu during their campaign, but they do not specify its effect upon the army's outward march. See Champion to Anderson, Ginani, 2 Jan. 1838 (ABC Arch.); 'Port Natal', [information from B. Norden], in *GTJ* (2 Nov. 1837); anon., in *GTJ* (21 Sept. 1837).

About thirty years later an Ndebele *impi* into Mashonaland was said to have suffered so much from the cold that forty men died in their sleep. See Leask, *Diary*, 195.

213. The *impi* left Zululand in late May and returned home in early September after having spent a longer time on the return journey, so it must have encountered the Ndebele in about late June. See Owen, *Diary*, 57; Wilson to Anderson, Ginani, 28 Sept. 1837 (ABC Arch.); Jnl. of H. J. Venable, 3 Sept. 1837 (ABC Arch.); Lindley to Anderson, Port Natal, 21 Aug. 1837, in Kotzé (ed.), *Letters*, 195.

214. Wilson to Anderson, *ibid.*; Lindley to Anderson, *ibid.*; *GTJ* (21 Sept. 1837).

Some modern authorities, *e.g.*, Bryant, *Olden Times*, 436, hold that the Zulu and Ndebele fought *at* Mosega—which is certainly wrong.

215. Evid. of Gatsietsoe, Cobejaan, and Magala, in Bloemhof, 189, 318, 327; Owen, *Diary*, 57-8; Schapera, 'Short history', 9.

216. Evid. of Cobejaan, Magala, and Jan Pienaar, in *Bloemhof*, 318, 327, 375; Mkulani, in D. Moodie, 'Matopo-Mawabeni: stat. report', 11 April 1898 (NAR, NB 6/1/1). Available evidence suggests that only one battle took place.

217. Magala and Cobejaan both say it was a 'drawn battle'. Harris, *Wild Sports*, 362, says that the Ndebele 'routed' the Zulu—a conclusion he may have formed from reading the *GTJ* (21 Sept. 1837), which reported that the Zulu suffered a 'severe defeat'. By contrast, Jnl. of Venable, 3 Sept. 1837 (ABC Arch.), says that the Zulu 'triumphed'.

218. 'Port Natal', in *GTJ* (2 Nov. 1837), estimated that the Zulu captured six to eight thousand cattle; Champion to Anderson, 2 Jan. 1838 (ABC Arch.), says 'several thousands'; A. Campbell to CNC, Insiza, 1 April 1898 (NAR, NB 6/1/1), says 'enormous herds'.

219. On Ndebele pursuit, see Evid. of Magala, in *Bloemhof*, 327; Mziki, *Mlimo*, 74. On significance of campaign in Dingane's career, see Gibson, *Story of the Zulus*, 56; Cope, *Izibongo*, 178-80, 188; A. T. Bryant, *Zulu-English Dict.*, 53.

220. See fn. 212 above. Among the Zulu officers killed was Khokhela, a son of Mncumbathe, the leading Ndebele *induna*. See Champion to Anderson, 2 Jan. 1838 (ABC Arch.); Fynn, *Diary*, 191; Posselt, *Fact & Fiction*, 171.

221. Correspondence between Dingane and Retief can be seen in the *GTJ* (28 Dec. 1837), and in Pretorius and Kruger (eds.), *Voortrekker-Argiefstukke*, 21-3. See also Owen, *Diary*, 58-9.

222. As the Ndebele were not again visited by literate observers for seventeen years, estimates of their losses are necessarily crude. See Bryant, *Olden Times*, 436; Mziki, *Mlimo*, 75.

At least a few women seem to have been captured by the Zulu and returned to Zululand; see Owen, *Diary*, 44; Gibson, *Story*, 56.

223. Barends may only have threatened to organize a commando as a bargaining point in his dispute with Waterboer over ownership of a settlement known as Daniel's Kuil. See P. Wright to D'Urban, Griqua Town, 6 Aug. 1837 (CA, GH

19/4); Wright to Stockenstrom, Griqua Town, 10 Oct. 1837 (CA, LG 495, no. 65).

224. Evid. of Jan Pienaar, in *Bloemhof*, 347-8; Theopolis Atkinson to Stockenstrom, Philippolis, 28 June 1837 (CA, LG 495, no. 42).

At least a few Philippolis Griqua did participate in the January commando. See Wright to D'Urban, Griqua Town, 6 Aug. 1837 (CA, GH 19/4).

225. Atkinson, *ibid*.

226. Evid. of Pienaar, in *Bloemhof*, 19, 348. Most sources agree that the commando was large; an anonymous letter, dd. Orange River, 20 Aug. 1837, in *GTJ* (14 Sept. 1837), estimates that the commando had 900 men when it passed through the Voortrekker camps in the Free State on its way north.

The commando appears to have left shortly before Wright wrote to Governor D'Urban on 6 Aug. 1837 (CA, GH 19/4). Jnl. of Venable, 3 Sept. 1837 (ABC Arch.), reports that some of the Zulu who were returning from their campaign against the Ndebele saw 'white men' in Ndebele territory. These people may well have been the Griqua.

227. Evid. of Pienaar and Magala, in *Bloemhof*, 19, 327-8, 347-8.

228. Evid. of Gatsietsoe, Moilo, and Magala, in *Bloemhof*, 189, 316-7, 327-8.

229. Evid. of Pienaar and Moilo, in *Bloemhof*, 19, 316-7, 347-8.

230. All the Bloemhof witnesses who testified on this commando support this conclusion, but they refer to Mzilikazi's being at a place called 'Loale', which I cannot identify (it could *not* have been the distant Lwale Pan).

231. Bloemhof witnesses; Wright to D'Urban, Griqua Town, 10 Oct. 1837 (CA, CO 464, no. 52). 'The Griquas', in *GTJ* (5 Oct. 1837), is the only source to describe a Griqua defeat (Harris, *Wild Sports*, 362-3, appears merely to follow this newspaper account).

232. Evid. of Magala, in *Bloemhof*, 327.

233. Wright to D'Urban, 10 Oct. 1837 (CA, CO 464, no. 52).

234. Evid. of Gatsietsoe, in *Bloemhof*, 189.

235. For general accounts of this period, see Walker, *Great Trek*, 138-9; 157-8; Nathan, *Voortrekkers*, 158ff.; Potgieter and Theunissen, *Potgieter*, 79ff.

236. Harris, *Wild Sports*, 361.

237. 'The emigrant farmers' [anon. letters, dd. Thaba Unchu, 17 & 21 April 1837], in *GTJ* (1 June 1837).

238. Potgieter and Theunissen, *Potgieter*, 82-3; Evid. of J. G. J. van Vuuren, in *Bloemhof*, 257.

239. Evid. of Moroko, Mongala, and Matlabi, in *Bloemhof*, 137, 140, 262; S. M. Molema, *Moroka*, 54.

240. Potgieter and Theunissen, *Potgieter*, 84ff. (see also their map, p. 80); P. Kruger, *Memoirs*, 9.

241. In the absence of satisfactory contemporary documentation of this episode, I shall not attempt to reconstruct it in detail. Potgieter and Theunissen, *Potgieter*, 87-92, give the most complete account; for an English version, see Bulpin, *Lost Trails*, 58-62. Unfortunately, neither of these accounts is very convincing.

242. Testimony of Moroko, in *Bloemhof*, 137. T. M. Thomas, Jr., Untitled paper on Ndebele history (CA, Acc. 302, vol. 24, pt. 2), gives an account similar to that of Moroka; however, he identifies the Tswana allies as Kwena rather than Rolong.

243. Afrikaner claims by right of conquest are well-documented; see, *e.g.*, Evid. of D. F. Kruger, in *Bloemhof*, 219; Walker, *Great Trek*, 158; *etc.*

Ironically, Dingane himself claimed the western Transvaal to be his by right of conquest, and he suggested that Voortrekkers might settle there rather than in Natal. See Owen, *Diary*, 59-60, 65. A number of Europeans also agreed that the Zulu should have had an equal claim to Ndebele territory. See, *e.g.*, Livingstone, *Family Letters*, I, 112; Edwards to Tidman, Kuruman, 8 Dec. 1841 (LMS, SA 18/2/B).

After most Ndebele had migrated across the Limpopo, the Voortrekkers returned to the western Transvaal to make sure they were all gone. See Preller, *Lobengula*, 32; Kruger, *Memoirs*, 32; Thomas, *Eleven Years*, 162-3.

244. Cilliers, in Bird (ed.), *Annals*, I, 240;Evid. of Moroko, in *Bloemhof*, 137.

245. For estimates of the numbers of cattle captured by the Voortrekkers, see Walker, *Great Trek*, 158; Potgieter and Theunissen, *Potgieter*, 94; Bryant, *Olden Times*, 437.

NOTES FOR CHAPTER V

1. It is sometimes mistakenly asserted that Mzilikazi founded a town called Bulawayo when he arrived in Matabeleland, but the first such town was actually founded by his successor, Lobengula, in 1870. For discussion of the sites of the central towns through the nineteenth century, see O. Ransford, *Bulawayo*, 164-7; Summers and Pagden, *The Warriors, passim*.

2. There are, however, occasional pieces of contemporary, second-hand documentation, recorded by Europeans who travelled around the peripheries of Ndebele territory, or who got information indirectly from these regions. Among the most important of these figures was David Livingstone. His travels and those of other early travellers are summarized usefully in E. C. Tabler, *Pioneers of Rhodesia*, (Cape Town, 1966).

3. This subject is discussed at length in William F. Lye, 'The distribution of the Sotho peoples after the Difaqane', in L. M. Thompson (ed.), *African Societies in Southern Africa*, 191-206.

4. On Sebitwane's interest in settling by the Marico River, see Edwin Smith, 'Sebetwane and the Makololo', in *Great Lion of Bechuanaland* (London, 1957), 377-8. On Molitsane's career, see his statement in G. M. Theal (ed.), *Basutoland Records* (Cape Town, 1883), I, 517-32.

5. Lye, 'Distribution', 199, argues that the Ndebele state 'prevented the development of a Tswana paramountcy which might have countered the encroachments of the Trekboers [*sic*]'. This argument, while intriguing, ignores the possibility that a hypothetical Tswana state might have responded to the coming of the Voortrekkers as did the Ndebele. Furthermore, the history of the Kololo demonstrates that the Sotho/Tswana were as capable of migrating out of South Africa as were the Nguni-dominated Ndebele.

6. The activites of the Voortrekkers during these years are well covered in the body of general literature on the Trek movement cited in the previous chapter. See Lye. 'Distribution', 204-5, for a discussion of how the gradual Voortrekker occupation of the western Transvaal affected various Tswana communities in different ways.

7. F. Owen, *Diary*, 151; A. Waterboer to Gov. P. Maitland, Griqua Town, 24 April 1846 (CA, GH 14/1).

8. P. Lemue, Mothetho, 21 Sept. 1839, in Germond (ed.), *Chronicles*, 140; I. Schapera, 'Short History', 9–10.

9. S. M. Molema, *Moroka*, 61–2; J. T. Brown, *Nomads*, 220.

10. R. Edwards to Tidman, Kuruman, 8 Dec. 1841 (LMS, SA 18/2/B).

11. These raids began in mid-1841 and continued, apparently annually, through at least 1845. See Edwards to Tidman, *ibid.*; David Livingstone, *Missionary Correspondence*, 7, 25, 33, 37, and *Family Letters*, I, 69, 111–2, *et passim*; R. Arkwright, *Sport & Service in South Africa*, ed. by E. C. Tabler (Cape Town, 1971), 46, 65; J. Mackenzie, *Ten Years*, 359–63; Mziki, *Mlimo*, 96–7; *etc.*

12. I use the term 'Ndebele' here to indicate any person who would have acknowledged that Mzilikazi was his sovereign (see Appendix, below).

13. Andrew Smith to Gov. D'Urban, Black River, 15 Dec. 1835 (CA, GH 19/4); Smith, *Diary*, II, 150, 152; R. Moffat, *Matabele Jnls.*, I, 74, 81, 87, 96; Moffat to Ellis, Kuruman, 17 Sept. 1835 (LMS, MM 1/1/A).
   One effect of such epidemics was that Mzilikazi resided in remote posts to avoid contagion in population centres. See Moffat, *Missionary Labours*, 578–9.

14. Moffat, *Missionary Labours*, 588.

15. Moffat, *Matabele Jnls.*, II, 80. This statement was written in reference to Mzilikazi's disinclination to participate in slave trading.

16. Thomas, *Eleven Years*, 162.

17. Evid. of Cobejaan and Magaal [Magala], in *Bloemhof*, 318, 327–8. Cobejaan left Mzilikazi in Ngwato country; Magala left him at the Limpopo River.

18. Evid. of W. P. Grobbelaar, in *Bloemhof*, 326, names nine Tswana chiefs said to have deserted Mzilikazi; however, at least one of these—the Kgatla chief Pilane—was never under Mzilikazi's direct rule. For further references to Tswana refugees, see Breutz, *Rustenburg*, 219, 257, 291; TNAD, *Short History*, 43; Lemue, in Germond (ed.), *Chronicles*, 140; Edwards to Tidman, 8 Dec. 1841 (LMS, SA 18/2/B).

19. Evid. of Cobejaan and Magaal, in *Bloemhof*, 318, 327–8.

20. Smith, *Diary*, II, 246.

21. Hughes and van Velsen, 'The Ndebele', 45. They quote these figures: Zansi (Nguni-derived Ndebele)-15%; Enhla (Sotho)-25%; Holi (Shona)-60%.

22. Mziki, *Mlimo*, 78, identifies an uncle of Mzilikazi named 'Hosana'. This is probably the 'Gozane' whose descendants were interviewed in the Transvaal more than a hundred years later; see Breutz, *Rustenburg*, 182, 457–8.
   Some of these remnant groups were later enlarged by political refugees from Matabeleland, particularly during the succession crisis following Mzilikazi's death; see TNAD, *Short History*, 43.
   On Nguni who deserted Mzilikazi when he was moving away from earlier settlements, see N. van Warmelo, *Transvaal Ndebele Texts*, 16; C. Schulyer to M. Clarke, Fort Weeber, 31 May 1879 (Pretoria Arch., SN 1A).

23. The first written evidence of Ndebele population after early 1837 was recorded in 1854 by Robert Moffat. Unfortunately, he says very little about this subject, giving only the impression that significant changes had occurred *after* the migration. See, *e.g.*, *Matabele Jnls.*, I, 360–1.
   I know of only two previous estimates of the number of people to migrate north. In 1867 Karl Mauch estimated that Mzilikazi was accompanied by about 30,000 migrants, but he does not explain how he arrived at this figure; *Karl*

Mauch, trans. & ed. by F. O. Bernard (Cape Town, 1971), 80. Lye, 'Ndebele kingdom', 96, estimates 'between 10,000 and 20,000 people'. He also does not explain the basis of his estimate, which contrasts markedly with his figure of 60,000 to 80,000 as a 'reasonable' estimate of the peak Ndebele population during the 1830s.

24. This story is given in his 1905 draft article and in his book, *Mlimo* (p. 63). See page 77, above, for a relevant quotation on this subject.

25. Campbell to CNC, Insiza, 1 April 1898 (NAR, NB 6/1/1). A possibly related story is in Hawubasa ka Kumalo, 'The first visit of the Mandebele to Rhodesia', *Nada*, 5 (1927), 21, which actually concerns a purported expedition from the Transvaal to the Zambezi River.

26. To reiterate: the Ndebele *impi* returned home from north of the Limpopo in 1831 to find that their homes had been attacked by the Griqua of Barend Barends.

27. D. Lindley, *et al.*, to Anderson, Mosika, 18 Aug. 1836 (ABC Arch.), reprinted in Kotzé (ed.), *Letters*, 140.

This same letter was printed in the ABC's *Missionary Herald* (May 1837; pp. 187-93), but it seems unlikely that Campbell ever saw it. It is perhaps significant that Campbell never even alludes to the ABC missionaries, although he has much to say about the LMS mission founded in 1859 in Matabeleland (*Mlimo*, pp. 131-4). Hence his evidence about the Ndebele 'spies' is probably uninfluenced by written records.

28. E. Marais, 'The blood trail in the Transvaal', *The Star* (17 Oct. 1925), 5. The Afrikaner hunter was Jan Viljoen.

Note how similar this passage is to Mzilikazi's purported description of what he had expected to find when he entered the Transvaal (quoted from the same article on p. 49, above).

29. Mziki, *Mlimo*, 63. The context of this quotation in *Mlimo* actually places it at the time of Moffat's first visit to Mzilikazi in 1829; the 'Boers' mentioned actually refer to Griqua. Nevertheless I cite this passage here for two reasons: first, it is a representative and succinct statement of the whole Myth; second, it typifies the confusion of Afrikaners and Griqua which pervades traditions. Significantly, Cambell wrote approximately the same passage in 1898, but he then placed it in the context of the 1836-37 Voortrekker troubles; Campbell to CNC, 1 April 1898 (NAR, NB 6/1/1).

30. For a variety of examples, see A. W., 'Expulsion of Nkulumana', *Nada*, 13 (1935), 93; E. H. B., 'Notes on the Matabele occupation of Southern Rhodesia', *Nada*, 13 (1935), 15; J. A. Pitout, 'The arrival of the Mandebele in S. Rhodesia, as told by Siatsha', *Nada*, 30 (1953), 57; P. S. Mahlangu, *Umthwakazi* (Cape Town, 1957), 14-5; Statements of Ginyalitsha, Ngungu, Ntabeni, and Siatcha, *et al.*, *passim*, in R. F. Windram Papers (NAR, WI 8/1); *etc.*

31. Mtompe Khumalo, in Mhlagazanhlansi, *My Friend Kumalo*, 8.

32. The earliest written reference to this story I have seen is in C. H. S. Stabb's Ms. notes, written in 1875 [no pagination] (NAR, ST 12/4/4). Hughes and van Velsen, 'The Ndebele', 49, indicate that the story was still widely believed by the Ndebele during the 1950s. That the Myth is still alive is shown by L. W. B.[olze]'s reference to it in his introduction to the reprint edition of *Mlimo* (1972).

33. See, *e.g.*, Posselt, *Fact & Fiction*, 172-3; Summers and Pagden, *The Warriors*, 66ff.; R. Brown, 'External relations', 264-5.

34. J. S. Moffat, *The Lives of Robert & Mary Moffat*, 212ff., 298ff.; Edwin W.

Smith, *Robert Moffat* (London, 1925), 162ff., 208ff.; Cecil Northcott, *Robert Moffat* (London, 1961), 165–6, 213ff. I know of no indication either in Moffat's writings or in any other contemporary documents that Moffat travelled north of the Limpopo before 1854.

35. J. S. Moffat, Ms. Diary, 5 Dec. 1887, p. 3 (NAR, MO 1/3/1/1). The younger Moffat had worked as a missionary in Matabeleland from 1859 to 1865, so his knowledge of the Ndebele ran much deeper than what he learned during his 1887 visit as a government agent. It is perhaps significant to dating the origins of the Myth that Moffat does not mention its having been current during the 1860s.

36. J. S. Moffat to S. Shippard, 12 Dec. 1887, cited in R. Brown, 'External relations', 264. The younger Moffat drew heavily upon his father's papers to write his joint biography, *The Lives of Robert & Mary Moffat*, several years earlier.

37. Moffat, *Missionary Labours*, 587.

38. Moffat, draft letter to *British Banner*, Feb. 1853, cited in Brown, 'External relations', 264.

39. This point is discussed in the previous chapter's section on the 1835–6 embassy to Cape Town. See p. 113, above.

40. Moffat, *Missionary Labours*, 586; D. Lindley to Anderson, Port Natal, 21 Aug. 1837 (ABC Arch.), reprinted in Kotzé (ed.), *Letters*, 197.

41. See, *e.g.*, Moffat, *ibid.*, 586–7; Northcott, *Robert Moffat*, 165; H. M. Hole, *Passing of the Black Kings*, 57.

One wonders if when Moffat wrote his letter to the *British Banner* in early 1853 (see fn. 38, above) he was especially incensed by the recent Afrikaner sacking of his son-in-law David Livingstone's mission station. See Livingstone, *Family Letters*, II, 184–6.

42. Note that Moffat did not mention his having advised Mzilikazi to move north in his 1842 book, but he did so only in his 1853 letter. I believe the reason for this difference lies in his ignorance of what had become of Mzilikazi at the time he wrote his book. Moffat left South Africa for England in 1839; Mzilikazi was at that moment thought by Europeans to be finished, possibly even dead. By contrast, in 1853 Mzilikazi's successful resettlement in Matabeleland was general knowledge; Moffat was probably ready—consciously or unconsciously—to take credit for the Ndebeles' survival as a nation.

On early rumours of Mzilikazi's ruin, see Lindley to Anderson, Port Natal, 1 Dec. 1837 (ABC Arch.), reprinted in Kotzé (ed.), *Letters*, 214; Jnl. of F. Owen, 6 May 1839 (Cory Library Mss., Acc. no. 1113 [seen on microfilm in CA]).

Moffat returned to his mission station in 1843. At least as late as 1844 he did not know where Mzilikazi was living. See H. H. Methuen, *Life in the Wilderness* (London, 1846), 265.

43. Moffat, *Matabele Jnls.*, I, 195, 328, 361. See also quote from *Mlimo*, above in this section.

44. A. W., 'Expulsion', 93. A. W.'s informant was an Ndebele named Kanyemba, estimated to be ninety years old in 1935. Note that Thabazinduna is actually northeast from Mosega, not north.

45. Mtompe Khumalo, in Mhlagazanhlansi, *My Friend Kumalo*, 8; Statement of Ntabeni, p. 4 (NAR, WI 8/1); Pitout, 'Arrival', 57; A. W., 'Expulsion', 93. Mahlangu, *Umthwakazi*, 14, gives the same story and specifies that Moffat had previously visited the location.

Thabazinduna is famous in Ndebele tradition as the location where Mzilikazi purportedly had a number of dissident *indunas* executed shortly after his arrival in Matabeleland. See, *e.g.*, Titus J. Hlazo, 'The naming of the hill, "Intaba Yezinduna," Matabeleland', *Nada*, 12 (1934), 72-3.

46. Statement of Mkulani, in D. Moodie, 'Matopo-Mawabeni Statistical Report', 11 April 1898 (NAR, NB 6/1/1); E. H B., 'Notes' (draws directly on Mkulani's statement); Pitout, 'Arrival'; Statements of Ngungu, Ntabeni, and Siatcha (NAR, WI 8/1).

47. Statement of Ngungu, p. 1 (NAR, WI 8/1).

48. Summers and Pagden, *The Warriors*, 66.

49. E. Marais, 'Blood trail'.

50. Another possible manifestation of his reputation was the assertion that Mzilikazi named (or renamed) his heir 'Nkulumane' in honour of Moffat's mission station 'Kuruman'. That the son's name was Nkulumane is true; however, the similarity between this name and 'Kuruman' may only have been a coincidence. In Zulu *-nkulumane* means 'white rhinoceros' (Doke & Vilakazi, *Zulu-English Dictionary*); it is not impossible that Mzilikazi's son received the name as a child, before Mzilikazi even met Moffat (Nguni naming customs are discussed in the section on Gundwane Ndiweni; see pp. 152-4, below.) During the 1830s several Europeans apparently met Nkulumane, but only Andrew Smith identified him by name; see Smith, *Diary*, II, 39. Other visitors' estimates of the boy's age would place his birth date well before 1829, the year Moffat first met Mzilikazi. See Harris, *Wild Sports*, 162; Burrow, *Travels*, 50, 70, 72. Nkulumane's name seems to have been associated with the town of Kuruman only after Mzilikazi's death—a possible indication that the connection was tied to the then-developing Moffat Myth.

51. Statement of Mkulani, in D. Moodie, 'Matopo-Mawabeni: Stat. Report', 11 April 1898 (NAR, NB 6/1/1); Mziki, *Mlimo*, 78; Statement of Siatcha, p. 1 (NAR, WI 8/1).

Mzilikazi apparently left all his wagons behind; there is no evidence that he took any with him, and in 1854 Moffat reported that he possessed none. *Matabele Jnls.*, I, 258.

52. Ellenberger, *History*, 210; Mziki, *Mlimo*, 78. Generally, Ellenberger's account of the Ndebele migration borrows from Campbell's 1905 draft article; however, Ellenberger's assertion that Mzilikazi was a lone straggler was not made by Campbell in that article.

53. Ellenberger, *History*, 211; Bryant, *Olden Times*, 438; Summers and Pagden, *The Warriors*, 67.

54. This point is tenuous. N. van Warmelo, *The Bakgatla ba ga Mosetlha* (Pretoria, 1944), 5, refers to the Kgatla later fleeing the Voortrekkers, going 'to the North-West, in the same direction that Mzilikazi had already taken.'

55. Statement of Ngungu, p. 1 (NAR, WI 8/1); Statement of Mkulani (NAR, NB 6/1/1); Mziki, *Mlimo* 78; Ellenberger, *History*, 211; Bryant, *Olden Times*, 438. Mtompe Khumalo, in Mhlagazanhlansi, *My Friend Kumalo*, 8, makes the same point, but he adds the incorrect assertion that the Ndebele attacked the Kwena of Sechele along the way and captured the Ngwato prince Macheng. Macheng is known to have been captured in 1842; Livingstone, *Family Letters*, I, 69; Mackenzie, *Ten Years*, 361-2.

56. Mackenzie, *ibid.*, 359; Mackenzie to Chas. Warren, Mafeking, 9 June 1885, 'Summary of the history of Bechuanaland', in C.4588, 66; E. Smith, 'Sebetwane', 387-9; W. F. Lye, 'Sotho wars', 227.

57. Mackenzie to Warren, *ibid.*; Evid. of Khama, taken 3 Sept. 1888, in C.

5918, 67; Matambo to Posselt, Bulawayo, 8 Jan. 1914 (NAR, Misc/PO 9); Statement of Mkulani (NAR, NB 6/1/1). A contrary view is expressed in A. Sillery, *The Bechuanaland Protectorate* (Cape Town, 1952), 118, 180. Sillery possibly confuses earlier Ndebele attacks on the Ngwato with the period of the migration, however.

58. Statement of Ntabeni, p. 65 (NAR, WI 8/1).

59. Mziki, *Mlimo*, 78. The earliest recorded description of these Ndebele rites is in Smith, *Diary*, II, 307. Smith did not actually observe the rites, but got his information from Mncumbathe. Among the many later first-hand descriptions, see 'The Matabele soldier's dance', anon. letter, dd. Bulawayo, 13 Feb., in *Diamond Fields Advertiser* (12 May 1890), 3; W. A. Elliott, '"Feast of the first fruits" in Amandebeleland', *Juvenile Missionary Magazine* (London, Sept. 1885), 101-3; Elliott, *Gold from the Quartz*, 86-93; David Carnegie, *Among the Matabele*, 70ff.; Thomas, *Eleven Years*, 301-3; Mhlagazanhlansi, *My Friend Kumalo*, 29-32.

60. This inference is based upon the impression given in traditions that the Ndebele did not linger in Ngwato country.

61. The fact that a two-fold division took place is supported by virtually all traditional authorities. Gundwane's identity is discussed below.

62. See, *e.g.*, Statement of Ntabeni, pp. 1, 3 (NAR, WI 8/1).

63. See the maps in Becker, *Path of Blood*, 276; Omer-Cooper, *Zulu Aftermath*, 132; Ransford, *Bulawayo*, 16; Mziki, *Mlimo* [reprint ed. only], 62.

64. Mackenzie to Warren, in C.4588, 66.

65. See, *e.g.*, Hlazo, 'Naming', 72.

66. The emphasis on exploration is especially evident in the Statements of Ginyalitsha and Ngungu (NAR, WI 8/1); Mziki *Mlimo*, 78-9; Ellenberger, *History*, 211; Bryant, *Olden Times*, 438. See also Moffat, *Matabele Jnls.*, I, 372.

67. Statement of Ginyalitsha, p. 2 (NAR, WI 8/1); Hlazo, 'Naming', 72-3. By contrast, Mtompe Khumalo, in Mhlagazanhlansi, *My Friend Kumalo*, 8, suggests that it was the other division which became lost.   •

68. Moffat, *Matabele Jnls.*, I, 289; Thomas, 'Mission to the Matebele', 288; F. C. Selous, *A Hunter's Wanderings in Africa* (London, 1881), 31-2.

69. This point is far from certain. One current which runs through the traditions is that the other division waited for Mzilikazi until they thought he was dead. Evidence for this is cited below.

70. This subject is treated at greater length in my article, 'A lost man in Southern African history: Kaliphi/Gundwane of the Ndebele', *International Jnl. of African Historical Studies*, X, 1 (1977), 96-110.

71. Statement of Ginyalitsha, p. 1 (NAR, WI 8/1); Mtompe Khumalo, in Mhlagazanhlansi, *My Friend Kumalo*, 8; Mziki, *Mlimo*, 84-5; A. W., 'Expulsion', 94; *etc.*

Campbell does not mention Gundwane by name in his 1905 draft article—an omission reflected in Ellenberger and Bryant's books, which draw upon Campbell.

The earliest written reference to Gundwane of which I am aware is in Campbell to CNC, Insiza, 1 April 1898 (NAR, NB 6/1/1): 'The tribe separated into two . . . "Magundana" [*sic*] in charge of half, making for Thabas Induna . . . '

72. Statement of Ntabeni, pp. 29, 41 (NAR, WI 8/1).

73. Doke & Vilakazi, *Zulu-English Dictionary*; J. N. Pelling, *Practical Ndebele Dictionary*.

74. On naming customs, see Bryant, *Olden Times*, 15, 39; Peter Nielsen, *The Matabele at Home* (Bulawayo, 1913), 4; Cope, *Izibongo*, 25-6; Hughes and van Velsen, 'The Ndebele', 96; E J. Krige, *Social System of the Zulus*, 73-4.

75. For descriptions of Kaliphi's authority during the 1830s, see Moffat, *Matabele Jnls.*, I, 62, 70, 85; Harris, *Wild Sports*, 84; Smith, *Diary*, II, 79, 139, 141; Burrow, *Travels*, 47; Jnl. of Venable, 8 Feb. 1836 (ABC Arch.).

76. The mystery of Kaliphi's fate is commented upon in P. L. Breutz's biographical sketch, 'Mkalipi', in W. J. de Kock (ed.), *Dictionary of South African Biography* (Johannesburg, 1968), I, 545. See also Storry, *Shattered Nation*, 18-9.

Ntabeni (quoted above) is the only traditional authority to mention Kaliphi by name, but he seems to have done so only in response to an explicit question posed by his interviewer. Campbell, 1905 draft article, and *Mlimo*, 70ff., mentions Kaliphi by name as commander of the Ndebele force at the Battle of Vegkop in 1836. Curiously, he also identifies 'Gundwane' as the sub-commander at that battle. I suspect that Campbell got the name Gundwane from an authentic Ndebele tradition, but that he got Kaliphi's name from a contemporary European document (probably Harris, *Wild Sports*, in which Kaliphi's role in the battle is discussed extensively). Not recognizing that Kaliphi and Gundwane were one person, Campbell then reconciled his apparently contradictory evidence by placing both names in his account and assigning to 'Gundwane' the lesser role of sub-commander. His conclusion is followed by many later writers.

77. Moffat, *Matabele Jnls.*, I, 305.

78. On Monyebe's death, see T. M. Thomas to Tidman, Inyati, 23 Sept. 1862 (LMS, MM 1/2/A); R. Moffat to Tidman, Kuruman, 25 Dec. 1862 (LMS, MM 1/2/A); J. S. Moffat to J. S. Unwin, Bloemfontein, 1 March 1863, in J. P. R. Wallis (ed.), *The Matabele Mission . . . of John and Emily Moffat* (London, 1945), 188-9; J. Mackenzie, *Ten Years*, 326-7.

A brilliant analysis of family rivalries in Ndebele politics through this whole period is Lance F. Morrow's 'Pre-Mfecane carry-overs in subsequent Ndebele politics', in *Collected Seminar Papers on the Societies of Southern Africa in the 19th & 20th Centuries*, Vol. 3 (Univ. of London, Institute of Commonwealth Studies, 1972), 85-95.

79. Some traditional authorities specify that the migrants separated into two equal-sized groups, but most give the impression that Kaliphi/Gundwane's group was somewhat the larger.

Although I contend that 'Kaliphi' and 'Gundwane' were merely variant names for one person, I shall not argue that either name is necessarily a preferable form to use. Instead, I shall hereafter combine the two as 'Kaliphi/Gundwane'. It should be reiterated that hitherto the name Kaliphi has not been associated in print with the events discussed below.

80. For details, see Statements of Ginyalitsha, Ntabeni, Ngungu, and Siatcha (NAR, WI 8/1); Mziki, *Mlimo*, 84; Hlazo, 'Naming', 73; Pitout, 'Arrival', 57; Mhlagazanhlansi, *My Friend Kumalo*, 8. See also Cobbing, 'The evolution of Ndebele Amabutho', 622-4.

81. Summers and Pagden, *The Warriors*, 67, hold that this division had all the women and children; Statement of Ngungu, pp. 3-4 (NAR, WI 8/1), specifies that Mzilikazi's group had women and children in it.

82. Statements of Ngungu, p. 8, and Ntabeni, pp. 1, 41 (NAR, WI 8/1); A. W., 'Expulsion', 94.

83. Statements of Ngungu, p. 8, and Ntabeni, pp. 2-3 (NAR, WI 8/1);

Mhlagazanhlansi, *My Friend Kumalo*, 9.

84. For an excellent analysis of the relevance of the Shona background to the Ndebele invasion, see D. N. Beach, 'Ndebele raiders and Shona power', *Jnl. of African History*, XV, 4 (1974), 633ff.

85. For a mainly Ndebele-derived perspective, see Mziki, *Mlimo*, 79ff.; Mhlagazanhlansi, *My Friend Kumalo*, 9; Statement of Mkulani (NAR, NB 6/1/1); Campbell to CNC, 1 April 1898 (NAR, NB 6/1/1).

For Shona-derived perspectives, see Statements of Nkani, and Umzila, p. 1 (NAR, WI 8/1); C. T. Stuart to CNC, Gwelo, 16 Feb. 1906 (NAR, A 3/18/28).

86. Beach, 'Ndebele raiders', 638ff.; R .Kent Rasmussen, *Mzilikazi of the Ndebele* (London, 1977), Chapters 5–7; N. M. B. Bhebe, 'Some aspects of Ndebele relations with the Shona in the 19th century', *Rhodesian History*, 4 (1973), 31ff.

87. Statement of Ntabeni, p. 1 (NAR, WI 8/1); Mhlagazanhlansi, *My Friend Kumalo*, 9; Ransford, *Bulawayo*, 166.

88. This impression is pronounced in Bryant, *Olden Times*, 438. For a colourful, if somewhat inaccurate, picture of the confusion during the migration, see 'The story of Ndansi Kumalo', in Margery Perham (ed.), *Ten Africans* (London, 1936), 64–5. See also fn. 67, above.

89. Campbell, 1905 draft article; Mziki, *Mlimo*, 79; Ellenberger, *History*, 211; Mhlagazanhlansi, *My Friend Kumalo*, 8.

This clash is apparently confirmed from the Tawana side; see James Chapman, *Travels in the Interior of South Africa*, rev. & ed. by E. C. Tabler, 2 vols. (Cape Town, 1971), II, 178–9.

90. Statement of Ginyalitsha, p. 11 (NAR, WI 8/1).

91. Statements of Ntabeni, p. 3, and Siatcha, p. 1 (NAR, WI 8/1); A. W., 'Expulsion', 94; C. L. Carbutt, 'A brief account of the rise and fall of the Matabele', *Nada*, 25 (1948), 39. Panda Matenga is another location frequently mentioned in accounts of Mzilikazi's travels, but it is probable that he did not get quite that far north.

92. Campbell, 1905 draft article; Mziki, *Mlimo*, 79ff.

93. These conclusions are speculative, but they are supported to some extent by the obvious interest in crossing the Zambezi which the Ndebele retained through the ensuing decades. For a discussion of this subject, see R. Brown, 'External relations', 265–6.

94. Statements of Ginyalitsha, p. 11, and Ngungu, pp. 1, 9 (NAR, WI 8/1); Mhlagazanhlansi, *My Friend Kumalo*, 8.

95. Moffat, *Matabele Jnls.*, I, 289, 371–2. Recall that on two earlier occasions (c. 1822 and c. 1827) Mzilikazi's northward migrations appear to have been halted by tsetse fly (see Chapters 2–3 above).

96. Statement of Ginyalitsha, p. 11 (NAR ,WI 8/1).

97. Becker, *Rule of Fear*, 183; Omer-Cooper, *Zulu Aftermath*, 147; Hole, *Passing of the Black Kings*, 84, 102–3; Ransford, *Bulawayo*, 19; R. Brown, 'External relations', 266–7.

98. Mhlagazanhlansi, *My Friend Kumalo*, 8, is the most widely cited example.

99. Statement of Ntabeni, p. 51 (NAR, WI 8/1); Mziki, *Mlimo*, 99.

100. Livingstone, *Travels*, 99–100; E. Smith, 'Sebetwane', 398; Ellenberger, *History*, 312; Mutumba Mainga, *Bulozi Under the Luyana Kings* (London, 1973), 65, 69–70. Livingstone—who interviewed Sebitwane shortly before the latter's death in 1851—appears to be the primary authority for all these

accounts.

101. For example, Hlazo, 'Naming', 72, holds that Mzilikazi's division reached the Zambezi, following it to its confluence with the Gwai, thence up to the Bembezi, *etc.*

102. Moffat, *Matabele Jnls.*, I, 233, 239–40, 297; Mziki, *Mlimo*, 99ff.; Statement of Ginyalitsha, p. 11 (NAR, WI 8/1); R. Lanning, 'Statistical report . . . 1898', p. 8 (NAR, NB 6/1/1); Livingstone, *Travels*, 100ff.; E. Smith, 'Sebetwane', 399; Mainga, *Bulozi*, 70.

103. Mhlagazanhlansi, *My Friend Kumalo*, 8. Dating Mzilikazi's difficulties at the Nata River to this time of the year also conforms to the seasonal patterns of tsetse fly infestation; see Tabler, *The Far Interior*, 80-1.

104. Statement of Siatcha, p. 1 (NAR, WI 8/1), and Hlazo, 'Naming', 73, give us the name of the settlement. The concusion that Mzilikazi halted at the Bembezi is also supported by Pitout, 'Arrival', 57.

105. Moffat, *Matabele Jnls.*, I, 372; T. M. Thomas, 'Mission to the Matabele', 288; Alex C. Bailie to Chief Clerk, Gubulawayo, 31 Dec. 1876 (CA, GH 19/12), reprinted in C.2220; Statement of Ngungu, p. 2 (NAR, WI 8/1); Campbell, 1 April 1898 (NAR, NB 6/1/1); Mziki, *Mlimo*, Chapter 12; Mhlagazanhlansi, *My Friend Kumalo*, 9, 15; Hlazo, 'Naming', 73; Pitout, 'Arrival', 57; *etc.*

106. Hlazo, 'Naming', 73.

107. There is a fairly considerable literature on this subject. In addition to numerous articles in *Nada*, see especially Morrow, 'Pre-Mfecane carry-overs'.

Cobbing, 'Evolution', 624, describes the crisis which developed upon Mzilikazi's arrival as a 'civil war'. However, I have seen no evidence which persuasively counters the impression that Mzilikazi restored his authority quickly and without significant resistance.

108. Statement of Ntabeni, p. 4 (NAR, WI 8/1), gives 'autumn' as the time of Mzilikazi's arrival. Hlazo, 'Naming', 73, says the reunion occurred shortly after the *inxwala*.

Cobbing, 'Evolution', 624, typifies modern historians in giving c. 1841 as the date of Mzilikazi's arrival in Matabeleland, thereby implying his migration had lasted about four years. One problem with such a chronology is accounting for what Mzilikazi was doing during all those years.

109. When this book was going to the printer, I received a copy of Julian Cobbing's Ph.D. thesis, 'The Ndebele under the Khumalos, 1820-1896' (University of Lancaster, 1976). As Professor Ranger indicates in the Foreword to the present book, Dr Cobbing's work is the first significant study of the Ndebele kingdom during its trans-Limpopo history. I heartily endorse his work to all readers who wish to pursue Ndebele history past 1839.

Notes for Appendix

1. See, *e.g.*, Hughes & van Velsen, 'The Ndebele', 44.

2. The latter term (usually spelled *Matabele*) is still frequently used in southern Africa, particularly by white writers. See, *e.g.*, Summers & Pagden, *The Warriors*; Storry, *The Shattered Nation*. Both books claim to be up-to-date treatments of Ndebele history, but insist on using the outmoded term 'Matabele' throughout.

3. Lye, 'Sotho wars', 153; N. J. van Warmelo, *A Preliminary Survey of the*

Bantu Tribes of South Africa (Pretoria, 1935), 87. Other suggested definitions of 'Matabele' include: 'the destroyers'; 'those who stab'; 'those who sink down out of sight behind their shields'; 'those who disappear'; *etc.*

4. According to E. Smith, 'Sebetwane', 371n: 'The BaTswana [*i.e.*, western Sotho] applied the terms "BomMma-Ntatisi" [or "Mantatee"] and "Matabele" indiscriminately to all marauders or wandering foreigners coming from the east.'

5. Mzilikazi's connections with the 'Transvaal Ndebele' are discussed at length in Chapter 2, above.

6. See, *e.g.*, Mahlangu, *Umthwakazi*, 10; Kotzé (ed.), *Letters*, 105; and Arbousset & Daumas, *Narrative*, 134.

Significantly, when Mzilikazi's ambassador Mncumbathe signed a treaty with the governor of the Cape Colony in 1836 (see Chapter 4), no variant of 'Ndebele' or 'Matabele' was written into the document. Instead, Mzilikazi was described as the 'King of the Abaqua Zooloo or Qua Machoban' [Mashobane was his father]. The original treaty can be seen in the Cape Archives (GH 19/5).

7. In 1885 the missionary John Mackenzie, who had visited Matabeleland in 1863 and 1873, wrote that the 'names Matabele and Basuto were originally terms of reproach, but are now accepted as proper names by those who are addressed by them.' See British Parliamentary Paper, C.4588, p. 63. A year later, however, Lobengula told a white hunter that ' "Amandebeli is an Abusuto word, the proper name for my people is Zulu." ' See Walter Montagu Kerr, *The Far Interior*, 2 vols. (Boston, 1886), I, 67.

8. Fittingly, the Ndzundza of Magodongo, who were among the first people Mzilikazi encountered, may have been the first to call his followers 'Matabele'. See Mziki, *Mlimo*, 53.

BIBLIOGRAPHY

The bibliography is arranged as follows:
I.   Bibliographies and archival guides
II. Archival sources
III. Unpublished theses and manuscripts
IV. Government publications
V.   Periodicals and newspapers
VI. Published articles and books (including individually authored government publications)

Abbreviations used throughout this book, such as 'NAR' for 'National Archives of Rhodesia', are given in square brackets next to their referents. Wherever possible unpublished sources are listed with the same abbreviations and reference numbers employed in their respective repositories. An alphabetical list of the most frequently used abbreviations is offered on page x, above.

This bibliography does not list all sources consulted in the preparation of this study. It does, however, attempt to list all sources cited in footnotes. For additional materials relevant to Ndebele studies and related topics, readers should consult the bibliographies and archival guides in the first section.

I. BIBLIOGRAPHIES AND ARCHIVAL GUIDES

Baxter, T. W. (ed). *Guide to the Public Archives of Rhodesia*. Vol. I: *1890–1923*. Rev. Ed., Salisbury: National Archives of Rhodesia, 1969. 262p.
—— and E. E. Burke. *Guide to the Historical Manuscripts in the National Archives of Rhodesia*. Salisbury: National Archives of Rhodesia, 1970. 527p.
Bevan, Elizabeth Joan (comp.). *Mzilikazi, 1790–1878: A Bibliography*. Johannesburg: University of Witwatersrand, 1969. 32p.
Hess, Robert L. and Davan M. Conger. *A Bibliography of Primary Sources for 19th Century Tropical Africa*. Stanford: University Press, 1972, 800p.

Matthews, Noel and M. Doreen Wainwright (comps.). *A Guide to Manuscripts and Documents in the British Isles Relating to Africa*. Ed. by J. D. Pearson. London: Oxford University Press, 1971. 321p.

Mendelssohn, Sidney. *South African Bibliography*. 2 vols. London: Kegan, Paul, Trench, Trübner, 1910.

Schapera, I. *Select Bibliography of South African Native Life and Affairs*. London: Oxford University Press, 1941. 249p.

Thompson, Leonard, Richard Elphick and Inez Jarrick. *Southern African History Before 1900: A Select Bibliography of Articles*. Stanford: Hoover Institute, 1971. 102p.

II. ARCHIVAL SOURCES

A. *American Board of Commissioners for Foreign Missions* [ABC], Houghton Library, Harvard University

1. *South African Missionary Correspondence*, 1835-8 (seen on microfilm no. ZD/A. 4-5 in Cape Archives)

B. *Cape Archives* [CA], Cape Town

1. *Accessions* [Acc.]
Acc. 302   Orpen Papers
Acc. 519   D'Urban Papers
Acc. 1336   Letter from [Mzilikazi] to D'Urban (photocopy).

2. *Colonial Office* [CO]
CO 455   Letters received; military and naval officers, 1836.
CO 464   Letters received; consistories, clergymen and missionaries, 1837.
CO 2649   Letters received; drostdy, Graaff Reinet, 1823.
CO 2658   Letters received; drostdy, Graaff Reinet, 1824
CO 2721   Letters received; civil commissioners and resident magistrates, Albany and Somerset, 1830.
CO 2743   Letters received; civil commissioners and resident magistrates, Graaff Reinet, 1833.
CO 2750   Letters received; civil commissioners and resident magistrates, Graaff Reinet, 1834.

3. *Government House* [GH]
GH 1/23   Secretary of State, London: despatches received, 1836.
GH 8/1   Lt Governor: despatches, 1836.
GH 8/2   Lt Governor: despatches, 1837
GH 14/1   Border tribes and diplomatic agents, 1835-46.
GH 14/8   Letters received; native chiefs in Bechuanaland, 1860-81.
GH 18/6   Misc. letters; private individuals, 1850-62.
GH 19/4   Border tribes & treaties, 1834-45.
GH 19/5   Treaties with native chiefs (originals), 1836-46.
GH 19/12a   Correspondence re Mr Bailie's mission to the north (Matabeleland), 1877.

GH 23/11   Secretary of State, London: despatches to, 1833–8.
GH 26/19   Cape of Good Hope, duplicate despatches, 1831–2.

4. *Graaff Reinet* [GR]
GR 10/16   Misc. letters received, 1832.
GR 10/35   Letters from Adam Kok, Capt A. Waterboer and Griqua papers, 1816–36.

5. *Lt Governor* [LG]
LG 2–3   Letters received; Colonial Office, Cape Town, 1829–33.
LG 9   Commission of Enquiry into reports of cruelty towards native tribes beyond the Orange River, March 1830
LG   207 Letters received; civil commissioner, Cradock, 1836–7.
LG   219 Letters received; civil commissioner, Graaff Reinet, 1836–7.
LG   495 Letters received; private individuals, 1836–7.

C. *London Missionary Society Archives* [LMS], London (now housed in the library of the School of African and Oriental Studies, London). Citations give box no./folder no./jacket letter.

1. *Matabele Mission* [MM]. Correspondence, 1835–97. 2 boxes.
2. *John Philip Papers*. In 'Odds, Africa', boxes 5–7.
3. *South Africa (including Bechuanaland) Missions* [SA]. Correspondence, 1823–45, boxes 9–21.
4. *South Africa, Journals*. 1824–92, box 4.

D. *National Archives of Rhodesia* [NAR], Salisbury.

1. *Historical Manuscripts Collection*.
BA 10/2/1   Journal of Alex Bailie, 1876–8.
FR 2/2/1   Reminiscences of Ivon Fry, told to R. F. Windram, 1938.
JA 5/2/4   S. N. G. Jackson, Notes on the military organization of the Matabele.
MISC/PO/9   F. W. T. Posselt, correspondence with Matambo, 1913–14.
MO 1/3/1/1   J. S. Moffat, diary in Matabeleland, 1887–92.
MO 5/1/1   Robert Moffat, correspondence.
WI 1/1/1   George Wilkerson, 'The Matabele Nation', ts., 2 vols.
WI 8/1   R. Foster Windram, Reminiscences.
WO 1/4/1   Joseph Garbett Wood, ts. Jnl. of visits to Matabeleland and Mashonaland in 1887 and 1888
—— A. A. Campbell, Reminiscences (unnumbered accession).

2. *Public Archives*
A 3/18/28   British South Africa Company Administrator's Office, Correspondence: 'History of the Matabele Tribes', 1904–6.
NB 6/1/1   Chief Native Commissioner for Matabeleland: Annual reports for 1898.

E. *Pretoria Archives* [PA], Pretoria.

1. C. Schulyer, Asst. Native Commissioner, to Capt M. Clarke, Fort Weeber, 31 May 1879, in Secretary for Native Affairs [SN 1A].

F. *Wesleyan Methodist Missionary Society* [WMMS], London.
1. South African and Bechuanaland Missions, Correspondence.

III. UNPUBLISHED THESES AND MANUSCRIPTS

[Campbell, A. A.]. [apparently unpublished article on Ndebele history, intended for *Bulawayo Chronicle*, c. 1905. Detailed notes taken from a draft of this article are in J. M. Orpen to D. Fred Ellenberger, 2 January 1906, in Documents Historiques, Grand Format, II, 3, Ellenberger Papers (the present author has drawn upon the notes of William F. Lye, who consulted the Ellenberger Papers in Lesotho)].
Hughes, A. J. B. 'The restructuring of Ndebele society under European control'. n.d. [c. 1956], ts. 424 p. [seen on microfilm no. 269, in NAR].
Lye, William Frank. 'The Sotho Wars in the interior of South Africa, 1822-1837'. Ph.D. Thesis in History, University of California, Los Angeles, 1969. 277p.
Rasmussen, R. Kent. 'A political history of the Philippolis Griquas, 1825-1861'. Seminar paper presented at University of California, Los Angeles, 1968. 52p.
Smith, Andrew. 'Journal of Expedition'. Vol. X-XI of Smith manuscripts [MSS], in South African Museum, Cape Town.
——. 'Memoranda A; notes on Tswana, Sotho and Matabele tribes'. Vol. XII of *ibid*.
Stow, G. W. 'The intrusion of the stronger Bantu races, cont.'. Ms. and ts. in Africana Collection of South African Library, Cape Town [ts. copy is cited in this book].
Thomas, [Thomas Morgan, Jr]. Untitled paper on Ndebele history. n.d. [c. 1910?]. Ts. 14p. In Orpen Papers (CA, Acc. 302, vol. 24, pt. 2).
Wilkerson, George. 'The Matabele Nation'. n.d. [c. 1909]. ts. 2 vols. 470p. (NAR, WI 1/1/1).

IV. GOVERNMENT PUBLICATIONS

A. *Miscellaneous* (note that individually authored government publications are listed under 'Articles and Books', below).
Cape of Good Hope. *Evidence Taken at Bloemhof before the Commission appointed to Investigate the claims of the South African Republic, Captain N. Waterboer, Chief of West Griqualand, and Certain other Native Chiefs, to Portions of the Territory on the Vaal River, now known as the Diamond-Fields*. Cape Town: Saul Solomon & Co, 1871. 392p. [copies of this volume can be found in CA, GH 21/1, and CA, HA 89].
Transvaal. Native Affairs Department [TNAD]. *Short History of the*

Native Tribes of the Transvaal. Facsimile reprint, Pretoria: State Library, 1968 (first pub.,Pretoria: Government Printer, 1905). 67p.

United States Board on Geographic Names. *Rhodesia and Nyasaland.* Washington, DC: Office of Geography, Dept of the Interior, 1956. 214p.

——. *South Africa.* 2 vols. Washington, DC: Division [*sic*] of Geography, Dept of the Interior, 1954.

B. *British Parliamentary Papers.*

503. *Caffre War* . . . n.l. [London], 1837.

C.1748. *Correspondence respecting the war between the Transvaal Republic and neighbouring tribes.* London, 1877.

C.2220. *Further correspondence respecting the affairs of South Africa.* London, 1879.

C.4588. *Further correspondence respecting the affairs of the Transvaal and adjacent territories.* London, 1885.

C.4643. *Further correspondence respecting the affairs of the Transvaal and adjacent territories.* London, 1886.

C.5918. *Further correspondence respecting the affairs of Bechuanaland and adjacent territories.* London, 1890.

C.8130. *Matabeleland: Report of the Land Commission of 1894; and correspondence relating thereto.* London: 1896.

V. PERIODICALS AND NEWSPAPERS

Evangelical Magazine and Missionary Chronicle (1824-35); (retitled:) *The Missionary Magazine and Chronicle* (1836-66); (retitled:) *The Chronicle of the London Missionary Society* (1867-   ). London: London Missionary Society. Monthly.

Grahamstown Journal [*GTJ*]. Grahamstown, Dec. 1831-Dec. 1837. Weekly.

Journal of African History. London: Cambridge University Press, 1960-   . quarterly.

Mbire; Historical Research South of the Zambezi. Salisbury: Historical Association of Central Africa, 1971-. Irregular annual.

Nada. Salisbury: Department of Native Affairs, 1923-63; Ministry of Internal Affairs, 1964   . Annual.

VI. PUBLISHED ARTICLES AND BOOKS

Abrahams, Peter. *Wild Conquest.* Harmondsworth: Penguin, 1966 (First published London, 1950). 348p. [novel].

Arbousset, T. & F. Daumas. *Narrative of an Exploratory Tour to the Northeast of the Colony of the Cape of Good Hope.* Trans. by J. C. Brown. Facsimile reprint, Cape Town: C. Struik, 1968 (First published in French, Paris, 1842; first published in English, Cape Town, 1846). 330p.

Arkwright, Robert. *Sport and Service in South Africa: The Diary of Lieutenant Robert Arkwright, 1843-1846.* Ed. by E. C. Tabler. Cape

Town: A. A. Balkema, 1971. 98p.

A. W. 'The expulsion of Nkulumana', *Nada*, 13 (1935), 93–5.

Bain, Andrew Geddes. *Journals of Andrew Geddes Bain: Trader, Explorer, Soldier, Road Engineer and Geologist.* Ed. by Margaret Lister. Cape Town: Van Riebeeck Society, 1949. 246p.

Baines, Thomas. *The Gold Regions of South Eastern Africa.* Facsimile reprint, Bulawayo: Books of Rhodesia, 1968 (First published, London, 1877). 187p.

——. *The Northern Goldfields Diaries of Thomas Baines.* Ed. by J. P. R. Wallis. 3 vols. London: Chatto & Windus, 1946. 779p.

Barnes, J. A. *Politics in a Changing Society: A Political History of the Fort Jameson Ngoni.* Manchester: Manchester University Press, 1967 (First published 1954). 245p.

Beach, David. 'Ndebele history in 1971'. *Rhodesian History,* I (1970), 87–94.

——. 'Ndebele raiders and Shona power', *Jnl. of African History*, XV, 4 (1974), 633–51.

Becker, Peter. *Hill of Destiny: The Life and Times of Moshesh.* London: Longman, 1969. 294p.

——. *Path of Blood: The Rise and Conquests of Mzilikazi.* London: Longmans, 1962. 289p.

——. *Rule of Fear: The Life and Times of Dingane.* London: Longmans, 1964. 283p.

Bhebe, Ngwabi M. B. 'Ndebele trade in the nineteenth century', *Jnl. of African Studies*, I, 1 (1974), 87–100.

——. 'Some aspects of Ndebele relations with the Shona in the nineteenth century', *Rhodesian History*, 4 (1973), 31–8.

Bird, John (ed.). *The Annals of Natal, 1495–1845.* 2 vols. Pietermaritzburg: P. Davis & Sons, 1888.

Boyce, William B. *Notes on South African Affairs.* Facsimile reprint, Cape Town: C. Struik, 1971 (First published, 1838).

B.[reutz], P. L. 'Mkalipi', in *Dictionary of South African Biography*, ed. by W. J. de Kock (Johannesburg: National Council for Social Research, 1968), I, 544–5.

Breutz, P. L. *The Tribes of Mafeking District.* Pretoria: Department of Native Affairs, 1955 (Ethnological Publications, No. 32). 315p.

——. *The Tribes of Marico District.* Pretoria: Department of Native Affairs, 1953 (Ethnological Publications, No. 30). 266p.

——. *The Tribes of Rustenburg and Pilansberg Districts.* Pretoria: Department of Native Affairs, 1953 (Ethnological Publications, No. 28). 501p.

Broadbent, Samuel. *A Narrative of the First Introduction of Christianity Amongst the Barolong Tribe of Bechuanas, South Africa.* London: Wesleyan Mission House, 1865. 204p.

Brookes, Edgar H. & Colin de B. Webb. *A History of Natal.* Pietermaritzburg: University of Natal Press, 1965. 371p.

Brown, J. Tom. *Among the Bantu Nomads: A Record of Forty Years Spent Among the Bechuana.* London: Seeley, Service, 1926. 272p.

Brown, Richard. 'The external relations of the Ndebele kingdom in the pre-partition era', in *African Societies in Southern Africa*, ed. by L. M. Thompson (London: Heinemann, 1969), 259-81.

——. *The Ndebele Succession Crisis, 1868-1877*. Reprint, Salisbury: Central Africa Historical Association, 1966 (First published in *Historians in Tropical Africa*, Salisbury, 1962). 18p.

Bryant, A. T. *A History of the Zulu and Neighbouring Tribes*. Cape Town: C. Struik, 1964. 157p.

——. *Olden Times in Zululand and Natal*. London: Longmans, Green, 1929. 710p.

——. *A Zulu-English Dictionary . . . and a Concise History of the Zulu People*. Pinetown, Natal: Mariannhill Mission Press, 1905.

Bullock, Charles. *The Mashona and the Matabele*. Cape Town and Johannesburg: Juta, 1950. 310p.

Bulpin, T. V. *Lost Trails of the Transvaal*. Johannesburg: Nelson, 1965. 474p.

Burrow, John. *Travels in the Wilds of Africa; being the diary of a Young Scientific Assistant who accompanied Sir Andrew Smith in the Expedition of 1834-1836*. Ed. by Percival R. Kirby. Cape Town: A. A. Balkema, 1971. 90p.

Campbell, A. A. [see Mziki].

Carbutt, C. L. 'A brief account of the rise and fall of the Matabele', *Nada*, 25 (1948), 38-44.

Carnegie, David. *Among the Matabele*. London: Religious Tract Society, 1894. 128p.

Casalis, Eugene. *The Basutos, or Twenty-three Years in South Africa*. London: James Nisbet, 1861 (First published in French, Paris, 1859). 355p.

Chapman, James. *Travels in the Interior of South Africa, 1849-1863*. 2 vols. Rev. and ed. by E. C. Tabler. Cape Town: A. A. Balkema, 1971 (First published London, 1868). 258, 244pp.

Chase, John Centlivres. *Natal: A Re-print of all the Authentic Notices*. Facsimile reprint, Cape Town: University of Cape Town and South African Library, 1955 (First published in two parts, Grahamstown, 1843). 135, 310pp.

——. 'Substance of the journal of two trading travellers, and of the communications of a missionary', *South African Quarterly Journal*, I, 4 (1830), 402-7.

Cloete, Stuart. *African Portraits*. Cape Town: Constantia, 1969. 366p.

Cobbing, Julian. 'The evolution of Ndebele Amabutho', *Jnl. of African History*, XV, 4 (1974), 607-31. (See also p. 237, n. 109, above.)

Colquhoun, Archibald R. *The Renascence of South Africa*. London: Hurst & Blackett, 1900. 299p.

Cope, Trevor (ed.). *Izibongo: Zulu Praise-Poems*. Oxford: Clarendon Press, 1968. 230p.

Cumming, R. Gordon. *Five Years of a Hunter's Life in South Africa*. 2 vols. 2nd ed., London: John Murray, 1850. 388, 381pp.

Denoon, Donald, 'with' Balam Nyeko. *Southern Africa Since 1800*. London: Longman, 1972. 242p.

Depelchin, H. and Ch. Croonenberghs. *Trois Ans dans L'Afrique*

Australe, Tome I: *Le Pays des Matabélés . . . 1879-1881*. Brussels: Polleunis, Ceuterick et Lefebure, 1882. 428p.

Doke, C. M. & B. W. Vilakazi. *Zulu-English Dictionary*. Johannesburg: University of Witwatersrand Press, 1948 [various editions have been used in this book].

Du Plessis, J. *A History of Christian Missions in South Africa*. London: Longmans, Green, 1911. 494p.

E.H.B. 'Notes on the Matabele occupation of Southern Rhodesia', *Nada*, 13 (1935), 14-7.

Ellenberger, D. Fred. *History of the Basuto: Ancient and Modern*. Written in English by J. C. Macgregor. London: Caxton, 1912. 396p.

Elliott, W. A. ' ''Feast of the first fruits'' in Amandebeleland', *Juvenile Missionary Magazine* (London: LMS, Sept. 1885), 101-3.

——. *Gold From the Quartz*. London: London Missionary Society, 1910. 223p.

——. *Handbooks to our Mission Fields: South Africa*. London: London Missionary Society, 1913. 115p.

——. *Notes for a Sindabele Dictionary and Grammar*. Bristol: Sindabele Publishing Co, n.d. [1911]. 589p.

Engelbrecht, J. A. *The Korana*. Cape Town: Maskew Miller, 1936. 239p.

'Facts about the world's oldest man', in *The Star* (Johannesburg, 18 October 1937).

Fourie, H. C. M. *Amandebele van Fene Mahlangu*. Zwolle: La Riviere and Voorhoeve, 1921. 214p.

Fuller, Claude. *Tsetse in the Transvaal and Surrounding Territories: An Historical Review*. Pretoria: Government Printer, 1923 (Dept of Agriculture, Entomology Memoirs No. 1). 68p.

Fynn, Henry. *The Diary of Henry Francis Fynn*. Ed. by James Stuart and D. Mck. Malcolm. Pietermaritzburg: Shuter & Shooter, 1969 (First published, 1950). 341p.

Gann, L. H. *A History of Southern Rhodesia: Early Days to 1934*. London: Chatto & Windus, 1965. 354p.

Gardiner, Allen F. *Narrative of a Journey to the Zoolu Country*. London: William Crofts, 1836. 412p.

Germond, Robert C. (ed.). *Chronicles of Basutoland*. Morija: Sesuto Book Depot, 1967. 583p.

Gibson, J. Y. *The Story of the Zulus*. Pietermaritzburg: P. Davis & Sons, 1903. 276p. (Rev. ed. also used).

Gluckman, Max. 'The rise of a Zulu empire', *Scientific American*, 202, 4 (1960), 157-68.

Gray, Richard. 'Annular eclipse maps', *Jnl. of African History*, IX, 1 (1968), 147-57.

——. 'Eclipse maps', *Jnl. of African History*, VI, 3 (1965), 251-62.

Harris, William Cornwallis. *The Wild Sports of Southern Africa*. London: John Murray, 1839. 387p.

Hawabusa Ka Kumalo. 'The first visit of the Mandebele to Rhodesia', *Nada*, 5 (1927), p. 21.

Hlazo, Titus J. 'The naming of the hill ''*Intaba Yezinduna*'',

Matabeleland', *Nada*, 12 (1934), 72-3.

Hole, Hugh Marshall. *Lobengula*. London: Philip Allan, 1929. 211p. [novel].

——. *The Passing of the Black Kings*. Facsimile reprint, New York: Negro Universities Press, 1969 (First published, London 1932). 322p.

Holub, Emil. 'Die Ma-Atabele', *Zeitschrift für Ethnologie* (1893), 177-206.

Hughes, A. J. B. *Kin, Caste and Nation among the Rhodesian Ndebele*. Manchester: Manchester University Press for the Rhodes-Livingstone Institute, 1956. 86p.

—— and J. van Velsen. 'The Ndebele', in *The Shona and Ndebele of Southern Rhodesia*, by Hilda Kuper, A. J. B. Hughes and J. van Velsen (London: International Africa Institute, 1954), 41-129.

Hunt, D. R. 'An account of the Bapedi', *Bantu Studies*, V, 4 (1931), 275-326.

Isaacs, Nathaniel. *Travels and Adventures in Eastern Africa*. Ed. by Louis Herman and P. R. Kirby. Cape Town: C. Struik, 1970 (First published, 1836). 349p.

Johnson, Frank. *Great Days: The Autobiography of an Empire Pioneer*. London: G. Bell & Sons, 1940. 366p.

Jones, Neville [see Mhlagazanhlansi].

Kerr, Walter Montagu. *The Far Interior*. 2 vols. Boston: Houghton Mifflin, 1886. 316, 318p.

Kirby, Percival R. *Sir Andrew Smith, MD, KCB: His Life, Letters, and Works*. Cape Town: A. A. Balkema, 1965. 358p.

Kotzé, D. J. 'Die eerste Amerikaanse sendelinge onder die Matebeles', *Argief-jaarboek vir Suid-Afrikaanse Geskiedenis*, 13de jaargang, deel I (Pretoria: Staatsdrukker, 1950), 129-318.

—— (ed.). *Letters of the American Missionaries, 1835-1838*. Cape Town: Van Riebeeck Society, 1950. 276p.

Krige, Eileen Jensen. *The Social System of the Zulus*. Pietermaritzburg: Shuter & Shooter, 1965 (First published, 1936). 420p.

Kruger, Paul. *The Memoirs of Paul Kruger*. Trans. by A. Teixeira de Mattos. New York: The Century Co, 1902. 440p.

Kuper, Hilda. *An African Aristocracy: Rank Among the Swazi*. London: Oxford University Press, 1961 (First published 1947). 251p.

Leask, Thomas. *The Southern African Diaries of Thomas Leask, 1865-1870*. Ed. by J. P. R. Wallis. London: Chatto & Windus, 1954. 253p.

Lewis, D. G. 'Nkulumana, Umta ka Umziligazi', *Nada*, 33 (1956), 11-2.

Liesegang, Gerhard. 'Nguni migrations between Delagoa Bay and the Zambezi River, 1821-1839', *African Historical Studies*, III, 2 (1970), 317-37.

Lindblom, K. G. *The Use of Oxen as Pack and Riding Animals in Africa*. Stockholm: Riksmuseets Etnografiska Avdelning, 1931. 77p.

Livingstone, David. *Family Letters, 1841-1856*. Ed. by I. Schapera. 2 vols. London: Chatto & Windus, 1959. 266, 320p.

——. *Livingstone's Missionary Correspondence, 1841-1856*. Ed. by I.

Schapera. London: Chatto & Windus, 1961. 342p.
——. *Missionary Travels and Researches in South Africa*. 25th ed. New York: Harper & Bros, 1859. 755p.
Lloyd, Edwin. *Three Great African Chiefs (Khâmé, Sebelé, and Bathoeng)*. London: T. Fisher Unwin, 1895. 271p.
London Missionary Society. *Papers Respecting the Matebele Mission, South Africa* (Printed for the Directors only). London: Yates & Alexander, 1873. 316p. [copies can be found in the British Museum (reference, 4766.ff.16) and the NAR].
Lovett, Richard. *The History of the London Missionary Society*. 2 vols. London: Henry Frowde, 1899.
Lye, William F. 'The Difaqane: the Mfecane in the Southern Sotho area, 1822-24', *Jnl. of African History*, VIII, 1 (1967), 107-31.
——. 'The distribution of the Sotho peoples after the Difaqane', in *African Societies in Southern Africa*, ed. by L. M. Thompson (London, 1969), 190-206.
——. 'The Ndebele kingdom south of the Limpopo River', *Jnl. of African History*, X, 1 (1969), 87-104.
Macgregor, James C. *Basuto Traditions*. Cape Town: Argus Printing & Pub Co, 1905. 67p.
Mackenzie, John. *Ten Years North of the Orange River . . . 1859 to 1869*. Edinburgh: Edmonston & Douglas, 1871. 523p.
Mackenzie, W. Douglas. *John Mackenzie: South African Missionary and Statesman*. London: Hodder & Stoughton, 1902. 564p.
Macmillan, William M. *Bantu, Boer, and Briton*. Rev. ed., Oxford: Clarendon Press, 1963 (First published, London, 1929). 382p.
Mahlangu, P. S. *Umthwakazi*. Cape Town: Longman, 1957. 76p.
Mainga, Mutumba. *Bulozi Under the Luyana Kings*. London: Longmans, 1973. 278p.
Marais, Eugene. 'The blood trail in the Transvaal; tales of the Matabele recalled by a man who may be the last survivor of those who saw them march nearly a century ago', *The Star* (Johannesburg, 17 October 1925), p. 5.
Marais, J. S. *The Cape Coloured People, 1652-1937*. Johannesburg: Witwatersrand University Press, 1962 (First published, 1939). 296p.
Marks, Shula. 'The traditions of the Natal "Nguni": a second look at the work of A. T. Bryant', in *African Societies in Southern Africa*, ed. by L. M. Thompson (London, 1969), 126-44.
Mauch, Karl. *Karl Mauch: African Explorer*. Trans. and ed. by F. O. Bernard. Cape Town: C. Struik, 1971. 247p.
[Merensky, Alexander]. 'Beiträge zur Geschichte der Bapeli', *Berliner Missionsberichte*, 20 (1862), 327-42.
Merensky, Alexander. 'Esquisse geographique et naturelle du sud-est de L'Afrique', Trans. by F. Polchet, *Bulletin Société Belge de Geographie*, 2 (1878), 437-71.
Methuen, Henry H. *Life in the Wilderness, or Wanderings in South Africa*. London: Richard Bentley, 1846. 318p
Mhlagazanhlansi [Neville Jones]. *My Friend Kumalo*. [Bulawayo:

Rhodesian Publishing Co, c. 1946]. 54p.

Mönning, H. O. *The Pedi*. Pretoria: J. L. van Schaik, 1967. 365p.

Moffat, John S. *The Lives of Robert & Mary Moffat*. 2nd ed. London: T. Fisher Unwin, 1885. 484p.

——. 'The Matebele', *Juvenile Missionary Magazine* (London, September–October 1874), 176–9, 192–6.

—— and Emily Moffat. *The Matabele Mission: A Selection from the Correspondence of John and Emily Moffat, David Livingstone and others, 1858–1879*. Ed. by J. P. R. Wallis. London: Chatto & Windus, 1945. 268p.

Moffat, Robert. *The Matabele Journals of Robert Moffat, 1829–1860*. Ed. by J. P. R. Wallis. 2 vols. London: Chatto & Windus, 1945. 382, 295p.

——. *Missionary Labours and Scenes in Southern Africa*. London: John Snow, 1842. 624p.

—— and Mary Moffat. *Apprenticeship at Kuruman; being the Journals and Letters of Robert and Mary Moffat, 1820–1828*. Ed. by I. Schapera. London: Chatto & Windus, 1951. 308p.

Molema, S. M. *The Bantu Past and Present*. Edinburgh: W. Green & Son, 1920. 398p.

——. *Chief Moroka: His Life, His Times, His Country and His People*. Cape Town: Methodist Publishing House, n.d. [1951]. 210p.

Moore, W. G. *A Dictionary of Geography*. Baltimore: Penquin, 1963 (First published, 1949). 196p.

Morrow, Lance F. 'Pre-Mfecane carry-overs in subsequent Ndebele politics', in *Collected Seminars Papers on the Societies of Southern Africa in the 19th and 20th Centuries*, vol. 3 (University of London, Institute of Commonwealth Studies, October 1971–June 1972), 85–95.

[Moss, Joseph]. 'The origin and rise of Matabeleland' (Paper read by Mr Joseph Moss, Interpreter in the High Court of Griqualand, at a meeting and native concert in Kimberley Town Hall), *Diamond Fields Advertiser* (Kimberley, 12 June 1889), p.3.

Msebenzi. *History of Matiwane and the Amangwane Tribe, as told by Msebenzi to his Kinsman, Albert Hlongwane*. Ed. by N. J. van Warmelo. Pretoria: Department of Native Affairs, 1938 (Ethnological Publications, No. 7). 275p.

'Mziki [A. A. Campbell]. *'Mlimo: The Rise and Fall of the Matabele*. Facsimile reprint, Bulawayo: Books of Rhodesia, 1972 (First published Pietermaritzburg, 1926). 193p.

Nathan, Manfred. *The Voortrekkers of South Africa*. South Africa. Central News Agency; London: Gordon & Gotch, 1937. 428p.

Ndansi Kumalo. 'The story of Ndansi Kumalo of the Matabele tribe, Southern Rhodesia', recorded by J. W. Posselt and Margery Perham, in *Ten Africans*, ed. by M. Perham (London: Faber & Faber, 1936), 63–79.

Nielsen, Peter. *The Matabele at Home*. Bulawayo: Davis & Co., n.d. [1913]. 73p.

Northcott, Cecil. *Robert Moffat: Pioneer in Africa, 1817–1870*. London: Lutterworth Press, 1961. 357p.

Omer-Cooper, John D. 'Aspects of political change in the nineteenth-century Mfecane', in *African Societies in Southern Africa*, ed. by L. M. Thompson (London, 1969), 207–29.

——. *The Zulu Aftermath: A Nineteenth Century Revolution in Bantu Africa*. London: Longmans, 1966. 208p.

Otterbein, Keith F. 'The evolution of Zulu warfare', in *Law and Warfare*, ed. by Paul Bohannon (Garden City, NY, 1967), 351–7 (First published, 1964).

Owen, Francis. *The Diary of the Rev. Francis Owen, M.A.: Missionary with Dingaan in 1837–38*. Ed. by Geo. E. Cory. Cape Town: Van Riebeeck Society, 1926. 180p.

Pelling, J. N. (comp.) *A Practical Ndebele Dictionary*. Bulawayo: Daystar Publications, 1966. 148p.

Pettman, Charles. *South African Place Names, Past and Present*. Queenstown: Daily Representative Ltd., 1931. 194p.

Pitout, J. A. 'The arrival of the Mandebele in S. Rhodesia as told by Siatsha', *Nada*, 30 (1953), 57–8.

Plaatje, Soloman T. *Mhudi: An Epic of South African Native Life a Hundred Years Ago*. Facsimile reprint, New York: Negro Universities Press, 1970 (First published, Lovedale, 1930). 225p. [novel].

Posselt, F. W. T. *Autumn Leaves*. Bulawayo: Privately printed, 1942. 105p.

——. *Fact and Fiction: A Short Account of the Natives of Southern Rhodesia*. Bulawayo: Rhodesian Printing & Publishing Co, 1935. 210p.

——. *Upengula the Scatterer, or Lobengula and the Amandebele*. Bulawayo: Rhodesian Printing & Publishing Co, 1945. 140p.

Potgieter, Carl and N. H. Theunissen. *Kommandant-Generaal Hendrik Potgieter*. Johannesburg: Afrikaanse Pers Beperk, 1938. 271p.

Preller, Gustav S. *Lobengula: The Tragedy of a Matabele King*. Johannesburg: Afrikaanse Pers-Boekhandel, 1963. 318p.

—— (ed.). *Voortrekkermense . . . Dokumente oor die Geskiedenis van die Voortrek*. 4 vols. Kaapstad: De Nationale Pers, 1920–5.

Pretorius, H. S. and D. W. Kruger (eds.). *Voortrekker-Argiefstukke, 1829–1849*. Pretoria: Staatsdrukker, 1937.

Ranger, T. O. 'The historiography of Southern Rhodesia', *Trans-African Jnl. of History*, I, 2 (1971), 63–76.

——. 'The nineteenth century in Southern Rhodesia', in *Aspects of Central African History*, ed. by T. O. Ranger (London: Heinemann, 1968), 112–53.

Ransford, Oliver. *Bulawayo: Historic Battleground of Rhodesia*. Cape Town: A. A. Balkema, 1968. 182p.

——. *The Rulers of Rhodesia*. London: John Murray, 1968. 345p.

Rasmussen, R. Kent. 'From Cillicaats to Zelkaats: the orthographic odyssey of Mzilikazi', *Rhodesiana* (September, 1975). 52–61.

——. 'A lost man in Southern African history: Kaliphi/Gundwane of the Ndebele', *International Jnl. of African Historical Studies*, X, 1 (1977), 96–110.

——. *Mzilikazi of the Ndebele*. London: Heinemann, 1977. 48p.

——. Mzilikazi's migrations south of the Limpopo, c. 1821-7: a reassessment', *Trans-African Jnl. of History*, V, 1 (1976), 52-74.

Ritter, E. A. *Shaka Zulu*. London: Panther Books, 1971 (First published, London, 1955). 316p.

Samkange, Stanlake. *Origins of Rhodesia*. New York: Praeger, 1969. 292p.

Sanders, Peter. *Moshweshwe of Lesotho*. London: Heinemann, 1971. 54p.

Schapera, I. *Praise-Poems of Tswana Chiefs*. Oxford: Clarendon Press, 1965. 255p.

——. 'A short history of the Bangwaketse', *African Studies*, I, 1 (1942), 1-26.

——. *The Tswana*. London: International African Institute, 1971 (First published, 1953). 81p.

Scully, William Charles. 'Fragments of native history', *The State* (Johannesburg, September, October, and November, 1909), 284-92, 435-41, 595-603.

Selby, John. *Shaka's Heirs*. London: George Allen, 1971. 232p.

Selous, Frederick Courteney. *A Hunter's Wanderings in Africa*. Facsimile reprint, Bulawayo: Books of Rhodesia, 1970 (First published, London, 1881). 455p.

Sibree, James, *London Missionary Society: A Register of Missionaries, Deputations, etc. from 1796 to 1923*. 4th ed., London: London Missionary Society, 1923 (Based upon earlier editions by J. O. Whitehouse). 221p.

Sigola, Simon. 'How Lobengula came to rule the Matabele', *Nada*, 36 (1959), 87-91.

Sillery, Anthony. *The Bechuanaland Protectorate*. Cape Town: Oxford University Press, 1952. 236p.

——. *Sechele: The Story of An African Chief*. Oxford: George Ronald, 1954. 224p.

Smit, Erasmus. *The Diary of Erasmus Smit*. Trans by W. G. A. Mears. Ed. by H. F. Schoon. Cape Town: C. Struik, 1972 (First published in Dutch, [location?], 1897; reprinted in G. S. Preller [ed.], *Voortrekkermense*, II, 60-278). 189p.

Smith, Andrew. *Andrew Smith and Natal: Documents Relating to the early History of that Province*. Ed. by P. R. Kirby. Cape Town: Van Riebeeck Society, 1955. 253p.

——. *Andrew Smith's Journal of His Expedition into the Interior of South Africa/1834-36*. Ed. by W. F. Lye. Cape Town: A. A. Balkema, 1975. 323p.

——. *The Diary of Dr. Andrew Smith, 1834-1836*. Ed. by P. R. Kirby. 2 vols. Cape Town: Van Riebeeck Society, 1939-40. 413, 342p.

——. *Report of the Expedition for Exploring Central Africa from the Cape of Good Hope, June 13, 1834*. Cape Town: Government Gazette Office, 1836. 68p. [A copy can be found in the South African Library (Cape Town)].

Smith, Edwin W. *The Life and Times of Daniel Lindley (1801-80)*. London: Epworth Press, 1949. 456p.

——. *Robert Moffat: One of God's Gardeners*. London: Student

Christian Movement, 1925. 256p.

——. 'Sebetwane and the Makololo', in *Great Lion of Bechuanaland*, by E. W. Smith (London: London Missionary Society, 1957), 367–410 [First published in *African Studies*, 15, 1 (1956), 49–74].

Stabb, Henry. *To Victoria Falls via Matabeleland: The Diary of Major Henry Stabb, 1875*. Ed. by Edward C. Tabler. Cape Town: C. Struik, 1967. 268p.

Steedman, Andrew. *Wanderings and Adventures in the Interior of Southern Africa*. 2 vols. Facsimile reprint, Cape Town: C. Struik, 1966 (First published, London, 1835). 330, 358p.

Stent, Vere. *A Personal Record of Some Incidents in the Life of Cecil Rhodes*. Facsimile reprint, Bulawayo: Books of Rhodesia, 1970 (First published, Cape Town, 1925). 98p.

Storry, J. G. *The Shattered Nation*. Cape Town: Howard Timmins, 1974. 175p.

Stow, George W. *The Native Races of South Africa*. Ed. by George McCall Theal. London: Swan Sonnenschein, 1905. 618p.

Summers, Roger and C. W. Pagden. *The Warriors*. Cape Town: Books of Africa, 1970. 181p.

Tabler, Edward C. *The Far Interior: Chronicles of Pioneering in the Matabele and Mashona Countries, 1847–1879*. Cape Town: A. A. Balkema, 1955. 443p.

——. *Pioneers of Rhodesia*. Cape Town: C. Struik, 1966. 185p.

Taylor, Guy A. 'The Matabele head ring (Isidhlodhlo) and some fragments of history', *Nada*, 3 (1925), 37–42.

Theal, George McCall (ed.). *Basutoland Records*. Vol. I: *1833–1852*. Cape Town: W. A. Richards, 1883. 637p.

——. *South Africa*. 4th ed. London: T. Fisher Unwin, 1899 (First published, 1894). 442p.

Thom. H. B. *Die Lewe van Gert Maritz*. Kaapstad: Nasou Beperk, 1965 (First published, 1947). 234p.

Thomas, Thomas Morgan. *Eleven Years in Central South Africa*. 2nd ed., with new introduction by Richard Brown. London: Frank Cass, 1971 (First published, London, 1872). 418p.

——. 'Mission to the Matebele', *Missionary Magazine & Chronicle* (London, October 1864), 281–9.

Thompson, George. *Travels and Adventures in Southern Africa*. Ed. by Vernon S. Forbes. 2 vols. Cape Town: Van Riebeeck Society, 1967–8 (First published, London, 1827).

Thompson, Leonard (ed.). *African Societies in Southern Africa*. London: Heinemann, 1969. 336p.

——. 'Co-operation and conflict: the Zulu kingdom and Natal', 'Co-operation and conflict: the High veld', in *The Oxford History of South Africa*; Vol. I: *South Africa to 1870,* ed. by M. Wilson and L. M. Thompson (Oxford, 1969), 334–446.

Tylden, G. 'Vegkop, 2 October 1836: analysis', *Africana Notes & News*, 10, 4 (1953), 136–9.

——. 'Vegkop, 2 October 1836: a reconstruction', *ibid*, 14, 5 (1961), 180–2.

Vansina, Jan. *Oral Tradition: A Study in Historical Methodology.* Trans. by H. M. Wright. London: Routledge & Kegan Paul, 1965. 226p.

van Warmelo, Nicolaas J. *The Bahwaduba.* Pretoria: Dept. of Native Affairs, 1944 (Ethnological Publications, No. 19), 23–32.

——. *The Bakgatla ba ga Mosetlha.* Pretoria: Dept. of Native Affairs, 1944 (Ethnological Publications, No. 17), 3–11.

——. *A Genealogy of the House of Sekhukhune.* Pretoria: Dept. of Native Affairs, 1944 (Ethnological Publications, No. 21), 45–55.

——. *The Ndebele of J. Kekana.* Pretoria: Dept. of Native Affairs, 1944 (Ethnological Publications, No. 18), 13–21.

——. *A Preliminary Survey of the Bantu Tribes of South Africa.* Pretoria: Dept. of Native Affairs, 1935 (Ethnological Publications, No. 5). 123p.

——. *Transvaal Ndebele Texts.* Pretoria: Dept. of Native Affairs, 1930 (Ethnological Publications, No. 1). 108p.

Vaughan-Williams, H. 'A short history of Lobengula, Umziligazi and the Matabeles', Chapter XVI in *A Visit to Lobengula in 1889* (Pietermaritzburg: Shuter & Shooter, 1947), 109–13.

Walker, Eric Anderson. *The Great Trek.* 5th ed., London: Adam & Charles Black, 1965 (First published, 1934). 389p.

——. *A History of Southern Africa.* 3rd ed., London: Longmans, 1962 (First published as *A History of South Africa*, 1928). 973p.

Walter, Eugene Victor. *Terror and Resistance: A Study of Political Violence, with case studies of some primitive African Communities.* New York: Oxford University Press, 1969. 385p.

Widdicombe, John. *Fourteen Years in Basutoland.* London: The Church Printing Co, n.d. [1891]. 306p.

Wills, A. J. *An Introduction to the History of Central Africa*, 2nd ed., London: Oxford University Press, 1967 (First published, 1964). 412p.

Wilson, Monica. 'The Nguni people', in *The Oxford History of South Africa*, Vol. I: *South Africa to 1870*, ed. by M. Wilson and L. M. Thompson (Oxford, 1969), 75–130.

—— and Leonard Thompson (eds.). *The Oxford History of South Africa.* Vol. I: *South Africa to 1870.* Oxford: Clarendon Press, 1969. 502p.

Winter, Johannes August. 'The history of Sekwati', in *Report of the Tenth Annual Meeting of the South African Association for the Advancement of Science,* X (Cape Town, 1913), 329–32.

——. 'The tradition of Ra'lolo', in *ibid*, 87–100.

Young, Robert B. *The Life and Work of George William Stow.* London: Longmans; Cape Town: Darter Bros, 1908. 123p.

INDEX

(Note: References to material contained in the footnotes are selectively limited to substantive issues which are not also cited in their corresponding sections of the text.)